Reaffirming Rehabilitation

Reaffirming Rehabilitation

Francis T. Cullen

Karen E. Gilbert

The 30th Anniversary Edition

Routledge
Taylor & Francis Group

LONDON AND NEW YORK

First published 2013 by Anderson Publishing

Published 2015 by Routledge
2 Park Square, Milton Park, Abingdon, Oxon OX14 4RN

and by Routledge
711 Third Avenue, New York, NY 10017, USA

Routledge is an imprint of the Taylor & Francis Group, an informa business

Notices
No responsibility is assumed by the publisher for any injury and/or damage to
persons or property as a matter of products liability, negligence or otherwise,
or from any use of operation of any methods, products, instructions or ideas
contained in the material herein.

Practitioners and researchers must always rely on their own experience and
knowledge in evaluating and using any information, methods, compounds, or
experiments described herein. In using such information or methods they should
be mindful of their own safety and the safety of others, including parties for
whom they have a professional responsibility.

Product or corporate names may be trademarks or registered trademarks, and
are used only for identification and explanation without intent to infringe.

Library of Congress Cataloging-in-Publication Data
Application submitted

British Library Cataloguing-in-Publication Data
A catalogue record for this book is available from the British Library.

ISBN-13: 978-1-4557-3130-5 (pbk)

Dedication

For their love, support, and guidance, we dedicate this book to our families, past and present:

To Francis Cullen, Justine Cullen, Jordan Cullen, and Paula Dubeck by Francis T. Cullen

To Bernard Alesi, Jane Alesi, Caitlin Gilbert, Elisabeth Gilbert, and James Gilbert by Karen E. Gilbert

CONTENTS

Introduction to the Anniversary Edition

I

Most often, social institutions remain much the same, shifting only gradually in one direction or the other. The current way of doing things appears so natural, so taken for granted, that envisioning an alternative set of policies and practices is virtually unthinkable. But at certain historical junctures, such socially constructed realities are shattered—they lose their legitimacy and are vulnerable to be questioned. It is at these moments that much is at stake, because choosing a quite different future suddenly seems within reach, if not of urgent necessity.

When we authored *Reaffirming Rehabilitation* in 1982, American corrections was at such a juncture and was poised to be transformed in consequential ways. Indeed, the correctional system stood at a momentous policy fork in the road. A crisis was at hand, and a feverish debate raged over how best to fix what was obviously broken. At the time, crime had risen precipitously; the social fabric had been frayed by government malfeasance and persistent protest on college campuses and in city streets; and the nation's prisons were depicted as so inhumane and coercive as to be unsuitable for offender treatment. Because it was the reigning correctional ideology, the rehabilitative ideal was understandably blamed for all that was wrong in the correctional domain. To nearly all commentators—we were among the few contrarian criminologists—it made little sense to do more of the same and retain a system based on treatment. Rehabilitation, critics asserted, should not be revised and reaffirmed but rejected. A new vision for corrections was needed.

Toward this end, many wise scholars and policy-makers argued that the solution to the prevailing crisis was to take decision-making power away from correctional officials. They proposed a "justice model," built on the premise that if "doing good" was not possible, efforts should be made to "do justice" for offenders. Under the guise of the rehabilitative ideal, judges and correctional officials had been given almost unfettered discretion to prescribe the appropriate cures for offenders. But rather than engage, as a physician would, in expert individualized treatment, they too often abused their discretion. Judges were guilty of allowing their likes and dislikes—so-called extra-legal factors—to influence who was incarcerated and for how long. Sent to prison under indeterminate sentences, offenders were supposed to be released when they were reformed. However, wardens and parole boards lacked the expertise to distinguish the cured from the criminal. For the most part, obedience to authority—doing what one was told—and not being rehabilitated was the key to earning a parole.

In contrast, reformers believed that if offenders were accorded more legal rights that limited the discretion of state officials, then the system would, in the least, offer fair and certain punishment. In particular, they favored determinate sentencing, or similar schemes (e.g., sentencing guidelines), in which the statutes would list the precise penalty, including years spent in prison, for each offense. In this scenario, equality before the law would be ensured. Now punishing only the crime and not trying to cure each offender's problems, judges would be bound to give the convicted the sentence prescribed by the criminal code. They would have no leeway to sanction minorities and the poor differentially. Similarly, because prison terms would be fixed by law, offenders would know their release date when first entering the prison gates. They would not have to con wardens and parole boards into releasing them. The correctional system would not be perfect, but, again, there would be more justice.

When proposing a reform, it is natural to see the problems that inhere in the old way of doing things and to envision how a new model can avoid these difficulties and bring forth much good. It is harder, however, to be reflexive—to take a step back and to consider whether the new way of doing things might be pregnant with a host of negative, unanticipated consequences. In *Reaffirming Rehabilitation*, however, we engaged in this reflexive exercise. Our deliberations caused us to fear that the movement away from the treatment ideal in favor of the justice model would be, to use Sam Sieber's term, a "fatal remedy."

Most importantly, we were concerned that in abandoning rehabilitation, reformers were embracing a system whose sole purpose would be to punish offenders. Corrections thus would have no mandate or obligation to create therapeutic environments or to consider the welfare of offenders. The only issue at hand would be whether the punishment assigned to a defendant was just—that it was finely calibrated to match the seriousness of the crime and was handed out equally, regardless of race, class, or gender. In the prevailing context, we believed that this reasoning suffered a fatal flaw that in turn made it a fatal remedy.

Thus, the justice model reformers advocated lenient sanctions for offenders. In their view, prisons were inherently inhumane and criminogenic. They should be used sparingly, with only the most dangerous offenders locked up. Most other offenders should receive a measure of punishment administered in the community. This vision struck us as hopelessly naïve. Waiting in the wings were numerous conservative politicians prepared to replace rehabilitation not with a justice model sympathetic to offenders but with get tough penalties—including long prison terms—intended to deter the calculators and incapacitate the wicked. They promised to make citizens' streets safer and to restore "law and order." We cautioned that the outcome of this debate was beyond dispute. The conservatives' war on crime would prevail over the justice model's war on injustice. With the countervailing influence of rehabilitation forfeited, the floodgates to unfettered punishment would be opened. The result would be a correctional system that would become harsher but, ironically, do little to achieve its stated goal of enhancing public safety.

II

We were right—an evaluation that reflects neither hubris nor any sense of satisfaction. In the three decades that have passed, American corrections entered an unprecedented mean season. It is not hyperbolic to say that a punitive orgy ensued, in which elected officials feasted on citizens' fears and populist punitive rhetoric to win votes. A war on crime was expanded to include a war on drugs. The linchpin of these wars was the promise to lock up more people, especially more young, black men from the nation's increasingly poor inner cities. A non-falsifiable logic was employed. Any drop in crime was attributed to rising imprisonment; any increase in crime was *prima facie* evidence that prison sentences were not yet stiff enough. Either way, the intractable rise in incarcerated Americans was not to be questioned. The result was an unprecedented era of mass imprisonment. In 1982, the U.S. state and federal prison population was a little over 400,000; today it exceeds 1.5 million. Further, back then, 1.84 million were under some form of correctional supervision—prison, jail, probation, or parole. That statistic now stands at over 7.3 million.

Still, there is substantial reason for optimism. A growing consensus now exists—across the political spectrum—that the era of mass imprisonment must end. State prison populations have now declined for the first time in nearly four decades. In the wake of the financial crisis that hit the United States in 2008, many governors have confronted the stubborn fact that balanced budgets are not possible unless correctional spending is curtailed. It is common to hear that the current level of imprisonment is "unsustainable." There is a push to move as many low-risk offenders into the community as soon as possible. And there is a corresponding desire to be more judicious in who is sent to prison in the first place. Although resources are in short supply, rehabilitation necessarily is being trumpeted once again. If offenders are to be released or kept in the community, something responsible must be done with them. Placing them in treatment programs is an attractive solution.

More generally, it is realized that the punitive paradigm that had a vice grip on American corrections since 1982 is intellectually bankrupt. If hundreds of thousands of offenders are locked up, this alone will suppress the crime rate to a degree. But beyond this "incapacitation effect," little is gained—and much is lost. It is now clear that the most effective way to change high-risk offenders is to place them in evidence-based treatment programs. Punitive sanctions rarely serve their stated purpose of specifically deterring offenders from recidivating. This empirical reality has robbed punitive corrections of its legitimacy.

Thus, it is clear that American corrections took the wrong policy fork in the road in 1982. Now we have the rare chance for a "do-over." Once again, we are at a historical junction where real change is possible—a time when we have the opportunity to choose what our correctional future will be. And once again, we propose that reaffirming rehabilitation is the road to take.

In making this strong recommendation, we do not suggest that it is possible to return to 1982 and pick up where we left off. Much damage has been done. Corrections faces the daunting challenge of implementing responsible practices when the offender population in the system far outstrips the resources available. Still, difficulty should not be an excuse for inaction. The American economy will eventually rebound and replenish state treasuries. Further, in the past thirty years, important advances in offender treatment have been made.

The notion that "nothing works" has been put to rest. In fact, knowledge of how to rehabilitate offenders, and the technology to accomplish this task, are readily available. Implementing effective interventions on a large-scale basis remains a difficult task, but it is an enterprise worthy of our efforts.

In Chapter 8, we wrestle with the challenge of undertaking rehabilitation in the time ahead. The discussion begins by describing what has transpired in the past thirty years. The evidence paints a bleak picture. The mean season in corrections that flourished during this period resulted in unrestrained punitive rhetoric, questionable policies, a failed experiment in mass imprisonment, and a host of punishment-oriented interventions that were pure quackery. Nonetheless, also during this period, a smaller but consequential movement emerged to show that the nothing works doctrine in offender rehabilitation was false and to identify the principles of effective treatment.

In short, we demonstrate that rehabilitation has survived the mean season in corrections. The larger challenge is how to reaffirm rehabilitation responsibly. We make four recommendations to guide the future of rehabilitation. First, efforts should be made to capitalize on the public's continued embrace of rehabilitation as a core goal of corrections. Despite the many attacks over the past three decades, opinion polls reveal that the American citizenry firmly supports a correctional system that not only punishes but also saves the criminally wayward. Second, rehabilitation should be evidenced-based. Until an empirically stronger model arises, interventions should be based on the "RNR paradigm," whose acronym represents the model's three core principles. Thus, according to the risk principle, treatment should be directed at high-risk offenders; according to the need principles, treatment should target for change the major predictors of recidivism that are "dynamic" or malleable (e.g., antisocial attitudes, low self-control); and according to the responsivity principle, treatment should be employed that is "responsive to" and thus capable of changing criminogenic needs (e.g., cognitive-behavioral programs). Third, interventions with antisocial youths should start early in life and, as they age, continue into adulthood; it is "never too early and never too late" to rescue offenders from beginning or continuing a criminal career. Fourth, correctional officials must be made accountable for lower recidivism rates. In the end, corrections must become a profession that is based on the core mandates to use effective treatments and to do no untoward harm to offenders or to the public.

III

In revisiting *Reaffirming Rehabilitation*, we were delighted to confirm that the book, in its original form, retained much relevance for today. We did not revise the chapters, because this is a treatise that largely stands on its own and thus could be appropriately updated by the inclusion of an epilogue. As just noted, we undertake this discussion of the major policy happenings in the last thirty years in Chapter 8, which also provides guidance on where the future of rehabilitation might head.

For those unfamiliar with the original edition of *Reaffirming Rehabilitation*, it might be helpful for us to give a brief tour of its contents. We start with Chapters 2 and 3, because these lay the foundation for what is to follow. Chapter 2 provides the *conceptual foundation* for understanding criminal justice policy. It reviews the classical and positivist schools of criminology, what is meant by the ideological categories of conservative, liberal, and radical, and then how criminological schools and political ideologies are interrelated when it comes to criminal justice policy. Especially to newcomers to the study of corrections, this analysis illuminates why how we think about crime can have important policy ramifications.

Chapter 3 then supplies the *historical foundation* for the remainder of the book by examining the rise of the rehabilitative ideal. In colonial America, criminals were often punished publicly and physically. But in the 1820s, reformers invented a new institution, which they called the "penitentiary." They proposed that by placing offenders in a specially designed community from which there was no escape, it would be possible to transform them from troubled souls into morally upstanding citizens. In short, they married the notions of prisons and rehabilitation, essentially arguing that the core goal of institutionalizing offenders was to rescue them from a life in crime. The full contours of this rehabilitative ideal were fleshed out over the next century, especially the notion that treating offenders should be similar to treating medical patients. In this view, the key was individualized treatment in which the intervention was to address the unique factors causing each offender to break the law. To administer such cures, reformers in the Progressive era—the first two decades of the 1900s—created indeterminate sentencing, pre-sentence reports and probation supervision, parole boards and parole officers, and a separate juvenile justice system devoted exclusively to saving wayward youngsters. The rehabilitative ideal, and the sentencing and organizational structure it justified, dominated American corrections into the 1970s.

At this historical juncture, faith in rehabilitation suddenly collapsed. One moment everyone believed in rehabilitation; the next moment nobody seemed to do so. As we introduce in Chapter 1 and then elaborate in Chapter 4, a crisis gripped the criminal justice system. Confidence in the rehabilitative ideal hinges on citizens' belief that state officials—judges, wardens, parole boards—will use the discretion accorded them to treat offenders. But by the early 1970s—and as described above—many observers came to believe that this discretion was being abused, which led to inequitable sentencing, coercive prison environments, and parole release that was akin to playing the lottery.

Admittedly, objective reasons existed to criticize the administration of justice, but these had existed for many years. In the past, identifying problems was a prelude to pursuing reforms to fix them. Now, however, critics were prepared to throw the baby out with the bathwater—to replace rehabilitation with the justice model. In large part, this transformation from correctional reform to revolution was tied to the rising mistrust that Americans had in the state. In turn, this "legitimacy crisis" or "confidence gap"—as it was called—was nourished by the social and cultural upheaval that emerged in the 1960s and continued well into the 1970s. Names such as Watergate, the Vietnam War, and Attica came to signify government corruption and brutality. Thus, if the state could not be trusted to do good for offenders, then at least efforts could be made to stop its officials from harming offenders. The justice model promised to protect offenders by taking away officials' discretionary powers to harm and by forcing them to do justice.

Although we were aware of the shortcomings of the rehabilitative ideal, we believed that its critics failed to appreciate its central role in humanizing the correctional system. After all, criminals are, in a very real way, undeserving of our sympathy and efforts to bring them back into our community. Their actions harm others—sometimes in minor ways, sometimes in lethal ways. Victims rightly call for justice, if not vengeance, to be exacted. Our collective moves us to want to make offenders suffer just as they had made others suffer. Common sense also nourishes the belief that the more pain we inflict on them, the less likely they will be to do harm in the future. If these feelings and logic are not balanced, then what is to restrain punitive sentiments from running amok? And when politicians perceive that stirring up such ill feelings will win them votes, we have an interest group who benefits by campaigning for an increasingly harsh justice system.

Amazingly, Americans have often led the way in arguing that corrections must be about more than exacting retribution or trying to frighten offenders into conformity. Rather, we have been a people—from elites to the masses—who have long understood that a critical role of the correctional system is to correct. In very real ways, the long-standing embrace of rehabilitation has been rooted in the nation's Judeo-Christian tradition and the abiding conviction that redemption is possible for all wayward souls. Religious faith also has shaped the public's behavior, asking its members to refrain from vengeance and to turn the other cheek in hopes that love, not hate, would be a stronger cure for offenders.

Support for rehabilitation has a practical side as well. Criminology as a discipline has identified what many in the general public suspect to be true: that there are causes of crime. We now commonly call these "risk factors"—ranging from brain trauma during pregnancy and difficult temperaments evident at birth to dysfunctional family life, school failure, exposure to delinquent peers, and life in a disorganized neighborhood marked by concentrated disadvantage. Yes, crime is chosen, but this very choice is shaped intimately by personal traits and social circumstances that are beyond one's choice. The reality is that unless these criminogenic risk factors are targeted for change—unless rehabilitation is used—offenders will return to crime over and over and over again. Thus, it is in our enlightened self-interest to forgo vengeful punishments that may offer some momentary catharsis but that leave the underlying causes of crime untouched.

The key insight we had in 1982 was that there is a high cost to be paid when rehabilitation is purged from the correctional system. What compelling set of beliefs, we asked, would now have the power to temper feelings of vengeance? What rationale would exist to say that sanctioning offenders humanely actually is in our self-interest? In the absence of the rehabilitative ideal—a strong countervailing force to punitive ideology—there is little to restrain the harsh sentiments that are so easily visited upon offenders, a group that has no political lobby and that elicits little sympathy. As we have argued—and we return to this in Chapter 8—the critique of rehabilitation helped to unleash a truly awful policy era in American corrections.

In Chapter 5, we thus detailed the unanticipated consequences that would occur by moving away from the rehabilitative ideal. Taking a reflexive position, we cautioned justice model advocates that they were embarking on a reform that would create the very situation they ascribed to rehabilitation: the corruption of benevolence. To be sure, these reformers had noble intentions and were trying to change very real problems. But their prescription was, as we have argued, fatally flawed. Above all else, they sought to take discretionary power away from judges and correctional officials and to locate it in the hands of legislators and, unwittingly, of prosecutors. But legislators and, typically, chief prosecutors are elected officials who have a political interest in responding to and stirring up public anger, especially when a heinous crime has been committed. Because they do not deal with offenders day in and day out as correctional officials do, they are influenced far more by the harm a victim has suffered than by the humanity of the criminal. In our view, this was a recipe for a rash of get tough sentencing reforms. In Chapter 6, our analysis of the first round of determinacy in sentencing laws confirmed our suspicions.

Finally, in Chapter 7 we made a case for reaffirming rehabilitation. In the intervening three decades, nothing has occurred to change our minds. In fact, in 1982, we could not have envisioned how troubling crime control policy would become and how corrections would be overwhelmed by the tsunami of mass imprisonment. Over the years, rehabilitation did not fully disappear. For one thing, programs served to occupy inmates' time. But more importantly, there has always been a strong core of correctional practitioners who understood that rehabilitation offered a more moral and more effective way to sanction offenders. There also has been a small group of scholars—now expanding rapidly—who engaged in research to show that offender treatment reduced recidivism. Together, they formed a loosely-coupled community that did much to keep rehabilitation alive and moving forward.

IV

As noted, Chapter 8 builds on these themes, illuminating both the policy follies of the past thirty years and the reasons to be optimistic that rehabilitation will be integral in guiding correctional policy and practice in the time ahead. The challenge that awaits us all is to play an active role in choosing this correctional future. Rehabilitation will remain a viable option only so long as effective interventions are developed and implemented widely and with integrity. Doing so will involve a firm commitment to evidence-based corrections and to transforming corrections into a true profession marked by expertise and the embrace of an ethic of care. Much work thus remains to be undertaken. Let us spare no time in getting to it.

Foreword to the First Edition

This is more than a book about punishment versus rehabilitation of criminals. It is, to be sure, the first book to defend the notion that Americans acted unwisely and too hastily when they recently exorcised rehabilitation programs from prisons. But it also is an essay on how social movements go awry—on the unanticipated consequences of purposive social action. Further, it documents a proposition which humanitarian policy makers established centuries ago, namely that "government by law" always will, in the absence of "government by men," have gross injustice as its consequence. More generally, it pinpoints the tragic irony involved as humanitarians, bent on reducing pain and suffering in the world, have recently convinced Americans to inflict more pain and suffering on criminals, even if doing so allows criminals to inflict more pain and suffering on the rest of us.

The irony becomes apparent as Cullen and Gilbert share four insights with their readers in Chapter One, then in subsequent chapters go on to document or otherwise demonstrate the validity of the insights. First, they show that criminals are being hurt more by the political liberals' new "justice model" of dealing with offenders than they were hurt by the liberals' older "interventionist" and "treatment" models. Next they demonstrate that liberals have contributed to the construction of a new punitive policy that rests on a foundation of spite and hate rather than on assumptions about the effectiveness of punishment. Deterrence policy, long championed by political conservatives, asks that pain be imposed on criminals as a means of repressing crime—the assumption is that such pain will reduce crime rates both by reforming criminals (specific deterrence) and also by terrorizing bystanding citizens so much that they will be afraid to violate the law (general deterrence). But the idea now being implemented by liberals (some call them neo-conservatives) is that pain should be imposed on criminals simply because they deserve it ("just deserts," "retribution," "vengeance."). Third, the authors suggest that the new system of mandatory, flat, and presumptive sentences for criminals is producing more injustice than did the replaced system of indeterminate or discretionary sentencing. Finally, Cullen and Gilbert provide a factual basis for the belief that the new tactics of terror are not reducing America's skyrocketing crime rate. In sum, they show that "a criminal justice system rooted in retributive principles will be neither more just, more humane, nor more efficient than a system that, at least ideologically, had offender reform as its goal."

The old libertarian principle is that government ought to interfere in citizens' lives as little as possible and when it must interfere it ought to hurt them as little as possible.

Conservatives take this notion to mean that government regulation of citizens is nefarious and therefore should be minimal. Ironically, however, conservatives are now as in the past asking for increased government regulation in the form of more energetic enforcement of criminal laws and, thus, for more severe punishment of criminals. Liberals take the libertarian principle to mean that all citizens must be protected from unjust administration of essential government regulations designed to maximize the common good, the public interest, the general welfare. Ironically, however, liberals are now calling for elimination of the chief instrument used for such protection of citizens who are accused of crime or who are criminals—discretionary decision-making by police, prosecutors, judges, parole officials, and other members of the judicial and executive branches of government. "It is ironic," Cullen and Gilbert say, "that liberals who mistrust the state to administer rehabilitation in a just and humane manner are now placing their total faith in the same state (legislatures) to punish justly and humanely."

The importance of discretionary decision-making can be illustrated by taking a look at how things work in our courthouses. In modern nations every adult who is not mentally disturbed or retarded knows that bureaucracies never work as they are supposed to work. Whether the bureaucracy is that of a factory, an army, a corporation, a university, or a government office, something or someone always gums up the works. But Americans, knowing that, nevertheless have remarkably little insight into how and why courthouse personnel impose sentences on criminals. If they did, they would not heed the calls of justice model liberals for more uniform sentences.

We have learned in high school civics classes—and perhaps at our mothers' knees—that judges, prosecutors and defense lawyers make two decisions, and in a certain order. First, they decide as a matter of fact that a defendant is or is not "guilty as charged." Then they decide as a matter of policy what should be done with, to, or for the guilty person. It is proper, of course, to acknowledge that these two decisions are made hundreds of times each day in courthouses around the nation. But our perception of the sequence in which factual and policy matters come up for decisions is distorted. As Arthur Rosett and I showed in *Justice By Consent: Plea Bargains in the American Courthouse* (1976), criminal justice personnel *first* settle the policy issue and *then* make the factual decision regarding guilt.

Put simply, defense attorneys, prosecutors, and judges first agree on what the sentence should be for an individual defendant. The agreement stems from negotiations about the defendant's character and the circumstances of the offense. Then the trio, acting in concert, selects from the statute books a crime whose stipulated punishment is consistent with what has been decided upon as appropriate for the defendant at the bar. For example, if a man who broke into a house and stole a television set is defined as a "bad guy" who should be sent to prison, he is likely to be charged with, and found guilty of, burglary. But if a defendant who did the same thing is defined as a "good guy" who should be fined or sent to the county jail for a few days, he is likely to be charged with, and found guilty of, some lesser included offense such as trespassing.

Neither calls for the just deserts (retribution) model of sentencing nor legislation implementing such a model is going to change this sequence of fitting crime to the punishment rather than fitting punishment to a crime. The reason is compelling: the sequence is essential to fairness. It permits courthouse personnel to correct the injustice which always results when an abstract law, which cannot take into account the specific circumstances that are inherent in each case, is administered in a routine manner. President Lyndon Johnson's Commission on Law Enforcement and Administration of Justice put the matter this way:

> Framing statutes that identify and prescribe for any nuance of human behavior is impossible. A criminal code has no way of describing the difference between a petty thief who is on his way to becoming an armed robber and a petty thief who becomes one on a momentary impulse. Making such distinctions is vital to effective law enforcement. Therefore the law gives wide latitude to police and prosecutors in making arrests and bringing charges, judges in imposing penalties, and the correctional authorities in determining how offenders should be treated in prisons and when they should be released on parole. The law, in short, makes prosecutors, judges, and correctional authorities personally responsible for dealing individually with individual offenders, for prescribing vigorous treatment for dangerous ones, and for giving an opportunity to mend their ways to those who appear likely to do so.

But when citizens are free to make decisions they are bound to make some bad ones. Courthouse citizens are no exception. As Cullen and Gilbert point out in Chapter Four, justice model liberals must be credited with calling America's attention to the fact that discretionary sentencing has been blatantly discriminatory. What these indignant democrats introduced as a corrective is a different matter. Two problems arose as policy-makers tried to do something about the fact that when there is a discretionary choice between severity and leniency, poor people get severity and rich people get leniency. These problems are now in dire need of solution.

One problem arose because justice model liberals convinced legislators that there would be less injustice if sentences were mandatory and flat rather than discretionary and indeterminate. This is not the case. In democracies, nondiscretionary sentencing systems always give power to the legislative branch of government, as compared to the judicial and executive branches. The power is the same as that seized by dictators who tolerate no breaches of their orders. Tyranny is always implemented by rank-oriented bureaucracies in which each person is threatened with punishment for not obeying the commands issued by persons of higher rank. In such systems, injustices are rampant. And it does not matter, really, if the chieftain of the military-like bureaucracy is an elected legislative body rather than a self-appointed ruler. Currently, legislators are using the justice model of sentencing to restrict the freedom of courthouse personnel (and other criminal justice workers as well) to be wise, compassionate, innovative, judicious, and fair. Judges are being directed to impose fixed amounts of pain on criminals in a machine-like manner. The quality of justice is decreasing in direct proportion to the degree to which the judges are obeying their orders. As I said in a recently published Canadian book (*New Directions in Sentencing*, Brian A. Grosman, Editor, 1980), "What is important in the current drive to make judges into robot-like servants of legislators is not the fact that injustice is sometimes produced as judges select crimes to fit sentences. Injustice will always be with us. What is important is the question of whether the apparent reversal of expected procedure regarding crime and punishment produces more injustice than would strict enforcement of criminal statutes. There is no evidence that it does. On the contrary, it seems obvious that the legislators now implementing the classical school's computerized system for imposing sentences are unwittingly asking for an increase in the amount of injustice in the world."

A second problem also arose as justice model liberals trashed discretionary sentencing because it is so discriminatory. The problem is that liberals have, like conservatives, opted for terror rather than for nonpunitive means of reducing the crime rate. Many variables are involved when rich criminals are punished less severely than poor ones, whites less severely than blacks, women less severely than men. One of them is discrimination. Acting on the principle that discrimination is a more overpowering variable than all the others combined, liberals and radicals alike are demanding equality in sentencing. But to justice model liberals such equality is to be established by punishing more rich, white, and female criminals. As liberals and humanitarians, they should have, and still should, demand that we achieve equality in sentencing by punishing fewer poor people, blacks and males, thus supplementing their demand that these people be punished less severely than they are now being punished. The crime rates of those who are rich, white, or female seem to be lower than those who are poor, black, or male. One reason, perhaps, is that the criminals in the favored groups are not punished as frequently or severely as the others. Criminals who are not punished nevertheless change their ways, and it is reasonable to believe that they change their ways because they not punished. Thus, in matters of crime control, at least, forgiveness seems to be as effective as terror. It follows that all who heed the libertarian principle should be trying to make the rate of punishing disadvantaged groups more like the rate of punishing advantaged groups, not the reverse.

Perhaps this humanitarian option was overlooked, and still is being overlooked, because being soft on criminals is not a winning political stance. More generally, in the United States, humanitarianism alone is rarely a political winner. President Franklin D. Roosevelt voiced humanitarianism as the announced aim of social policy when he called for programs to alter the fact that one-third of all Americans were ill-housed, ill-clothed, and ill-fed. Ordinarily, however, any call for implementation of humanitarian ideals must be cloaked in utilitarian garb if it is to be adopted. In other words, humanitarians must argue that humanitarianism pays. For example, it will not do to insist that official U.S. aid should be given to the starving people of developing nations simply because people ought not to starve; it is more effective to argue that such largesse will win international allies. Consistently, it is not practical to say that slums ought to be cleaned up to free poor people from a life of squalor; it is practical to say that slums should be cleared because conventioneers will be attracted to a slum-free city and will leave their spending money in it. In short, merely saying that it is inhumane to let people starve or continue to live in miserable ghettos is not enough. To get humanitarian things done, Americans must be practical.

More to the point of Cullen and Gilbert's fascinating book is the possibility that rehabilitation of criminals was called for in the 1950s, 1960s and early 1970s because the rhetoric of rehabilitation promoted humanitarianism, not because rehabilitation programs were expected to change criminals into noncriminals. Thus, it is not too farfetched to postulate that after World War II humanitarians hit on an ingenious but practical plan for reducing the severity of pain in prisons. They called not for humanitarianism but for "treatment" of prisoners, and perhaps they did so in part because they were stirred by memories of how the invention of utilitarian "refuges" and "reformatories" for juveniles first led to isolated humanitarian laws designed to protect children from the harshness of the criminal law and then to humanitarian establishment of juvenile courts. Surely some of the reformers really believed that prisons which were said to reform criminals by inflicting pain on them (specific deterrence) could also be made to rehabilitate them. Nevertheless, what got into prisons was humanitarianism, not scientific methods of changing criminals.

In Chapter Seven, Cullen and Gilbert say, "Rehabilitation has historically been an important motive force underlying efforts that have increased the humanity of the correctional system." This means that all sorts of good things came into prisons when the rehabilitative ideal was introduced. Among them were better food and housing, higher levels of sanitation, radio, television, even pastel walls. More significant introductions were relaxed discipline, freedom to move about, and increased opportunities for inmates to affect what happens to them. Most important, however, was humanitarian reduction of the pains of imprisonment. It became acceptable, even fashionable, to say that nowadays persons are sent to prison *as* punishment (the psychological pain stemming from loss of liberty), not *for* punishment (the physical pain stemming from assaults on the body). But after the rehabilitative ideal made its appearance, leaders such as Sanger Powers (Wisconsin) and Richard McGee (California) could additionally keep telling guards, wardens, legislators, and others that any unnecessary restriction or deprivation of inmates would damage the treatment process and thus should be avoided.

Cullen and Gilbert note that close observers of our prisons recognized that the preeminence of rehabilitation in "treatment-oriented" prisons was more myth than reality. I was one of those observers. Over twenty-five years ago I wrote that, evaluated scientifically, treatment programs in prisons were both farces and failures. I based my claim on first-hand research observations suggesting that few inmates were getting rehabilitated. I attributed the failure to dominance of the punitive-custodial ideology and to the fact that the rehabilitation programs were based on a fundamental misconception about the nature of human personality. Thus, I agreed with the many persons arguing that "treatment" and "rehabilitation" had never been tried in prisons or, for that matter, in institutions for juveniles or in probation and parole work. It is still proper to argue, as Cullen and Gilbert do, that the rehabilitative ideal never was implemented. But it "worked" nevertheless. It worked because "treatment" came to mean "We treat them well here." Humanitarianism was introduced, and defended, in the name of treatment.

Until Robert Martinson published his 1974 "Nothing Works" article in a liberal magazine, not many people noticed the many sociological research studies and essays purporting to show that prisons do not rehabilitate. For example, Walter Bailey's 1966 review of reports on the effectiveness of 100 treatment programs concluded that correctional programs rarely correct, but few people paid any attention to the review. No one yelled, "Nothing works!" Now, dozens of people are handed salaries of up to $50,000 a year just for standing up in an occasional meeting on prison policy and shouting, "Nothing works!" Others are receiving gold stars, pay raises, and book royalties for writing essays whose only message is a negative one: "Nothing works."

Popularizing the idea that prisons fail to rehabilitate and, indeed, that the rehabilitative ideal produces injustice, has had unanticipated consequences. For one thing, as discussed, in matters of sentencing more power has been given to the legislative branch of government, to the detriment of the executive and judicial branches. Accordingly, injustice is more frequent and sentences are longer. An equally devastating and important consequence has been encouragement of policies which once again insist that persons be sent to prison as punishment or for incapacitation purposes and not for rehabilitation purposes. The rhetoric of rehabilitation and treatment has been deleted from policy statements pertaining to prisons. Therefore, it is no longer permissible for wardens and corrections directors to justify humanitarianism by saying "We treat them here" when they mean "We treat them well here." When the rehabilitative ideal disappeared, humanitarianism in prisons disappeared with it. Prisoners are now being hurt like they never were hurt before.

Contemporary inmates are being physically hurt by fellow inmates, and are being psychologically hurt by prison officials charged with depriving them of their liberty, to a much greater degree than was the case when rehabilitation was in vogue. In the 1950s I published a research report suggesting that guards in treatment-oriented prisons were protecting inmates from each other at least as effectively as were the guards working in the punitive-custodial prisons of the times. They did this by borrowing from the child-rearing techniques of middle-class people, thus giving love and affection to inmates who were not misbehaving, and withdrawing love and affection from inmates who misbehaved. Guards in punitive-custodial prisons functioned more like traditional police officers, protecting inmates from each other by arresting and taking misbehaving inmates to disciplinary court for conviction and sentencing. But now that the rehabilitation rhetoric is gone, guards systematically use neither of these control systems for protecting inmates from each other. Inmates are raping, assaulting, and killing each other like never before. The guards have retreated to the walls.

There are at least four different ways to make sense of the fact that contemporary prison guards and their bosses are concentrating on perimeter control rather than on keeping the prison crime rate down. The first is to observe that, in the absence of the rhetoric of rehabilitation, guards have no obligation to assist inmates. They ignore their needs because everyone else is ignoring their needs. Second, it is possible that poor policing and concordantly high inmate crime rates are deliberately being used to supplement the psychological pain of incarceration with bodily pain violently inflicted on inmates by inmates. Perhaps prison personnel, who long ago were prohibited from beating inmates, are letting inmates do their dirty work for them. Third, poor policing in prisons might be valuable to prison personnel because it functions to maximize inmate divisiveness, thus preventing inmates from joining hands against the staff. "If they are fighting each other, they aren't fighting me," a warden told me long ago.

The fourth hypothesis, which I favor, is that the guards' retreat to the walls is a way of allowing, perhaps even encouraging, inmates to develop in the prison yard the "just deserts" or vengeance system of justice that justice model liberals are advocating for the broader society. In that system, you give the offender his due by trying to hurt him as much as he hurt you, your friends, or your allies. In that system, you try to incapacitate the offender so he won't hurt you or your friends and allies again, at least not for a time. In that system, humanitarian considerations have no place. Inmates seem to have been left alone to adopt that system. As they have done so, violence among them has escalated. With increased violence, of course, comes increased pain and suffering.

Policing, whether in prison or on the outside, involves more than merely arresting, convicting, and hurting wrongdoers. It involves preaching and practicing humanitarianism, including racial equality, brotherly love, and forgiveness rather than hate. Outside our prisons, liberals have joined conservatives to preach hatred of criminals, and they have done so by calling for revenge ("just deserts") and for locking them up so they will hurt us no more ("incapacitation"). Inside our prisons, even inmates have heeded this call. They practice hatred of those who offend them, and some are sustained only by their dreams of revenge. Note that in matters of criminal justice, inmates always behave as their keepers behave. All of us, collectively, are their keepers. Note further that free citizens, like inmates, also behave as their governors behave. As legislatures increasingly escalate the use of violence in an attempt to control citizens, the citizens become increasingly violent.

What we need is a new rhetoric. Humanitarians, libertarians, and liberals must find some words which will once again let humanitarianism into the criminal justice system through the back door. Although Swedish Minister of Justice Herman Kling has said, "We must practice humanity without expecting anything in return," my observation is that, in America at least, plain humanitarian arguments—and even slogans such as "love thy neighbor"—are not effective. If this be true, then the new rhetoric must somehow reduce the pains of punishment—especially of imprisonment—without actually calling for such reductions, just as the rhetoric of rehabilitation did.

My hunch is that we will find such a new rhetoric by focusing on America's work ethic. We believe in work, and in addition we are now in need of a solution to the dilemma appearing whenever someone (usually an economist) notes that, as the state increases the cost of crime for criminals (longer and harsher prison terms for more offenders), it increases its own costs proportionately because it must build and man new prisons, pay board-and-room costs of prisoners for longer terms, and pay the costs of increased police and court work as well. If prisoners are required to earn their keep, the new rhetoric might insist, the costs of crime to criminals will remain high but the costs to the state will diminish. Once this rhetoric has been accepted by policymakers, at least two-thirds of the journey toward renewed humanitarianism in our methods of dealing with criminals will have been made. The remainder of the journey will be easily accomplished as humanitarians point out, logically enough, that the state will not get much work out of prisoners if they are kept chained to the floor or—at the other extreme—hardly policed at all.

It doesn't matter, really, that the financial costs of administering justice actually might not decrease as prisoners are put to work. What matters is that humanitarianism could again be made to dominate decision-making in the criminal justice process. Wardens would not be able to say, as they once did, "We treat them well here and as a result they are getting rehabilitated." But they could say—with an equal disregard for factual accuracy—"We treat them well here and as a result their work is reducing our costs." The world runs on healthy hypocrisies.

Donald R. Cressey
University of California,
Santa Barbara, California

January 2, 1982

Crisis in Criminal Justice Policy

In 1977, C. Ray Jeffrey, soon to be elected president of the American Society of Criminology, declared unhesitantly that "punishment has failed... treatment has failed."[1] This assertion is perhaps overly sweeping and, some might argue, empirically problematic. But whatever its factual merits, Jeffrey's statement accurately expressed the sentiments of many of his academic peers and, indeed, of much of the general public at this time. Nothing that was being done about the "crime problem" seemed either to prove or promise to be successful— our "war on crime" was in a shambles—and the public agitated for order to be restored. However, the uncertainties as to just what solution would rectify this troubling state of affairs were considerable; a crisis in American criminal justice policy prevailed.[2]

THE CRISIS EMERGES

There was good reason for people to doubt the wisdom and effectiveness of our policies. City streets became increasingly endangered, and drugs and delinquency were no longer seen to be exclusively confined to distant, disorganized urban slums—they penetrated as well into the communities, homes and lives of the affluent and "respectable." Indeed, by all accounts, the crime rate had burgeoned in recent years. Criminologists were now writing extensively and often with an air of inevitability about the "growth of crime" and the "relentless upsurge in crime."[3] Few would any longer disagree with Charles Silberman's conclusion that "since the early 1960s, the United States has been in the grip of a crime wave of epic proportions."[4]

One did not have to travel far for the statistics needed to confirm these observations. Data accumulated and published by the FBI in 1977 indicated that during the course of the preceding decade, the amount of serious violent crime rose over 80 percent, serious property crimes over 75 percent. In 1976, eleven million crimes were reported to police; the actual number of offenses (which include both crimes reported and not reported to police officials) perpetrated on the American public in that single year is estimated to have been at least two to three times higher than this eleven million statistic.[5] The magnitude of such crime figures is perhaps more understandable if placed in these terms: by the mid-1970s, approximately three Americans in every hundred could expect to be the victim of a violent

1

Reaffirming Rehabilitation. DOI: http://dx.doi.org/10.1016/B978-1-4557-3130-5.00001-5

crime each year and one household in ten to be burglarized.[6] Equally disturbing but of even greater drama, James Q. Wilson informed us in 1975 that "a typical baby born and remaining in a large American city is more likely to die of murder than an American soldier in World War II was to die in combat."[7]

But a soaring crime rate was not all that people saw. At the same time, the inhumanity and injustice of our correctional process were forced upon the public's consciousness. Attica accomplished this deed.

Now it has been persuasively argued that it is primarily through unrest that the powerless are able to move the powerful to yield material and political concessions.[8] The history of imprisonment has certainly demonstrated the viability of this principle. Countless times, it has taken a wave of inmate insurrections to publicize prison abuses, prick society's conscience, and prompt correctional officials to institute reforms—however cosmetic. And this lesson has not been lost on our incarcerated. Tom Murton, noted prison critic and former superintendent of Arkansas State Penitentiary, has observed that by failing to improve conditions until a riot occurs, the prison "administration clearly informs inmates that it must be forced to perform its duty. It also indicates that it can be manipulated by intimidation and coercion. From these revelations, the inmates learn the necessity of developing a power base in order to bring about change within the prison."[9] On this topic, a Pennsylvania steel worker has been equally perceptive: "I think that if they didn't pull off a riot and grab some hostages, they figure nobody would ever pay attention to their problems. And you know, they're probably right."[10]

Yet despite this knowledge that prison reform and protest are intimately intertwined, inmates do not always riot in an effort to secure greater advantages or, more accurately, in an effort to suffer fewer disadvantages. More frequently, they endure their painful environment rather than risk a confrontation with the power—in concrete terms, the guns—held by the agents of the state. At certain junctures in history, however, social circumstances prevail that allow for the inmates' pent-up frustrations and hostility to break through traditional constraints and to be unleashed in the form of an uprising against the custodial regime. In these unique eras, insurrections sweep across our nation's prisons.

Significantly, by the late 1960s, the climate was ripe for another rash of inmate disturbances protesting deplorable living conditions. While the walls of our prisons remained as high and as secure as ever and proved sufficient to keep all but the exceptionally ingenious inmates confined, they were no longer able to keep society out.[11] On the other side of the penitentiary gates, substantial segments of the populace questioned the fundamental legitimacy of governmental policies (Vietnam) and of social arrangements that resulted in gross disparities of wealth. These attitudes, based in part on radical ideologies, seeped through the cracks in the prison wall and provided inmates with a new vocabulary with which to explain their plight. They now suffered not "prison abuse" but "oppression"; rebellion against the "exploitive" order was called for.[12]

At the same time, investigative reporters, mobile camera crews, and nightly news were now common features. Inmates knew that more than ever before their uprisings would receive immediate and widespread attention, and that negotiations with administrators over long lists of grievances would appear on the television screens in the living rooms of many

American households. Brutalizing practices would be too open to be ignored; at least some changes could be won.[13]

Not surprisingly, then, beginning in 1968 in Salem, Oregon, a series of inmate uprisings spread throughout our prison system. "The horrifying climax" to this wave of riots came on September 13, 1971, at Attica Correctional Facility, located in the small, upstate New York town of Attica.[14]

Four days earlier on Thursday, September 9, shortly before 9 a.m., an attempt to direct a company of inmates headed for their daily yard privileges back into their cells precipitated an outbreak. An hour and a half later, 1,281 of Attica's 2,243 inmate population occupied D-Block Yard in the prison, holding 38 guards hostage. Over the course of the following weekend, the national media went into D-Block Yard and watched as an outside committee of "observers" (including such notables as radical attorney William Kunstler, news reporter Tom Wicker, and Black Panther leader Bobby Seale) was allowed to negotiate with the inmates. A list of demands was procured, and State Correctional Commissioner Russell G. Oswald quickly agreed to nearly all points. However, Oswald refused to grant the inmates' demand for complete immunity for crimes committed during the uprising. And when a young guard injured in the takeover died, this proved to be a crucial impediment to a negotiated and bloodless settlement.

On Monday morning, September 13, the fateful decision was reached to retake the institution. An armed assault by state troopers and some correctional officers was launched at 9:43 a.m. The firing ceased by 9:52 and by 10:30 the rebellious inmates had been cleared from D-Block Yard. The final toll was the largest in the 150 year history of the American penitentiary. Over 80 inmates were wounded and 29 lay dead or dying. Ten guards were also killed—not by inmates as threatened and as reported initially by prison officials—but by the crossfire of the assaulting troopers.[15]

Attica was not to be simply another unfortunate, grizzly, yet soon forgotten event in the dark history of American penology.[16] Instead, it quickly assumed a national character and joined those other events in our past that have produced deep anguish in the American conscience. Shortly after Attica, a *Time* correspondent prophetically remarked:

> Attica. For some time to come in the U.S., that word will not be primarily identified with the plain upon which ancient Athens nurtured philosophy and democracy. Nor will it simply stand for the bucolic little town that gave its name to a turreted prison, mislabeled a "correctional facility." Attica will evoke the bloodiest prison rebellion in U.S. history. It will take its place alongside Kent State, Jackson State, My Lai and other traumatic events that have shaken the American conscience and incited searing controversy over the application of force—and the pressure that provokes it.[17]

Thus, the tragedy of Attica did not remain hidden; it reverberated throughout our nation. In the year following the violent repression of the Attica insurrection, the American public, typically conservative on law and order issues, had become "essentially more sympathetic to the complaints of inmates than to the conduct of penal authorities."[18] In this vein, a Louis Harris survey indicated that 58 percent of the public attributed "recent takeovers of prisons by inmates" to the fact that "authorities don't understand the needs of prisoners," while only 23 percent stated that "authorities are too easy on inmates" (19 percent remained undecided).[19]

Beyond this, Attica revealed another truth to those who had not previously glimpsed into the world of imprisonment: prisons are populated overwhelmingly by racial minorities and the economically disadvantaged. Indeed, few white faces (not counting the all-white custodial force held hostage) and even fewer faces of the rich could be found among the prisoners occupying D-Block Yard.[20] With the civil rights movement still in memory, these demographic facts of prison life suggested, if not demanded, the conclusion that racism and class inequality permeated our criminal "justice" system.

But above all, "Attica became a code word for the failure of the entire apparatus of corrections,"[21] or in Gresham Sykes' words, "a symbol for the end of an era in correctional philosophy."[22] A century and a half before, America had forged ahead with a penal innovation: a penitentiary system that promised to reform its charges. This promise for the humane improvement of inmates remained largely unfulfilled, but nevertheless many believed it to be within reach. Attica shattered this hope. The violent encounter between the state and its captives made apparent to the nation that the prison had failed in its original mission. Brutality, not benevolence, seemed the governing principle of our prisons. As never before, the assumptions underlying our correctional policies came under careful scrutiny, and liberal as well as more radical prison reform movements with roots in the previous decade took on added meaning. Few could any longer dispute that changes were clearly in order.

Thus, Americans in the first half of the 1970s were faced with the prospect of an intractable crime rate and confronted with the reality—powerfully symbolized by Attica—that their prisons were both inhumane and grossly ineffective. In this context, a culprit was needed to take the blame, and a candidate was readily found. Rehabilitation would take the rap.

THE FAILURE OF CRIMINAL JUSTICE REHABILITATION

Over the course of the past century, the notion that we should rehabilitate lawbreakers had, on the surface, displaced punishment as the philosophy guiding the formulation of criminal justice policy. It had become something of a truth in criminological circles that punishing criminals for their transgressions—whether it was to balance harms inflicted on society (retribution), to teach that crime does not pay (deterrence), or to protect society by keeping the dangerous in secure cages (incapacitation)—had no moral legitimacy, scientific standing, or pragmatic benefit. Thus, writing in 1930, Harry Elmer Barnes, a pioneer in the field of criminology, voiced the opinion that "our entire system of criminal jurisprudence is wrong-headed and unscientific because, in the first place, it rests upon the fundamental assumption of the primary importance of detecting guilt and adjusting the punishment to the crime."[23] Similarly, over 35 years later, Karl Menninger asserted in his acclaimed work *The Crime of Punishment* that "crime problems have been dealt with too long with only the aid of common sense. Catch criminals and lock them up; if they hit you, hit them back. This is common sense, but it does not work."[24]

In practice, the ascendancy of rehabilitation meant that the components of the criminal justice system were now manifestly organized to effect the reformation of offenders. Criminals were supposedly placed on probation to allow for their treatment in the community; they were sent to prison not to pay for their crimes but to be cured of their criminogenic malady; and they were released on parole by a board of "experts" when this benevolent task of reform had been accomplished.

However, close observers of our correctional system would have recognized that the pre-eminence of rehabilitation was more myth than reality. They were well aware that probation was likely the result of an offender receiving a mild sentence in exchange for a guilty plea that would lighten the burden of a prosecutor's case load. And release from prison, where few rehabilitation programs actually operated according to plan, probably reflected the willingness of an inmate to cooperate with the custodial regime or perhaps the desire of the state to reduce the size of its prison population in order to save money. As historian David Rothman has illustrated, a look to our past clearly reveals that "convenience" far more often than "conscience" has controlled the daily workings of our correctional process.[25]

Nevertheless, as America entered the decade of the seventies, a substantial segment of the population believed that treatment philosophy was in fact the force that regulated criminal justice policy. A Louis Harris national poll in 1968 indicated that nearly half (48 percent) of the public thought that the primary purpose of prisons at that time was rehabilitation, compared with 24 percent who thought that prisons functioned to protect society and 13 percent who gave punishment as a response (15 percent answered "not sure").[26] Even more significantly, the same Harris poll revealed that fully 72 percent of the public thought that rehabilitation "should be the emphasis" of our prisons. As federal judge Marvin Frankel remarked in 1972, it is "fashionable nowadays to say that only rehabilitation of the offender can justify confinement."[27] Public confidence in criminal justice rehabilitation ran high.

But this abiding faith in rehabilitation was soon shattered by the realities of the day. Again, as rising crime rates incited increasing fear in the public and turmoil reigned in our prisons, it became all too clear that our criminal justice system was failing. And with this realization came the conclusion that what many believed to be the guiding principle of this system—rehabilitation—was responsible for this troubling state of affairs. Indeed, the disillusionment at both ends of the political spectrum was profound. For conservatives, rehabilitation undermined law and order by "coddling" the criminal element; it was the cause of our high crime rates. For liberals, rehabilitation was now seen not to allow for the betterment of society's captives but rather to be a major source of the coercive, discriminatory treatment suffered by prison inmates; it was the cause of America's Atticas. In this context, few defenders of criminal justice rehabilitation remained.

By the mid-1970s, then, many stood poised to cast aside the philosophy of rehabilitation. Yet if proclamations of the death of rehabilitation were widespread, this did not immediately resolve the issue of exactly what strategy should be employed to deal with the pressing problem of crime and its control; a crisis existed in criminal justice policy. Several alternative proposals vied to replace rehabilitation as the dominant paradigm in the field and thus put an end to this crisis.[28] But only one—determinate sentencing, rooted in the philosophy of punishment—captured the imagination of liberals and conservatives alike, and of both those who suggest policies (academics) and those who make policies (legislators). "By the mid-1970's," in Samuel Walker's words, "sentencing reform became the latest fad."[29] And as another commentator observed in 1977, "determinate sentencing is clearly an idea whose time has come."[30]

DETERMINATE AND INDETERMINATE SENTENCING

As we shall see later, "determinate" or "flat" sentencing is a complex concept that is used to refer to several different ways of handling a convicted offender. For our purposes here, however, it will suffice to outline only its most general meaning: after a defendant either enters a guilty plea or is tried and found guilty, the judge sentences the defendant to a specific number of years in prison. Thus, the exact penalty a criminal will endure is stated or "determined" at the time of sentencing. Further, in a pure flat sentencing format, the judge would not have the freedom or discretion to assign any sanction (s)he desires. Instead, it is the legislature's task to formulate a code that, based on the seriousness of each offense, prescribes precisely how much each act should be punished. In turn, the judge is bound to follow these directives. Concretely, this means that if the legislature decides that the crime of armed robbery deserves three years' imprisonment, then the judge must send a convicted armed robber to the penitentiary for three years.

Throughout the early part of our history, sentencing was, for the most part, determinate in nature. Unlike an ideal determinate sentencing scheme, the legislatures typically declined to specify a particular term of imprisonment for each criminal offense, choosing instead to set only the maximum number of years in prison that an offense could entail. This left a judge presiding over a criminal case free to select any sentence up to but not exceeding this legislatively-fixed maximum. Nevertheless, once a judge decided upon and assigned a particular sentence (for example, three years), an offender would be obliged to serve out this entire term. Only an executive pardon from the governor could spare the criminal this burden.[31]

By the 1870s, a revolution in sentencing practices began to develop, and by the first quarter of the 1900s, the change to a new way of dealing with convicted criminals had been all but completed. Convicts would now be given "indeterminate" (or "indefinite") sentences. Judges no longer sentenced an offender to a flat or exact term; the time to be spent in the penitentiary would not be determined prior to incarceration. Instead, at the sentencing hearing, a criminal was told the *range* of years that would be served, and hence the criminal entered prison not knowing when release back into society would occur. In contrast to the old sentencing procedures, then, a person convicted of armed robbery would not receive a flat term of three years but rather would be sent to the penitentiary for a term that could span anywhere from one to six years.

The movement in sentencing away from determinacy and toward indeterminacy was intimately related to the emergence of new ideas on how to achieve an offender's reformation. When penitentiaries first appeared in America during the 1820s, it was felt that a common regime of discipline, hard work, firm religious training, and isolation from criminal influences would provide every inmate with a moral fiber sufficiently strong to resist the ubiquitous temptations of vice and corruption that prevailed outside the prison walls. However, reformers at the turn of the next century—usually called "Progressives"—had a different agenda to press forward: the treatment of criminals should not be uniform but individualized. Since people commit crimes for different reasons—for instance, some might steal because they are poor, others because they are emotionally troubled—it made little sense, the Progressives argued, to expose offenders to exactly the same regime during their captivity. Instead, all logic pointed toward taking every inmate separately, then determining the unique set of factors that drove each one into crime, and, finally, of curing the individual offender of his or her specific pathological condition.

Two crucial and connected policies followed from the Progressives' vision of how to remedy an offender's misfortune. First, in proposing the individualized treatment of the convicted, the Progressives were, in essence, urging that the state's response to a criminal should not depend on the nature or seriousness of the crime committed (what an offender did) but on the nature of the criminal's condition (what is wrong with the offender) and on how quickly this can be cured. In short, the punishment should fit the criminal and not the crime. And second, this meant that, in practice, the exact length of a prison sentence should not be determined by a judge at the time of conviction. Just as people in hospitals recover at different rates, the Progressives reasoned, so do people in prisons. As such, the date of release could only be set after an inmate's progress in a rehabilitation program had been closely monitored, and a committee of "experts"—the parole board—had ascertained that an offender had achieved a clean bill of health. Thus, the Progressives' agenda mandated that criminals enter the penitentiary on indeterminate sentences, and that their length of captivity be regulated not by the gravity of the crime they had committed but by their willingness and capacity to be reformed.

The liberal reform movement of the Progressives succeeded in popularizing a philosophy of corrections that had a substantial impact on the everyday functioning of the criminal justice system—though, it must be added, not in ways fully anticipated by the Progressives. Nevertheless, the Progressives' proposals for indeterminate sentencing and parole boards (as well as for probation to effect community treatment and a separate justice system for the rehabilitation of juvenile offenders) all became, and still are, integral features of society's apparatus of social control.

Yet not everyone was pleased by this turn of events. Those holding a more conservative "law and order" perspective were disturbed by the prospect that inmates would be "coddled" rather than punished during incarceration and thus would fail to learn their lesson that "crime does not pay." Even more troubling in the conservative view was that parole boards would allow supposedly "rehabilitated," but in reality dangerous criminals to pass through the prison gates and into society where they would readily prey on good, innocent citizens. Social commentators called parole "the nation's Public Scandal No. 1." Meanwhile, newspapers were quick to capitalize on these sentiments and the fear they aroused by running cartoons headed by such captions as "Turning Criminals Loose," and which depicted parolees committing violent crimes.[32] But the conservatives' assault on the liberal reforms of the Progressives for the most part proved a failure. Their successes were occasional and usually came in the form of either pressuring judges and parole board members to be severe for a time with the criminals that had the misfortune to come their way or in obtaining passage of limited determinate sentencing laws (such as mandatory minimum prison terms for violent offenders, or mandatory life sentences for "habitual" criminals convicted of three felonies).

ATTACKING REHABILITATION: DETERMINATE SENTENCING SOLVES THE CRISIS

As we shift our attention back to more recent days and to the disillusionment surrounding the philosophy of rehabilitation, it should be of little surprise to learn that today's conservatives have given their wholehearted support to the movement to abandon indeterminate in favor of determinate sentencing. Like their predecessors, current conservatives are convinced that rehabilitation leads to the coddling of criminals and thus lowers the costs or pains of crime. From their vantage, this undermines the deterrent and protective powers of our criminal justice system and results in a higher crime rate. The conservatives thus conclude that society's futile efforts to treat criminals in a more humane manner are fostered at the expense of the increased victimization of good, innocent citizens; it is time that we ceased worrying about the criminals and started worrying about society.

For conservatives, the idea of determinate sentencing promises to make the welfare of the innocent and the sanctity of the social order our highest priorities once again, and thereby to remedy the ills initially spawned by Progressives and other liberal reformers over the past century. Remember, under a pure or ideal determinate or flat sentencing format, a conviction for a crime means that a defendant must serve the precise sentence that the legislature has prescribed for that particular offense. This ensures that judges would lose much of their discretion to return predatory criminals to the street on probation for "community treatment," and that parole boards would lack the power to prematurely terminate an inmate's stay in captivity. In the long run, criminals, as well as those pondering the commission of illegal acts, will be taught, the conservatives argue, that stern punishment inevitably follows conviction and hence that crime does not pay anymore. And for those who are unable or unwilling to learn this lesson, at least they will be confined in their cages where they can no longer wreak havoc on the law-abiding.

If it could be anticipated that conservatives would react favorably to calls for determinate sentencing, the same could not be said of liberals. After all, the liberals have traditionally resisted the passage of harsh, "law and order" statutes, and they are the very people who campaigned so long and hard to institutionalize treatment ideology. Yet by the middle part of the 1970s, an amazing philosophical transformation had occurred. Substantial segments of the liberal camp had rejected the ideal of rehabilitation and now embraced proposals for determinate sentencing as fully as their conservative counterparts.

In the past, liberals had often been unhappy with criminal justice rehabilitation. However, this displeasure was always of a particular flavor: the rehabilitative ideal is a sound one, but the way it is being put into practice is flawed; sufficient resources are lacking or an innovative technique must replace outdated modes of offender reformation. In contrast, current-day liberals decline to argue that the solution to the problems surrounding correctional rehabilitation is more and better programs. They voice instead a more profound critique which manifests that their faith in rehabilitation has been shattered at its very foundation: the rehabilitative ideal itself is inherently flawed.

More explicitly, while conservatives believe that rehabilitation has resulted in the coddling of criminals and the *victimization of society*, liberals assert the opposite: rehabilitation has eventuated in the *victimization of the criminal*. Though reform programs may have been the product of good intentions, they have had ugly consequences. Originally, liberals were convinced that the state should be granted the power to deprive inmates of their freedom pending their cure. Recalcitrant prisoners who resisted attempts to rehabilitate them would either have a change of heart or endure prolonged incarceration. Certainly, this might present some sticky problems. However, since the state was ultimately acting for the welfare or betterment of the inmate, it could be trusted to enforce an offender's therapy in a humane and efficient manner.

But their trust in the state, liberals now realize, was badly misplaced. It is clear that the state and its agents (judges, parole boards, correctional personnel), given broad discretionary powers under the guise that they were benevolently reforming offenders, have frequently abused these powers and neglected the needs of the criminal. Hence, "in the name of treatment," criminals have all too often been accorded few due process rights, warehoused in essentially custodial institutions for excessive lengths of time, subjected—on the basis of race, class or political conviction rather than their "condition"—to widely disparate "treatments" (punishments?) for the same offense, and had their minds and bodies violated "for their own good." Justice thus has not been well served by the movement to build a therapeutic state. Lionel Trilling captured the essence of the liberals' disappointment with the legacy of their reforms when he commented, "Some paradox in our nature leads us, once we have made our fellow men the objects of our enlightened interest, to go on to make them the objects of our pity, then of our wisdom, ultimately of our coercion."[33]

In light of the persisting and inherent evils of criminal justice rehabilitation, liberals argue that the time has come to ensure that the victimization of offenders is no longer justified by the ideology of rehabilitation. Rehabilitation must cease to be the guiding philosophy of penal practice, and only be permitted if voluntarily chosen by an offender. The goal of the criminal *justice* system must be the dispensing of *justice*, not the reformation of offenders. A "justice model" must be instituted in place of the rehabilitation model.

At the core of the liberals' justice model is the demand that all sentencing be flat or determinate. Again, from the liberals' perspective, the crux of the problem with the present system is that the rehabilitative ideal and its offspring, indeterminate sentencing, have given judges and parole boards extremely wide discretion on the grounds that such freedom is required to reform offenders by fitting the punishment to the criminal, not the crime. But this power has been abused. At best, judges and parole boards have made erroneous decisions about how much liberty an offender should lose because they lacked the wisdom or expertise to do otherwise; at worst, they have allowed political consideration and discriminatory criteria to influence their judgments. As such, true justice can only be achieved if this unfettered discretion is eliminated or severely constrained—a task which determinate sentencing accomplishes. Under this scheme, sanctions are legislatively-fixed. Judges are thus substantially constrained to follow the legislature's directives, and since sentences are served in their entirety, parole boards are not needed to assess which inmates should be released back into the community. Moreover, sentences are scaled according to the seriousness of the crime, and are not a function of who the person is. Hence, every criminal's punishment—whether black or white, rich or poor—is commensurate with the harm caused society. All offenders are equal before the law, and all receive their "just deserts"—nothing more, nothing less.

As we progressed into the latter part of the 1970s, the movement to scrap rehabilitation was well underway. By the end of the decade, twelve states—led most notably by California, always on the cutting edge of penal reform—had shifted decidedly away from indeterminate prison terms and toward some variation of determinate sentencing. A number of other states as well as the federal government were actively considering a change in this direction. Further, over half of the state legislatures around the country had passed laws prescribing flat or mandatory sentences for at least selected categories of offenses, and more than a few of their brethren assemblies were hurrying to try their own experiments with this strategy.[34]

And why not? Determinate sentencing had something for everyone, and at the same time, promised to resolve the crisis in criminal justice policy wrought by burgeoning crime rates and prison turmoil. For conservatives, concerned with the welfare of the victim and the preservation of social order, determinate sentencing would ensure a marked increase in the cost of violating the law and would thus afford a major reduction in an intolerably high level of crime. For liberals, concerned with the just and humane processing of criminals, it meant equal treatment before the courts and the elimination of the gross abuses inmates suffered during captivity "in the name of rehabilitation." There would be no more Atticas.

Now the two political camps did disagree in one fundamental respect: how severe (or long) prison sentences should be. This inconsistency was an outgrowth of the divergent reasoning that led each of these ideological rivals to support the same social policy of determinate sentencing. Since their principal priority was mitigating the horrors of crime by raising its costs, conservatives favored prison terms of lengthy duration. In contrast, believing that penitentiaries, even absent state enforced therapy, are bastions of inhumanity and desiring to minimize the harms visited upon inmates, liberals argued for restraint in the use of incarceration. Only serious offenders should be imprisoned, and then only for short periods of time.

However crucial this disagreement would prove to be in the future, in the enthusiasm of the moment, it could be overlooked or a temporary compromise struck. And those responsible for making criminal justice policy, the legislators, had every reason to do so. Not only, as academics advised, would determinate sentencing resolve all of the pressing problems surrounding crime and its control, but it would also save the day cheaply. In the past, reform proposals inevitably called for large amounts of expenditures. Adding staff to rehabilitate inmates costs money, and "changing society" to eliminate the criminogenic conditions burdening urban neighborhoods is even more expensive. But now the job could be done simply by manipulating the legal code, by matching a flat sentence to each criminal offense. A few consultants might have to be paid to assist in this task, but no large and immediate appropriations would be necessary. Crime control at no cost; surely the voters would be pleased.

REAFFIRMING REHABILITATION: THE FALSE APPEAL OF DETERMINATE SENTENCING

We find ourselves, then, in the midst of a potent movement that seeks to cast criminal justice rehabilitation aside and place its faith in the contrasting philosophy of punishment or "just deserts." Indeed, on the surface, all logic urges us to support this renovation of our criminal justice system. For one thing, there seems much to be excited about: determinate sentencing holds out the bright promise of a more rational, efficient, just and humane system of social control. Beyond this, defending rehabilitation is not an easy thing to do these days. After all, have not scholar followed by scholar—from John Bartlow Martin to Francis Allen to Marvin Frankel to Norval Morris—painstakingly illustrated the poverty of indeterminate sentencing and the rehabilitative ideal?[35] And have not the data scoured from research study after research study convincingly demonstrated that "rehabilitation doesn't work"?[36]

Certainly, these are persuasive arguments against the agenda for criminal justice rehabilitation first thrust forth by the Progressives. Nevertheless, our purpose for undertaking this volume is not to provide further enlightenment either about the inadequacies of state enforced therapy or about the viability of determinate sentencing. Instead, it is quite the opposite: to warn of the dangers of embracing a punishment philosophy and to propose that we should not reject rehabilitation but rather reaffirm a rehabilitation that is properly tempered by considerations limiting the coercive potential of the state.

This is not the place to detail the reasoning underlying our opposition to the new wave of criminal justice "reform"; this task will be accomplished in later pages. But for now let us suggest quite broadly that to abandon the rehabilitative ideal is to risk losing the invaluable ideological role it plays in trumpeting the call for humanity in a system that is by its very nature, by its prescribed function and daily workings, repressive. Further, if determinate sentencing appears at first glance to resolve the crisis in criminal justice policy that emerged in the 1970s, we believe that closer inspection will reveal that it is more a Pandora's Box than a panacea.

In this vein, three issues should be kept in mind as we progress through the pages to come. First, in basing punishment strictly on the crime and not the criminal, implicit in the determinate sentencing paradigm is the assumption that the state not only has no right but also *no obligation* to do anything about the condition or needs of an offender. Yet we may ask, is a philosophy that gives legitimacy to state neglect of individual needs likely to be more benevolent than one that mandates, however imperfectly, state concern? Second, it is highly ironic that those who mistrust the state to administer criminal justice rehabilitation in a just and humane manner are now placing their total faith in the state (the legislature in particular) to punish justly and humanely. We have searched in vain to discover the basis for this faith. And third, in the past, the failure of treatment programs has invariably evoked a plea among liberal reformers that inmates receive more and not less rehabilitation. When the new agenda for punishment fails to reduce crime at some point in the future, what will the call be for then? Less punishment—or more?

In disclosing that our intention is to argue for the reaffirmation of criminal justice rehabilitation, we are at the same time revealing our own political bias and designating the audience that we most wish to hear our words. Essentially, this is a liberal reformist tract written for fellow liberal reformists. We have tagged ourselves in this way because we fully embrace the fundamental liberal principles that the goal of our criminal justice system should be to improve rather than to damage an offender, and that for society's own welfare, criminal punishment should reflect not our basest instincts (vengeance) but our most noble values. Alternatively, we are speaking above all to liberals who so readily rejected rehabilitation in recent times and turned to determinate or "just deserts" sentencing as a strategy to more effectively institute these principles within the criminal justice system. In its bluntest terms, our message to such liberals is that they are playing into the hands of the more repressive forces in our society; determinate sentencing will result in less justice and more coercion for criminal defendants—the objects of their new "wisdom." Only the ideology of rehabilitation contains at its core a benevolence consistent with the tradition of liberal reformism. This benevolence can be corrupted, but it can also be capitalized upon; and it is to this latter task, we believe, that liberals should direct their energies.

Now those at both ends of the political spectrum may, we suspect, be tempted to close their books at this juncture. Conservatives may be prepared to dismiss our initial thoughts here as "bleeding heart liberalism." And, of course, this caricature is not totally false. Nevertheless, our assessment to follow in later pages possesses some pragmatics that hopefully will prompt the conservative to read onward: determinate sentencing will be an expensive innovation, perhaps even fiscally irresponsible, and will have a negligible impact on the overall crime rate in our society. On the other hand, radicals will likely counter that efforts to reform the workings of the criminal justice system are badly misplaced. Until there is social justice, there can be no criminal justice; until material and political resources are more equitably distributed, "the rich will get richer" and "the poor will get prison." We are inclined to agree with this reasoning. Yet the conclusion that true justice must await the arrival of a wider socioeconomic revolution should not be used to legitimate a profound disinterest in the consequences of the current and ongoing system of criminal justice. In the absence of a vast structural transformation of American society, it is certainly a worthy task to press for criminal justice policies that will eventuate in less injustice and be less repressive. Indeed, it is a task that can only be neglected at a cost of considerable human misery.

Closer to the end of this volume, we will undertake a more comprehensive review of the movement during the 1970s to abandon rehabilitation, and we will then present the details of our case against the determinate sentencing paradigm. First, however, we would like to acquaint the reader with both the major schools of criminological thought (Classical and Positivist) and criminal justice ideologies that have so long formed the underpinnings of the debate over whether we should punish or rehabilitate offenders. In turn, we will endeavor to chronicle the way in which these theories and ideologies have become embodied in the heart of the American criminal justice system over the past two centuries.

NOTES

[1]C. Ray Jeffrey, *Crime Prevention Through Environmental Design*. (Beverly Hills, Ca. Sage, 1977), p. 29. Again on page 80, Jeffrey commented that "At the end of the criminal justice process operates a correctional system that neither deters nor rehabilitates."

[2]James B. Jacobs has thus observed that "prison officials have lost confidence in themselves owing to the repudiation of both punishment and rehabilitation as justifications for imprisonment." See his "Race relations and the prisoner subculture." Pp. 1–27 in Norval Morris and Michael Tonry (eds.), *Crime and Justice: An Annual Review of Research, Volume I.* (Chicago: University of Chicago Press, 1979). Similarly, David A. Ward noted as early as 1973 that the "most common theme at the national conferences of American correctional administrators has become 'The Crisis in Corrections.' Clearly American prison systems are in trouble and the trouble is not only that there has been violence in the prisons but also that the claim that offenders could be 'rehabilitated' in prison has been exposed as a myth." See "Evaluative research for corrections." Pp. 184–206 in Lloyd E. Ohlin, *Prisoners In America.* (New York: The American Assembly, 1973), p. 184. See also Donald F. Anspach, "The crisis in American penology." Paper presented at the 1980 meeting of the American Society of Criminology, and Samuel Walker, *Popular Justice: A History of American Criminal Justice.* (New York: Oxford University Press, 1980), pp. 221–254.

[3]Sir Leon Radzinowicz and Joan King, *The Growth of Crime: The International Experience.* (New York: Basic Books, 1977), p. 3.

[4]Charles E. Silberman, *Criminal Violence, Criminal Justice.* (New York: Random House, 1978), p. 3.

[5]Federal Bureau of Investigation, *Uniform Crime Reports—1976.* (Washington, D.C.: U.S. Government Printing Office, 1977). p. 35. Victimization data, gathered by surveying the general public and asking respondents how many times they had been the victim of a crime, indicate that the actual amount of crime in America is at least two to three times greater than that reported by the FBI. See Peter Wickman and Phillip Whitten, *Criminology: Perspectives on Crime and Criminality.* (Lexington, Massachusetts: D.C. Heath and Company), pp. 83–85. Another useful resource on crime statistics is Michael Gottfredson, Michael Hindelang, and Nicolette Parisi (eds.), *Sourcebook of Criminal Justice Statistics—1977.* (Washington, D.C: U. S. Government Printing Office, 1978).

[6]Silberman, *Criminal Violence, Criminal Justice*, p. 4. Similarly, Bureau of Justice Statistics indicate that in 1975, "the number of U.S. households that were the site of a burglary or a theft or those in which a member was a victim of a theft or a violent crime" totaled 32 percent. U.S. Department of Justice, "30 percent of U. S. households hit by crime." *Justice Assistance News* 2 (May 1981), p. 1.

[7]James Q. Wilson, *Thinking About Crime.* (New York: Vintage, 1975), p. 19.

[8]Frances Fox Piven and Richard A. Cloward, *Regulating the Poor: The Functions of Public Welfare.*
(New York: Pantheon Books, 1971).

[9]Thomas E. Murton, *The Dilemma of Prison Reform.* (New York: Praeger, 1976), p. 30.

[10]Quoted in Louis Harris, "Public rejects force in quelling prison riots." *Chicago Tribune* (February 7, 1972), p. 18.

[11]See James B. Jacobs' discussion on the prison as part of "mass society" in his *Stateville: The Penitentiary in Mass Society*. (Chicago: University of Chicago Press, 1977).

[12]For comments on the politicization of inmates, see John Irwin, *Prisons In Turmoil*. (Boston: Little Brown, 1980), pp. 107–110. However, the question arises as to whether any substantial number of inmates actually internalized radical ideas or simply utilized leftist ideology to justify grievances that have long plagued our prisons. In this regard, see Miller's claim that the civil rights movement did not markedly politicize black gangs during the 1960s but rather functioned to provide gang members with "an important new kind of justificational vocabulary to the repertoire of traditional modes for explaining gang activity.. . .Black gang members continue, by and large, to do much the same kinds of things, but for some there have been changes in the ways they characterize and justify these practices." Walter M. Miller, "Youth gangs in the urban crisis era." Pp. 91–128 in James F. Short, Jr. (ed.), *Delinquency, Crime and Society*. (Chicago: University of Chicago Press, 1976), p. 113.

[13]Inmate access to the media is now a common feature of prison protests. For instance, in the February 1980 riot in New Mexico, a newsman was brought into the prison to conduct negotiations with inmates and television cameras later filmed an inmate reading the final agreement reached with the administration. See Michael S. Serrill and Peter Katal, "The anatomy of a riot: the facts behind New Mexico's bloody ordeal." *Corrections Magazine* 6 (April 1980), pp. 16, 21. Similarly, newsmen were recently allowed to conduct in-depth interviews with inmates staging a hunger strike on the protective custody wing (Cell Block 10) of Walpole (Ma.) State Prison. See Joe Heaney, "Cell Block 10's common denominator: 'bum raps'." *Boston Herald American* (July 13, 1980), p. B1.

[14]Silberman, *Criminal Violence, Criminal Justice*, p. 376.

[15]For accounts of the events of the Attica riot, see Tom Wicker, *A Time To Die*. (New York: Ballantine Books, 1975) and New York State Special Commission on Attica, *The Official Report of the New York State Commission on Attica*. (New York: Praeger, 1972).

[16]For instance, the recent riot at the Penitentiary of New Mexico that left 33 inmates dead and over 200 raped or beaten created an initial wave of much consternation but produced little change in correctional policy across the nation. For a report on the New Mexico riot, see the April 1980 edition of *Corrections Magazine*.

[17]"War at Attica: was there no other way?" *Time Magazine* (September 17, 1971), p. 19.

[18]Louis Harris, "Public rejects force in quelling prison riots," p. 18.

[19]*Ibid.*, p. 18.

[20]"At the time of the Attica uprising, at least 75 percent of the 2,250 prisoners were black or Puerto Rican." *Time Magazine*, "War at Attica: was there no other way?", p. 19. Similarly, James B. Jacobs notes that minorities are overrepresented in the prisoner population by a factor of five. See his "Race relations and the prisoner subculture," p. 19. See also Jeffrey H. Reiman, *The Rich Get Richer and the Poor Get Prison: Ideology, Class and Criminal Justice*. (New York: John Wiley, 1979).

[21]Samuel Walker, *Popular Justice*, p. 243.

[22]Gresham M. Sykes, *Criminology*. (New York: Harcourt, Brace, Jovanovich, 1978), p. 476.

[23]Harry Elmer Barnes, *The Story of Punishment: A Record of Man's Inhumanity to Man*. Second edition, revised. (Montclair, N.J.: Patterson Smith, 1972, originally published in 1930), p. 265. Sykes, *Criminology*, p. 459, has also commented that by 1950 "almost every criminology student was thoroughly indoctrinated with the idea that the punishment of criminals was a useless relic."

[24]Karl Menninger, *The Crime of Punishment*. (New York: Penguin Books, 1966), p. 5.

[25]David J. Rothman, *Conscience and Convenience: The Asylum and Its Alternatives in Progressive America*. (Boston: Little Brown, 1980).

[26]Louis Harris, *The Public Looks at Crime and Corrections*. (Washington, D.C: Joint Commission on Correctional Manpower and Training, 1968), p. 7.

[27]Marvin E. Frankel, *Criminal Sentences: Law Without Order*. (New York: Hill and Wang, 1972), p. 7.

[28]For instance, two alternative paradigms suggested at this time included radical or Marxist criminology and the manipulation of the environment (e.g., better street lighting, placement of building entrances) to reduce chances of victimization. For a discussion of these "new criminologies," see Gresham M. Sykes, "The rise of critical criminology," *Journal of Criminal Law and Criminology* 65 (June 1974), pp. 206–213; Richard Quinney, *Class State and Crime: On the Theory and Practice of Criminal Justice*. (New York: David McKay, 1977); Ian Taylor, Paul Walton, and Jock Young, *The New Criminology: For a Social Theory of Deviance*. (London: Routledge and Kegan Paul, 1973); Oscar Newman, *Defensible Space: Crime Prevention Through Urban Design*. (New York: Collier Books, 1973); Jeffrey, *Crime Prevention Through Environmental Design*.

[29]Walker, *Popular Justice*, p. 243.

[30]Michael Serrill, "Determinate sentencing: the history, the theory, the debate." *Corrections Magazine* 3 (September 1977), p. 3. Largely influenced by the discrepancy between the equality movement begun in the 1960s and the racial and class inequalities manifested in the criminal justice system, major academic statements favoring determinate sentencing by liberal and some radical scholars appeared between 1970–1972. However, wider acceptance of these reform proposals by their colleagues in the field as well as by criminal justice policy makers and practitioners did not transpire until the mid-1970s and beyond. The major conservative writings supporting a more punitive orientation to crime by James Q. Wilson and Ernest van den Haag were both published in 1975. A more detailed discussion of the conditions (including the general failure of American corrections as symbolized by Attica and rising crime rates) spanning the past two decades that gave rise to and sustained the rejection of rehabilitation as well as the acceptance of just deserts/determinate sentencing reform is presented in Chapter 4.

[31]*Ibid*, p. 4.

[32]Rothman, *Conscience and Convenience*, pp. 160–161.

[33]Quoted in David J. Rothman, "The state as parent: social policy in the Progressive era." Pp. 67–96 in Willard Gaylin, Ira Glasser, Steven Marcus, and David Rothman, *Doing Good: The Limits of Benevolence*. (New York: Pantheon Books, 1978), p. 72.

[34]Michael Kannensohn, *A National Survey of Parole-Related Legislation Enacted During the 1979 Legislative Session.* (Washington, D.C.: U.S. Department of Justice, 1979).

[35]John Bartlow Martin, *Break Down the Walls: American Prisons—Present, Past, and Future.* (New York: Ballantine Books, 1951), pp. 231–244 ("Rehabilitation—the dangerous myth"); Francis A. Allen, *The Borderland of Criminal Justice.* (Chicago: University of Chicago Press, 1964), pp. 25–41; Marvin E. Frankel, *Criminal Sentences*, pp. 86–102; Norval Morris, *The Future of Imprisonment.* (Chicago: University of Chicago Press, 1974), pp. 1–27.

[36]As will be discussed in detail at a later point, the most notable summary of research in this tradition is Robert Martinson's "What works?—questions and answers about prison reform." *Public Interest* (Spring 1974), pp. 22–54. See, more generally, Douglas Lipton, Robert Martinson, and Judith Wilks, *The Effectiveness of Correctional Treatment: A Survey of Treatment Evaluation Studies.* (New York: Praeger Publishers, 1975).

Criminal Justice Theories and Ideologies

The current controversy over the appropriate direction for American criminal justice policy does not exist in an ahistorical or apolitical vacuum. Contemporary debates concerning the causes of crime, the proper purpose of the criminal sanction, and over the pragmatics of criminal justice reform are outgrowths of the prescriptions and policies of past students of criminal justice. Hence, to facilitate our understanding of the issues which surround the current dispute over crime and punishment in America, we will examine two schools of criminology which have dominated thinking about crime and criminal justice for the past two hundred years. The classical and positivist schools are based on distinct sets of underlying ideological assumptions, posit differing rationales for punishment, and suggest unique social policies to deal with crime. Their disparate assumptions, as we shall see throughout these chapters, lie at the heart of the debate between supporters of rehabilitation and supporters of punishment.

In this chapter we will delineate three modern political ideologies which reflect vastly differing assumptions and value stances concerning crime and criminal justice. It should be noted that ideologies are unprovable sets of assumptions about the proper state of things. They are generally "unexamined presumptions" which shape an individual's stance on given issues, and are often highly emotionally charged.[1]

It is important to be able to recognize one's own ideological stance as well as those of others with respect to issues of crime and punishment. As Walter Miller has observed, "ideology and its consequences exert a powerful influence on the policies and procedures of those who conduct the enterprise of criminal justice, and ... the degree and kinds of influence go largely unrecognized. Ideology is the permanent hidden agenda of criminal justice."[2] In a similar vein, ideological concerns can have an impact upon social scientists studying crime and social policy. One's ideological stance can affect the type of problems selected for study, the process of theory construction, interpretation of research findings, and recommended social policies. One must thus be on guard against "statements forwarded as established conclusions [which] are based on ideological doctrine rather than empirically supportable evidence."[3]

Before discussing the conservative, liberal, and radical positions in more detail, however, we will first set out the central features of the classical and positivist schools of criminology.

Reaffirming Rehabilitation. DOI: http://dx.doi.org/10.1016/B978-1-4557-3130-5.00002-7

SCHOOLS OF CRIMINOLOGICAL THOUGHT

THE CLASSICAL SCHOOL

The classical school, represented most prominently by Cesare Beccaria and Jeremy Bentham, was at its core a movement to bring about the reform of the criminal justice systems of Europe in the eighteenth century. Legal and judicial institutions of that period were characterized by such abuses as trial by torture, secret accusations, presumptions of guilt before trial and arbitrary court procedures. Further, judges possessed virtually unrestrained discretion in setting penalties, and many of the penalties were barbarous indeed: death by burning, by the gibbet or by breaking on the wheel, punishment by such means as branding or amputation.[4]

The reformers of the classical school were influenced in their own views by such social contract theorists of the Enlightenment as Montesquieu, Rousseau, and Hobbes. Along these lines, Beccaria argued that in order to gain the security and liberty of an organized society, humans freely and willingly gave up part of their liberty to the state. Laws exist to ensure the maintenance of society, and when laws are broken and the state or its citizens thereby endangered, punishment is both necessary and justified. In this regard, "the true measure of crimes is . . . the harm done to society."[5] Laws that are not necessary for the welfare of the state and its citizens are unjust restrictions on individual liberty, however.

Equality was another theme central to Enlightenment thinkers which was adopted by the classical school. Since all men were created equal (in the state of nature) and are equally possessed of reason and free will, equality before the law (if not in property or rank) should be a fundamental principle of society.[6]

In light of these social and intellectual influences on Beccaria and Bentham, the central assumptions of the classical school included the following:

1. Only the legislator has the authority to make laws. Only laws, in turn, can set the punishment for crimes. Therefore it is the legislature, not the judge, which should fix the precise punishments for violations of the law. Prohibited acts and their attendant penalties should be matters of public knowledge. The role of the judge should be limited to the determination of guilt or innocence of the accused; thus, the judge is allowed little or no role in the determination of penalties for given offenses/offenders.

2. Human beings are both rational and possessed of free will, and can thus be held responsible for their actions. Humans are governed by the principle of *utility*; that is, they seek pleasure or happiness and avoid pain or unhappiness.[7]

3. Punishment should be based on the social harm of the act and not on the "intention" of the offender. Therefore, like offenses should receive like punishment; punishment should "fit the crime" and not the criminal.

4. The goal of punishment is primarily the prevention of crime and only secondarily to exact retribution for the harm an offender has caused. To prevent crime, punishments should be just severe enough for the pain or unhappiness created by the punishment to outweigh the pleasure or happiness obtainable from the crime. This is all that is

required for an offender to decide that "crime does not pay" and thus to be deterred from violating the law once again in the future ("specific deterrence"). Similarly, if the costs are higher than the benefits that can be derived from illegal behavior, those in the public contemplating criminal acts will also decide against pursuing such activities ("general deterrence"). Notably, Beccaria believed that any punishment beyond the minimum level needed to deter people from breaking the law unjustly restricts individual liberty, is non-utilitarian, and thus must be viewed as illegitimate.

5. Certainty and swiftness of punishment are more crucial to the prevention of crime than is severity; hence, "the certainty of a punishment, even if it be moderate, will always make a stronger impression than the fear of another which is more terrible but combined with the hope of impunity."[8]

6. The rights of accused persons should be protected against abuse. In particular, the accused should be presumed innocent until sufficient proof of guilt is introduced. Moreover, court hearings should be governed by clear and fair procedures.

In sum, Beccaria contended that "in order for punishment not to be, in every instance, an act of violence of one or of many against a private citizen, it must be essentially public, prompt, necessary, the least possible in the given circumstances, proportionate to the crimes, dictated by the laws."[9]

The proposals of the classical school met with some success in the years after their introduction. Beccaria's *Essay on Crimes and Punishments*, originally published in 1764, was translated into several languages shortly thereafter, including a French-language edition for which the introduction was written by Voltaire. Classical ideas also became an integral part of the French Code of 1791.[10]

Practical problems of implementing "pure" classical principles into the French Code provided the impetus for a modification of these principles. These modifications came to be embodied in a movement called the neo-classical school.

It must be remembered that in his desire to avoid the possibility of capricious and arbitrary punishments by judges, Beccaria argued that penalties should be set ahead of time by the legislatures. Equally "harmful" offenses were to receive equally "painful" penalties without regard to the characteristics of individual offenders. As these tenets were embodied in the French Code of 1791, circumstances of individuals were ignored to the extent that all offenders—whether first offenders or recidivists, children, insane, or incompetent—were dealt with only on the basis of the act committed. Proponents of the neo-classical school, while in the main accepting basic classical assumptions, modified these principles to allow for the consideration of certain individual circumstances as a pragmatic response to the exigencies of criminal sentencing. Thus, mitigated penalties and partial responsibility became possible for youth, the insane, the feeble-minded, and for other offenders under certain environmental or mental circumstances.

It has been suggested that this neo-classical model has formed the philosophical underpinnings of the agencies of social control in modern industrial societies.[11] Certainly this is true in that the classical school provided a *rationale* for punishment, although punishment as a feature of criminal justice systems antedated classical pronouncements.[12] A legalistic definition of crime is another characteristic common to the classical school and to modern criminal justice. And clearly, the neo-classical concept that criminals should be held responsible for (i.e., subject to punishment for) their actions, although less so in certain circumstances or for particular categories of individuals, is firmly embedded in our legal system.

Their accommodation of classical principles notwithstanding, the criminal justice and correctional systems of the industrialized Western world have also been influenced by a school of thought that arose to challenge classical assumptions: positivism.

THE POSITIVIST SCHOOL

The guiding concept of the positivist school of criminology has been the application of the scientific method to the study of the criminal. During the period between Beccaria's *Essay* (1764) and the publication of the positivists' first treatise—Lombroso's *The Criminal Man*—in 1876, science rather than reason alone had become the dominant means of understanding the world. Thus, it became the task of the early positivists of the Italian School—Lombroso, Garofalo, and Ferri—to extend the assumptions and methodology of science to the problem of criminal behavior.

Cesare Lombroso, often referred to today as the father of criminology, adopted a largely biological theory of crime causation. His early work emphasized the notion of the "born criminal," an individual more primitive and atavistic than the noncriminal and who could be identified by means of certain visible "stigmata." While never totally abandoning the idea of the born criminal and the biological basis for crime, his later work also cited the importance of social and environmental factors in the causation of crime. He is remembered today less for the specific content of his theories than for his insistence on the gathering of empirical data, emphasis on objectivity and the use of the scientific method, and stress on determinism rather than free will as the primary impetus to human action.

It is also important to note that positivism can take (and has taken) other forms than the biological variety. For example, psychological positivism, instead of locating the cause of criminal behavior within the biological makeup of an individual, might instead look for the cause in faulty personality development of the offender. Sociological positivism, conversely, might point to aspects of the social structure or the social environment as primary causal factors. Indeed, it has been concluded that "most contemporary scientific criminology is positivistic in method and in basic formulations."[13]

In order to understand more fully the impact of the positivist school on criminology and criminal justice in America, it is important to explicate the central features of this approach. First of all positivists, in seeking the source of criminal behavior, tend to assume that crime is *determined* by factors largely outside the control of the individual. Although they may differ as to whether the factors are primarily biological, psychological, or sociological in nature, they generally accept the idea of multiple factor causation—that is, that crime is caused by the interaction of a number of complex variables. Consequently, free-will explanations of crime are rejected in this model, and the differences between criminals and noncriminals are emphasized.

Second, since criminals did not freely choose their criminal behavior, it is inappropriate to punish them for their crimes. Early positivists argued that the small proportion of offenders whose behavior cannot be altered and who represent a danger to the community should be held in lifelong confinement.[14] For most others, individualized treatment of the offender is appropriate so that the underlying causes of criminal behavior may be eliminated. In this regard, the "medical model" provides a vocabulary with which positivists can talk about and understand crime:

> And as medicine teaches us that to discover the remedies for a disease we must first seek and discover the causes, so criminal science in the new form which it is beginning to assume, seeks the natural causes of the phenomenon of social pathology which we call crime: it thus puts itself in the way to discover effective remedies....[15]

Since individuals cannot be cured of their criminal tendencies through their own efforts, it is for the good of society as well as for the offenders' own good that the state undertakes to *rehabilitate* them. Allen has described the *rehabilitative ideal* as "the notion that a primary purpose of penal treatment is to effect changes in the characters, attitudes, and behavior of convicted offenders, so as to strengthen the social defense against unwanted behavior, but also to contribute to the welfare and satisfaction of offenders."[16]

Third, in the positivist scheme, more emphasis is placed on the offender than on the offense. Penalties are to be tailored to the unique and varied circumstances of each individual rather than to be based on considerations of social harm and deterrence. It is possible and even desirable that two persons committing similar offenses may receive varying dispositions if their individual conditions vary. In order that the goal of individualized treatment may be achieved, judges and correctional officials must be free to fit the type and duration of penalty to offender needs; in other words, punishments should not be immutably pre-set by legislatures. One important means for achieving this goal of particularized treatment is the indeterminate sentence: offenders remain in prison for as long as it takes to effect a "cure."

It is clear that the core assumptions and goals of the classical and positivist schools are frequently in conflict with one another. Table 2.1 points up the major areas of contrast between the two models.

Ostensibly, the positivist rehabilitative ideal has dominated criminal justice policy throughout the last century. The legacy of the positivists includes the indeterminate sentence, probation and parole, the reformatory, and the juvenile justice system. It is perhaps more correct to say, however, that our criminal justice and correctional apparatus represents a combination of classical and positivist principles. And most recently, as we shall see later in the chapter, positivist assumptions and policies have been giving way to a resurgence of classical thought in the United States.

POLITICAL IDEOLOGIES AND CRIMINAL JUSTICE POLICY

We have seen that the unique sets of assumptions of two predominant schools of criminological thought give rise to vastly different explanations of and prescriptions for the

Table 2.1 Early Schools of Criminology

	Classical	Positivist
1. Central concern of model's founders	reform of criminal justice system	scientific study of criminal
2. View of humans	free-will; utilitarian	deterministic: biological, psychological, sociological
3. Responsibility for actions	yes	no
4. Way to stop crime	insure that the costs of crime outweigh the benefits	eliminate factor causing crime
5. Focus of social control	(a) the law: make penalties severe enough to outweigh the benefits of crime (b) no judicial discretion; to insure that costs outweigh the benefits, punishment must be certain for everyone: punishment fits the crime (c) punishments fixed by law (implies the use of determinate sentences)	(a) the criminal and his/her condition: criminals are fundamentally different from the rest of us (b) judicial discretion; since each criminal & his/her condition may be different, the judge needs the leeway to fit the penalty to the needs of the individual criminal (c) indeterminate sentences rehabilitate the criminal
6. Purpose of social control	deterrence—if criminal is shown that the costs of crime outweigh the benefits (that "crime doesn't pay"), then the person will not commit any more offenses; punishment of offender can also serve to deter public from crime	

problem of crime. Likewise, both "expert" and "public" viewpoints about preferred criminal justice policy are frequently grounded in the political ideologies which are held by individuals. These ideologies tend to rest on sets of unexamined assumptions rather than upon solid empirical data, tend to have an emotional component, and are relatively resistant to change.[17] Thus, an understanding of criminal justice trends cannot rest on an examination of research results alone; the role of political viewpoints in the advocacy of particular policies toward crime also must be assessed.

In the course of this discussion, three varieties of political perspectives will be examined: conservative, liberal, and radical. Each will be defined with respect to its guiding principles and the implications of those principles for the control of crime. Then, current classical and positivist perspectives on crime will be analyzed in relation to their ideological bases.

CONSERVATIVE IDEOLOGY

Conservative thought places primary emphasis on the importance of maintaining social order; thus, the concerns of conservatism are more directed toward protecting society than toward aiding the offender. At the same time, the conservative assumes that existing social arrangements are basically sound and reflect widespread consensus among the members of society. The offender, then, is viewed as one who is "out of step" with the rest of the society.[18]

Conservatives tend to eschew rapid social change. They are likely to decry the breakdown of traditional values, and to seek to preserve traditional institutions. From their perspective, the sources of crime are often to be found in the erosion of discipline and respect for authority, coupled with an increase in permissive attitudes and practices throughout society.[19]

Individuals are seen as being responsible for their own actions—good or bad—in the conservative view. In this regard, self-reliance and individual achievement are to be encouraged. Conversely, a lack of faith in the ability of the government to solve individual and social problems abides in conservative thought. As a result of the foregoing premises, conservatives focus on punishment rather than rehabilitation as the proper goal of the criminal justice system.

In keeping with their emphasis on social order, system goals which focus on the protection of innocent citizens—that is, deterrence and incapacitation—are of primary importance. Sympathy is also directed toward the victim of crime. On the other hand, the criminal justice system is seen as being too lenient toward the offender. "Technicalities" which allow the guilty to go free should be minimized, and punishments should become both more certain and more severe in order to help reduce crime.

LIBERAL IDEOLOGY

According to proponents of liberalism, the central goals of society should be individual rights and equal opportunity for all. Liberals see current social arrangements as imperfect in that certain economic and social inequities persist in society. Although the social structure is probably not ultimately perfectible, improvements in the direction of greater equality are possible. Further, the state, through its programs, can provide the means to improve the condition of its citizens.

Moreover, there is a fundamental assumption in liberalism that crime is caused by the structural conditions of society rather than by the individual's calculation that crime pays. The long-term remedy for the crime problem, then, is fundamental social change. Short-term programs, favored by liberals, tend to focus on improving the situation of the offender as well as on reducing crime, and tend to be piecemeal in nature.[20]

Traditionally, liberals have placed their faith in rehabilitation as a central goal of criminal justice. However, the ebbing belief in the efficacy of rehabilitative programs among a number of liberals has served to divide the liberal camp. On the one hand, there are those who might be called the "traditional liberals" who argue that the goal of treatment of offenders is being prematurely jettisoned. Their contention is that the resources of the criminal justice system have never yet been fully committed to rehabilitation as a *real* goal of corrections. In addition, they argue, there are rehabilitative programs which have been shown to be effective with some offenders, but these successes have been glossed over by critics of treatment goals. On a philosophical level, rehabilitative programs represent a means of "doing good" for offenders; they also embody a rationale for humane treatment which opposes the conservative pressure to "get tough on crime."

Conversely, "justice model liberals" contend that the rehabilitative ideal is bankrupt as a strategy for reducing crime. Moreover, the structural concomitants of the philosophy of treatment—discretion and the indeterminate sentence—have brought about long penalties as well as real inequities in the penalties for similar offenses, thus undermining the "justice" of the system. As a remedy, liberals should thus abandon rehabilitation and instead embrace the more realistic and limited goal of just deserts, together with reductions in system discretion, short sentences commensurate with offense gravity, and determinate sentencing.

Finally, both liberal camps tend to agree in their support of decriminalization of victimless offenses, and of deinstitutionalization and expanded use of alternatives to incarceration.[21]

RADICAL IDEOLOGY

Radicals assume that their primary goals of true economic, social, and political equality for all cannot be achieved under the present capitalist system. The currently-dominant pattern of relations of production is designed to keep those who own the means of production in power, and to keep those who do not without power. Consequently, crime in capitalist society is due to the efforts of the powerful to maintain their power at all costs, as well as to the brutalization of the working class under capitalism or to their conscious resistance to exploitation by the powerful.[22]

Thus, the causes of crime are intimately connected to the fundamental flaws in the capitalist system. Programs of piecemeal reform which leave the relations of production unaltered are unlikely to achieve positive objectives. In fact, criminal justice and correctional reforms may have the effect of actually extending the domination of the powerful over the powerless in that these reforms may deflect attention away from the fundamental problems underlying capitalist systems.[23] That is, improvements that make current conditions more tolerable may, in the long-run, reduce the likelihood that the disadvantaged will push for revolutionary change in their material position. Notably, in the radical view, true social justice and a fundamental resolution of the problem of crime must await the demise of capitalism and the rise of the socialist state.

In order to further clarify the major points of comparison and contrast among the conservative, liberal, and radical ideologies with respect to crime causation and control, see Table 2.2.

CLASSICISM, POSITIVISM, AND POLITICAL IDEOLOGY

It is important to note that a bifurcation of the liberal camp was brought about by the justice model liberals' rejection of the rehabilitative ideal. For liberal justice model supporters, their defection represents a basic shift away from positivist and toward classical principles.

Table 2.2 Correctional Ideologies: Politics and Punishment

Issues	Conservative	Liberal	Radical
1. View of capitalism and the American political system	Principles fundamentally sound	Needs improvement; need greater economic and social equality	Principles fundamentally unsound and exploitive: Change to socialism
2. Reason for Crime	Social Disorder—Lack of Discipline in Society (a) Traditional Institutions and values have broken down (b) Lenient criminal justice system—"crime pays"	Poverty, racism, and other social injustices cause people to go into crime: Our society is not meeting the human needs of people and crime is a manifestation of this inadequacy in our system.	Capitalist exploitation Conditions lead the rich to exploit the poor and the poor to prey on one another
3. Way to Stop Crime	Re-establish social order and discipline (a) Re-assert traditional values that made America great (b) Increase costs of crime by stiffer punishments	Make a better social order through reform (a) Social programs to meet the needs of the disadvantaged (b) Establish a more humane and just system of criminal justice (Rehabilitation?)	Eliminate the capitalist system: Establish A New Social Order!
4. Focus of Attention	On the victim of crime and on innocent citizens — punish criminals in order to protect these groups	On the criminal — Help the disadvantaged criminal and prevent future victimization of society	On the inherent inhumanity of the system
5. Source of Crime Problem	Street crime	Street and White-collar crime	The crime of capitalism and the rich
6. Prime Values	Social Order—"Law and Order"	Protection of individual rights and humane treatment of the less advantaged; "doing justice" and "doing good"	Total economic and social equality. "No classes and no exploitation"

Thus, as in the classical paradigm, punishment and the assumption of criminal responsibility are embraced as the guiding tenets of the criminal justice system. Similarly, in both models punishment is to be based on the social harm of the offense, not the characteristics of the offender. Legislatures are to set penalties, punishment is not to be severe, judicial discretion is to be reduced, and sentences are to be determinate in both plans. Justice model proponents, however, assign a lesser role to deterrence in the determination of penalties than does the classical school.

Interestingly, conservative ideology also shares several common elements with the classical school. Each strongly emphasizes deterrence as a central goal of punishment, and each allows considerations of deterrence to influence the magnitude of penalties. Conservative ideology shares with classicism a view of crime as a willful act against the social order by an essentially rational individual. Conservative thinkers, however, tend to favor escalating criminal penalties to ensure maximum deterrent and incapacitative effects, while classical thinkers tended to downplay severity in favor of certainty and swiftness of punishment.

Given the close relationship of each to classical doctrine, it appears that the conservative and the liberal justice models share a number of common assumptions about the rationale for punishment. The most important area of disagreement between the two, it would seem, lies in the role of deterrence—which, in turn, is linked to the issue of magnitude of punishment. Given that these liberal justice model advocates now share an ideological base with conservatives, a fundamental problem arises for this group: how will these liberals now be able to effectively oppose the conservatives' call for more severe punishments? How will they avoid having their programs for criminal justice reform co-opted and penalties escalated by conservative interests in the name of "justice," amid cries of "get tough on crime?" What will happen to the needs of offenders now that liberals ask nothing of the correctional systems other than to punish the offenders therein? It is obvious that this liberal ideological shift will have profound effects on the structure and function of the criminal justice system in the years to come. It is this issue that will occupy much of our attention in the chapters to follow.

CONCLUSION

We have seen in this chapter that the ideologies represented in the classical and positive schools, as well as the political ideologies of conservatism, liberalism, and radicalism, are at the center of the current crisis in criminal justice policy discussed in the last chapter. Classical, conservative, and liberal justice models center around punishment and retribution as dominant criminal justice goals; traditional liberal and positivist models stress rehabilitation; and radical models call for the elimination of capitalism as the only effective means of system reform. Thus, it is clear that the treatment model is under attack from both the political left and right. But in order to fully understand the nature of the criticisms against rehabilitation, it is essential that we first investigate the rise of the therapeutic state itself.

NOTES

[1] Walter B. Miller, "Ideology and criminal justice policy: some current issues." Pp. 453–473 in Sheldon L. Messinger et al. (eds.), *The Aldine Crime and Justice Annual 1973*. (Chicago: Aldine Publishing Company, 1974), p. 454.

[2] *Ibid.*, p. 463.

[3] Miller, "Ideology and criminal justice policy: some current issues," p. 454.

[4] Coleman Phillipson, *Three Criminal Law Reformers: Beccaria/Bentham/Romilly*. (Montclair, New Jersey: Patterson Smith, 1975), pp. 30–32.

[5] Cesare Beccaria, *On Crimes and Punishments*. (Indianapolis: Bobbs-Merrill, 1978), p. 64.

[6] Leon Radzinowicz, *Ideology and Crime*. (New York: Columbia University Press, 1966), p. 5.

[7]Jeremy Bentham, *An Introduction to the Principles of Morals and Legislation*. Pp. 7—398 in *The Utilitarians*. (Garden City, New York: Doubleday, 1961), p. 18.

[8]Beccaria, *On Crimes and Punishments*, p. 58.

[9]*Ibid.*, p. 99.

[10]George B. Vold, *Theoretical Criminology*. Second edition prepared by Thomas J. Bernard. (New York: Oxford University Press, 1979), p. 25.

[11]Ian Taylor, Paul Walton, and Jock Young, *The New Criminology: For a Social Theory of Deviance*. (Boston: Routledge and Kegan Paul, 1973), pp. 9—10.

[12]Vold, Theoretical Criminology, p. 29.

[13]*Ibid.*, p. 47.

[14]Cesare Lombroso, "Crime and insanity in the twenty-first century." *Journal of Criminal Law and Criminology* 36 (May 1912), p. 60.

[15]Enrico Ferri, *Criminal Sociology*. (New York: Agathon Press, 1967), pp. 18—19.

[16]Francis A. Allen, *The Decline of the Rehabilitative Ideal*. (New Haven: Yale University Press, 1981), p. 2.

[17]Miller, "Ideology and criminal justice policy: some current issues," p. 454.

[18]Don C. Gibbons and Peter Garabedian, "Conservative, liberal, and radical criminology: some current issues." Pp. 51—65 in Charles E. Reasons, *The Criminologist: Crime and the Criminal*. (Pacific Palisades, California: Goodyear Publishing Company, 1974), p. 52.

[19]Miller, "Ideology and criminal justice policy: some current issues," p. 455.

[20]Neal Shover, *A Sociology of American Corrections*. (Homewood, Illinois: The Dorsey Press, 1979), p. 42.

[21]Gibbons and Garabedian, "Conservative, liberal, and radical criminology: some current issues," p. 56.

[22]Richard Quinney, *Class, State, and Crime*. Second Edition. (New York: Longman, 1980), pp. 57—66.

[23]Shover, *A Sociology of American Corrections*, p. 48.

The Rise of Rehabilitation

The determinate sentencing movement that emerged and then flourished over the course of the past decade-and-a-half represents a vigorous attack on the popular belief that rehabilitation should be the primary if not exclusive aim of our criminal justice system. These advocates of punitive justice have questioned both the viability of positivist thinking about crime and the wisdom of past reformers who held grand visions of transforming prisons into hospitals where the criminally "sick" would be benevolently cured. In contrast, the agenda of these critics calls for innovations that will effectively and severely constrain the unfettered discretion that court and correctional personnel have long exercised in the illusory attempt to effect the "individualized treatment" of the lawless. Soon, they hope, we will be rid of the indeterminate prison term and of parole boards that have labored futilely to distinguish which among the wayward have been saved and which remain chronically criminogenic. As disenchantment with the rehabilitative ideal becomes complete, punishing the criminal will replace treating the offender as the dominant purpose of the correctional process. No longer will we find anyone engaged in the well-intentioned but foolhardy enterprise of trying to fashion sanctions that "fit the offender"; now punishment will "fit the crime"—nothing more, nothing less. In their view, a new and promising era of American criminal justice policy will be upon us at last.

Some might imagine that by voicing a bold appeal to cast aside rehabilitation in favor of punitive principles, the proponents of determinate sentencing were proposing a new and untried concept. But to apply a revisionist label to these "reformers," it would be necessary to ignore that there was once a time when the prospect of curing offenders was given little thought and punishing the wicked was the sole concern of those meting out criminal sanctions. As such, the recent movement trumpeting the paradigm of just deserts and determinacy in sentencing is perhaps best seen not as providing truly novel ways of processing offenders but rather as returning us to an earlier age—of swinging the pendulum of criminal policy back more closely to its point of origin.

These considerations suggest the interesting question of how it came to pass that faith in the philosophy of punishment waned and preference was increasingly accorded to notions of saving the criminally deviant. That is, at what historical junctures did reformers zealously embark on crusades to build a "therapeutic state" in which lawlessness would provoke not

29

Reaffirming Rehabilitation. DOI: http://dx.doi.org/10.1016/B978-1-4557-3130-5.00003-9

a vengeance intent on inflicting pain but a rational effort to give the errant the desire to conform? Below, we endeavor to present a broad overview of the crucial turning points over the past two centuries that precipitated the rise of rehabilitation and the creation of a criminal justice system that ostensibly was devoted to the task of reforming those who had occasion to fall under its auspices.

CURIOUS PUNISHMENTS OF BYGONE DAYS

"The concept of rehabilitation," Alan Dershowitz has observed, "would have been entirely alien to the early colonists.... Society's duty was simply to punish the offender—swiftly, publicly and often quite harshly."[1] The cultural baggage that the early settlers brought with them to America did not include the conception that criminal sanctions had the power to save the wayward. Informed by religious doctrines teaching the natural wickedness of the human spirit, they could envision little prospect of reforming those who pursued a sinful path. As historian Samuel Walker has noted, "The colonists took a pessimistic view of humankind: man was a depraved creature cursed by original sin. There was no hope of 'correcting' or 'rehabilitating' the offender. An inscrutable God controlled the fate of the individual."[2] At best, the colonists believed, criminal punishments might scare offenders into mending their ways or convince those contemplating crime to resist such evil temptations. However, the more optimistic assumption that the lawless could be transformed into the law-abiding through reformative measures imposed by the state would not arise for nearly two centuries after the Pilgrims and similar pioneers first came to America's shores. It would take this long for reformers to invent a new mechanism that promised to make even the most hardened criminals repent for their transgressions: the penitentiary would be born.

Colonial Americans invoked a wide array of punishments to enforce public safety. Property offenders were frequently sanctioned with fines and compelled to pay restitution for the goods that had been stolen or damaged. This was particularly true for community residents caught for their first violation of the law and fortunate enough to possess sufficient resources to cover the cost of their penalty.[3] As those familiar with the workings of the current legal process are well aware, economic sanctions continue to be distributed with regularity in our courtrooms.[4] Yet if the administration of justice in modern and colonial times shares this common thread, large differences in the two legal systems remain. In this light, three central and distinguishing features of the nature of criminal punishment in bygone days deserve special attention.

First, apart from financial penalties, the bulk of the sanctions utilized by the colonists intentionally inflicted physical pain by damaging or inconveniencing an offender's body.[5] Perhaps the most favored corporal punishment of this era was whipping, which was often used in conjunction with or in place of fines. Its attractiveness lay in the fact that it held the capacity to subject a criminal to searing pain within moments, could be administered cheaply and easily, and could be imposed on those who lacked the property or means to pay economic sanctions. Yet other punitive measures, more curious by modern standards, were also available to the colonists.

Nearly every community, for instance, was equipped with stocks, a device that forced offenders to sit in a cramped position while their feet and usually their hands also were fastened in a locked wooden frame. A similar form of punishment was the pillory. Miscreants would stand upright and have their head and hands immobilized in openings cut out of a wooden frame. Those with the misfortune of being placed in this instrument could also expect that they might have their "ears nailed to the beams of the pillory and when released they would be compelled to tear their ears loose or have them carelessly cut away by the officer in charge."[6] They could anticipate as well that they would be assaulted by the jeers of their fellow townspeople and, if especially unpopular, risked being pelted with vegetables or perhaps harder and more dangerous objects.

Many offenders, including some of the victims of the stocks and pillory, were branded on the hand and for repeat or serious crimes on the face. For example, the crime of blasphemy in Maryland called for imprinting a "B" on the offender's forehead, while thieves in New York had a "T" branded on their thumb. A milder form of identifying the lawless, one made famous in Hawthorne's novel *The Scarlet Letter*, was to force an offender to weave a letter onto his or her garment that symbolized the particular crime that had been committed (e.g., "A" for adultery). Any woman prone to "violence of the tongue" had an additional hazard to avoid: the ducking stool. "To cool her immoderate heat," a village scold or gossip would first be strapped into a chair attached to a lever resting on a post located on the bank of a stream or pond. Then, much to the delight of an onlooking crowd, she would be plunged repeatedly into the water until all were convinced that this bothersome woman would exercise more prudence in the future.[7]

For those who failed to be discouraged by corporal punishment, the colonists displayed no reluctance to resort to surer means to deal with these sinful creatures and thereby preserve the social peace. Similar to the British practice of transporting criminals to America and later to Australia, the colonists simply banished many offenders from living in their community. In particular, strangers convicted of noncapital crimes could rarely avoid a court order mandating that they be flogged and then expelled. Those who were raised within the community yet persisted in recidivating would, if not banished first, inevitably earn a trip to the gallows. In Massachusetts, for instance, a thief convicted of a first offense would be fined or whipped, while the next crime would bring another fine, thirty lashes, and an hour's stay on the scaffold with a rope around one's neck. A further transgression would prove an offender incorrigible and lead to his or her execution.[8]

A second feature of colonial punishments is that they were carried out in public. This tells us that the purpose of imposing sanctions was not simply to exact retributive justice but also to create a spectacle that would humiliate offenders and deter others who feared the prospect of undergoing a similar fate. Punishing the criminal was a truly collective experience in which community members would congregate around the whipping post, stocks, pillory, ducking stool, or gallows—usually located in the town square—to witness the ridicule and suffering of the criminally deviant. The identity of the wayward would be established for all to see and the offender would undergo complete social degradation. In the small, tightly-knit colonial communities "where men ordered their behavior in fear of a neighbor's scorn,"[9] this public spectacle made for a rational and potent response to crime.

Of interest is how drastically we have moved away from the concept of ceremoniously disciplining offenders before the public's eyes. With the exception of such oddities as road gangs working on highways, only rarely is today's citizen privy to the actual punishment offenders endure. Michel Foucault has captured the essence of this shift that has caused punishment to become "the hidden part of the penal process":

> It is the conviction itself that marks the offender with the unequivocally negative sign: the publicity has shifted to the trial, and to the sentence; the execution itself is like an additional shame that justice is ashamed to impose on the condemned man; so it keeps its distance from the act, tending always to entrust it to others, under the seal of secrecy. It is ugly to be punishable, but there is no glory in punishing. . . . Those who carry out the penalty tend to become an autonomous sector; justice is relieved of responsibility for it by a bureaucratic concealment of the penalty itself.[10]

A third and final distinguishing characteristic of colonial criminal justice is the sparse use of imprisonment as a punitive measure. Many counties did find the time and resources to erect a local jail. However, except under unusual circumstances, confinement to these structures was not employed as a means of punishing the convicted; nor was it anticipated that incarcerating offenders in an institutional environment could bring about their reform. Instead, jails were utilized almost exclusively to detain debtors and those awaiting either trial or the discharge of their penalty (e.g., hanging). As Harry Elmer Barnes observed, "they were rarely used for the incarceration of what were regarded as the criminal classes. At each session of the court, there occurred what was called a 'gaol delivery,' when the jail was practically emptied of its inmates, only to be filled again during the interval between the delivery and the next session of the court."[11]

It is thus of little surprise that the jail facilities built by the colonists were ill-suited to deprive offenders of their liberty for more than a short period. Architecturally, they resembled a regular household; moreover, it was common practice for the keeper and his family to live on the premises. Inmates were free to roam unchained and uncuffed about the jail. Escapes were frequent and only those held on the most serious charges such as murder would warrant a special guard. Prisoners were given no special clothes to wear and were often required to provide for their own food and living necessities. The prison as we are accustomed to visualizing it today was simply nonexistent. As David Rothman has remarked, "Even at the close of the colonial period, there was no reason to think that the prison would soon become central to criminal punishment."[12]

ENLIGHTENED PUNISHMENT

However, in the years surrounding the American Revolution, the legitimacy and sensibleness of state administered corporal punishment became increasingly difficult to sustain. Influenced by the advent of the Enlightenment and, more particularly, by the writings of British utilitarians and French philosophes, the citizens of the new nation began to develop revisionist conceptions of human nature, the social order, and the origins of criminality. Calvinist doctrines preaching the natural depravity of man and woman were largely cast aside and replaced by the more optimistic image of humans as rational beings in control of their own destinies. Political power could no longer be justified by appeals to traditional authority and to the "Divine Right of Kings." Instead, society's members were endowed with inalienable rights and the government's survival was made contingent on its ability to fulfill its part of the social contract. More generally, established institutional patterns and practices were now open to public scrutiny and became vulnerable to change if it could not be shown that they were grounded in principles of rationality.

In this context, it made little sense to trace the cause of crime to the natural sinfulness burdening all of God's human creations. Significantly, Americans in the last quarter of the eighteenth century did not have to search far to arrive at a new understanding of why illegality flourished. Even a cursory inspection of the colonists' legal system, they believed, revealed that criminal punishments were both brutalizing and irrationally administered. Such an archaic system had little hope of deterring humans that were at once free and calculating. It thus seemed urgent that steps be taken to sweep away the barbarous and ineffective sanctioning practices previously mandated by a repressive British monarchy. In the new nation, punishing criminals would finally become an enlightened enterprise.[13] In the words of Harry Elmer Barnes, "the criminal jurisprudence and penal administration of the time could not long remain immune from the growing spirit of progress and enlightenment."[14]

The design to be followed in renovating the legal system inherited from colonial days was supplied in the works of European writers, most notably in Cesare Beccaria's *On Crimes and Punishments* (1764; first published in America in 1777). Their message to American reformers was clear: (1) Fashion a criminal code in which sanctions are commensurate with the level of social harm produced by each offense. (2) Certainty of punishment is the most important ingredient in insuring that the costs of crime outweigh the benefits. (3) Excessively severe penalties are both illegitimate and undermine the deterrent powers of the courts. Thus, Montesquieu, as Barnes has noted, "condemned the barbarous injustice of the French penal code and advocated reforms which would make punishments less severe and more nearly adapted to the specific crimes for which they were imposed."[15] Similarly, Beccaria spoke of the need for "mildness of punishment." He asked, "Who, in reading history, can keep from cringing with horror before the spectacle of barbarous and useless torments, cold-bloodedly devised and carried through by men who called themselves wise?" He then asserted that, "For punishment to attain its end, the evil which it inflicts has only to exceed the advantage derivable from the crime.... All beyond this is superfluous and for that reason tyrannical." Moreover, Beccaria warned that overly harsh sanctions lead only to inhumanity and pervasive lawlessness. "The severity of punishment of itself emboldens men to commit the very wrongs it is supposed to prevent; they are driven to commit additional crimes to avoid the punishment of a single one." Indeed, it is instructive that "the countries and times most notorious for severity of penalties have always been those in which the bloodiest and most inhumane deeds were committed, for the same spirit of ferocity that guided the hand of the legislator also ruled that of the parricide and assassin."[16]

Inspired by the ideas of Beccaria and other enlightenment thinkers, reformers enthusiastically set about the task of dismantling the colonial justice system and of constructing a correctional process that was to be both more rational and humane. Much effort was devoted to revising criminal codes so that they would better reflect the principle of certainty and to insure that the punitiveness of sanctions would be proportionate to the harmfulness that any given crime engendered.[17] However, an additional problem presented itself: what could be substituted for the brutal and unreasonably harsh corporal punishments that had been so wantonly imposed by their colonial predecessors? Post-Revolutionary reformers solved a portion of this quandary by eliminating the use of the death penalty for all but the most serious offenses. But again, this still left open the question of how felons should be sanctioned now that public whippings, brandings, and similar sorts of state responses were deemed unacceptable.

It was not long, however, before an alternative was suggested that not only avoided the distasteful mutilation of an offender's body and the dehumanization of public humiliation but seemed eminently rational as well: criminals could be punished by being incarcerated. County jails, used for years as detention facilities for those awaiting trial, had become a permanent feature of the American landscape. It took only a short jump for reformers to imagine that such structures, if built to be sturdier and more secure, could be relied upon to perform the added function of confining those whom the court might wish to sentence to a more prolonged period of captivity. Further, imprisonment possessed the decided advantage of greatly facilitating the chore of devising a criminal code that made punishment commensurate with the gravity of each crime. Now a simple yet precise formula could be applied: the more serious the offense, the longer the deprivation of liberty.[18]

What is important to remember is that however innovative a measure, the prison was viewed as an instrument of punishment and not one of rehabilitation. Scant consideration was given to how the internal workings of a jail might affect the correction of offenders. The reformers of this day, David Rothman has remarked, "hardly imagined that life inside the prison might rehabilitate the criminal.... A repulsion from the gallows rather than any faith in the penitentiary spurred the late eighteenth century [prison] construction."[19] Instead, their major concern was how to resolve the exigency of developing and operating a custodial regime that did not resort to the cruelties of bygone punishments. Faced with this pressing yet quite unfamiliar task of administering an institutional order—after all, even Beccaria had offered no advice as to what the character of imprisonment should be[20]—reformers enjoyed little success in their endeavors. Typically, they evolved facilities that were, in Ralph England's apt description, "dreadful."[21] Perhaps the worst of these early experiments in incarceration was tried from 1776-1826 near East Granbury, Connecticut. Here, inmates were housed deep within the belly of a worked-out copper mine. These poor unfortunates found themselves:

> confined at night in little sheds erected in the mine tunnels, and making nails and shoes above ground during the day. The mine was entered by descending a nineteen-foot ladder into Stygian black and chilling damp. Fractious prisoners were flogged at a surface whipping-post or shackled to the wall of an unlighted chamber at the end of one of the tunnels, where the shackling-hasps are still in place.[22]

Yet reformers in one state, Pennsylvania, proved to be more resourceful and progressive than this. Led by the Quakers and other liberal elements, they embarked on a project to build a prison that would be capable of more than merely punishing its charges. Their efforts eventually came to fruition in the Walnut Street Jail, a structure that Negley Teeters later called "the cradle of the penitentiary." It was here that the idea of using incarceration to reform the criminally deviant received its beginning test in the new nation.

A decade after the close of the Revolutionary War, the local jail situated on Walnut Street in Philadelphia could give the residents of the "City of Brotherly Love" little of which to be proud. Within this gloomy structure, the sexes intermingled freely, the young and naive sat side-by-side with the hardened criminal, jailers sold liquor to all takers, and inmates often stripped their more vulnerable counterparts of their clothes and sold the garments to purchase alcohol.[23] Appalled by these deplorable conditions, Dr. Benjamin Rush asked a group of leading citizens to meet at Benjamin Franklin's home on March 9, 1787 to hear his ideas for criminal justice reform. Rush, a signer of the Declaration of Independence and considered by many to be the father of American psychiatry, urged that a prison be established that would bring about the cure rather than the degradation of its captives. Anticipating developments that would not blossom fully for another century, he called for a therapeutic program that included the classification of inmates for housing, prison labor, indeterminate sentencing, and individualized treatment.[24]

Rush's provocative presentation proved to be the stimulus for the creation two months later of The Philadelphia Society for Alleviating the Miseries of Public Prisons. In all, thirty-seven prominent Philadelphians banded together on May 8, 1787 to found this reform organization. Notably, the preamble to the Society's constitution reflected not only the optimism and humanity inherent in Quakerism but also the conviction that the criminally wayward could be reclaimed.

> When we consider that the obligations of benevolence, which are founded on the precepts and example of the author of Christianity, are not cancelled by the follies or crimes of our fellow creatures... it becomes us to extend our compassion to that part of mankind, who are the subjects of these miseries. By the aids of humanity, their undue and illegal sufferings may be prevented... and such degrees and modes of punishment may be discovered and suggested, as may, instead of continuing habits of vice, become the means of restoring our fellow creatures to virtue and happiness.[25]

One large question, however, remained for this nascent reform group to confront: how should the prison be altered to make it conducive to correction rather than to corruption? Evidence suggests that they gained an answer to this problem from their familiarity with the recommendations proposed by the famous British prison reformer, John Howard.[26] Now Howard had become initiated into the pathologies of imprisonment when, at forty-seven years of age, he assumed the position of Sheriff of Bedford, England. After inspecting the three local jails under his authority, he was thoroughly dismayed by the disease, filth, exploitation, and disorder that flourished within these structures. In search of a more adequate mode of prison organization, he set forth between 1773 and 1790 on several extensive tours of jails both in England and on the European continent. He was most impressed by the facility at Ghent in Flanders and by the St. Michele House of Correction for boys in Rome, both of which advocated the betterment of offenders through hard work, prayer, silence, and isolation in separate cells at night. In this light, Howard's own blueprint for prison reform championed the cause of rehabilitation over punishment as well as the curative potential of nightly solitude in a single cell: "If it be difficult to prevent their being together in the daytime, they should by all means be separated at night. Solitude and silence are favorable to reflection, and may possibly lead them to repentance."[27]

The members of the reform Society in Philadelphia had little reason to dispute the wisdom of Howard's faith in cellular incarceration. After all, their own observations of the Walnut Street Jail had amply demonstrated that it is pure folly to allow inmates to interact with one another and thereby reinforce their criminal inclinations. Further, the Quakers could well remember the stories of their ancestors who were cast into British jails as part of their religious persecution. Here, these early Quakers endured vile living conditions and witnessed the tragedy of forcing offenders of all sorts to live within the same confines.[28]

Society members thus launched an enthusiastic campaign announcing the therapeutic advantages of single-cell imprisonment. "Solitary confinement to hard labor," they claimed, "will prove the means of reforming these unhappy creatures."[29] Exercising substantial political influence, their labors proved productive shortly afterwards. On April 5, 1790, they secured passage of a law mandating that a cell block be raised in the yard of the Walnut Street Jail. In all, sixteen individual cells were to be constructed, eight on each of two floors. These new domiciles were to be reserved to house the "more hardened and atrocious offenders" in solitary confinement.[30] Further, reflecting a broader trend toward the centralization of governmental powers, the Walnut Street Jail was now given state-wide responsibilities. Although still made to pay for the keep of all criminals sentenced in their local jurisdictions, counties were instructed to send their more confirmed offenders to do penance in the lonely solitude of the Walnut Street Jail.[31] The notion of a state penitentiary had finally emerged in America.

The innovation at this Philadelphia prison quickly received substantial acclaim and attracted a stream of interested parties from both other states and foreign lands. Yet this initial optimism gradually turned into a profound despair. Beset by a flood of commitments, the core principle of solitary confinement no longer proved pragmatic and was violated repeatedly by those managing the institution. The Walnut Street Jail had been transformed into a den of idleness and criminal contamination. In the face of these disheartening circumstances, many stood poised "to throw the whole thing overboard and return to the simpler and swifter methods of dealing with criminals which had previously prevailed."[32] However, this was not what was to occur in the years ahead.

THE INVENTION OF THE PENITENTIARY: THE GREAT AMERICAN EXPERIMENT

Today, the fact of imprisonment is deeply enmeshed within the taken-for-granted side of social life. For most of us, it strains the imagination to conceive of what could be done to serious felons if they were not incarcerated. Talk of abolishing prisons might provide some good argumentative fun, but "everyone knows" that in the end such ideas must be dismissed as merely utopian. Indeed, the conclusion that we must place offenders behind bars is such an accepted wisdom in our culture that one question on the Wechsler I.Q. Test for Children (Revised) is: why should criminals be locked up?

For Americans living in the first part of the nineteenth century, however, being able to supply an answer to this query would not necessarily have been looked upon as a sign of intelligence. The expanded use of jail sentences as a means of punishing criminals had accomplished little other than the creation of another social problem. Prison facilities were proving to be financial burdens, custodial nightmares, and incubators of crime and vice. Even the progressive reform at the Walnut Street Jail was wallowing in failure. The place of the social institution of imprisonment within society remained tenuous, and many could readily see the advantages of returning to earlier and less troublesome methods of inflicting punishment. "Our favorite scheme of substituting a state prison for the gallows," one New York lawyer remarked in 1818, "is a prolific mother of crime.... Our state prisons, as at present constituted, are grand demoralizers of our people."[33] It seems unlikely that more than a few of his contemporaries would have found reason to voice any disagreement with this claim.

Further, when Americans glanced abroad, they could discover scant evidence that the sanction of imprisonment was either an efficacious or humane response to the problem of crime. European nations displayed a reluctance to embrace the prison sentence as the normative or preferred penalty to be imposed on adult felons, and no country had made offender reform the expressed goal of its criminal justice system. In Great Britain, for example, efforts to operationalize John Howard's design for a truly reformative institution had met with little success. While Englishmen committing minor property offenses did begin to receive short prison terms beginning in the 1770s, those convicted of more grievous felonies continued to be hanged or sent to Australia (which from 1787 to 1867 saw 163,000 convicts come to its shores). While awaiting transportation, many offenders were kept for much of each day within the dreary holes of "Hulks," decommissioned warships moored at dockyards. It was not until 1842 that the first real penitentiary appeared at Pentonville, and not until the 1850s that Britain would institute a national system of prisons and punish major crimes with long-term sentences.[34]

Yet however bleak the future of the American prison appeared in the early portions of the 1800s, by the third decade of this century public opinion had experienced a remarkable reversal. Faith suddenly ran high that the errant could be restored to conformist ways if placed within an orderly prison that facilitated penitence through a regimen of discipline, religion, hard work, and separation from all criminal influences. The "penitentiaries" that emerged were now held up as sources of national pride. Foreign nations felt compelled to send emissaries—the most notable being the French observers Gustave de Beaumont and Alexis de Tocqueville[35]—to study this "great American experiment" in penal reform. In this context, prison construction surged ahead, and Americans soon witnessed the invention of the first large-scale, state-administered penitentiary system that ostensibly had offender rehabilitation as its overriding concern.

What engendered this precipitous rise of prisons dedicated to the cure of its captives? One necessary condition was clearly the development of increasingly powerful and centralized state governments. Within an expanding capitalist economy, these new administrative structures possessed the authority and bureaucratic machinery to accumulate the huge sums of money required to construct and to operate large incarcerative institutions.[36] Yet the special fervor that surrounded the notion that criminals should be saved and not simply punished through imprisonment can perhaps be traced more directly to another set of circumstances: changes in American society provided the populace with revised understandings of the origins of crime, which in turn enabled them to see the logic of pursuing an innovative control policy. The prospect of rehabilitating criminals in the prison was no longer to appear either futile or farfetched to Americans of the 1830s.

In his *The Discovery of the Asylum*, historian David Rothman has thus suggested that the fixed order and familiar ways of colonial days suffered a deep erosion as the new nation proceeded into the Jacksonian era.[37] Americans found themselves residing in a more open and fluid society marked by geographical as well as socioeconomic mobility, urban growth, and the beginnings of modernization. With roots and memories extending back to an earlier and more stable era, many responded to these changes with considerable apprehension. It seemed that the social fabric was becoming unglued; disorder, not order, prevailed before them.

In this atmosphere, there was little mystery to Jacksonian Americans as to the origins of crime and deviance. Unlike their predecessors, they did not see these as resting in either the natural depravity of the human spirit, or in the existence of an irrationally formulated and administered criminal law. Instead, the lawlessness threatening communal peace was now held to be symptomatic of a pervasive breakdown in the social order. With discipline attenuated and values in flux, the young and morally vulnerable were being readily exposed to the corrupting influences of an increasingly secular society.

Again, Americans in the 1820s and 1830s felt that they had good reason to be anxious about society's capacity to weather the severe strains it endured. Yet while they despaired at the passing of a life which was at once quieter and more cohesive than the one they now experienced, they nevertheless manifested a firm sense of optimism that criminal deviance could be eradicated from their midst. Notably, their conviction that the pressing problem of crime could be solved emanated directly from their understanding that social disorder was the root cause of all lawlessness. For this explanation immediately suggested what seemed a foolproof strategy for crime control: the casualties of the disorderly society should be placed within an orderly environment that would effect their reform by furnishing them with the strong moral fiber needed to resist the corrupting influences that were rampant in the wider community. As David Rothman has commented, Americans were convinced that the intimate connection between social chaos and criminality could be severed if only "a special setting for the deviant" could be fashioned. "Remove him from his family and community and place him in an artificially created and therefore corruption-free environment. Here he could learn all the vital lessons that others had ignored, while protected from the temptations of vice."[38] The prison, of course, presented an ideal locale in which to pioneer this new reformative society.

The most urgent task confronting reformers was to restructure the internal routine of the penitentiary so that it would affirm the principles that had made for an orderly society in colonial times. It was clear that offenders would have to experience the discipline absent in their defective upbringing. Respect for authority would be mandated, and obedience to unbending rules demanded. Idleness, an inevitable occasion for vice and mischief, would be replaced by hard and steady labor aimed at instilling good habits that inmates could carry with them upon release. The value of religion would similarly be emphasized, with all offenders being amply educated in Christian doctrines. And above all, inmates would be totally separated from contacts that might result in their further contamination and commitment to criminal ways. The prison must not degenerate into a school for knavery and licentiousness.

Two competing reform movements emerged, each trumpeting a distinct program for how the core principles of an orderly society of captives could best be satisfied. As might be expected, the Quakers and other liberal elements in Pennsylvania combined to form one of the groups at the forefront of this quest to establish a truly rehabilitative institution. Learning from their dismal failure at the Walnut Street Jail, these reformers were adamant that freedom from debasing criminal interactions could only be attained through a system of total solitary confinement that was never to be compromised. They proposed that each inmate be housed in a separate cell, day and night, for the entire term of incarceration. No communication with either fellow captives or outside visitors would be permitted. Even contact with guards and prison authorities was to be kept to a bare minimum. Inmates would be compelled to work alone in their cells at such tasks as spinning or shoemaking. The Bible was to be the only reading material that would be made available, and it was anticipated that its teachings would facilitate the process of penitence as offenders reflected upon their errant ways in the loneliness of their cells.

The Pennsylvania plan was put into practice when the state legislature approved the construction of two prisons, one to be located in Pittsburgh and the other at Cherry Hill in Philadelphia. The latter institution, designed by John Haviland and completed in 1829, proved to be the more renowned of the two new "penitentiaries." Here, inmates resided in cells nearly twelve feet long, seven and one-half feet wide, and sixteen feet high. They were released from confinement for one hour each day to exercise in a yard adjoining their cells and enclosed by a high barrier that precluded sight in or out. The remainder of their tenure in captivity was spent working, eating, sleeping, Bible reading, and contemplating within the boundaries of their thick-walled rooms.

Meanwhile, a rival scheme of prison organization, the "silent" or "congregate" system, had evolved in New York. A new state prison had been erected in 1817 within the town of Auburn. Influenced by Quaker thinking, Auburn officials soon introduced the practice of total solitary confinement. Between 1821 and 1823, the "oldest and most heinous offenders" were held in a small seven by three and one-half by seven feet cell in complete seclusion and without the possibility of passing the time through labor. The results of this experiment were disastrous. Several inmates attempted suicide, and numerous others suffered mental collapse. The governor eventually intervened and pardoned those enduring the horrifying fate of idle solitude.

With the abandonment of solitary confinement at Auburn, an alternative mode of reformative discipline was desperately needed. Auburn warden Elam Lynds, assisted by his deputy John Cray, was quick to supply a prescription for tackling this exigent task. Inmates would now sleep alone in their cells, but congregate during the day for meals, hard labor, and Sunday worship. However, in Lynds's regime, inmates were not allowed to utter a single word and were taught to march about the prison in a lock-step shuffle with eyes downcast. Where the Quakers sought to separate offenders from corrupting criminal conditions through secure and sturdy walls, Lynds and his fellow Auburn reformers relied upon the rule of silence, backed by a ready willingness to inflict the pain of the whip, to bring about this paramount end.[39]

Advocates of the Quaker "solitary" model and of the Auburn "silent" system engaged in heated and at times vitriolic debate in their efforts to convince others—including foreign visitors—of the greater merits of their particular reform programs. The New Yorkers asserted that their plan was both more efficacious and economical, and accused their competitors of building an apparatus certain to induce insanity. The proponents of the Pennsylvania design dismissed this latter charge and typically leveled one of their own: congregate living violates the sacred principle of absolute insulation from criminal contamination and hence is doomed to failure. Yet whatever their disagreements over the specifics of what constitutes a preferred institutional routine, it must be remembered that both camps embraced the common vision that an orderly prison community would save the errant from a life of crime. They shared as well a belief that has persisted in varying degrees of intensity to this very day: the purpose of the criminal justice system should be to rehabilitate offenders and not merely to subject them to the irrationality of aimless punishment.

THE NEW PENOLOGY

By the time the maturing American republic advanced into the Civil War period, much of the penitentiary's initial glitter had badly waned. In stark contrast to the confident and ebullient atmosphere that had reigned just three decades before, few enthusiasts could now be located that would pronounce this "great" experiment in correctional reform a success. More common if not ubiquitous among social commentators was the conclusion reached by the noted penologists Enoch C. Wines and Theodore Dwight in their *Report on the Prisons and Reformatories of the United States and Canada.* After completing an extensive survey of existing penitentiaries, they declared that "There is not a state prison in America in which the reformation of the convicts is the one supreme object of the discipline, to which everything else must bend.... There is not a prison system in the United States, which... would not be found wanting. There is not one, we feel convinced... which seeks the reformation of its subjects as a primary object."[40]

Several factors combined to leave the grand promise of reformers that penitentiaries will save the wayward substantially unfulfilled. Because congregate living was less expensive than unbroken solitary confinement and permitted the establishment of group work arrangements that proved to be more productive and hence profitable than the labors of single inmates, the Auburn design served as the blueprint for nearly all American prisons that were built in the middle portion of the 1800s. However, the wardens of these institutions were not always equal to the task of enforcing the regime of deafening silence prescribed by Elam Lynds and his fellow New York reformers. These wardens were often faced with the problem of severe overcrowding, which in turn undermined the pragmatics of providing nightly solitude for each of their charges and fostered idleness that gave inmates both the chance and need to communicate with their compatriots. Moreover, to effect the cure of the incarcerated, prison officials were equipped with an unproven theory of rehabilitation—isolation from social intercourse—which, even if applied in good faith, few experts of today would see as enhancing the reintegration of convicts back into the eminently social world that prevails outside the penitentiary. This chore of changing the lawless into the law-abiding was further complicated by the courts' reluctance to place the best candidates for reform—the young and beginning criminals—under the wardens' supervision. Rather, only the older and habitual offenders were to be the objects of their enlightened concern. To make matters still worse, these more refractory creatures were bereft of any incentive to strive for their betterment while in captivity. Since they all served flat or determinate sentences and thus their release from prison was not contingent on their showing signs of being cured, there was little a warden could do, short of physical abuse, to move inmates to undertake a concerted effort to forsake their sinful ways. Confronted with these diverse and seemingly insurmountable barriers to administering a reformative environment, officials soon abandoned therapeutic ends and instead concentrated their energies on the more pressing demand of maintaining peace and security within their prison communities.

It is notable as well that few in the more affluent and influential classes objected to this displacement of goals. For when they had occasion to scrutinize the composition of the penitentiary populace, they could see that only immigrants and the native poor were being held captive. There was some sentiment that these incarcerated souls suffered from hereditary defects that made them incurably treacherous, and considerable agreement that they were drawn from the worst element of the dangerous classes mired at the bottom reaches of the social order. Many among the advantaged thus felt thankful that the high and impenetrable walls of society's fortress-like penitentiaries, once built to insulate inmates from corrupting influences, could now be used to insure that these menacing criminals would remain securely caged and unable to prey upon the defenseless public. While "the promise of reform had built up the asylums," Rothman has remarked, "the functionalism of custody perpetuated them."[41]

Yet just when it appeared that American corrections might discard the vision of doing good through rehabilitation and regress to the point of again espousing a purely punitive crime control ideology, a wave of fresh ideas holding out exciting possibilities burst upon the scene. In their attempt to reaffirm the viability of prison rehabilitation, the advocates of this "new penology" set forth an agenda that exalted an innovative reformative tool: the indeterminate sentence. They asserted that the founders of the initial penitentiaries had erred when they embraced the fallacious assumption that merely encapsulating offenders within the boundaries of an orderly and disciplined prison environment is sufficient to achieve their reformation. From their perspective, the flaw in this early theory of corrections is that it gave scant consideration to the problem of how the process of sentencing is intimately involved in the process of reform. The proponents of the Quaker and Auburn designs had thus accepted the classical school's conception of criminal law shaped in the days of the Enlightenment. They simply had not perceived the need to be critical of a system that allowed judges, operating within the strictures of more or less specific criminal codes prescribed by legislators, to assign each offender a flat or determinate sentence.[42] Those at the head of the movement for a new penology, however, were certain that fixed-terms did little to make reform foremost in the minds of inmates. Knowing their exact release-date prior to entering the penitentiary, convicts quickly learned that once they survived their sentence, they would be turned free, cured or not. As such, they could afford to be passive if not resistant actors in the process of reform as they shuffled in silence about the prison.

To rectify this counterproductive situation, post-Civil War reformers were clear that "The prisoner's destiny should be placed, measurably, in his own hands; he must be put into circumstances where he will be able, through his own exertions, to continually better his own conditions. A regulated self-interest must be brought into play, and made constantly operative."[43] This could be readily accomplished, they proposed, by making all sentences indeterminate and by investing powers of release in the hands of prison officials. In this way, inmates would be struck by the forceful reality that they would be deprived of their liberty until they were fully fit to resume their place in society. With the link between freedom and cure manifest, they would now have good reason to work diligently for their self-improvement. Meanwhile, prison officials would exercise their discretion to reward reformed inmates with release, while keeping their more incorrigible brethren safely incarcerated until the time when they too would bend to the therapeutic powers of the indeterminate sentence. A system that could promise both the reform of offenders and the protection of society was thus suddenly within reach.

The various threads of this new penology first coalesced into a coherent correctional philosophy at the National Congress on Penitentiary and Reformatory Discipline in October of 1870. Organized by Enoch C. Wines, this meeting attracted 130 delegates from 24 states, Canada, and South America. Over the course of a week, they listened to forty papers authored by the leading penologists of this era. Among the more influential were several papers, including one made available by Crofton himself, which described Sir Walter Crofton's famous "Irish Progressive System."[44]

A Britisher by birth, Crofton had been appointed the director of the Irish prison administration in 1854. A short while later, he instituted a scheme that allowed inmates to gradually prove their reform and thereby win early release from their prison sentence. Upon arriving at the penitentiary, all offenders were immediately placed in solitary confinement for a period of eight to nine months. To appreciate the pains of idleness and, by comparison, the fruitfulness of labor, no work was allowed in the first three months of incarceration. After completing this initial stay in solitude, inmates were then advanced to a second stage. Here, each was allowed to be the "arbiter of his own fate." Similar to the token economies that modern-day behavior modifiers construct, inmates were rewarded with "marks" for industriousness and were penalized by having marks subtracted if they engaged in disruptive behavior or evidenced a defiant attitude. Once a sufficient number of marks had been accumulated, offenders would progress to an open-prison in which guards were unarmed and few restrictions were imposed on the inmates' lives. Crofton conceptualized this "intermediate" institution as "a filter between the prisons and the community." Those who "misconduct themselves are at once reconsigned to more penal treatment," while those who continue to display self-discipline are "restored to liberty."[45] The final stage was for inmates to be granted a conditional discharge on a "ticket-of-leave." These offenders were expected to register with the local police and could be returned to prison for a failure to adjust properly (e.g., unemployed, consort with bad companions, commit another offense) to their newly-earned freedom. Since a total indeterminate structure of sentencing was not operative, inmates who were unable to progress through all of the stages were released once the maximum limit of their sentences had expired.[46]

Significantly, Crofton drew many of the core features of his plan from the bold experiment in correctional reform previously undertaken by Alexander Maconochie. Yet he was not alone in borrowing from this pioneer in reformative penology. As John Barry recognized, many of the ideas promulgated at the 1870 Cincinnati Congress "were taken from Maconochie's writings, the language sometimes lifted bodily."[47] Now Maconochie was granted the opportunity to embark on his innovative program of reform at the penal colony located on Norfolk Island, Australia. Appointed Superintendent in 1840, a position he had sought, he welcomed the task of attempting to rehabilitate the criminal population that the English courts had seen necessary to transport to this distant continent. He promptly abolished the punitive and degrading practices that had been in use, and introduced in their place a "mark system" that would permit inmates to move incrementally toward a future of decreasing restrictions and, ultimately, of freedom. A firm believer in the indeterminate term, he commented that "When a man keeps the key to his own prison, he is soon persuaded to fit it to the lock,"[48] He voiced as well the conviction that we accomplish little by simply repressing the lawless. Using a medical metaphor that later writers would employ with regularity, he thus commented that:

> When a man breaks a leg, we have him into a hospital, and cure him as speedily as possible, without even thinking of modifying his treatment, so as to make his case a warning to others. We think of the individual, not of society. But when a poor fellow-creature becomes morally dislocated, however imperious the circumstances to which he may have fallen victim, we abandon all thought of his welfare, and seek only to make "an example" of him. We think of society, not of the individual. I am persuaded that the more closely and critically we examine this principle, and whether abstractly, and logically, or above all Christianly and politically, the more doubtful it will appear;—Yet it lies at the root of nearly all our Penal institutions, and reasoning on which they are founded.[49]

By all accounts, Maconochie's experiment in the humanistic, rehabilitative treatment of offenders proved a resounding success. Yet despite such favorable results as low recidivism rates and a peaceful prison order, the controversy surrounding his "coddling" of criminals led to his dismissal in 1844. Within two year's time, floggings and then riots had returned to the penal colony at Norfolk Island.[50]

It is clear, however, that the most discussed and energizing of all of the Congress's presentations was the one delivered by Zebulon R. Brockway. As Superintendent of the Detroit House of Correction, he had already succeeded in securing the passage of a variation of the indeterminate sentence. After much agitation, he had convinced the legislature to grant him the power to detain women over the age of fifteen and convicted of prostitution for a period of up to three years. The exact date of release for any individual inmate would then be regulated by her progress toward reform. Writing in 1868 on behalf of the law, Brockway had contended that "To commit these persons to the House of Corrections until they are reformed will be a strong inducement for them to enter immediately upon the work of self-improvement."[51]

Now at the Congress in 1870, Brockway was prepared to offer the delegates both a compelling defense of reformatory penology and a strategy for putting this hopeful theory into practice. Entitling his talk "The Ideal of a True Prison System for a State," he began by noting that if we are to believe that "punishment, suffering, degradation are... deterrent... then let prison reform go backward to the pillory, the whipping post, the gallows, the stake; to corporal punishment and extermination!" Brockway, however, was aware that we should be capable of much more than this. "But if the dawn of Christianity has reached us, if we have learned the lesson that evil is to be overcome with good, then let prisons and prison systems be lighted by this law of love." Indeed, to solve the crime problem we must abandon "the thought of inflicting punishment upon prisoners to satisfy so-called justice, and turn toward the real objects of the system: the protection of society by the prevention of crime and reformation of criminals." Yet Brockway followed up his appeal for the goal of inmate rehabilitation with the stern warning that efforts in this direction will inevitably founder until the time comes that prison stays are made indeterminate. "The remedy cannot be had," he argued, "so long as a determinate sentence is imposed at the time of trial.... The writer's experience of more than twenty years... forces the conviction that a reformatory system cannot exist without it, and that it is quite indispensable to the ideal of a true prison system."[52]

Based in large part on Brockway's imaginative thinking and the pathbreaking experiments of Crofton and Maconochie, the Congress concluded by setting forth a "Declaration of Principles." Thirty-seven in number, these principles elucidated the core parameters of the "new penology" that had crystallized during the fervor of the previous week's meetings. The delegates called for the creation of prison orders which embodied the Irish Progressive System, and provided inmates with industrial labor and training as well as with academic and religious education. They asserted that offenders should live in sanitary and humane conditions while incarcerated, and should be given assistance at finding employment and "regaining their lost position in society" when discharged. They felt also that separate institutions should be forged for women, juveniles, and the less hardened criminals. Further, they suggested that political influences be purged from the correctional system and that guards be supplied with more adequate training. But again, underlying these varied recommendations were two central doctrines: a firm belief in the curative powers of the indeterminate sentence and a fundamental conviction that the "supreme aim" of American criminal justice should be "the reformation of criminals, not the infliction of vindictive suffering."[53]

The tenets of the new penology received their fullest expression in the reformatory that opened at Elmira, New York in 1876. None other than the eminent Zebulon Brockway was lured to supervise the establishment of this enterprising institution. By design, Elmira was to hold first-offenders from the ages of 16-30; in practice, much of the inmate population was composed of recidivists. Further, while Brockway would have preferred that all of his charges be given purely indeterminate sentences, he settled for a system of maximum terms prior to which cured inmates might be allowed to re-enter the community. To facilitate inmate correction and following Crofton's lead, an elaborate mark scheme was developed. Brockway placed arriving offenders in the middle of three grades. Those exhibiting continued progress toward reform earned marks that advanced them to the first stage and eventually led to their conditional release. Alternatively, troublesome inmates were lowered one level, and then were faced with the tedious task of climbing their way back up to the higher stages where they could be considered for a "ticket-of-leave" or what Americans now termed "parole." Finally, all inmates were exposed to a strenuous daily schedule that included a combination of such diverse activities as industrial labor, vocational training, schoolwork, religious instruction and prayer, military drill, and methodical physical exercise. This regimen meshed nicely with Brockway's desire to insure that offenders were left with not a "moment's idleness for either hand or head."[54]

Despite the intense intellectual excitement that characterized the emergence of the new penology of the 1870s, this reform paradigm did not immediately spark a major renovation of the American system of crime control. Elmira did succeed in prompting a number of other states to erect reformatories for younger criminals. However, the principles drafted in Cincinnati found their way less quickly into the wider domain of adult corrections; life in the state penitentiaries remained much the same.[55] Nevertheless, it must be recognized that the champions of the new penology played a large role in bolstering the legitimacy of rehabilitative ideology at a time when it appeared vulnerable to being discredited and swept aside. Moreover, they contributed a forceful therapeutic program that would constitute the starting point for a major reform movement which would arise in the very next generation ahead.

THE PROGRESSIVE ERA: INDIVIDUALIZED TREATMENT

The first two decades of the 1900s witnessed the ascendancy of a potent spirit of reform that reverberated throughout American society. It was a time, according to Richard Hofstadter, in which the "impulse toward criticism and change... was everywhere so conspicuous."[56] Those who pledged allegiance to what would become known as "Progressivism" were attracted to this movement from diverse backgrounds and for equally diverse motives.[57] Nevertheless, they embraced the common vision that the social order was in desperate need of amelioration, and shared as well the conviction that the maladies afflicting society were surmountable within the broad boundaries of existing institutional arrangements. Liberal though speedy reform, not revolutionary class warfare, would solve the difficulties facing the nation and bring forth the dawn of a new age of social progress.

For the Progressives, "big business" posed the gravest danger to the sanctity of American democratic ideals. The increasing concentration of corporate wealth and power now threatened both to make a mockery of the principle of free-enterprise and to enable the "robber barons" to exert such inordinate influence on politicians as to fundamentally corrupt the cherished process of representative government. The corporate menace could only be diminished, the Progressives cautioned, if the public sector were fortified to the point where it could dominate the private sector. They thus argued that the state must be endowed with sufficient authority to regulate business practices and, when necessary, to bust perilous trusts.

The Progressives' faith in the state extended to other realms as well. The advent of a burgeoning and heartless capitalist industrialism had produced a variety of casualties, particularly among urban immigrants vulnerable to exploitation. "Insanitary housing, poisonous sewage, contaminated water, infant mortality, the spread of contagion, adulterated food, impure milk, smoke-laden air, ill-ventilated factories, dangerous occupations, juvenile crime, unwholesome overcrowding, prostitution, and drunkenness," Jane Addams zealously wrote, "are the enemies which the modern city must face and overcome would it survive."[58] Christian charity might help to mitigate the harshness of these conditions, and social activists could uplift some unfortunates by manning settlement houses in the midst of slum neighborhoods. But the very enormity of the social problems besetting the urban environment demanded that larger measures be pursued that possessed the capacity to bring about more lasting and far-reaching improvements. In their crusade for social justice against entrenched interests, the Progressives had little choice but to turn to the government for support. They now billed the state as an "agency whose positive assistance is one of the indispensable conditions of human progress."[59] Their strategy, successful in many instances, was to prompt legislators into passing laws that would give the injured worker compensation, ban child labor, supply financial aid to widows with children, provide for old-age pensions, and establish boards of community hygiene. In their efforts to humanize the industrial society, they thus helped to launch the start of the welfare state.[60]

For those disturbed by the plight of the criminal and delinquent within the correctional system, the coming of the Progressive era and its ethic of reform furnished a firm sense of optimism that meaningful changes could be won. In a presentation in 1911 entitled "The Future Attitude Toward Crime," George W. Kirchwey commenced by telling his audience that "We are met at a fortunate time. The moral atmosphere... is electric with impulses toward a better understanding and a better ordering of the relations of society to the individual."[61] But in this favorable context, what specifics should constitute the reform agenda to be followed? The beginning answer to this question, the Progressives felt, could be found in the "new" penology first espoused several decades before. It was clear that rehabilitation, not retributive punishment, should guide the sanctioning process. At the turn of the century, Charlton T. Lewis voiced sentiments that would be echoed repeatedly in the years to come when he asserted that "The method of apportioning penalties according to degrees of guilt implied by defined offenses is as completely discredited, and is as incapable of a part of any reasoned system of social organization, as is the practice of astrology or... witchcraft." He then continued, "The entire abandonment of retribution as a motive is the first condition of a civilized criminal jurisprudence."[62] Further, there was a uniformly strong reaffirmation of the value of the indeterminate sentence. Again, Lewis's words prove a worthy example of Progressive thinking: "the time will come when the moral mutilations of fixed terms of imprisonment will seem as barbarous and antiquated as the ear-lopping, nose-slitting and head amputations of a century ago."[63]

However, the Progressives were not content simply to apply the penological principles inherited from their predecessors, and hence they soon moved to embellish the new penology with the ideas of their own generation. In this regard, the incipient disciplines of psychology and sociology revealed how this earlier therapeutic paradigm could be fleshed out. Suggesting a Positivist School approach to crime and its control, the logic of these behavioral sciences instructed Progressives to begin by investigating the factors which precipitate criminal involvement. Since the life experiences of one offender will inevitably differ from the next, the source of crime in any given instance could be expected to vary. This meant that every lawbreaker would have to be processed on a case-by-case basis. It would be necessary to study an offender closely and then to diagnose the particular criminogenic condition—perhaps the sordid influences of a slum home, perhaps a mental conflict—responsible for the person's waywardness. Once the cause of the problem was discovered, then the offender would be subjected to a treatment program specifically designed to eliminate the abnormality giving rise to the criminal inclinations in question. To administer this program of individualized treatment, correctional personnel would have to be invested with the unbridled discretion required to fit the "punishment" to the criminal rather than to the crime. Much like a physician exercises wide latitude in prescribing a cure for a patient, so too would the treaters of crime be given these powers to cure their "patients." Pursuing this medical analogy still further, many began to suggest that the very concept of prisons should be forfeited, and these institutions for criminals turned into hospitals. The flavor of the Progressives' perspective is well illustrated in these 1912 remarks by Warren F. Spaulding, Secretary of the Massachusetts Prison Association:

> Each criminal is an individual, and should be treated as such. . . . Character and not conduct is the only sound basis of treatment. Fundamental in the new scheme is. . . individualism. In the old system, the main question was, What did he do? The main question should be, What is he? There can be no intelligent treatment until more is known than the fact that a man did a certain thing. It is as important to know why he did it. Diagnosis is as necessary in the treatment of badness as it is in the treatment of illness.[64]

Notably, the Progressives did not possess the overriding enthusiasm for incarceration that had been so characteristic of the Jacksonian reformers who initially built the penitentiary or of the new penologists who had continued to popularize the stance that a well-ordered asylum was the most essential ingredient in the reform of the errant. While the Progressives agreed that many offenders required the strictures of the prison and the experience of the indeterminate sentence to be rehabilitated, they were equally adamant that many others could best be treated within the confines of the community. As a consequence, they called for the creation of parole boards, the increased use of parole-release from the penitentiary, and the establishment of supervision programs that would both facilitate an offender's reintegration into society and would insure that the uncured would be returned to their cells. Similarly, they urged that the practice of probation be expanded drastically. As an alternative to imprisonment, offenders would now be placed under the guidance of a probation officer who was to act as a counselor and policeman—someone sensitive enough to understand an individual's problems but stern enough to lock offenders up if they persisted in criminal or profligate ways. However, probation officers were to perform an additional function as well. It was to be their duty to research the social and personal background of each convicted defendant, and then to provide judges with a detailed presentence report that would aid the court in assigning the correct treatment to each offender.

It should be recognized that the Progressives' commitment to the policy of individualized treatment was at the heart of their desire to give special life and legitimacy to "community corrections." Parole would permit the decarceration of the cured and the continued institutionalization of the incorrigible, while probation afforded judges a new sanctioning option and, through the officers attached to the court, access to the information required to make a sound sentencing decision. As William G. Hale commented in 1918, "As redemptive measures, our probation and parole laws have added vital wheels to our machinery of justice. They have gone far toward enabling us to deal with the individual as an individual and not as mere human grist, to be fed into an unthinking machine, and have thus made possible more ample provision for his reformation."[65]

A final and significant feature of the Progressives' therapeutic agenda was an abiding belief that the state would carry out this agenda in good faith. Just as they trusted the state to bust corporate monopolies and to be an invaluable ally in the crusade for greater social justice, now they were convinced that the state and its agents could be trusted to bring about the humane and scientific cure of the criminally deviant. As such, they did not hesitate to grant court and correctional personnel the wide discretionary powers required for the individualized rehabilitation of offenders. In this same vein, they did not actively entertain the possibility that this discretion would be corrupted to serve organizational and class interests and not be used to do good as they had planned. Neither did it strike the Progressives that the practice of state enforced therapy—where an inmate's cure is coerced and not volunteered—might suffer from any inherent theoretical defects or, still worse, that it might result in the physical and psychological abuse of the very people it intended to "save." As David Rothman has observed:

> The most distinguishing characteristic of Progressivism was its fundamental trust in the power of the state to do good. The state was not the enemy of liberty, but the friend of equality—and to expand its domain and increase its power was to be in harmony with the spirit of the age. In criminal justice, the issue was not how to protect the offender from the arbitrariness of the state, but how to bring the state more effectively to the aid of the offender. The state was not a behemoth to be chained and fettered, but an agent capable of fulfilling an ambitious program. Thus, a policy that called for the state's exercise of discretionary authority in finely tuned responses was, at its core, Progressive.[66]

In the context of America's "age of reform," to use Richard Hofstadter's designation, the Progressives' ideas for altering the correctional system did not fall idly by the wayside. By the end of this era, a flurry of legislative activity had transpired that instituted major portions of their reform program. In 1900, for instance, only five states allowed for indeterminate sentencing; a little over two decades later, the number had climbed to 37.[67] The concept of parole, which had its origins in the ticket-of-leave systems of Maconochie and Crofton[68] as well as in Brockway's reformatory system, had been adopted in only a handful of states at the turn of the century. By the middle part of the 1920s, 44 states provided for parole and over half of the inmates in the nation were discharged in this manner.[69] The beginnings of probation extend back to the 1840s when an affluent Boston shoemaker, John Augustus, voluntarily took errant youths under his care and supervision. In 1878, Massachusetts honored Augustus's pathbreaking work by becoming the first jurisdiction to pass a probation law. However, it was not until 1897 that another state followed suit.[70] In contrast, by 1920 probation was permitted in two-thirds of the states for adults and in every state for juveniles.[71]

It should be noted that the Progressives' therapeutic model received its most complete expression in the measures formulated to control delinquent behavior. Starting in 1899 in Cook County, Illinois, state after state created a separate legal system for processing youthful offenders. By the year 1920, all but three had established a special court for hearing juvenile cases.[72] Now for the Progressives, rehabilitation was to be the exclusive concern in this newly-created realm of juvenile justice. Under the guise of the concept of *parens patriae*, the Progressives wished to place the state in the role of a kindly parent that would nurture the wayward back to conformity. They felt as well that the task of "child saving" could best be accomplished if efforts were made to detect youths with such delinquent tendencies as truancy and illicit sexual activity prior to their falling into a life of more serious criminality.

In line with these assumptions, the Progressives were able to secure passage of legislation mandating that the state would no longer take an adversarial posture toward juvenile offenders. Since the state would now act in the best interests of delinquent youths, criminal trials, defense attorneys, rules of evidence, standards of guilt, and other due process protections were all stripped away in the daily rounds of the juvenile court. Judges were given the unfettered discretion to investigate what was wrong with a particular youth and then to prescribe the most corrective treatment available. This might involve supervision within the community or a stay in a special reformatory constructed just for juveniles where inmates could be kept until they achieved adulthood. Further, the powers of the state to intervene in the lives of troubled youths were greatly expanded. Unlike adults, juveniles could be brought before the court not only for violations of the criminal law, but also for engaging in a range of misbehaviors (known today as status offenses) which indicated that they were in a pre-delinquent stage and would soon be venturing into more nefarious activities. The court was also instructed to minister to those unfortunate youths who had been abandoned, neglected, or abused by their parents.

In sum, the Progressives succeeded in a major renovation of the criminal justice system. Within the space of two decades, their innovations reformulated sentencing practices in the direction of indeterminacy, established the new bureaucratic structures of probation and parole, created a separate system of juvenile justice, introduced wide discretionary powers throughout the legal process, and reaffirmed the vitality of the rehabilitative ideal. At the end of their era, nearly all of the elements of the criminal justice system familiar to today's students of crime control were securely in place. Of equal significance, the Progressives bequeathed a powerful rationale for the individualized treatment of offenders that would dominate American correctional policy until very recent times. As David Rothman has concluded, "the synthesis achieved in the 1900-1920 years dominated reform thinking and action down until yesterday."[73]

THE LEGACY OF REFORM

The Progressives' version of a criminal justice system fully dedicated to the rehabilitation of criminal offenders was never achieved. While the framework of a therapeutic state had been erected, the substance in many instances was lacking. The Quakers' penitentiary did not become a modern hospital. Treatment programs in prisons frequently lacked integrity, and treatment personnel were often undertrained or sparse in number. In 1954, for example, there were only 23 full-time psychiatrists employed to run counseling sessions for the 161,587 inmates in state and federal prisons.[74] Although California made advances in this direction, a pure system of indeterminate sentencing was not instituted in any state (all employed maximum limits for most prison terms handed out).[75] Few offenders on probation or parole received intensive care. Moreover, it appears that the emergence of community corrections did not lessen the use of incarceration, but rather provided the state with the means to increase its surveillance of offenders who previously would have been either set totally free after serving their time in the penitentiary or given an unsupervised suspended sentence.[76] Additionally, the problems within the arena of juvenile justice became so pervasive that the Supreme Court was eventually compelled to grant youthful delinquents an array of due process rights that would reduce the risk of their being abused by their "kindly parent," the state.

Yet if the reality of offender treatment only infrequently approximated the therapeutic design articulated by the Progressives, the philosophy of rehabilitation nevertheless continued to retain, if not expand, its appeal throughout much of the current century. Scarcely a decade ago, large proportions of both the general public and correctional workers believed that rehabilitation should be the primary goal of our prisons.[77] One 1972 survey of juvenile correctional superintendents revealed that only 15 percent endorsed the abolition of the indeterminate sentence.[78] Faith in treatment, though not absolute, was especially pronounced among liberal academics and similar leftist interest groups. For example, after reviewing ten of the leading criminology texts, Jackson Toby observed in 1964 that "students reading these textbooks might infer that punishment is a vestigal carryover of a barbaric past and will disappear as humanitarianism and rationality spread."[79]

As America pushed into the late 1960s, rehabilitation thus remained unchallenged as the dominant correctional ideology. There seemed to be little chance that there would be a call either to revert to the punitive principles of bygone days or to abandon the quest to build upon the foundation of the therapeutic state laid by the Quakers, new penologists, and Progressives. The long rise of rehabilitation seemed certain to proceed unabated in the immediate, if not into the distant future. A decade later, however, the philosophy of rehabilitation had been substantially discredited, and concerted efforts were well underway to find a solution to the crisis in criminal justice policy precipitated by the demise of treatment ideology. How rehabilitation came to suffer such a sudden decline in recent times, particularly within the liberal community, is the issue that will next capture our attention.

NOTES

[1] Alan M. Dershowitz, "Background paper." Pp. 67–130 in Twentieth Century Task Force on Criminal Sentencing, *Fair and Certain Punishment*. (New York: McGraw-Hill, 1976), p. 83.

[2] Samuel Walker. *Popular Justice: A History of American Criminal Justice*. (New York: Oxford University Press, 1980), p. 13.

[3] David J. Rothman, *The Discovery of the Asylum: Social Order and Disorder in the New Republic*. (Boston: Little, Brown and Company, 1971), p. 48; Dershowitz, "Background paper," p. 83.

[4] For instance, Malcolm M. Feeley, *The Process is the Punishment: Handling Cases in a Lower Criminal Court*. (New York: Russell Sage Foundation, 1979), p. 137 has reported that 45 percent of all offenders sentenced in the lower criminal court he studied received fines.

[5] For reviews of the corporal punishments used in colonial times, see Alice Morse Earle, *Curious Punishments of Bygone Days*. (Montclair, N.J.: Patterson Smith, 1969, originally published in 1896). More generally, see Graeme Newman's discussion of the "rise of curious punishments" in his *The Punishment Response*. (Philadelphia: J. B. Lippincott Company, 1978), pp. 112–123, and Harry Elmer Barnes and Negley K. Teeters' chapter on corporal punishment contained in their *New Horizons in Criminology*. Third edition. (Englewood Cliffs, N.J.: Prentice Hall, 1959), pp. 285–293.

[6] Barnes and Teeters, *New Horizons in Criminology*, pp. 292–293.

[7] Earle, *Curious Punishments of Bygone Days*, pp. 11–28.

[8] Rothman, *The Discovery of the Asylum*, p. 52.

[9] *Ibid.*, p. 50.

[10] Michel Foucault, *Discipline and Punish: The Birth of the Prison*. (New York: Pantheon Books, 1977), pp. 9–10.

[11] Harry Elmer Barnes, "The historical origin of the prison system in America." *Journal of the American Institute of Criminal Law and Criminology* 12 (May 1921), p. 36.

[12] Rothman, *The Discovery of the Asylum*, p. 56 and, more generally, pp. 46–56.

[13] *Ibid.*, pp. 59–61. See also Walker, *Popular Justice*, pp. 35–36.

[14] Harry Elmer Barnes, *The Story of Punishment: A Record of Man's Inhumanity to Man*. (Montclair, N.J.: Patterson Smith, 1972; originally published in 1930), p. 121.

[15] Barnes, "The historical origin of the prison system in America," p. 42.

[16] Cesare Beccaria, *On Crimes and Punishments*. (Indianapolis: Bobbs-Merrill, 1963; originally published in 1764), pp. 42–44.

[17] Dershowitz, "Background paper," p. 85.

[18] Rothman, *The Discovery of the Asylum*, p. 62.

[19] *Ibid.*, p. 62.

[20] Blake McKelvey, *American Prisons: A History of Good Intentions*. (Montclair, N.J.: Patterson Smith, 1977), p. 4.

[21]Ralph W. England, "John Howard and his influence in America." Pp. 25−33 in John Freeman (ed.), *Prisons Past and Future*. (London: Heinemann, 1978), pp. 29−30.

[22]*Ibid.*, p. 30.

[23]Negley K. Teeters, "The Pennsylvania Prison Society — a century and a half of penal reform." *Journal of the American Institute of Criminal Law and Criminology* 28 (No. 3, 1937), p. 376.

[24]Howard B. Gill, "Correctional philosophy and architecture." *Journal of Criminal Law, Criminology, and Police Science* 53 (September 1962), pp. 312−313.

[25]McKelvey, *American Prisons*, p. 7.

[26]England, "John Howard and his influence in America," pp. 30−31, and Barnes, "The historical origin of the prison system in America," pp. 42−45.

[27]Quoted in Torsten Eriksson, *The Reformers: An Historical Survey of Prisoner Experiments in the Treatment of Criminals*. (New York: Elsevier, 1976), p. 37.

[28]For an account of the Quaker experience with imprisonment in the 1600s, see John Sykes, *The Quakers: A New Look at Their Place in Society*. (Philadelphia: J. P. Lippincott Co., 1958), pp. 146−154, and John L. Nicholls (ed.), *The Journal of George Fox*. (London: Cambridge University Press, 1952), pp. 252−258.

[29]Quoted in McKelvey, *American Prisons*, p. 8.

[30]Barnes, *The Story of Punishment*, p. 129.

[31]Paul Takagi, "The Walnut Street Jail: a penal reform to centralize the powers of the state." *Federal Probation* 39 (December 1975). pp. 18−26.

[32]Gill, "Correctional philosophy and architecture," p. 313.

[33]Quoted in Rothman, *The Discovery of the Asylum*, p. 93.

[34]See Michael Ignatieff, *A Just Measure of Pain: The Penitentiary in the Industrial Revolution, 1750−1850*. (New York: Pantheon, 1978), pp. 81, 200−201, and Thorsten Sellin, *Slavery and the Penal System*. (New York: Elsevier, 1976), pp. 97−106.

[35]For an account of their visit, see Gustave de Beaumont and Alexis de Tocqueville, *On the Penitentiary System in the United States and Its Application in France*. (Carbondale: Southern Illinois University Press, 1964; originally published in 1833).

[36]Andrew T. Scull, *Decarceration: Community Treatment and the Deviant — A Radical View*. (Englewood Cliffs, N.J.: Prentice Hall, 1977), pp. 31−32.

[37]The following discussion of the emergence of the American penitentiary system is derived primarily from Rothman's *The Discovery of the Asylum*, pp. 62−108.

[38]*Ibid.*, p. 71.

[39]For accounts of the Auburn and Quaker systems, see Barnes, *The Story of Punishment*, pp. 125−144; McKelvey, *American Prisons*, pp. 11−21; Eriksson, *The Reformers*, pp. 47−80; and Ronald L. Goldfarb and Linda R. Singer, *After Conviction*, (New York: Simon and Schuster, 1973), pp. 24−31.

[40]Quoted in Rothman, *The Discovery of the Asylum*, pp. 240−242.

[41]*Ibid.*, p. 240.

[42]Dershowitz, "Background paper," pp. 87−89.

[43] "Declaration of principles promulgated at Cincinnati, Ohio, 1870." Pp. 39—63 in Charles R. Henderson (ed.), *Prison Reform*. (Dubuque, Iowa: Brown Reprints; originally published in 1910), p. 39.

[44] McKelvey, *American Prisons*, p. 89.

[45] Quoted in Snell Putney and Gladys J. Putney, "Origins of the reformatory," *Journal of Criminal Law, Criminology, and Police Science* 53 (December 1962), p. 439.

[46] For a review of Crofton's system, see Eriksson, *The Reformers*, pp. 89—97.

[47] Quoted in Barnes and Teeters, *New Horizons in Criminology*, p. 425, fn. 8.

[48] Quoted in Putney and Putney, "Origins of the reformatory," p. 437.

[49] Quoted in Eriksson, *The Reformers*, p. 88.

[50] *Ibid.*, pp. 81—88.

[51] Quoted in McKelvey, *American Prisons*, p. 81.

[52] Zebulon R. Brockway, "The ideal of a true prison system for a state." Pp. 389—408 in his *Fifty Years of Prison Service*. (Montclair, N. J.: Patterson Smith, 1969; originally published in 1912), pp. 391, 400, 403.

[53] "Declaration of principles promulgated at Cincinnati, Ohio, 1870," in Henderson (ed.), *Prison Reform*, pp. 39—63.

[54] Quoted in Eriksson, *The Reformers*, p. 100.

[55] Barnes, *The Story of Punishment*, p. 147.

[56] Richard Hofstadter, *The Age of Reform*. (New York: Alford A. Knopf, 1955), p. 5.

[57] In this regard, see the writings contained in Arthur Mann (ed.), *The Progressive Era: Liberal Renaissance or Liberal Failure?* (New York: Holt, Rinehart and Winston, 1963).

[58] Quoted in Arthur A. Ekirch, Jr., *Progressivism in America: A Study of the Era from Theodore Roosevelt to Woodrow Wilson*. (New York: New Viewpoints, 1974), pp. 75—76.

[59] Quoted in John D. Buenker, *Urban Liberalism and Progressive Reform*. (New York: Charles Scribner's Sons, 1973), p. 43.

[60] *Ibid.*, pp. 42—79.

[61] The presentation was later published in the *Journal of the American Institute of Criminal Law and Criminology* 2 (1912), pp. 501—504.

[62] Charlton T. Lewis, "The indeterminate sentence." *Yale Law Journal* 9 (October 1899), pp. 18—19.

[63] Quoted in David J. Rothman, *Conscience and Convenience: The Asylum and Its Alternatives in Progressive America*. (Boston: Little, Brown and Company, 1980), p. 60. For a similar example, see Eugene Smith, *Criminal Law in the United States*. (Dubuque, Iowa: Brown Reprints, 1971; originally published in 1910), pp. 65—74.

[64] Warren F. Spaulding, "The treatment of crime — past, present and future." *Journal of the American Institute of Criminal Law and Criminology* 3 (May 1912), p. 378. More generally, see Rothman, *Conscience and Convenience*, pp. 43—81, and Walker, *Popular Justice*, pp. 150—151.

[65] William G. Hale, "Crime: modern methods of prevention, redemption and protection." *Journal of the American Institute of Criminal Law and Criminology* 9 (August 1918), p. 244.

[66] Rothman, *Conscience and Convenience*, p. 60.

[67]David J. Rothman, *Incarceration and Its Alternatives in 20th Century America*. (Washington, D.C.: U.S. Government Printing Office, 1979), p. 21.

[68]In this regard, see Stephen White, "Alexander Maconochie and the development of parole." *Journal of Criminal Law and Criminology* 67 (March 1976), pp. 72–88.

[69]Rothman, *Incarceration and Its Alternatives in 20th Century America*, p. 21, and his *Conscience and Convenience*, p. 44.

[70]Eriksson, *The Reformers*, p. 156.

[71]Rothman, *Conscience and Convenience*, p. 44.

[72]*Ibid.*, p. 215; Walker, *Popular Justice*, p. 155. See also Anthony M. Platt, *The Child Savers: The Invention of Delinquency*. (Chicago: University of Chicago Press, 1969).

[73]Rothman, *Incarceration and Its Alternatives in 20th Century America*, p. 1.

[74]David F. Greenberg, *The Problem of Prisons*. (Philadelphia, Pa.: National Peace Literature Service, 1970), p. 16.

[75]Richard A. McGee, "A new look at sentencing: part II, a plan for maximum justice with minimum capriciousness." *Federal Probation* 38 (September 1974), p. 3.

[76]David F. Greenberg, "Problems in community corrections." *Issues in Criminology* 10 (Spring 1975), p. 12; Rothman, *Conscience and Convenience*, pp. 110–111.

[77]Louis Harris, *The Public Looks at Crime and Corrections*, p. 7 and *Corrections 1968: A Climate for Change*, p. 15, both published by Washington, D.C.: Joint Commission on Correctional Manpower and Training, 1968.

[78]Gerald R. Wheeler, *Counter-deterrence: A Report on Juvenile Sentencing and Effects of Prisonization*. (Chicago: Nelson Hall, 1978), p. 92.

[79]Jackson Toby, "Is punishment necessary?" *Journal of Criminal Law, Criminology, and Police Science* 55 (September 1964), p. 332.

Attacking Rehabilitation

Successive generations of reformers advocating the rehabilitative ideal have repeatedly been successful in spawning a sense of confidence and optimism that the lawless could be corrected and made law-abiding. Yet consensus on the wisdom of building a therapeutic state has never been complete. Conservatives have frequently been suspicious of efforts aimed at regenerating offenders, fearing that they will furnish an excuse to release the wicked back into society where they once again will prey on the defenseless. Though objections have been raised less often by more liberal elements, disenchantment with the prospect of molding a criminal justice system around the rehabilitative ideal has long sprinkled the writings and speeches of those on the left. Indeed, on occasion, these liberal critiques have penetrated to the very premises that form the foundation of the therapeutic state.

Thus, in *Break Down the Walls*, a 1954 tract arguing for the abolition of imprisonment, John Bartlow Martin termed rehabilitation "the dangerous myth.... The truth is that a rehabilitation 'program' in today's prison is utter nonsense. Prison is a place to keep people locked up. It can never be more."[1] Two decades earlier, Frank Tannenbaum proclaimed that "We cannot do good to the evil-doer either by doing evil or by merely doing good,"[2] while Ray Simpson, a prison psychologist in Illinois, observed that "there is very little evidence that the routine procedures mentioned above have done much to alter the deep-seated delinquent tendencies of reformatory and, penitentiary inmates.... Prison methods of today are stupid and inadequate."[3] In 1925, lawyer Edward Lindsey expressed many of the same reservations regarding indeterminate sentencing that later critics would come to voice. For instance, he illuminated the potential problems of giving "unlimited discretion to parole boards to determine by their rules what shall entitle the prisoner to discharge" and questioned whether the suspense of an uncertain release date might not constitute the "cruel and unusual punishment" of prison inmates. Based on these and other observations, he warned that "It is probably best not to be dogmatic at present as to what is the best form of the sentence."[4] More generally, Francis Allen has noted that "most of the counts in the modern indictment of the rehabilitative ideal were expressed by one person or another before the outbreak of the American Civil War."[5]

But if the criticism of rehabilitation has roots that extend from the distant to the more recent past, it never proved sufficient to check the emergence of the therapeutic state nor to

Reaffirming Rehabilitation. DOI: http://dx.doi.org/10.1016/B978-1-4557-3130-5.00004-0

dissuade many from embracing the thought that the reformation of the criminal was within reach. As we turned into the 1970s, nearly a century-and-a-half after the penitentiary became a permanent feature of the American landscape, faith in rehabilitation ran high. In *Struggle for Justice* published in 1971, a committee of authors antagonistic to state enforced therapy was nevertheless compelled to conclude that "the treatment approach receives nearly unanimous support from those working in the field of criminal justice."[6]

However, as the very appearance of volumes like *Struggle for Justice* signaled, the groundwork for an unprecedented attack on criminal justice rehabilitation had already been laid. The turbulence of the 1960s was spreading into the decade of the seventies, and taken together, the various threads of this disruption questioned the legitimacy of the social order in fundamental ways and on many fronts. As we shall explore below, liberals and conservatives interpreted this broad crisis in authority besetting the state through vastly different lenses. And in the arena of corrections, this resulted in their evolving quite distinct visions of what was wrong with the methods used to administer criminal sanctions: for liberals, the prevailing "justice" system was seen to victimize the offender; for conservatives the system permitted the intolerable victimization of the innocent citizen. But for members of both political camps, the social disorder of the times would lead, if for divergent reasons, to a similar prescription as to how to solve the failures of American criminal justice: rehabilitation and the indeterminate sentence must be abandoned and replaced by the principles of just deserts and determinacy.

The unity achieved by the left and right at this historical juncture—an unusual occurrence in any matter of criminal policy—has proven to be of no small significance. For it formed the underpinnings of a reform movement that has succeeded in putting the prescription for desert and determinacy into practice and in seriously weakening the tenacity of the rehabilitative ideal. Indeed, it has become fashionable for today's commentators to speak of the "sudden demise of the unassailable place that indeterminacy held in penal thought only a decade ago"[7] and to observe that in "the course of a decade, perhaps less, the rehabilitative ideal suffered a precipitous decline in its capacity to influence American penal practice and, more important, in its potency to define commonly held aspirations in the penal area."[8] In the pages that follow, we will endeavor to investigate both the origin and parameters of the movement that has shaken the therapeutic state at its very foundation and led more than one author to ask, "Is rehabilitation dead?"[9]

THE CONSERVATIVE ATTACK: GETTING TOUGH ON CRIME

The years spanning the middle part of the 1960s to the latter portion of the decade were troubling times for Americans with conservative inclinations. While yearning for their cherished goal of a stable and tranquil society, those leaning to right were forced to witness widespread and poignant challenges to the prevailing social order. Indeed, direct confrontation with state authority became commonplace. Marches trumpeting the rights of diverse minority groups and protesting the U.S.'s military intrusion into Vietnam were ubiquitous events. The turmoil in the ghettos and on university campuses emerged as not infrequent fe____s on network news, with police and national guard troops outfitted in riot gear as leading actors in the dramas that unfolded across the nation. The practice of civil disobedience was now a favorite strategy of many insurgent movements, and few Americans missed the sight of the limp bodies of demonstrators being carried by authorities from draft boards, welfare headquarters, the offices of college presidents, and the entrances of nuclear power plants. An even more menacing threat to the sanctity of the social order seemed to be posed by radical political groups, which spouted frightening revolutionary rhetoric and punctuated the peace, sporadically but vividly, with bombings, shootouts, and hijackings. With fear of terrorism and piracy heightening, police departments quickly fashioned S.W.A.T. units, while airports soon made negotiating detectors an expected routine of travel.

Assaults on the legitimacy of the established order, however, were not confined to dramatic moments of political protest. Less spectacular but fundamental alterations in existing social relations taught conservatives that traditional moral values and lines of authority were suffering deep erosion. In the matter of a few years time, abortions, "living together," premarital sex, and divorce became normative, while teenage parenthood had the makings of a national problem. Patriarchal dominance in families was called into question as "women's liberation" came upon the scene and women began to seek "fulfillment" not as homemakers but as careerists. Within the field of education, A.S. Neill's *Summerhill*[10] became standard reading and instructional philosophy shifted away from strict and structured learning to the "open classroom." The courts saw fit to constrain the absolute powers of principals to discipline students and moved as well to secularize schools. School dress codes vanished as students donned the preferred uniform of long hair and blue jeans. Restrooms became places where pupils smoked pot, not cigarettes, and in some institutions teachers and students alike feared for their safety. These and other changes led conservatives like Edward Banfield to comment in dismay, "One wonders what may be the effect on boys and girls brought up to respect authority of the advice (given by an ex-nun in the magazine *Seventeen*) to 'hold always the openness of questioning the president of the college, of questioning the dean of students, of questioning fair housing, divorce laws and birth control.'"[11]

In this context, crime assumed new meaning and significance. As discussed in Chapter 1, offense rates during this period climbed at an alarming pace and exacted a noticeably higher toll on the public in the damage done to their bodies, property, and minds. The threat of victimization thus came to be of increasing relevance in the everyday lives of many citizens, particularly city dwellers. But the salience of the "crime problem" flowed only partially from its objective consequences. With conservative politicians of the era warning of imminent social and political collapse, criminality was now held up, in Richard Quinney's words, as "the ultimate crack in the armor of the existing social order."[12] "Crime" became a codeword for all that was wrong with American society, a symbol of the disruptive forces that were undermining traditional patterns of authority and precipitating the decay of the social fabric. "What is crucial in this discussion," James Finckenauer observed, "is the fact that it was not crime per se that became an issue in the 1960s, but rather 'law and order.'" It was a social issue that involved a "backlash, reaction against youth, malaise, and alienation. It was a potent, political program, and it has persisted into the seventies. Crime was not a simple or single issue, but rather included race, lawlessness, civil rights, and other emotional issues."[13]

Signifying wider social disorder, crime thus became an intense and escalating concern for those on the right. And increasingly, conservative leadership demanded that action be taken. On its broadest level, their agenda called for an assault on the "permissive society" that had deflated the legitimacy of old morals and ways, and had allowed disrespect for the law to flourish. Youths should be subjected to firm discipline while growing up and educated in schools that have gone "back to basics." They must be taught the value of patriarchal family life, religion, hard work, individual responsibility, and, ultimately, a genuine respect for authority. The "moral majority" must not, they believed, allow humanists and hedonism to loosen the glue that holds American society together.

While this larger task of reformulating the traditional order was in progress, however, there was a manifest need to find a more immediate and direct solution to the lawlessness that was ripping apart the fabric of communal life. A "war on crime" was required that would re-establish "law and order." In this regard, conservatives warned that the permissiveness evident in other institutional spheres had crept into our correctional apparatus. Parole boards showed a disturbing proclivity to decarcerate violent felons prematurely, while judges displayed a reluctance to send even habitual offenders to the penitentiary. The leniency pervading the criminal justice system permitted dangerous men to walk free in our neighborhoods and informed them as well that there was little prospect of their being punished should they commit another offense. From the right's vantage, crime burgeoned because, quite simply, it was a paying enterprise. Statistics could be quoted revealing that less than 19 percent of all criminal offenses resulted in an arrest and that "less than one percent of the arrested are tried."[14] Speaking in 1975, Ronald Reagan thus remarked that "If you want to know why crime proliferates in this nation, don't look at the statistics on income and wealth; look at statistics on arrests, prosecutions, convictions, and prison populations. . . . The primary problem is in a criminal justice system that seems to have lost much of its capacity to determine the truth, prosecute and punish the guilty, and protect society."[15] This viewpoint has been echoed more recently by conservative columnist Patrick Buchanan, "Crime has tripled in two decades because crime pays. It is the nation's growth industry because it is an exciting, enjoyable profession where the criminal element runs little risk of being forced to pay an unacceptable price. In a decade, tens of thousands of men, women and children have been murdered. In retaliation, our defender, the state, has executed exactly one killer."[16]

At the core of the problem, conservatives argued, is that the criminal justice system has become more concerned with benefiting the criminal than with preventing the victimization of innocent citizens. This is strikingly apparent in the long list of rights that liberal justices accorded criminal defendants over the past two decades. Protections such as the exclusionary rule have, in the eyes of conservatives, unduly hampered the investigative abilities of police and reduced a prosecutor's capacity to win convictions. Some years ago, Barry Goldwater captured this sentiment when he sarcastically commented that legal rights were instituted "just to give criminals a sporting chance to go free,"[17] while more recent times have seen Supreme Court Justice Warren Burger voice the opinion that "too much concern for the rights of criminal defendants may be nourishing America's growing crime rate."[18] A similar conclusion has been reached by Republican Senator William V. Roth, Jr., "For too long, law has centered its attention on the rights of the criminal defendant—not on the victim or would-be victim of crime. It is time for law to concern itself more with the rights of the people it exists to protect."[19]

While the rights given to criminals are seen as a major obstacle in the state's quest to guard the lives and material possessions of the public, conservatives have maintained that a more fundamental reason exists as to why the criminal justice system coddles law-breakers at the considerable expense of the law-abiding: acceptance of the notion that criminals should be rehabilitated and not punished. The remarks of Republican Representative Sam Steiger are instructive in illustrating the reasoning underlying the right's dissatisfaction with the administration of American criminal justice.

In a 1976 presentation to the U.S. House of Representatives, Steiger commenced his talk with the observation that "one of the national problems the American people are frustrated about is the crime problem." While disturbed by soaring crime rates, "what really frustrates them is the perception that our criminal justice system, as presently administered, not only fails to solve the crime problem... but actually promotes and sustains the problem." The blame for this state of affairs can first be laid at the feet of academic criminologists who "have preached the doctrine of rehabilitation" and "have not hesitated to blast as stupid and reactionary any call for a toughening of the laws or procedures governing the treatment of offenders." These criminologists have had a marked impact on judicial attitudes and hence have achieved their goal of mitigating the harshness of criminal sanctions. Indeed, the frequency with which judges grant habitual felons probation and suspended sentences "appears to stem from the success, within the American judiciary, of the offender treatment philosophy that says, 'The only major purpose of a penal system is rehabilitation.'" And yet "where does this leave the public? It leaves them with the same bunch of thugs turned loose on them again and again." The time has come to "admit we do not know how to rehabilitate and start thinking about the criminal's victims for a change." Judges therefore can no longer be trusted to possess the freedom to send offenders back into society. After all, "how often do we read or hear about the crime committed by a person on probation or who has a felony sentence suspended?" Severe constraints must be imposed on "judicial discretion." While "there are certain problems with shackling the judges in this regard, the courts have left us no alternative."[20]

Yet what strategy could be used to eliminate the discretion that had so long received legitimation from a robust rehabilitative ideal and was now so firmly entrenched in the judiciary as well as in parole boards across the nation? For conservatives like Representative Steiger, the answer was clear: "I think that there is no alternative left to lawmakers but to turn to mandatory (or determinate) penalties."[21] While the rise of the therapeutic state had promoted the expansion of the discretionary powers of court and correctional personnel so that individualized treatment could be effected, the failure of rehabilitation meant that these powers could no longer be justified. To prevent further abuses that would only result in the continued victimization of the public, politicians must move to severely limit the discretion exercised by lenient judges and liberal parole boards. This could be accomplished by lawmakers themselves passing legislation that affixed a strict sanction to each criminal offense and make it mandatory that these specific sanctions be assigned in the event of a conviction. Judges would then have no choice but to impose the penalties that the legislature had prescribed in the criminal code; no coddling of the guilty could take place. Moreover, with the exception of good time credits, all offenders sent to prison would learn the exact length of their sentence at the time of their trial and would serve their terms in their entirety. The indeterminate sentence would thus become an anachronism and be replaced by the determinate sentence. Finally, since no early release for being "cured" would be permitted, parole hearings for inmates would cease and parole boards would be disbanded.

Significantly, conservatives were confident (and remain so today) that a criminal justice system that abandoned the futile goal of offender rehabilitation and set about the task of rationally punishing lawbreakers could achieve substantial reductions in the crime rate. By instituting a code of firm, legislatively-fixed determinate sentences, a two-pronged attack would be launched against the rampant lawlessness plaguing the social order. First, this strategy promised to bolster the deterrent capabilities of the state by insuring that crime no longer pays. Now those on the ideological left, conservatives asserted, have succeeded in convincing many that criminals are driven to violate the law by social and personal circumstances beyond their control. This has fostered the notion that every offender is burdened by a special criminogenic condition and that none is individually responsible for the criminal fate (s)he must endure. It has led as well to the evolution of a correctional system that seeks, in large measure, not to punish but to cure its charges.

Conservatives, however, vehemently rejected this positivist reasoning that criminals are pathological and that moral blame for the crime problem ultimately rests with society.[22] While it can be admitted that a few criminal acts are precipitated by uncontrollable passion or by mental defect, the vast majority of offenders break the law only after they have used their rational faculties to calculate that the benefits of an illegal enterprise outweigh the potential costs. Notably, conservatives were able to draw two conclusions from this classical image of the criminal. For one thing, since free will is exercised in the commission of all but the exceptional crime, lawbreakers—not society—should be held responsible for their actions and thus fully deserve to be legally sanctioned by the state. For another, to the extent that criminals and conformists alike are utilitarian creatures, it is clear that all but the irrational in society will be deterred if the pains of engaging in crime are made to exceed the pleasures.

In this light, people located on the right of the political spectrum held that the very existence of a soaring crime rate was explicit evidence that those administering our criminal justice system had tilted the utilitarian calculus in crime's favor: crime in America paid and paid well! Again, the source of the problem could be traced to our attempts to rehabilitate the wayward. Under the guise of individualized treatment, "bleeding heart" judges have placed serious felons on probation, while parole boards have mitigated the harshness of penal sanctions through early-release policies. Such leniency, however, has done little to effect offender reformation. Instead, it has succeeded only in informing the criminal element that the costs of disregarding the law are not as great as they might have once imagined; there is little to fear from a life in crime.

Despite the intolerably high price that Americans suffered daily as a result of a seemingly intractable crime rate, conservatives nevertheless believed that there was reason to be optimistic. There appeared to be a way to raise the costs of illegal activity substantially and thus to make crime a non-utilitarian and irrational behavioral choice: impose strict determinate sentences. Those who come before the court will now be granted no leniency. They will be held responsible for the crime committed and punished accordingly. Felons, particularly robbers, rapists, and murderers, as well as those who persist in repeating lesser violations, will be subject to mandatory incarceration with no prospect of parole. Under this system, offenders will soon learn that their punishment will be certain and, if their crime is serious, severe. Having been taught a painful lesson, they will think twice in the future before again violating the law. Further, those contemplating an initial excursion into the criminal domain will be struck by the new reality that crime in America no longer pays and will put their illegal thoughts and plans aside. In short, determinacy in sentencing will allow us to "get tough" with crime and thereby to enhance our ability to secure both the "specific" deterrence of convicted offenders and the "general" deterrence of the remaining portion of the American populace.

But this was not all that advocates felt that determinate or mandatory sentences could accomplish. Conservatives were convinced that this crime control strategy would attack lawlessness in a second way as well by markedly increasing the incapacitative effects of imprisonment. In vain attempts to rehabilitate criminals, judicial and parole officials have too often permitted the predatory to walk free in our communities where they have preyed on the law-abiding and pierced the sanctity of our homes. Yet if these dangerous men were uniformly sent to prison and kept securely in captivity, conservatives reasoned, then would not the victimization of the public be diminished and the social order be afforded greater protection? Answering in the affirmative, conservative commentators then asserted that the passage of strict, legislatively-fixed determinate penalties would achieve the previously elusive goal of incapacitating hardened criminals behind bars. Specifically, a criminal code could be fashioned that makes it mandatory for judges to impose lengthy prison terms on all defendants convicted of a violent street-crime or of repeated felonies. The end result would be that more criminals will be in jail where they belong, and the safety of the public will be commensurately enhanced.

These proposals were taken one step further by Harvard political scientist James Q. Wilson. In his widely-read *Thinking About Crime*, Wilson observed that liberals had long asserted that lawlessness will remain pervasive unless the rehabilitation of offenders is taken seriously and larger social reforms are undertaken that eradicate the injustices and inequalities at the root of criminality. From Wilson's vantage point, however, the liberals' agenda for crime control is destined for failure. Rehabilitation, he argued, has proven to be ineffective in denting recidivism rates, while the "root causes" of crime have displayed a remarkable immunity to attack. Wilson thus concluded that it would be more "prudent" and "realistic" to forsake these grander designs and to explore ways in which readily available criminal punishments might be manipulated to achieve meaningful reductions in the crime rate. In his words, "I argue for a sober view of man and his institutions that would permit reasonable things to be accomplished, foolish things abandoned, and utopian things forgotten."[23]

According to Wilson, incapacitation is the most potent crime weapon currently within the reach of policy-makers. His enthusiasm for this strategy stems predominantly from his interpretation of a study conducted by Marvin Wolfgang, Robert Figlio, and Thorsten Sellin and published under the title *Delinquency in a Birth Cohort*.[24] These researchers investigated the criminal involvement that occurred among a group of nearly 10,000 boys in Philadelphia in 1945. One of the more telling findings they reported was that merely six percent of those studied (18 percent of the boys in the sample who actually became delinquent) accounted for 52 percent of all offenses and two-thirds of the violent offenses engaged in by the entire cohort. For Wilson, the policy implications of this result were clear: if a small corps of chronic offenders commit a large proportion of all violations, a marked reduction in the crime rate could be obtained by incapacitating these offenders at the earliest possible time. Mandatory prison terms for serious offenders, he maintained, are central to achieving this end. Admittedly, such a policy would necessitate "substantial additional expenditures for new correctional facilities." Nevertheless, the rewards to be reaped are considerable. "Were we to devote these resources to a strategy that is well within our abilities—namely, to incapacitating a larger fraction of the convicted serious robbers—then not only is a 20 percent reduction possible, but even larger ones are conceivable."[25] After all, "Wicked people exist. Nothing avails except to set them apart from innocent people." And thus far, "We have trifled with the wicked, made sport of the innocent, and encouraged the calculators. Justice suffers, and so do we all."[26]

The logic underlying the right's attack on rehabilitation and their trumpeting of determinate sentencing can perhaps best be summarized by examining a 1976 presentation given by President Gerald Ford.[27] Speaking before the Yale Law School, Ford chose to focus on what he considered to be the most pressing legal issue of the day: the need, as the title of his talk indicates, "To Insure Domestic Tranquility" through the use of the "Mandatory Sentence for Convicted Felons." Paralleling other conservative thinkers of this moment (as well as those of today), Ford expressed the following observations which, when taken together, comprise the core assumptions of the right's vision of crime and its control. (1) Lawlessness is rising and poses a fundamental threat to the social order: "Have we achieved on our streets and in our homes that sense of domestic tranquility so essential to the pursuit of happiness?... If we take crime rates as an indication, the answer is no." (2) The gravest offenses are street-crimes committed by the disadvantaged and not white-collar crimes committed by the rich and powerful: "America has been far from successful in dealing with the sort of crime that obsesses America day and night. I mean street crime... the kind of brutal violence that makes us fearful of strangers and afraid to go out at night." (3) Greater concern must be shown the victims of crime: "The victims are my primary concern." (4) Crime flourishes because the criminal justice system, under the influence of treatment ideals, is too lenient on offenders: "Imprisonment too seldom follows conviction for a felony." (5) More punishment, not less, will bolster the deterrent and incapacitative powers of our legal apparatus and cause crime in America to decrease: "The crime rate will go down if persons who habitually commit most of the predatory crimes are kept in prison.... Six percent of them accounted for two-thirds of all the violent crime" (reference to Wolfgang et al. study). (6) Strict, legislatively-fixed, determinate sentencing is the solution to the nation's crime problem: "Make more sentencing mandatory and, therefore punishment more certain for those convicted of violent crimes."

One final comment regarding the right's attack on rehabilitation and call for stiff determinate sentences deserves mention. The events of the past fifteen years have clearly moved "crime" to the forefront of the political discussions held in conservative circles. With escalating crime rates creating fears in the minds of many citizens and symbolizing a penetrating challenge to the stability of the social fabric as well as to the legitimacy of traditional patterns of authority, those on the right have displayed a keen sensitivity to the need to re-establish "law and order." Yet if concern with lawlessness has been unusually intense during this era and has resulted in more frequent proposals to restore discipline in the criminal justice system, it must be realized that conservatives historically have been both disenchanted with rehabilitation and in favor of getting tough with crime. "Excessive leniency toward law-breakers," Walter Miller has commented, "is a traditional complaint of the right."[28] Indeed, although their previous plans typically lacked the comprehensiveness of the determinate sentencing schemes suggested in more recent times, conservatives have long campaigned to institute mandatory minimum prison terms for selected offenses (e.g., violent, sex) and categories of offenders (e.g., habitual).

However, something was to be different this time around. In the past, conservatives could anticipate that their efforts to punish rather than treat lawbreakers would meet with strong opposition from liberals equating punitive practices with vengeance and arguing that rehabilitation constitutes a more enlightened and scientific response to crime. Yet as the 1970s progressed, liberal resistance to the principle of punishment all but vanished. In a remarkable transformation of correctional ideology, the left rejected rehabilitation and sought to join with the right in tearing down the therapeutic state. Writing in 1977 about the growing movement to introduce determinate sentencing reform, Michael Serrill could offer an observation that one would not have thought possible merely ten years before: "Today, it is difficult to find a prominent member of the academic, prison reform, or liberal political community who does not favor a drastic reduction in the amount of discretion exercised within the criminal justice system."[29] Thus, in the space of a decade, the leading liberal interest groups that had so long fought in support of the rehabilitative ideal and indeterminacy in sentencing now converged with their conservative counterparts in believing that standards of desert and determinacy should guide the administration of justice. To move toward understanding this unprecedented shift in the left's criminal justice policy is the next task that we will attempt to take up.

THE LIBERAL ATTACK: DOING JUSTICE

While the turmoil of the sixties and seventies taught conservatives that the social order was in desperate need of fortification, the happenings of this era conveyed a vastly different message to those with a leftist orientation. These were times in which their experiences would eventually lead liberals to doubt both the willingness and capacity of the government to achieve an equitable and humane society. The liberals' trust in the state to do good would turn into a profound mistrust, while their optimism about the possibilities for genuine reform within the confines of existing institutional arrangements would be replaced by a deep sense of pessimism. The harsh realities they uncovered would force them to speak of the "limits of benevolence" and to admit that paternalistic measures aimed at saving the wayward had resulted in unconscionable abuses.[30] Reluctantly, they would abandon the hope of state benevolence and conclude that they had little choice but to devote their energies to expanding the rights of society's deviants so as to minimize the inclination of the state to victimize this vulnerable population. For if the government could not be relied upon to treat its outcasts kindly, then it might at least be possible to compel it to treat these people more fairly. In the end, "doing justice" and "due process" would supplant "doing good" and "rehabilitation" as the goal of liberal reform.

Now the emergence of the civil rights movement marked the beginning of a period in which the legitimacy of state authority was subjected to continued and widespread debate among liberal forces. By itself, the crusade for civil rights illuminated gross disparities in distributive justice and exposed the image of America as an open-class system as mere ideology. It unmasked as well the government's role in tolerating and at times actively perpetuating pernicious patterns of racism, sexism, and inequality. The violence unleashed in ghettos across the nation signified the depths to which faith in the prevailing order had fallen.

For those on the left, Vietnam served to quicken the pace at which their belief in the moral justification of the state was diminishing. By supporting what amounted to a dictatorial regime, America forfeited its claim as the defender of democratic ideals. It was clear that we were prepared to sacrifice human rights in the ruthless pursuit of self-interest; it was equally apparent that our political leadership was ethically bankrupt. This latter conclusion was vividly reinforced by the methods deployed by the state to control dissent over the war. As the use of undercover agents as well as unlawful break-ins and wire-taps against suspected radical elements became known, the threats to freedom suddenly seemed real and trust in the government waned. However, more dramatic proof of the coercive potential of the state was revealed by its willingness to utilize violence to suppress protest. The sight of police assaulting fleeing demonstrators during the anti-war rally at the 1968 Democratic National Convention came as a shocking reminder of the repressive powers that the government retains and will exercise when threatened by insurgent movements. The tragedy at Kent State nearly two years later proved even more disturbing. As a horrified public learned, it was not just the poor, the black, or the radical that the state would shoot down to insure the sanctity of its order.

At the same time, youthful "alienation" from "the system" was becoming pervasive. "The establishment" was now something of a dirty expression, and it was often uttered that "you can't trust anyone over thirty." Social analysts spent their time documenting the rise of a "counterculture." Resentment toward legal authority intensified as the government moved to squelch the use of even recreational drugs. For many on college campuses, there was little mystery as to why the social lubricant of their parents, alcohol, was legal while their preference, pot, was not: the state protects the values and interests of the more powerful.

Notably, this theme received fuller attention as the linkages between corporations and politicians were unraveled. The existence of a "power elite" that operated to enrich the advantaged at the expense of the less advantaged no longer seemed farfetched. Few liberals had trouble believing that our political leaders were substantially compromised by economic interests and were willing partners in big business' rape of the environment, daily deception of consumers, and massive accumulation of wealth and influence.

The erosion of state authority reached its most advanced stage as the veil hiding the Watergate scandal was torn away. The Nixon resignation and prison terms for numerous high ranking officials was prima-facie evidence that even those who make righteous calls for "law and order" and for a "war on crime" cannot be entrusted to administer a morally sound government. Particularly among liberals, the series of events over the previous decade that culminated in and were symbolized by Watergate left confidence in the state badly shaken. Commentators now talked of the existence of a "legitimacy crisis"[31] and of "a pervasive distrust in the legitimacy of the authority of a whole series of persons and institutions."[32]

With skepticism toward the state permeating the liberal community, leftists now encountered a disillusioning obstacle in their quest for a more equitable and humane social order: the growing fiscal crisis haunting the welfare state. In the past, a prosperous and expanding economy had generated a sense of optimism that sufficient resources abounded to solve pressing social problems and to create the "Great Society." But the seventies did much to make this liberal vision seem little more than an illusion. The advent of "stagflation," "double-digit inflation," "balanced budgets," "Proposition 2," and politicians winning elections on platforms of "fiscal conservatism," all signaled a collapse in the state's ability to untangle the contradictions of the U.S.'s capitalist economy and bring about another cycle of affluence. The time ahead promised to be one of retrenchment in which the powerless and the powerful would battle for scarce resources. In this competition, it was manifest whose side the state could be "trusted" to take. Hopes for bettering the lot of society's disadvantaged and dependent populations were thus severely dashed. Faced with these difficult realities, optimism declined and a deep pessimism crept into the minds and hearts of many liberals.[33]

In this context, as David Greenberg and Drew Humphries have observed, "liberal assumptions about the benevolence of the state could no longer be sustained."[34] Few in leftist circles doubted that the government lacked the will if not the capacity to "do good" for the casualties of the inequitable order over which it presided. Mistrust and pessimism led all but the most old-fashioned and idealistic liberals to anticipate that harm, not beneficence, will result when the poor, the aged, the sick, the retarded, and the mentally ill are brought under the auspices of state welfare programs or institutional care. This same thinking and sentiment informed the posture taken by the left toward the criminal justice system and its announced attempt to rehabilitate lawbreakers. Here, liberals saw scant indication that state enforced therapy was being conducted in a meaningful way or with the offenders' best interests at heart. Instead, it was apparent that therapeutic ideology was being used to justify both gross disparities in the administration of justice and inhumanity within the confines of custodial warehouses misnamed "penitentiaries" and "correctional" facilities. If the state once retained visions of being a kind parent to its captives, it was now clearly guilty of their abuse. The American criminal justice system did little to save and much to victimize those who had the misfortune of falling within its grasp.

Attica cemented these themes in the consciousness of the left. Traditionally, reformers had championed the infusion of the rehabilitative ideal into the criminal justice system and the expansion of discretionary powers that would allow for the individualized treatment of offenders. While the difficulties surrounding correctional programs were not ignored in the past, many liberals nevertheless had held tenaciously to the belief that the state could ultimately be induced to exercise these powers in a benevolent manner. But the bloody suppression of the uprising at Attica compelled even the most adamant supporters of enforced therapy to re-examine this assumption. In focusing attention on the plight of society's captives, Attica revealed how badly the liberals' faith in the state had been misplaced. It was now clear that the state used its discretion not to better inmates but to brutalize them, not to effect individualized treatment but to incarcerate only the poor and non-white. It was clear as well that the state could comfortably create a shameful penal environment that would drive even the most patient person to protest and then resort to terrifying violence to coerce obedience. As Michael Ignatieff poignantly remarked, these events raised "the issue of the morality of state power in its starkest form."[35] And for liberals of that day, the conclusion was unavoidable that within the arena of criminal justice, the state could not be trusted to act according to ethical principles; visions of doing good must be abandoned.[36]

The general "legitimacy crisis" besetting the government combined with the shock of Attica exerted a transforming influence on liberal thinking about American correctional policy. Scathing critiques of enforced therapy appeared at the inception of the 1970s,[37] written by authors sensitized by the events of the past decade to the coercive potential of the state. In the context of the post-Attica era, these works increasingly acquired wide readership and ready acceptance within a liberal community that was now prepared to hear the message being conveyed. Meanwhile, literature exposing the corruption of therapeutic measures mounted, while older writings that had expressed serious reservations about the rehabilitative ideal were resurrected and the foresight of their authors admired.[38] "By the mid-seventies," Samuel Walker noted, "a profound retreat from rehabilitation swept through public and professional thinking. For the first time in one hundred and fifty years, both the experts and the public questioned the fundamental assumptions of American corrections."[39]

Below, we will first explore the specific criticisms that disillusioned liberals of this period leveled at state enforced therapy, and then proceed to examine how liberals sought to resolve the crisis in criminal justice policy precipitated by the demise of the rehabilitative ideal.

THE LIBERAL CRITIQUE: VICTIMIZING THE OFFENDER

Again, liberal disapproval of the functioning of criminal justice rehabilitation is not a novel occurrence. However, while exceptions can be found, liberals in past years did not as a rule assert that rehabilitation should be cast aside as the legitimate goal of corrections. Now with their liberal brethren of more recent days, they did share the realization that the criminal justice system does more harming than saving of the wayward. Karl Menninger in his celebrated *The Crime of Punishment* could thus conclude that "I suspect that all the crimes committed by the jailed criminals do not equal in total social damage that of all the crime committed against them."[40] What is notable, though, is that such dismaying insights did not lead liberals like Menninger to crusade for the dismantling of the therapeutic state. The source of the inhumanities in our prisons, they often repeated, cannot be traced to the existence of the rehabilitative philosophy but rather to its inadequate or faulty implementation. More rational and better financed treatment programs, not less commitment to enforced therapy, is the answer to society's crime problem. Indeed, only when the irrational feelings of vengeance and the thirst for retributive punishment are no longer allowed to guide penal policy and principles of rehabilitation are fully embraced will the penitentiary actualize the good intentions of its founders. Thus, Menninger voiced the opinion that "Reformation of the individual is still not the purpose of our system. The infliction of vindictive suffering has not been repudiated. . . . And a prison whose primary aim is to make offenders into 'industrious, free men rather than orderly and obedient prisoners' is yet to be born!"[41] Similarly, years of imprisonment taught Nathan Leopold (of the famous Leopold and Loeb case) that "The prisons of today are a failure, for they are not effective instruments of rehabilitation of their inmates. To remedy this failure requires a complete revision of our penal philosophy and a firm adherence to rehabilitation as the only function to be served."[42]

Yet for liberals in the seventies, it became increasingly difficult to accept the premises espoused so confidently just a few years before by Menninger, Leopold, and nearly all other leading commentators. Shaken by the turmoil of the times to take a fresh look at old assumptions, those on the left went far in reconsidering their traditional belief—one held for close to a century and a half—that the benevolent cure of offenders will ineluctably follow should society make saving rather than punishing the wayward the sole purpose of its control efforts and pursue this end with vigor. In a radical transformation of perspective, liberals now rejected the notion that the deficiencies in the criminal justice system can be blamed on the *absence* of a genuine commitment to treatment. Instead, they asserted that it is the very *presence* of rehabilitative ideology and practice that is responsible for the most debasing features of American corrections. It is not the implementation of the theory of rehabilitation that is faulty, they argued, but the theory itself. As such, state enforced therapy will inevitably foster the abuse of offenders and result in gross inequalities in the administration of justice. We should no longer talk of the "crime of punishment" but, in the words of the authors of *Struggle for Justice*, of the "crime of treatment."[43]

1. Problems in Theory. In 1974, Robert Martinson reported the results of an extensive research project that had investigated the effectiveness of correctional treatment.[44] In essence, Martinson and his team of research associates were attempting to answer a question that was simple to state but far-reaching in its implications: Does rehabilitation work? After analyzing 231 treatment studies conducted from 1945 to 1967, Martinson could offer reformers little to be optimistic about. His data were clear in pointing to the conclusion that "With few and isolated exceptions, the rehabilitative efforts that have been reported so far have had no appreciable effect on recidivism."[45]

The notion that "nothing works" quickly became an established doctrine in the field and dealt a devastating blow to the legitimacy of the rehabilitative ideal. Martinson's assertion of the lack of treatment effects confirmed the suspicions of many liberals who had come to mistrust the benevolent intentions of the state and forced those who had been wavering on the rehabilitation issue to admit the futility of pursuing an illusory goal. Moreover, it placed those who persisted in advocating state enforced therapy in a terrible ethical quandary: in the face of sound empirical evidence showing that "nothing works," how can one justify depriving offenders of their liberty on the grounds that they are being cured?

What is of interest, however, is that researchers examining the impact of treatment programs on recidivism had, some years ago, reached much the same conclusion as that voiced by Martinson.[46] In 1959, for instance, Barbara Wootton's review of existing studies led her to observe, "As to the effectiveness of the comparatively humane methods now in use, surprisingly little evidence is available." Yet in the past, the scarcity of statistical support for offender reformation did not trigger a campaign to repudiate treatment but rather served as an impetus for the development of more adequate therapeutic measures. In short, knowledge that rehabilitation "does not work" simply meant that we must "do a better job to make it work." As Wootton went on to state, "At least we can say that, so far as offenders themselves are concerned, nothing yet has transpired which should discourage anyone, whether psychiatrically-minded or not, from urging further development of humane methods of treatment. . . . Clear evidence that reformative measures do in fact reform would be very welcome."[47]

But this time around, things were quite different. Martinson's dictum that "nothing works" was not looked upon as the starting point for yet another liberal campaign to save the criminal and the delinquent. Rather, "nothing works" became a code word for the more sobering belief that rehabilitation *cannot work*. Martinson's own interpretation of his findings is instructive in this regard. After revealing the negligible impact of treatment on recidivism rates, he admitted the possibility that the dearth of effects may arise because "our programs aren't yet good enough" and hence that "what our correctional system needs is simply a more full-hearted commitment to the strategy of treatment." Yet he was not sanguine about this conclusion. Instead, he felt compelled to caution that larger issues may be at the core of the repeated failures to make the lawless into the law-abiding. Reflecting liberal sentiment of the day, he remarked, "It may be. . . that there is a more radical flow in our present strategies—that education at its best, or that psychotherapy at its best, cannot overcome, or even appreciably reduce, the powerful tendency for offenders to continue in criminal behavior."[48]

In this vein, liberal critics labored to illuminate several fundamental reasons why criminal justice rehabilitation is inherently flawed and therefore cannot be expected to exert a salutary influence on an offender's criminal involvement. First, they proposed that an incorrect theory of crime underlies existing treatment programs. According to these critics, correctional rehabilitation is firmly rooted in the logic of the Positivist School or "medical model" and hence is based on the assumption that inmates are "sick" or "abnormal." In turn, it is held that offenders can be changed into conforming citizens if each one's pathological, criminogenic condition is treated and cured. But for liberal critics, such an image of the criminal is badly distorted. The vast majority of those who violate the law, they argued, are psychologically normal and have no "crime disease" to be healed. Instead, offenders exercise their rationality and free-will like the rest of us and fall into crime only because their social circumstances make this a normal—not pathological—behavioral choice. As a consequence, the way to reduce criminality is not to define the lawbreaker as sick and in need of cure, but rather to focus on the structural features of an unjust society that give some people little stake in the conventional order and make a life that risks captivity a reasonable alternative. In short, general social reform, not individual reform, is the solution to the problem of crime.[49]

Second, a treatment paradigm presupposes that an offender's progress in institutional programs is a good indicator of whether an inmate will have the capacity to stay straight if released. Those who gain "insight" into their emotional pathology, work to obtain an occupational skill, and avoid making trouble are good candidates for freedom; those who resist the advice of helping professionals and persist in disrupting the prison peace obviously are not yet fit to function without careful supervision. But for liberal critics, the link between prison adjustment and community adjustment is not as intimate as the rehabilitators would have us believe; rather, it is quite tenuous. The regimen and realities of the society of captives have little or nothing in common with life in the wider society. As such, many who might be model citizens within the confines of a structured environment may not possess the skills or personal strength to negotiate the rigors of an independent existence. Alternatively, those who fall prey to the intense pressures of imprisonment and respond with sporadic outbursts of resentment and rebelliousness may, notwithstanding, be equipped to adapt far better upon release. Norval Morris has cogently summarized the liberal concerns here: "Prison behavior is not a predictor of community behavior."[50]

Now these considerations, the critics continued, create a sticky dilemma for criminal justice rehabilitators. Although only presented with the opportunity to observe offenders within the context of the unusual social setting of the penitentiary, they nevertheless must make daily judgments regarding which inmates are cured and prepared for re-entry into society and which are not. Further, it is clear that our present understanding of criminal behavior has not advanced to the stage where it will make this task of distinguishing the rehabilitated from the criminal any more facile. The technology for accurately predicting conformity simply has not been developed to the point where it can be employed with even minimal confidence.[51] Indeed, given the complexity of the causal forces that underly the criminal choices of any one offender, evolving such technology may constitute an insurmountable obstacle. As a consequence, decision-makers in the treatment process are faced with the precarious chore of assessing who is cured with little reliable information at their disposal. Mistakes are thus inevitable: the dangerous will too often be set free and many harmless offenders will be kept needlessly caged.

To illustrate the pitfalls of attempting to cull the healthy from an institutionalized population, liberals had to search no further than David Rosenhan's provocative work, "Being Sane in Insane Places." Although conducted in a mental health setting, Rosenhan's research served as a powerful indictment of all behavioral scientists who claimed to have acquired the talent to discriminate the deviant from the non-deviant. In order to evaluate the expertise of treatment personnel, Rosenhan sent eight sane people into a variety of psychiatric facilities. All of these confederates were instructed to complain of having heard voices at their admissions screening but then to act perfectly normal once situated inside. Notably, "despite their public 'show' of sanity, the pseudopatients were never detected." Diagnosed as schizophrenic, they were kept hospitalized an average of nineteen days and were subsequently discharged not as sane but as suffering "schizophrenia in remission."

But Rosenhan did not halt his investigation here. The staff at one psychiatric facility "had heard of these findings but doubted that such an error could occur in their hospital." Taking up this challenge, Rosenhan informed the staff that during the next three months, one or more healthy confederates would be admitted to their institution. At the close of this period, staff members, including psychiatrists and trained psychologists, confidently identified nearly ten percent of the patient population as feigning illness. Rosenhan, however, had been less than honest with the staff: he actually had sent no new confederates into the hospital! That is, where treatment "experts" had previously failed to detect the sane among the insane, now they were discovering many "sane" people in a population that under normal circumstances would have been presumed to be entirely in need of cure. To Rosenhan, the conclusion demanded by these events was unavoidable: "One thing is certain: any diagnostic process that lends itself so readily to massive errors of this sort cannot be a very reliable one.... It is clear that we cannot distinguish the sane from the insane in psychiatric hospitals."[52]

For liberal critics, a third inherent defect in the theory of criminal justice rehabilitation is that it is enforced. Since earning release from prison under this system is contingent on being rehabilitated, inmates have little choice but to participate in treatment programs. Yet linking liberty to cure corrupts the very process of reform. For many inmates, a goal displacement occurs in which the end of therapy is shifted from genuine self-improvement to simply procuring their freedom. Rehabilitation becomes merely a means to be manipulated or a "game" to be played in the quest to win relief from the pains of imprisonment. Outwardly, offenders thus display enthusiasm about taking advantage of treatment services and serious concern about their "progress"; inside, however, they harbor a profound cynicism about the whole process. For other inmates, enforced therapy presents an even more difficult barrier to reform. The very experience of being forced to toil in programs creates deep resentment toward treatment professionals and a firm resistance to giving in and abiding by the rules of their captors. We should have learned by now, the critics warned, that people cannot be reformed against their will; only those who want to be helped can benefit from our offer to assist in their betterment. As Norval Morris and James Jacobs observed, "The concept of 'coerced cure' in the correctional field is also a dangerous delusion. In the field of psychological medicine it is widely agreed that psychotherapy, particularly if it is of the psychoanalytic variety, must be voluntarily entered into by the patient if it is to be effective."[53]

Finally, liberals argued that however appealing the principles of enforced therapy might seem on the surface, one reality remained which insured that efforts to cure offenders would inevitably end in disappointment: the very structure of the prison is antithetical to the reclamation of the wayward. When the Quakers proudly opened the gates of their first "penitentiary," they imagined that they had succeeded in creating a truly therapeutic environment. But the tragic history of their invention has shown that the prison resembles not a hospital where the benevolent cure of patients is effected but a warehouse that stores human flesh in degenerative conditions. Indeed, the daily regimen of incarceration culti-vates not responsibility but dependency, and teaches little about the skills needed to remain at liberty and much about the ways of surviving in a repressive and dangerous community. As one inmate wrote, "No bird ever learned to fly in a cage. Prisons do not, cannot rehabili-tate by virtue of the very nature of imprisonment which is to confine and restrict."[54] Beyond this, total institutions are intrinsically dehumanizing and thus necessarily sabotage even the sincerest attempts on the part of rehabilitators to humanize their clients. "Prisons," David Rothman observed in 1972, "brutalize inmates, humiliate them, and educate them in the ways of crime. Moreover, an impressive sociological literature... demonstrates that these characteristics are inherent in institutions, which by their very nature are infantalizing or corrupting."[55]

Liberals received compelling support for this image of the penitentiary from the imagina-tive research of social psychologist Philip Zimbardo. Desiring to gain insight into the condi-tions that underly our perpetual failure to evolve a rational and humane correctional institution, Zimbardo set out to construct a mock prison at Stanford University that would "simulate the psychological state of imprisonment." From over 75 students who volun-teered to participate in the experiment, 21 were selected to fill the positions of 11 guards and 10 inmates. Notably, all of the actual participants were "judged to be emotionally sta-ble, physically healthy, mature, law-abiding citizens."

The results of the study proved as disturbing as they did revealing. Within a short space of time, these normal students "gave up their identities and allowed their assigned roles and the social forces in the situation to guide, shape and eventually to control their freedom of thought and action." The guards, in particular, moved quickly to assert their authority and thereby to secure complete dominance over the inmates. "Typically the guards insulted the prisoners, threatened them, were physically aggressive, used instruments (night sticks, fire extinguishers, etc.) to keep the prisoners in line and referred to them in impersonal, anonymous, deprecating ways." Less than 36 hours into the experiment, a disorganized and depressed student-inmate had to be sent home. On each successive day, it was necessary to release additional inmates suffering similar symptoms. Most other prisoners responded to the arbitrary and capricious discipline exerted by the guards by withdrawing and becoming passive. With the psychological and physical dangers of living in this "mock" prison rising, the experiment which was to run two weeks had to be terminated after just six days.

For liberals, the lesson that must be drawn from Zimbardo's research was inescapable. Even when the most healthy and normal are placed within the roles typically populated by criminals and uneducated, authoritarian guards, a humane environment does not ensue. Instead, the very structure of imprisonment is so inherently corrupting that it constrains even good people to brutalize one another. In Zimbardo's words,

> The potential social value of this study derives precisely from the fact that normal, healthy, educated young men could be so radically transformed under the institutional pressures of a "prison environment." If this could happen in so short a time, without the excesses that are possible in real prisons, and if it could happen to the "cream-of-the-crop of American youth," then one can only shudder to imagine what society is

doing both to the actual guards and prisoners who are at this very moment participating in that unnatural "social experiment."[56]

2. Doing Harm. Liberal opposition to rehabilitation did not rest exclusively on the belief that flaws in the theory of enforced therapy make offender reformation a futile undertaking. Of equal or greater concern was that the current therapeutic state not only leaves recidivism rates impervious to assault but also visits immeasurable damages upon those it purports to save. While early reformers may have wished to formulate a system that would do good for offenders, in practice the system is using the mask of benevolence to do considerable harm.

Those on the left took special pains to vilify the indeterminate sentence.[57] As discussed, because it allows correctional officials to keep inmates incarcerated until genuine therapeutic advances are achieved, the indeterminate prison term is the linchpin of the policy of state enforced rehabilitation. In contrast, determinate sentencing would mean that, cured or not, all inmates re-enter society once their specific, fixed terms are completed. Now in the eyes of liberal critics, indeterminacy and the discretionary powers it places at the disposal of correctional decision-makers has had a long record of facilitating not cure but coercion. For one thing, the evidence is strong in suggesting that prison stays lengthened after the "progressive reform" of indeterminate sentencing replaced fixed-term statutes.[58] For another, inmates serving an indeterminate sentence have little idea of when they will be granted release. Already suffering the pains of a rigorous prison life, now they must endure the added burden of sitting in torturous suspense until the parole board deems them worthy of citizenship.[59] Further, without firm knowledge of their release date, they are unable to plan their return to society with their spouses and loved ones. Under the pressure of such uncertainty, family ties often disintegrate, thus precipitating a difficult crisis in an inmate's life and making reintegration into society more problematic once parole is granted.

Even more troubling, however, is that while correctional officials publically portray the indeterminate sentence as an invaluable therapeutic device, in their daily rounds behind the cover of the prison walls, they employ it as a ruthless weapon to coerce inmate conformity. Close observers of institutional realities are well aware, the liberals contended, that wardens do not earn economic security by reforming offenders. Instead, their job tenure is intimately dependent on their ability to maintain peace within the community of captives they supervise. As a consequence, prison administrators will appropriate any resources within reach that will enhance their capacity to satisfy custodial demands—even if this entails debasing the integrity of the treatment enterprise. In this light, the indeterminate sentence has been fundamentally corrupted and transmuted into one of the most tyrannical tools available to prison officials. While originally freedom was to be linked to an inmate's prospect for success on the outside, now the criterion for release has been drastically altered from cure to institutional conformity. Indeed, the message conveyed to all inmates is eminently clear: those who remain obedient and pose no threat to the equilibrium of the prison order will be rewarded with early release. Alternatively, those who persist in causing disruptions—"the political nonconformist, the malcontent, the inmate leader of an ethnic group, the persistent writ-writer, the psychotic, the troublemaker"—will be deprived of their cherished liberty until they acquire the wisdom to follow the rules dictated by the custodial regime.[60]

Capturing liberal sentiment in recent times, David Rothman has written of the prison that, "In the end, when conscience and convenience met, convenience won. When treatment and coercion met, coercion won."[61]

For liberals, the celebrated case of black inmate George Jackson provided a vivid example of the repressiveness that permeates the usage of the indeterminate sentence.[62] Arrested in the early 1960s for his part—sitting in a getaway car—in a $70 gas station robbery, Jackson was convicted and given an indeterminate term in the California correctional system. Not long into his sentence, Jackson organized a food strike among inmates. In the years ahead, he would emerge as a dynamic inmate leader and, informed by Marxist writings, would speak out forcefully against the pernicious effects of the radical and class injustices that pervaded prisons as well as the larger social order. His book *Soledad Brother* would bring him national attention and, in some quarters, acclaim.[63] But the price he would pay for such persistent resistance to prison authorities would be immense. For a $70 robbery, he would spend *eleven years* behind bars because he displayed no signs of being "rehabilitated."[64] He was not, however, set free after this lengthy stay. Vowing that the state would never permit him to leave captivity alive, he proved to be tragically prophetic. In 1971, George Jackson was gunned down in an aborted escape attempt. For many on the left, the events surrounding his death revealed that Jackson was seduced into escaping and then purposefully assassinated by his custodians. Where the oppressiveness of the indeterminate sentence had failed in this instance to silence George Jackson, the state had turned to surer means to keep the peace.

Liberal critics were able to point to yet another disquieting feature of state enforced therapy: the nature of the rehabilitative techniques that correctional officials are prepared to employ in their efforts to change the lawless into the law-abiding. Today, we cringe when we hear that well-intentioned Quakers zealously placed offenders in total solitary confinement for years on end in the confident belief that they would reform these errant people. Yet if our therapeutic strategies have the appearance of greater sophistication and scientific rationality, liberals cautioned, they are no less dehumanizing and forthrightly harmful. Under the guise of benevolence, we have evolved chemical and behavioral measures that too often leave irreversible physical and psychological scars and thus rob inmates of their health and personalities. The days of "clockwork orange" are upon us. In the words of Morris and Jacobs, "The search for a 'cure' for the criminal has sometimes even taken us beyond the bounds of civilized treatment. Drugs, electroshock therapy, sterilization, and even psychosurgery have all been used to 'reform' the prisoner's behavior."[65] Echoing these fears, David Fogel has observed that,

> On the dim horizon one sees a group of the newest enthusiasts clamoring for their place in the torturously convoluted history of prisons. They are generally known as "behavior modifiers." Though not new, their language is not well known because they are just now emerging from animal laboratories and the back wards of hospitals in search of defectives. Their therapeutic arsenal is equipped with positive and negative reinforcements, pills, chemicals, electrodes, and neurosurgical instruments.[66]

Further, the liberals asserted, we can anticipate that the primary use of these dangerous devices will not be to effect the betterment of the offender. Just as the indeterminate sentence has been corrupted into a coercive custodial weapon, so too will the same fate befall these new "therapies." Already in our prisons, the logic of behavior modification has become an excuse to deny recalcitrant inmates basic human rights, the "adjustment center" has become a handy euphemism for what is actually "the hole," and drugs have become an efficient way of inducing passive compliance. Indeed, the message of *One Flew Over the Cuckoo's Nest* should not be casually ignored. As this story by Ken Kesey nears to an end, the once rambunctious, refractory, and thoroughly human Randle P. McMurphy is wheeled into the hospital ward. On the medical chart hanging from his bed "was written in ink, Lobotomy.... We looked up to the other end at the head dented into the pillow, a swirl of red hair over a face milk-white except for the heavy purple bruises around the eyes.... 'There's nothin' in the face. Just like one of those store dummies.'" The Chief was certain that McMurphy "wouldn't have left something like that sit there in the day room with his name tacked on it for twenty or thirty years so the Big Nurse could use it as an example of what can happen if you buck the system. I was sure of that." It might be remembered that in the face of such dehumanization and in defiance of the "Big Nurse's" oppressive institutional regime, the Chief chose to smother McMurphy to death.[67]

3. *The Administration of Injustice.* As discussed, state enforced rehabilitation is based on the principle that the punishment should fit the criminal and not the crime. Performing this task requires that state officials be entrusted with sufficient discretion to develop an individualized treatment program for each offender that passes through the criminal justice system. But for liberals, it was manifest that the exercise of this broad discretionary power had eventuated in little treatment and much abuse within the confines of the prison. Moreover, this was not, liberals argued, the only station in the criminal justice system in which the existence of unfettered discretion was having deleterious consequences. In looking to the courts, they discovered that judges operated under few constraints and were making a mockery of the principle of equal justice before the law. "Law without order," Marvin Frankel wrote, prevailed in our courtrooms and threatened to undermine the very legitimacy of our system.[68]

Again, within the context of a rehabilitative model, it would be expected that judges would assign discrepant sanctions to offenders convicted of the same crime. Based on keen insight developed from years on the bench and equipped with a probation officer's presentence report, a judge might decide that one robber could best be treated in the community while another would derive more benefit from a stay in the penitentiary where a structured therapeutic community would be available. Increasingly, however, liberals came to perceive that treatment considerations had little or nothing to do with the "widely unequal sentences [that] are imposed every day in great numbers for crimes and criminals not essentially distinguishable from each other."[69] For one thing, liberals noted, judges fail to undergo specialized training aimed at providing them with the scientific expertise to prescribe the correct curative measures for each offender; indeed, as Martinson's finding that "nothing works" indicates, this skill has escaped even the most gifted in the treatment profession. Further, there is good evidence to suspect that judicial decision-making is highly idiosyncratic. It is apparent that each judge possesses his or her own particular set of biases (e.g., a "get tough" vs. "lenient" disposition), and hence any two judges are quite likely to mete out divergent sentences for crimes identical in nature and circumstance.[70] In this regard, one researcher selected files from actual cases and then asked federal judges to state what penalty they would impose on the defendants. The findings were instructive in illustrating the unruliness that pervades sentencing practices: "In the case of a middle-aged union official convicted on several counts of extortionate credit transactions, one judge proposed a sentence of 20 years' imprisonment plus a $65,000 fine. And another judge proposed a 3-year sentence with no fine."[71]

Yet what weighed most heavily on the conscience of many liberals was not that the administration of justice was excessively arbitrary and capricious—an admittedly troubling fact—but that it was also blatantly discriminatory. By taking even a cursory glance at our prisons, one could gain incontrovertible proof that judges believe that these are places more suited for the poor than the rich and for the nonwhite than the white. Ample case evidence is also available to show convincingly that discretionary justice is the equivalent of discriminatory injustice. For instance, "in two marijuana cases," the authors of *Fair and Certain Punishment* reported, "the same judge sentenced a white youth to one year's probation and a $400 fine; a black male received a two-year sentence; again, both were first offenders."[72] Articulating the left's view of sentencing, David Greenberg observed that the exercise of "unreviewed and unchecked" judicial discretion, "ostensibly justified as meeting the needs of the individual defendant—treating the criminal, not the crime," has "at best led to gross disparities in the sentencing of people with comparable offenses and previous records; at worst, it has been a respectable cover for letting off the upper- and middle-class criminal with a slap on the wrist, while reserving the full weight of law enforcement for those without money or power to fight back."[73]

THE LIBERAL SOLUTION: THE JUSTICE MODEL

While those who participated in the founding of the therapeutic state may have been blessed with admirable motives, for liberals in the seventies it had become disturbingly clear that the aims of these past reformers had been fundamentally corrupted. In a naive display of faith, the liberal community had trusted the government to evolve a system that would effect the benevolent cure of the aberrant. But now liberals had learned the difficult lesson, as the writers of *Struggle for Justice* lamented, that "out of the best intentions in the world can grow an increase in human misery."[74] The harsh reality, they argued, is that rehabilitation is a dangerous myth that has long been used by the state to justify the unconscionable victimization of offenders. Indeed, the paradigm of enforced therapy continues to permit gross inequities in criminal sanctioning to flourish and each day presents prison custodians with fresh opportunities not only to coerce their charges but also to damage them physically and psychologically. For liberals, the time had finally come to abandon their false hopes for a criminal justice system that would do good. The rehabilitative ideal must be cast aside as the program for liberal reform, and a replacement decided upon. In this light, the "justice model" emerged as the most promising candidate.

With mistrust of the government running rampant, the most pressing item on the left's reform agenda was to constrain the immense power the state exerted over the lives of its criminal members. "By now we should know," Ira Glasser warned, that "power is the natural antagonist of liberty, even if those who exercise power are filled with good intentions."[75] Again, for liberals, the source of the state's dangerous domination in the legal sphere can be traced directly to the unbridled discretion that has been placed—in the name of individualized treatment—at the disposal of criminal justice operatives. Despite disastrous consequences, judges, correctional officials, and parole boards remain free to dispense "treatment" more according to whim than to rule of law. To diminish this unwarranted concentration of power in the hands of the state's agents of social control, it is thus essential to discredit rehabilitation—the rationale that has traditionally justified the investment of broad discretion at nearly every juncture of the criminal justice system. As such, enforced therapy must be unmasked as being both ineffective and repressive, and then discarded. With the demise of rehabilitative ideology accomplished, there will be no legitimate reason to continue to permit court and correctional personnel to possess the discretion that was previously required to "fit the punishment to the criminal." Purging the system of its vast discretion will appear to be a sensible policy and thus become an attainable reform.

And what will govern the sentencing process once the goal of individualized treatment is forfeited? The liberal response to this query was unanimous: the philosophy of "just deserts" should be embraced as the new rationale guiding criminal sanctioning. In this view, punishment will now fit the offense and not the offender. The severity of penalties will be strictly commensurate with the seriousness of the crime committed, and all offenders, irrespective of position in society, will be treated exactly the same. In short, when citizens come before the court, they will receive only the punishment they deserve—no more, no less. "Simple" and equal justice will finally prevail in the nation's courts.[76]

Notably, a variety of liberal commentators labored to outline the specifics of what a legal system would entail that sought not to do good through rehabilitation but rather to do justice through retributive punishment.[77] While these authors differed occasionally on the particulars of their proposals, they nevertheless evidenced wide consensus regarding the central parameters that must comprise a liberal "justice model for corrections."[78] These shared assumptions are set forth below:

1. *For justice to be possible, all sentences must be "determinate" or "flat."* The most crucial ingredient to eradicating discretion in the criminal justice system and thereby protecting offenders from the abuse of state power is to eliminate the indeterminate sentence. Without exception, every offender must be informed prior to imprisonment exactly how long his or her stay in the penitentiary will be.

2. *The principle of just deserts and not that of individualized treatment will regulate the sanction an offender receives.* This means that the time inmates spend incarcerated will in no way be influenced by their prospects for reform. The link between cure and liberty, so dominant under state enforced therapy, will be unalterably severed. Instead, the nature of the crime committed will regulate the punishment that is "justly deserved" and can be legitimately imposed by the state. All sanctions will be proportionate to the gravity of the infraction in question: minor offenses will justify light penalties, serious offenses, harsher penalties. Similarly, first offenses should be sanctioned less severely than second or repeated violations of the law.

3. Sentences will be legislatively-fixed and narrow in range. Legislators (or sentencing commissions they appoint) must undertake an extensive revision of existing criminal codes. In renovating these codes, they must first rank offenses according to their relative seriousness and then develop a commensurate scale of sanctions. Of equal importance, however, is that lawmakers assign a specific sentence or very narrow range of possible sentences to each criminal offense. For instance, prior to the passage of determinate sentencing in Illinois, the penalty for a Class 3 felony was an indeterminate term of anywhere from one to ten years. In contrast, justice model advocate David Fogel has proposed that this penalty be narrowed to a flat term of three years with an option to increase the sentence one year if an aggravating factor (e.g., use of a gun) is present and to decrease the sentence one year if a mitigating factor (e.g., provocation by the victim) is present.[79] Ideally, the legislators would also delineate the exact factors which would have to occur for a sentence to be either heightened or lessened. Finally, the legislators would mandate that all offenders be given an exact determinate sentence (e.g., three years) and not an indeterminate sentence in which a judge imposes a sentence that contains a minimum and maximum stay in the penitentiary (e.g., two to eight years).

4. Compared to current sentencing practices, the lengths of prison terms should be substantially reduced. The deprivation of liberty in a free society is an extremely severe sanction and thus should be used parsimoniously. With the exception of offenses involving bodily harm or in repeated instances of theft, incarceration should be avoided altogether. When prison terms are warranted, they should not exceed five years, "save perhaps for the offense of murder—with sparing use made of sentences of imprisonment for more than three years."[80]

5. The discretion exercised by judges will be severely restricted. Because sentences will now be legislatively-fixed and very narrow in range, judges will be furnished with quite limited options in the sanctions they may choose to impose. Compelled to follow the mandates set down by the legislature in the revised criminal code, judges will thus lose the bulk of their discretionary powers. They will no longer have the luxury of "fitting the punishment to the offender," but instead will be forced to mete out equal justice to all—whether they be black or white, rich or poor, male or female, old or young. To illustrate the impact of fixed-term legislation on judicial discretion, we can again examine the options available to a judge under the old Illinois indeterminate sentencing law. For a Class 3 felony, a judge could have imposed virtually any indeterminate term within a range of one to ten years' imprisonment. In contrast, Fogel's plan for justice would set the penalty at a firm three years, plus or minus one.[81] Similarly, the Twentieth Century Task Force on Criminal Sentencing, authors of *Fair and Certain Punishment*, have proposed that judges be limited to imposing "presumptive sentences": the particular sanction which the legislature has decided that committing a given crime should "predictably incur" (e.g., ten years for a murder). Judges would be powerless to increase or decrease this sentence unless they were able to establish "specific mitigating or aggravating factors." Moreover, to be considered by a judge, these factors would first have to fall within legislative guidelines of what constitutes a relevant mitigating-aggravating circumstance and then their existence proven "beyond a reasonable doubt."[82]

6. Parole-release will be abolished. Since all sentences will be strictly determinate, parole boards will no longer conduct hearings for the purpose of determining whether an inmate is reformed and prepared for re-entry into the community. With discretion totally eliminated at this stage in the criminal justice system, offenders will simply serve the exact sentence they received at the time of conviction. One qualification of this general rule should be mentioned. As a concession to correctional officials faced with the difficult task of maintaining order in our prisons, most justice model advocates support the concept of "good time." Typically, this means that for every day (or several days) of good behavior or conformity while incarcerated, an inmate has one day subtracted from his or her sentence. Because this is a fixed ratio, inmates are still able to predict how long their sentences will be. For instance, in a day-for-day good time model, an offender serving a four-year term would know upon arrival at the penitentiary that counting good time credit, his or her sentence would actually run only two years. Lastly, while justice model authors firmly support the elimination of parole-release, there is more disagreement about whether the board's function of parole supervision after an offender is discharged into society should also be scuttled. Some argue that it provides a useful integrative and social control device, while others assert that it will simply serve as an excuse for the state to reincarcerate offenders after they have already paid their just due back to society.

7. *Voluntary rehabilitation programs should be supported and expanded.* Under determinate sentencing, every inmate receives a precise sentence prior to entering prison. With the exception of good time, correctional and parole authorities are stripped of their discretion and hence possess no power to extend or reduce this sentence. As a consequence, whether offenders do or do not participate in rehabilitation programs can have absolutely no influence on how long their term of incarceration will be. Enforced therapy will thus totally disappear: inmates have nothing to fear if they choose to forego reformative opportunities. They simply cannot be forced to experience harmful, unpleasant, or unrewarding "treatments." Further, the advent of flat terms also eliminates the possibility that the state can corrupt the rehabilitative ideal and use the indeterminate sentence not as a tool to enhance reform but as a custodial weapon ("behave or you don't get out") that aids in maintaining prison order. However, while "coerced cure" is strictly ruled out by the policy of just deserts and determinacy in sentencing, "facilitated change" should be strongly encouraged.[83] All offenders should be provided with the fully *voluntary* choice to participate in meaningful programs that will allow for genuine self-improvement. Those inmates who seriously desire to help themselves must be given the chance to do so.

8. *All inmates should reside in a just and humane environment.* Under the principle of just deserts, the exclusive purpose of a prison sentence is to punish offenders by depriving them of their liberty. Beyond the pain associated with loss of liberty, no additional suffering can be legitimately imposed. As such, it is the state's responsibility to evolve a prison environment in which offenders are not brutalized but rather are treated fairly and humanely during their stay in captivity. To insure that this occurs, inmates must be granted the complete array of constitutional rights and legal protections that are enjoyed by the non-convict population, with the exception of those rights that can be shown to be inherently inconsistent with the operation of a safe and secure prison. In the words of David Fogel, "All the rights accorded free citizens consistent with mass living and the execution of a sentence restricting the freedom of movement should follow a prisoner into prison."[84] Further, correctional

officials will not be permitted to employ custodial sanctions (e.g., revocation of good time, use of segregation, transfer of a troublesome inmate to another institution) in an arbitrary or capricious manner; instead, they will be mandated to apply such penalties according to due process principles. For instance, good time could only be revoked if an inmate first violated a specific rule written into the institution's code of conduct and then was given an opportunity to appeal the revocation decision at an open hearing and with the assistance of legal counsel. Finally, every effort should be made to reformulate the current method of administering prisons which concentrates all formal authority in the hands of the custodial regime and leads inmates to seek control over their existence through more informal and destructive means (e.g., riots, the corruption or extortion of guards). More consistent with our democratic ideals, a system of participatory management should be established in which inmates, guards, and administrators share power and join together in the governance of the prison community.[85]

A NOTE ON RADICAL REFORM AND DETERMINATE SENTENCING

In contrast to conservatives and liberals, radical thinkers have displayed little enthusiasm for determinate sentencing reform.[86] While they have been highly critical of the coercion intrinsic in and legitimated by state enforced therapy, they have been skeptical of the notion that the advent of the justice model will bring forth any meaningful improvements in the American correctional apparatus. Even those who had previously imagined that justice principles might advance "prisoners' interests and contribute to a broader process of radical social change" have now agreed that this reform agenda has had the "opposite effect."[87]

For radicals, the conservatives' call for harsh flat terms can be quickly dismissed as a naked attempt to increase the repressiveness of a criminal justice system that seeks to preserve an unjust capitalist order. In their eyes, however, the fallacy corrupting the liberals' justice model, though no less profound, is more subtle. Instructive in this regard is the analysis of the liberals' core value of due process by socialist Erik Olin Wright. Although noting that "due process of law is a sound principle," Wright then went on to observe that "in a society in which many people are desperately poor, it loses much of its significance. The fact that a poor person accused of stealing bread—or burglarizing a home—is tried under 'due process of law' does not reduce the oppressiveness of the system; it merely systemizes that oppression." Concluding, he remarked that "the fault in the legal system lies not in the concept of due process, but in the social context in which due process operates.... The core values of liberal justice... can be fully realized only where there is underlying social justice."[88]

Thus, radicals like Wright are convinced that until true social justice prevails attempts to do justice for individual citizens will inevitably fail, or worse, will intensify the repression of the disadvantaged. The real issue to be confronted, therefore, is not how to evolve a "just" correctional system but rather how to create a social order in which resources will be distributed equally and the human wants of all individuals will be adequately addressed. The insidious potential of the liberals' call for determinate sentencing is that it inadvertently deflects attention away from the intrinsic deficiencies of capitalist America and hence from the need for basic structural reform, and in turn insures that true criminal justice will remain an elusive goal. Commenting on the current movement toward punishment, Richard Quinney has captured the essentials of the radical position:

> As the "rehabilitation" ideal proves itself bankrupt in practice, liberals and conservatives alike (all within the capitalist hegemony) resort to the utilitarianism of pain. . . . We have the reconstruction of a reality that takes as given the existing social order. Rather than suggesting an alternative order, one based on a different conception of human nature, political economy, and social justice, we are presented with schemes that merely justify further repression within the established order. The solutions being offered can only exacerbate the conditions of our existence.[89]

CONCLUSION: DOING JUSTICE OR GETTING TOUGH?

The events of the period spanning the middle 1960s into the latter part of the next decade served to intensify the conservatives' dissatisfaction with the prevailing correctional philosophy of rehabilitation and prompted liberals to abandon their long-standing conviction that criminals should be saved and not punished. Following very divergent lines of reasoning, both those on the left and those on the right of the political spectrum agreed that the solution to the crisis besetting the criminal justice system rested in severely restricting the pervasive discretion inherent in the "therapeutic state" by introducing a system of legislatively-fixed determinate sentences. Indeed, the appeal of this new correctional paradigm of deserts and determinacy was so extensive that we could find political leaders as ideologically disparate as Gerald Ford and Edward Kennedy forcefully endorsing proposals for flat prison terms for convicted offenders.[90] In this context, it is not surprising that determinate sentencing emerged as a major reform movement that continues to this day to exert a profound influence on correctional policy across the nation. Few ardent supporters of rehabilitation remain to be heard.

Again, it is important to realize that conservatives and liberals embraced determinacy in sentencing for fundamentally different reasons and with fundamentally different goals in mind. For conservatives living in a time of protest and change, soaring crime rates vividly signified the attenuation of traditional patterns of authority and the fragility of the social order. With sensitivity to "law and order" mounting, politicians on the right demanded that more stringent measures be invoked to reduce the lawlessness that threatened the very fabric of communal life. It was clear to them that the existing criminal justice system coddled criminals and thus did little to prevent and much to contribute to the victimization of innocent citizens. Moreover, the source of the deterioration of discipline in our legal process, they argued, was not hard to uncover. Bestowed with considerable discretion and given the mandate to rehabilitate offenders, judges could be observed passing out lenient punishments (probation) that teach offenders that crime pays while parole boards all too often were returning the dangerous to society prematurely. To bolster the sanctioning process, it was thus essential to eliminate the discretionary decision-making that undermined the certainty and severity of criminal punishment. By compelling judges to impose mandatory prison terms and by keeping violent and habitual offenders incarcerated for lengthy tenures, the policy of stiff determinate sentencing promised to serve these crime control ends admirably. Indeed, it appeared that the goal of "getting tough" and making our streets safe once again was finally within reach.

Yet as we have seen, liberals interpreted the events of the 1960s and 1970s in much different terms. The turmoil of this era did not cause them to become nervous that the sanctity of a social order based on cherished and proven values was in jeopardy of collapse. Instead, it was a time when the left was led to question the very legitimacy of this traditional order as the state's willingness to use its power to protect vested political and economic interests was revealed. Within the realm of criminal justice, Attica symbolized the frightening capacity of the state to brutalize its most disadvantaged and defenseless members. The conclusion that the government could not be trusted to do good was now inescapable. In this light, enforced therapy was unmasked as a dangerous ideology that justified the unconscionable victimization of offenders and not their benevolent cure as liberals had long hoped. Invested with broad discretion under the guise of the rehabilitative ideal, the state's agents of social control had employed their unfettered powers to administer "justice" that was at once coercive, harmful, and inequitable. It was apparent that notions of saving the wayward would have to be surrendered and the less grand but more urgent task of protecting them from state abuse and insuring their equitable sanctioning undertaken. By constraining the discretionary powers of judges, correctional officials, and parole boards, legislatively-fixed determinate sentences based on strict principles of just deserts offered the real prospect that the victimization of offenders could be mitigated. While it was manifestly futile to have faith that the state would do good through rehabilitation, the goal of doing justice through a model of desert and determinacy now seemed both attainable and quite worthy of pursuit.

Significantly, the left's abandonment of rehabilitation as the guiding philosophy of criminal justice policy represented a dramatic shift in perspective and raised new concerns for the future. In the past, liberal academics, politicians, corrections' professionals, and citizen interest-groups united to resist the persistent attempts by conservatives to make our legal system expressly punitive in its purpose. They invariably attacked punishment as unscientific and as constituting a retreat from humanistic values. Admittedly, this liberal coalition was not sufficiently formidable to prevent fully the passage of harsh laws or the corruption of good intentions behind the penitentiary walls. Nevertheless, these liberal activists made strides in undermining the tenacious belief that repression will solve the crime problem and were successful in convincing large segments of society that rehabilitation ought to be the pre-eminent goal of American corrections. As discussed, a poll in 1972 revealed that nearly three-fourths of the public felt that rehabilitation "should be the emphasis" of our prisons.[91]

In this light, it seems highly problematic that the current disenchantment with rehabilitation could have become so profound and the popularity of determinate sentencing so pronounced without the firm backing of the liberal community. As Marc Plattner observed in 1976, "The subsequent turn against rehabilitation cannot be explained primarily as a conservative reaction to rising crime rates. It was made possible only by a discrediting of rehabilitation by the left."[92] Indeed, for over a decade now, liberals have inveighed against enforced therapy, trumpeted the principle of retributive justice, served as consultants to legislatures fashioning flat-term criminal codes, and sponsored as well as voted for the passage of these codes. It is perhaps not too much to assert that liberal support has been the crucial ingredient underlying the origin and continued vitality of the determinate sentencing movement.

However, one very large question emerges at this point. Have liberals followed a wise course in abandoning their traditional opposition to the right through the ideology of rehabilitation and then joining with conservatives in endorsing punishment as the paramount function of the criminal justice system? Clearly this bipartisan alliance has been remarkably successful in advancing the cause of deserts and determinacy and in fostering legislative reforms that have made noticeable inroads toward the dismantling of the

Table 4.1 Crisis in Criminal Justice Policy: Competing Perspectives

Policy	Conservatives	Justice Model Liberals	Traditional Liberals
1. School of Criminology	Classical	Classical	Positivist
2. Type of Rehabilitation Supported	Not a prime consideration but must be unrelated to release.	Voluntary	Enforced or involuntary
3. Criticism of Rehabilitation	Enforced rehabilitation is by its nature ineffective and dangerous, because it results in the coddling of criminals and therefore undermines the deterrent and incapacitative power of the criminal justice system. In the end, it leads to the victimization of good innocent citizens.	Enforced rehabilitation is by its nature theoretically flawed, coercive, and unjust. In the end, it results in the victimization of criminals, not in their betterment.	Rehabilitation will work if the correct treatment techniques are used and if the state will provide sufficient resources to run the programs adequately.
4. Type of Sentencing Supported	Determinate but with longer prison terms than are now handed out.	Determinate but with less use of incarceration and much shorter prison terms than are now handed out.	Indeterminate
5. Purpose of Sentencing	Establishing Law and Order—(A) Deterrence: make the punishment certain and severe enough so that criminals and potential criminals will learn that crime does not pay. (B) Incapacitation: lock dangerous offenders away for a long period so they will be unable to walk free on the streets where they can victimize innocent citizens.	Doing Justice—If we cannot make criminals into better people, then the least we can do is to make certain that our criminal justice system does a good job of dispensing justice. Everyone should be treated equally by our courts and receive only that punishment that their crime justly deserves.	Doing Good—Individualized treatments must be developed that bring about the rehabilitation of offenders.

therapeutic state. Yet while both the left and the right share a belief in determinate sentencing, it is essential to remember that they disagree dramatically on the *kind* of determinate sentencing that should be instituted. Conservatives look upon legislatively-fixed, flat terms as a strategy to repress crime through longer and more certain stays in prison; alternatively, liberals advocate this reform as a way of introducing more lenient and fairly administered sanctions. (For a summary of these competing perspectives, see Table 4.1.)

What remains to be determined in the political arena, therefore, is whose version of determinate sentencing will take precedence. That is, have liberals embarked on a path of reform that will lessen the victimization of offenders that occurred under enforced therapy or have they unwittingly helped to launch a movement that ultimately will result in a correctional system that assumes the very qualities they have so long opposed? In short, will "doing justice" or "getting tough" become the dominant concern of American criminal justice?

NOTES

[1] John Bartlow Martin, *Break Down the Walls: American Prisons—Present, Past, and Future.* (New York: Ballantine Books, 1954), p. 244.

[2] Frank Tannenbaum, *Crime and the Community.* (New York: Columbia University Press, 1938), p. 478.

[3] Ray Mars Simpson, "Prison stagnation since 1900." *Journal of the American Institute of Criminal Law and Criminology* 26 (March-April, 1936), p. 870.

[4] Edward Lindsey, "Historical sketch of the indeterminate sentence and parole system." *Journal of the American Institute of Criminal Law and Criminology* 16 (May 1925), pp. 9–126.

[5] Francis A. Allen, *The Decline of the Rehabilitative Ideal: Penal Policy and Social Purpose.* (New Haven: Yale University Press, 1981), p. 16. In this regard, David Rothman has reported that prison officials of the 1850s perceived incarceration as the "worst possible treatment." See his *Discovery of the Asylum: Social Order and Disorder in the New Republic.* (Boston: Little, Brown and Company, 1971), p. 244. Similarly, a government committee in Great Britain concluded in 1828 that "As places of reform only, goals have not succeeded; as places of reform only they ought not to be considered." Quoted in Michael Ignatieff, *A Just Measure of Pain: The Penitentiary in the Industrial Revolution, 1750–1850.* (New York: Pantheon Books, 1978), p. 175. Michel Foucault in *Discipline and Punish: The Birth of the Prison.* (New York: Pantheon Books, 1977), pp. 264–265 has added that "the prison, in its reality and visible effects, was denounced at once as the great failure of penal justice... the critique of the prison and its methods appeared very early on, in those same years 1820–1845; indeed, it was embodied in a number of formulations which—figures apart—are today repeated almost unchanged."

[6] American Friends Service Committee Working Party, *Struggle for Justice: A Report on Crime and Punishment in America.* (New York: Hill and Wang, 1971), p. 83.

[7] Marvin Zalman, "The rise and fall of the indeterminate sentence, parts I and II." *Wayne Law Review* 24 (No. 1, 1977), p. 47.

[8] Allen, *The Decline of the Rehabilitative Ideal*, pp. 1–2.

[9]Seymour L. Halleck and Ann D. Witte, "Is rehabilitation dead?" *Crime and Delinquency* 23 (October 1977), pp. 372–383; Michael S. Serrill, "Is rehabilitation dead?" *Corrections Magazine* 1 (May-June 1975), pp. 21–32.

[10]A. S. Neill, *Summerhill.* (New York: Hart, 1961).

[11]Edward C. Banfield, *The Unheavenly City Revisited.* (Boston: Little, Brown and Company, 1974), p. 193.

[12]Richard Quinney, *Class, State, and Crime: On the Theory and Practice of Criminal Justice.* (New York: David McKay Company, 1977), p. 13.

[13]James O. Finckenauer, "Crime as a national political issue: 1964–76— from law and order to domestic tranquility." *Crime and Delinquency* 24 (January 1978), pp. 15, 17. See also Allen, *The Decline of the Rehabilitative Ideal*, p. 38, and Ronald Bayer, "Crime, punishment, and the decline of liberal optimism." *Crime and Delinquency* 27 (April 1981), p. 177.

[14]Ernest van den Haag, *Punishing Criminals: Concerning a Very Old and Painful Question.* (New York: Basic Books, 1975), pp. 157–158.

[15]Quoted in Finckenauer, "Crime as a national political issue," p. 23.

[16]Patrick J. Buchanan, "Civil rights and murder." *Peoria Journal Star*. See also Nicholas Pileggi, "Inside the juvenile-justice system: how fifteen-year-olds get away with murder." *New York Magazine* 10 (June 13, 1977), pp. 36–44.

[17]Quoted in Finckenauer, "Crime as a national issue," p. 17.

[18]"Too much concern for criminals causing U.S. crime increase?" *Peoria Journal Star* (February 9, 1981), p. A-2.

[19]William J. Roth, Jr., "Is expanded use of mandatory prison sentences a sound approach to reducing crime—pro." *Congressional Digest* 55 (August-September 1976), p. 218.

[20]Sam Steiger, "Is expanded use of mandatory prison sentences a sound approach to reducing crime—pro." *Congressional Digest* 55 (August-September 1976), pp. 220, 222.

[21]*Ibid.*, p. 222.

[22]For an example of this mode of thinking, see the lead editorial of the December 14, 1980 issue of the *Peoria Journal Star* entitled "Our no-fault-society," p. A-6 or a letter-to-the-editor in the January 2, 1981 issue of the *Boston Herald American* headlined "Why violence is a way of life," p. A-15 in which a reader states, "we commiserate with the criminal because life has dealt a bad hand . . .. The result has been that responsibility for one's actions has been removed from the shoulders of the individual and placed squarely on the shoulders of society . . . . Only when the individual is again forced to be master of his own actions. . .. can we begin to deal with violence."

[23]James Q. Wilson, *Thinking About Crime.* (New York: Random House, 1975), pp. 222–223. For a stinging critique of this perspective, see Tony Platt and Paul Takagi, "Intellectuals for law and order: a critique of the new realists." *Crime and Social Justice* 8 (Fall-Winter 1977), pp. 1–16.

[24]Marvin E. Wolfgang, Robert M. Figlio, and Thorsten Sellin, *Delinquency in a Birth Cohort.* (Chicago: University of Chicago Press, 1972).

[25]Wilson, *Thinking About Crime*, pp. 194, 202–203, 223. For a similar conclusion, see Shlomo and Reuel Shinnar, "The effects of the criminal justice system on the control of

crime: a quantitative approach." *Law and Society Review* 9 (1975), pp. 581−611. Notably, a federal task force on which James Q. Wilson served has recently embraced the theory of incapacitation and urged that $2 billion be allocated for prison construction that will permit the more certain "quarantine of violent offenders." Reported in "Harsher treatment urged for violent criminals." *Peoria Journal Star* (August 18, 1981), p. 1 and "Crooks belong in jail," *Peoria Journal Star* (August 25, 1981), p. A-4.

[26]Wilson, *Thinking About Crime*, pp. 235−236. For views on crime control similar to those expressed by Wilson, see Ernest van den Haag, *Punishing Criminals* and Edward C. Banfield, *The Unheavenly City Revisited*, pp. 179−210.

[27]Gerald R. Ford, "To insure domestic tranquility: mandatory sentence for convicted felons." *Vital Speeches of the Day* 41 (May 15, 1975), pp. 450−452.

[28]Walter B. Miller, "Ideology and criminal justice policy: some current issues." Pp. 453−473 in Sheldon Messinger et al. (eds.), *The Aldine Crime and Justice Annual—1973*. (Chicago: Aldine Publishing Company, 1974), p. 454. Similarly, Newman F. Baker noted of J. Edgar Hoover that "the general tenor of his public statements runs like this: (a) I hate slimy criminals; (b) I believe in long prison terms as the only means of punishment; (c) I abhore rehabilitation; (d) Everybody else is either sentimental or crooked; (e) My outfit is the only one which is worth anything." See "Editorial: J. Edgar Hoover." *Journal of the American Institute of Criminal Law and Criminology* 28 (January-February 1938), p. 629.

[29]Michael Serrill, "Determinate sentencing: history, theory, debate." *Corrections Magazine* 3 (September 1977), p. 11.

[30]See, for instance, Willard Gaylin, Ira Glasser, Steven Marcus, and David Rothman, *Doing Good: The Limits of Benevolence*. (New York: Pantheon Books, 1978).

[31]David O. Friedrichs, "The law and the legitimacy crisis: a critical issue for criminal justice." Pp. 290−311 in R. G. Iacovetta and Dae H. Chang (eds.), *Critical Issues in Criminal Justice*. (Durham, N.C.: Carolina Academic Press, 1979). See also, Richard Speiglman, "Prison drugs, psychiatry and the state." Pp. 149−171 in David F. Greenberg (ed.), *Corrections and Punishment*. (Beverly Hills: Sage, 1977), p. 151.

[32]David J. Rothman, "The state as parent: social policy in the Progressive era." Pp. 67−96 in Gaylin et al., *Doing Good*, p. 84.

[33]Ronald Bayer, "Crime, punishment, and the decline of liberal optimism," pp. 169−190; Marvin Zalman, "The rise and fall of the indeterminate sentence, parts III and IV." *Wayne Law Review* 24 (March 1978), pp. 930−931; Platt and Takagi, "Intellectuals for law and order." p. 13.

[34]David F. Greenberg and Drew Humphries, "The cooptation of fixed sentencing reform." *Crime and Delinquency* 26 (April 1980), p. 209.

[35]Ignatieff, *A Just Measure of Pain*, p. xii.

[36]As Bayer has observed in "Crime, punishment, and the decline of liberal optimism," p. 180, "Attica... accelerated the growth of discontent.... In the post-Attica period, many began to assert that it was the ideology of rehabilitation itself that lay at the root of the most undesirable features of prevailing penal practice."

[37]See, for instance, American Friends Service Committee, *Struggle for Justice* (1971); David F. Greenberg, *The Problem of Prisons*. (Philadelphia: National Peace Literature Service, 1970),

pp. 32–33; Nicholas Kittrie, *The Right to Be Different: Deviance and Enforced Therapy*. (Baltimore: Penguin Books, 1971); Alan M. Dershowitz, "Psychiatry in the legal process: a knife that cuts both ways." *Trial* 4 (February-March 1968), pp. 29–33; Marvin E. Frankel, *Criminal Sentences: Law Without Order*. (New York: Hill and Wang, 1972); Sol Rubin, "Illusions of treatment in sentences and civil commitments." *Crime and Delinquency* 16 (January 1970), pp. 79–92.

[38]A good example can be seen in the attention given to Francis A. Allen's *The Borderland of Criminal Justice: Essays in Law and Criminology*. (Chicago: University of Chicago Press, 1964).

[39]Samuel Walker, *Popular Justice: A History of American Criminal Justice*. (New York: Oxford University Press, 1980), p. 244.

[40]Karl Menninger, *The Crime of Punishment*. (New York: Penguin Books, 1968), p. 28.

[41]*Ibid.*, p. 220.

[42]Nathan Leopold, "What is wrong with the prison system?" *Nebraska Law Review* 45 (No. 1, 1966), p. 56. For similar examples, see Harry Elmer Barnes, *The Story of Punishment: A Record of Man's Inhumanity to Man*. (Montclair, N.J.: Patterson Smith, 1972, originally published in 1930), and Seymour L. Halleck, *Psychiatry and the Dilemmas of Crime: A Study of Causes, Punishment and Treatment*. (New York: Harper and Row, 1967), pp. 340–349. More generally, see Gordon Hawkins' discussion of a school of penological thought he labels "reformism": "In speaking of reformists, I am referring to those traditional penal reformers who have for the most part taken the line that although most correctional or rehabilitative programs have proved unsatisfactory, this is due not to any defect in the underlying theory but to failure to implement adequately or properly that theory." *The Prison: Policy and Practice*. (Chicago: University of Chicago Press, 1976), p. 16.

[43]American Friends Service Committee, *Struggle for Justice*, p. 83.

[44]Robert Martinson, "What works?—questions and answers about prison reform." *Public Interest* (Spring 1974), pp. 22–54.

[45]*Ibid.*, p. 25; Douglas Lipton, Robert Martinson, and Judith Wilks, *The Effectiveness of Correctional Treatment: A Survey of Treatment Evaluation Studies*. (New York: Praeger, 1975). For research reaching a similar conclusion, see James Robison and Gerald Smith, "The effectiveness of correctional programs." *Crime and Delinquency* 17 (January 1971), pp. 67–80; David A. Ward, "Evaluative research for corrections." Pp. 184–206 in Lloyd E. Ohlin (ed.), *Prisoners in America*. (Englewood Cliffs, N.J.: Prentice Hall, 1973); Martin Gold, "A time for skepticism." *Crime and Delinquency* 20 (January 1974), pp. 20–24; David F. Greenberg, "The correctional effects of corrections: a survey of evaluations." Pp. 111–148 in David F. Greenberg (ed.), *Corrections and Punishment*. Beverly Hills: Sage, 1977); Robert Fishman, "An evaluation of criminal recidivism in projects providing rehabilitation and diversion services in New York City." *Journal of Criminal Law and Criminology* 68 (No. 2, 1977), pp. 283–305.

[46]For instance, see Donald R. Cressey, "The nature and effectiveness of correctional techniques." *Law and Contemporary Problems* (Autumn 1958), pp. 754–771.

[47]Barbara Wootton, *Social Science and Social Pathology*. (London: George Allen and Unwin, 1959), p. 334.

[48]Martinson, "What works?—questions and answers about prison reform," p. 49.

[49]*Ibid.*, p. 49; American Friends Service Committee, *Struggle for Justice*, pp. 40–41. See also Thomas S. Szasz, *Law, Liberty, and Psychiatry.* (New York: Collier Books, 1968). It should be noted, however, that social disadvantages that make crime a reasonable choice could conceivably be counteracted by rehabilitation programs that were oriented not toward curing hidden psychological pathology but toward providing job and educational skills that would enable an offender to achieve a genuine stake in conformity. As such, arguing that crime is a rational response to social circumstances and not an irrational response to internal abnormality does not preclude support of treatment theory or programs. That is, social and individual reform are not mutually exclusive concerns.

[50]Norval Morris, *The Future of Imprisonment.* (Chicago: University of Chicago Press, 1974), p. 16.

[51]In this regard, see Andrew von Hirsch, *Doing Justice: The Choice of Punishments.* (New York: Hill and Wang, 1976), pp. 19–26; Simon Dinitz and John P. Conrad, "Thinking about dangerous offenders." *Criminal Justice Abstracts* (March 1978), pp. 99–130; Bernard L. Diamond, "The psychiatric prediction of dangerousness." *University of Pennsylvania Law Review* 123 (December 1974), pp. 439–452; Alan A. Stone, *Mental Health and Law: A System in Transition.* (Washington, D.C.: U.S. Department of Health, Education, and Welfare, 1975), pp. 25–40.

[52]David L. Rosenhan, "On being sane in insane places." *Science* 179 (January 19, 1973), pp. 252, 257.

[53]Norval Morris and James J. Jacobs, *Proposals for Prison Reform.* Public Affairs Pamphlet No. 510. (New York: Public Affairs Committee, 1974), p. 12. See as well Jack Meyerson, "The board of prison terms and paroles and indeterminate sentencing: a critique." *Washington Law Review* 51 (1967), p. 627, and John R. Manson, "Determinate sentencing." *Crime and Delinquency* 23 (April 1977), pp. 204–207.

[54]Don Nickerson, "The indeterminate sentence: a medical model." *Fortune News* (February-March 1981), p. 9.

[55]David J. Rothman, "Of prisons, asylums and other decaying institutions." *Public Interest* 26 (Winter 1972), p. 13. More generally, see Erving Goffman, *Asylums: Essays on the Social Situation of Mental Patients and Other Inmates.* (Garden City, N.Y.: Anchor Books, 1961).

[56]Phillip G. Zimbardo, W. Curtis Banks, Craig Haney, and David Jaffe, "A pirandellian prison: the mind is a formidable jailer." *New York Times Magazine* (April 8, 1973), pp. 38–40.

[57]See, in particular, Jessica Mitford, *Kind and Usual Punishment: The Prison Business.* (New York: Vintage Books, 1973), pp. 87–103. Of interest here is that Lynne Goodstein has recently reported that inmates prefer determinacy in their sentences but that support for fixed terms diminishes substantially if such terms would mean spending a longer tenure behind bars. Getting out early and not knowledge of the specific date of release thus appears to be the dominant concern of most inmates. See Goodstein's "How important to prisoners is predictability of release?—A test of a presumed benefit of the determinate sentence." Paper presented at the 1980 meeting of the American Society of Criminology.

[58]Mitford, *Kind and Usual Punishment*, p. 92; Greenberg, *The Problem of Prisons*, p. 32; Allen, *The Borderland of Criminal Justice*, p. 35; Rubin, "Illusions of treatment in sentences and civil commitment," p. 81; Alan M. Dershowitz, "Indeterminate confinement: letting the therapy fit the harm." *University of Pennsylvania Law Review* 23 (December 1974) pp. 303–304; David Fogel, *"We Are the Living Proof": The Justice Model for Corrections*. Second edition. (Cincinnati: Anderson Publishing Company, 1979), p. 194.

[59]David Greenberg, "Rehabilitation is still punishment." *The Humanist* 32 (May-June 1972), p. 29.

[60]Mitford, *Kind and Usual Punishment*, p. 91.

[61]David J. Rothman, *Conscience and Convenience: The Asylum and Its Alternatives in Progressive America*. (Boston: Little, Brown and Company, 1980), p. 10.

[62]For details of this case, see Karen Wald, "The San Quentin Six case: perspective and analysis." Pp. 165–175 in Tony Platt and Paul Takagi (eds.), *Punishment and Penal Discipline: Essays on the Prison and the Prisoners' Movement*. (Berkeley, Ca.: Crime and Social Justice Associates, 1980), and Debby Begal, "An interview with Willie Tate." Pp. 176–183 in the Platt and Takagi volume.

[63]George Jackson, *Soledad Brother*. (New York: Bantam Books, 1970).

[64]Instructive in this regard is the reaction of one high-ranking California prison official to Jackson's *Soledad Brother* which was widely circulated in a corrections department memo: "This book provides remarkable insight into the personality makeup of a highly dangerous sociopath who sees himself not as a criminal but as a Revolutionary dedicated to the violent destruction of existing society. . . . This is one of the most self-revealing and insightful books I have ever read concerning a criminal personality." Quoted in John Irwin, *Prisons in Turmoil*. (Boston: Little, Brown and Company, 1980), p. 141.

[65]Morris and Jacobs, *Proposals for Prison Reform*, p. 13.

[66]Fogel, *"We Are the Living Proof"*, p. 180. See Mitford, *Kind and Usual Punishment*, pp. 129–150.

[67]Ken Kesey, *One Flew Over the Cuckoo's Nest*. (New York: Signet, 1962), pp. 269–271. See also Edward M. Opton, Jr., "Psychiatric violence against prisoners: when therapy is punishment." *Mississippi Law Journal* 45 (June 1974), pp. 605–644; Richard Speiglman, "Prison drugs, psychiatry, and the state"; Kenneth Wooden, *Weeping in the Playtime of Others: America's Incarcerated Children*. (New York: McGraw-Hill, 1976); Wendell Rawls, Jr., *Cold Storage*. (New York: Simon and Schuster, 1980). More generally, the deleterious effects of state social control were noted in detail by "labeling" theorists during this era. In this regard, see Edward M. Schur, *Labeling Deviant Behavior*. (New York: Harper and Row, 1971), and Francis T. Cullen and John B. Cullen, *Toward a Paradigm of Labeling Theory*. Monograph No. 58. (Lincoln: University of Nebraska Studies, 1978).

[68]Frankel, *Criminal Sentences: Law Without Order*.

[69]*Ibid.*, p. 8.

[70]See Willard Gaylin, *Partial Justice: A Study of Bias in Sentencing*. (New York: Vintage Books, 1974).

[71]The Twentieth Century Fund Task Force on Criminal Sentencing, *Fair and Certain Punishment*. (New York: McGraw-Hill, 1976), p. 5.

[72] *Ibid.*, p. 5.

[73] Greenberg, "Rehabilitation is still punishment," p. 29.

[74] American Friends Service Committee, *Struggle for Justice*, p. 19.

[75] Ira Glasser, "Prisoners of benevolence: power versus liberty in the welfare state." Pp. 97–170 in Gaylin et al., *Doing Good*, p. 123.

[76] John P. Conrad, "Corrections and simple justice." *Journal of Criminal Law and Criminology* 64 (No. 2, 1973), pp. 208–217. See also Conrad's "We never should have promised a hospital." *Federal Probation* 39 (December 1975), pp. 3–9.

[77] Fogel, *"We are the Living Proof": The Justice Model for Corrections*; American Friends Service Committee, *Struggle for Justice*; von Hirsch, *Doing Justice: The Choice of Punishments*; Morris, *The Future of Imprisonment*; Twentieth Century Task Force on Criminal Sentencing, *Fair and Certain Punishment*; Richard A. McGee, "A new look at sentencing: part II, a plan for maximum justice with minimum capriciousness." *Federal Probation* 38 (September 1974), pp. 3–11; Christopher T. Bayley, "Good intentions gone awry: a proposal for fundamental change in criminal sentencing." *Washington Law Review* 51 (1976), pp. 529–563; Constance Baker Motley, "'Law and order' and the criminal justice system." *Journal of Criminal Law and Criminology* 64 (September 1973), pp. 259–269; Richard Singer, "In favor of 'presumptive sentences' set by a sentencing commission." *Crime and Delinquency* 24 (October 1978), pp. 401–427 and *Just Deserts: Sentencing Based on Equality and Desert.* (Cambridge, Ma.: Ballinger, 1979).

[78] For a useful summary of the justice model, see Barton L. Ingrahan, Margaret Evans, and Etta Anderson, "Discretion and rehabilitation: fads and fixtures?" Pp. 89–106 in Margaret Evans (ed.), *Discretion and Control.* (Beverly Hills: Sage, 1978), pp. 97–98. It should also be noted here that the core features of the justice model advocated by liberals converge quite closely with the "due process model of the criminal process" summarized by Herbert L. Packer in *The Limits of the Criminal Sanction.* (Stanford, Ca.: Stanford University Press, 1968), pp. 163–173.

[79] Fogel, *"We Are the Living Proof"*, pp. 250, 255.

[80] von Hirsch, *Doing Justice*, p. 136.

[81] Fogel, *"We Are the Living Proof"*, pp. 250, 255.

[82] Twentieth Century Task Force on Criminal Sentencing, *Fair and Certain Punishment*, pp. 20, 44–45, 57.

[83] Morris, *The Future of Imprisonment*, p. 13.

[84] Fogel, *"We Are the Living Proof"*, p. 202. See also John Conrad, "Where there's hope there's life." Pp. 3–21 in David Fogel and Joe Hudson (eds.), *Justice As Fairness: Perspectives on the Justice Model.* (Cincinnati: Anderson Publishing Company, 1981), pp. 18–19.

[85] See Phyllis Jo Baunach, "Participatory management: restructuring the prison environment." Pp. 196–218 in Fogel and Hudson (eds.), *Justice as Fairness*; Joseph E. Hickey and Peter L. Scharf, *Toward a Just Correctional System: Experiments in Implementing Democracy in Prisons.* (San Francisco: Jossey-Bass, 1980).

[86] However, some have favored reforming the criminal justice system in this direction. See David F. Greenberg, "A reply." *The Prison Journal* 52 (Spring-Summer 1972), pp. 33–41,

and Jeffrey H. Reiman, *The Rich Get Richer and the Poor Get Prison: Ideology, Class and Criminal Justice.* (New York: John Wiley and Sons, 1979), pp. 195–200.

[87] Greenberg and Humphries, "The cooptation of fixed sentencing reform," pp. 206, 222.

[88] Erik Olin Wright, *The Politics of Punishment: A Critical Analysis of Prisons in America.* (New York: Harper and Row, 1973), pp. 339–340.

[89] Richard Quinney, *Class, State, and Crime: On the Theory and Practice of Criminal Justice.* (New York: David McKay Company, 1977), pp. 16–17.

[90] Gerald R. Ford, "To insure domestic tranquility: mandatory sentences for convicted felons"; Edward M. Kennedy, "Toward a new system of criminal sentencing: law with order." *American Criminal Law Review* 16 (Spring 1979), pp. 353–382.

[91] Louis Harris, *The Public Looks at Crime and Corrections.* (Washington, D.C.: Joint Commission on Correctional Manpower and Training, 1968), p. 7.

[92] Marc F. Plattner, "The rehabilitation of punishment." *Public Interest* 44 (Summer 1976), p. 105.

The Poverty of the Justice Model: The Corruption of Benevolence Revisited?

"Beautiful theories," Thorsten Sellin once observed, "have a way of turning into ugly practices."[1] In this regard, liberal critics have poignantly illustrated how the benevolent intentions of past reformers advocating the rehabilitative ideal have been only infrequently realized. Rehabilitation, it is now held, has more often served as an ideology that has both legitimated and created fresh opportunities for the repression of society's wayward members. Current liberal critics have thus offered the "justice model" as an alternative correctional paradigm, and on the surface, their arguments are persuasive that this strategy will allow us to achieve greater equality and less inhumanity in the administration of justice.

However, if Sellin is correct in his observation—and there is little contradictory evidence to be found in historical records—then we must immediately question whether the justice model itself may not constitute yet another "beautiful theory" that stands to be corrupted in fundamental ways and hence engender practices that are perhaps "uglier" than those presently in existence. While "the concerns and caution stimulated by penal rehabilitationism" should not be forgotten, Francis Allen has recently warned that "alternative theories of penal justice—retributive, deterrent, those of social defense—likewise contain potentialities for debasement and serious abuse."[2] In this light, it is significant that a revisionist movement of growing strength has emerged on the left that is debating the wisdom of liberals embracing the philosophy of deserts and determinacy as a means of achieving the traditional liberal correctional goals of justice and humanity.[3] The message being conveyed is that the liberals' call for a "justice model" promises neither to mitigate the injustices burdening the politically excluded and economically disadvantaged nor to lessen the victimization of society's captives. If implemented, the model will facilitate a program of sentencing and penal "reform" that in its pragmatics is distinctly conservative and oriented toward the introduction of more stringent crime control measures.

The latter portion of this book is devoted to a consideration of the danger of explicitly rejecting rehabilitation and instead affirming punishment as the exclusive, legitimate justification for state legal control. Consistent with the stance of liberals who are opposing their brethren's justice model, we will endeavor to demonstrate that a criminal justice system rooted in retributive principles will be neither more just, more humane, nor more efficient than a system that, at least ideologically, had offender reform as its goal. This will lead us

Reaffirming Rehabilitation. DOI: http://dx.doi.org/10.1016/B978-1-4557-3130-5.00005-2

to the conclusion that despite its disadvantages, rehabilitation should not be so readily cast aside but rather reaffirmed. In the next chapter, an analysis is undertaken of the wave of determinate sentencing legislation that has emerged in recent times and of the specific problems that these codes are or are not likely to engender. In contrast, the current chapter presents a more general discussion of how the benevolent intentions of the proponents of the justice model risk being corrupted should the agenda of deserts and determinacy guide correctional policy and practice in the coming generation.

RECONSIDERING THE JUSTICE MODEL: PROBLEMS WITH DETERMINATE SENTENCING

Below, we attempt to outline five major difficulties surrounding the justice model which, when taken together, furnish scant optimism that the swing in the American criminal justice system toward determinacy will ultimately qualify as a liberal reform. Later, it will be argued as well that, while the current movement is clearly conservative in its thrust, it will do little to advance the ideological right's goal of efficient crime control and enhanced protection of the social order. Before addressing these issues in greater detail, it must be admitted that the full and complex effects of the movement back to punishment—as in the case of policies instituted in the name of rehabilitation—will not become fully apparent for years. Moreover, we can anticipate that some of the problems to be outlined below could be avoided by reasonable planning[4] or, more likely, by the operation of organizational interests within the criminal justice system that corrupt the spirit of the reform and insure that "business proceeds as usual." Further, there are perhaps some jurisdictions that will experience an improvement in the quality of justice that will be administered. Nevertheless, the wisdom of pursuing any reform must ultimately rest in evaluating the full array of possible benefits and harms that surround the suggested policy. And despite the caveats mentioned above, in the case of determinate sentencing, the evidence is weighty in indicating that this "reform" will be less a panacea for the ills confronting the criminal justice system and more a Pandora's Box.

LONGER SENTENCES: THE POTENTIAL FOR REPRESSION

As mentioned, conservatives see the current sentencing movement as an opportunity to reduce the payoff from crime by stiffening criminal penalties. Liberal critics of the indeterminate sentence argue that it has been utilized in the past to increase prison terms in America, and they now see fixed sentencing as a way of limiting the use of incarceration. For example, von Hirsch in *Doing Justice* has proposed that "sentences above five years would be barred altogether—except for certain murders."[5] Ultimately, then, the most crucial issue in assessing the political flavor of the determinate sentencing movement is: will these measures mitigate or aggravate the current level of severity in penal sanctioning?

At present, nearly all projections lend credence to Judge David Bazelon's assertion that "mandatory incarceration, determinate sentencing, and the like are the first steps in a thousand-mile journey, but in precisely the wrong direction: towards repression. Mandatory incarceration means nothing more than locking up those manifesting symptoms of the underlying ill."[6] Indeed, Greenberg and Humphries now speak of the "cooptation of fixed-sentencing reform" and state that "the new legislation will increase rather than reduce sentence lengths"—a conclusion reached by a number of other authors as well.[7] Empirical research also supports the view that inmate stays will be inflated. A 1978 study by the House Criminal Justice Subcommittee found that proposed federal legislation "does not encourage alternatives to prison and ... could result in a significant (62.8 percent to 92.8 percent) increase in the federal prison population."[8] Similarly, an analysis of a flat-time bill in Ohio indicates that if instituted, the prison population would rise 21 percent, while legislation passed in Indiana may result in sentences being 50 percent longer for some first-time felony offenders.[9] A subcommittee of the New York State Bar Association reported that the new sentencing schemes in California, Indiana, and Illinois should all lead to increases in inmate populations.[10] Even an ardent supporter of just deserts principles was forced to conclude that a "review of present proposals or actions taken with regard to sentencing reform" constitutes a "rather unhappy picture."[11] Finally, when one adds to this the realization that a variety of states have passed strict mandatory, minimum sentencing laws for selected offenses (violent, drug) and offenders (habitual), it is clear that the liberals have suffered a "serious political defeat" in the current wave of sentencing "reform."[12] As William Nagel has observed, "The liberals want to get rid of the glaring disparities. The conservatives like that because they want to raise minimum sentences and be punitive. When they both get married, the result is that the uniform four-year sentence the liberal wants turns out to be the punitive ten-year minimum the conservative wants."[13]

But should we expect otherwise? It is ironic that liberals who mistrust the state to administer criminal justice rehabilitation in a just and humane manner are now placing their total faith in the same state (legislatures) to punish justly and humanely. We have searched in vain to discover the basis for this faith. As Conrad has remarked, "it is a common-place of criminal law-making that there are no votes for politicians in the reduction of sentences for felonies."[14] Indeed, one survey has indicated that fully 79 percent of those sampled said that they were more likely to vote for a candidate who advocated "tougher sentences for law breakers."[15] Similarly, a 1980 Gallup Poll reported that 86 percent of the nation's whites and 76 percent of all black citizens felt that "the courts in this area do not deal harshly enough with certain criminals."[16] In a time of rising crime rates and the hardening of public attitudes regarding crime,[17] and in light of the fact that state elites both view the public as being even more punitive than is actually the case and are "sensitive to the possibility of political losses resulting from support of reform,"[18] it is difficult to imagine that more than a few legislators would risk calling for a reduction in prison terms.

Yet this is what would have to occur under determinate sentencing reform for penalties to remain at even their present level of severity. The current system, as Zimring has noted, "seems addicted to barking louder than it really wants to bite": the sentences listed on the books and announced in court are later substantially lessened by parole boards.[19] However, when penalties are legislatively-fixed and parole boards abolished, the terms specified in the criminal code ideally are those that will be served. Whether legislators would, in today's political context, adjust determinate sentences downward a sufficient amount to match the real time inmates currently receive (even if good time is retained) seems problematic at best. Unless state elites are willing to bark less—despite the fact that barking loudly often reaps valuable political rewards—the bite will be more severe.

It should be noted as well that in the view of Marxist theorists Jeffrey Reiman and Sue Headlee, the current economic crisis besetting the welfare state insures that the reigning deserts philosophy will inevitably be manipulated to justify heightened state legal repression. Times of economic hardship, they have argued, precipitate intense rivalries for scarce resources throughout the social structure. In turn, "as the crisis forces businesses to engage in even more blatant forms of competitive grabbing, the belief in the moral distinction between these and ordinary crimes is threatened." To protect the legitimacy of the prevailing economic order, elites must move forcefully to illuminate this distinction by utilizing the law to portray conventional lawbreakers as individually responsible for their crimes and to dramatize the evil of offenders through harsh but "deserved" sanctions. Hence there is a call for "a return to basics, doing simple justice, holding individuals responsible for their deeds, and punishing the wicked, no more, no less." The "aims" of the advantaged in the competitive struggle, Reiman and Headlee believe, are thus well "served by the justice model"; indeed, it is "precisely what one would expect during the crisis."[20]

Beyond these particular considerations, one must question whether a movement that seeks to give a new legitimacy to punishment could ever have humane results. There is the immediate danger that a punitive philosophy does not readily suggest non-penal measures. Community sanctions are too easily identified as "letting the criminals off easily without really punishing them." Indeed, it remains an anomaly when such sanctions are called community "punishment" and not "treatment." Further, when the current agenda for punishment, like those before it,[21] fails at some point to solve the crime problem, the logic of the punishment perspective will demand that venturing outside the law be made even more costly. To legislators, this has characteristically meant sending more people to prison and for longer tenures.[22] It is a troubling reminder that "once a determinate sentencing bill is before a legislative body, it takes only an eraser and pencil to make a one-year 'presumptive sentence' into a six-year sentence for the same offense."[23]

Yet there is also a larger danger to be considered. By locating the source of illegality in the willful calculation of the costs and benefits of crime, the deserts paradigm abandons the humanistic spirit inherent in the traditional liberal appreciation of the social injustices that victimize the less advantaged and constrain them to follow a destructive path that ends in imprisonment. It is this sensitivity to the ravaging effects of inequality, racism, and youth that has allowed liberals to speak of the "crime of punishment" and to argue that the state has an obligation to undertake general social reform as well as the reform of both its captives and the conditions in which they are held. In contrast, the model of deserts and determinacy ultimately obligates the state to do no more than to make criminal pursuits unprofitable and to provide offenders of similar sorts with the solace that they are paying their debt to society in roughly equal (though, if necessary, heavy) amounts. Efficient justice and evenhanded justice for "responsible" individuals brought before the law become the focal—and as we shall see unattainable—concerns of the system. Meanwhile, the larger issues of the pervasive injustices prevailing in society and of our concomitant social responsibility to those victimized by crime and by a life in crime recede in importance.[24]

While it is tempting to forecast that a wave of draconian legislation will occur, there are several factors that *may* operate to minimize the coercive potential of determinate sentencing. One possibility is the creation of special sentencing commissions that would revise criminal codes and thus insulate legislators from political attacks for "leniency." However, few assemblies have abdicated the responsibility of sentencing reform to such commissions, and even if they were so inclined, there are no assurances that legislators would not simply reject the commissions' more liberal proposals and substitute harsher measures.[25] The economics of incarceration, however, may prove effective in setting an upper boundary to the severity of sentencing. With the annual cost for maintaining a single inmate in confinement now exceeding $10,000[26] and construction costs for new cells running between $35,000 and $50,000 apiece,[27] the expense of an inflated prison population is enormous and thus unlikely to be greeted with equanimity by those who have promised their constituencies lower taxes and a balanced budget. This contradiction between fiscal (low expenditures) and penal (high sentences) conservatism may at some point force a retreat from strict determinate sentencing principles and allow for more discretion in the early release of inmates from prison.[28] Similarly, it seems likely that legislative directives for the application of fixed sentences will not be unquestioningly followed by judges and prosecutors. In all jurisdictions, court personnel have evolved strategies to handle case load demands as well as normative conceptions of what constitutes a "just" sanction for certain types of offenses and offenders.[29] Laws that threaten to disrupt the way in which justice is customarily and most comfortably administered are thus likely to meet with resistance and evasion.[30]

In sum, the repressive potential of determinate sentencing may be mitigated to some degree but, quite significantly, only if its aims are thwarted by the pragmatics of the criminal justice system. Despite this small sense of optimism, there remains the grave risk that notions of just deserts will in the end "provide little more than an apologia for the prolonged imprisonment of common criminals."[31] Indeed, the current sentencing reform movement appears almost certain to eventuate in more offenders being sent to prison and for longer terms. As such, it is in the most fundamental respect a conservative reform.

RIGIDITY IN SENTENCING: IS JUSTICE SERVED?

A cornerstone of the liberal attack on the rehabilitative ideal is that it necessarily provides social control agents with "unfettered discretion" in their decision-making (e.g., to decide who should be incarcerated, or when an inmate is "cured" and deserving of release). Liberals assert that due to social bias, political pressures, custodial considerations, and lack of knowledge, this discretion has been abused and has resulted in gross inequities in punishment; thus, there has been "law without order." The solution is to discard notions of individualized treatment in favor of a scheme that eliminates or severely limits the exercise of discretion. Determinate sentencing would fulfill this goal; sanctions would be legislatively-fixed and the severity of the penalty would not be a function of assessments of the nature of an offender but exclusively of the seriousness of the crime committed and other relevant legal variables (e.g., number of previous offenses).

Apart from the issue of whether fixed sentencing would result in greater equality before the law—an issue that will be examined below—it is important to question the very possibility of developing a criminal code that can adequately scale penalties according to the "seriousness" of a crime. As research on this topic suggests, assessments of seriousness depend on a variety of factors and on the unique interaction of these factors in a given instance.[32] As such, it may simply be an insurmountable task to introduce the necessary complexity for handling diverse cases into a criminal code. Zimring has captured the essence of this difficulty:

> The problem is not simply that any such penal code will make our present statutes look like Reader's Digest Condensed Books; we lack the capacity to define into formal law the nuances of situation, intent, and social harm that condition the seriousness of particular criminal acts.... I am not suggesting that these are problems of sloppy drafting. Rather, we may simply lack the ability to comprehensively define in advance those elements of an offense that should be condensed in fixing a criminal sentence.[33]

A code based on determinate sentencing, then, is likely to suffer from excessive rigidity. Court personnel are robbed of the discretion that is needed to distinguish the nuances in a case and arrive at an assessment of what constitutes a just disposition. As a Massachusetts district attorney commented, "Every criminal that comes before us is different. Every case is different. Mandatory sentences put people in pigeonholes. It just doesn't work that way."[34] Fixed sentencing thus heightens the chance that crimes of different natures will be forced into a single, un-discriminating category and, in turn, that in the name of equal justice, dissimilar crimes will receive the same punishment. The remarks of Manhattan Supreme Court Justice Burton Roberts are instructive in this regard:

> [Fixed jail terms] would create an artificial system of justice—for there is no way to program into cold words of a statute all the nuances of each category of crime, be it robbery, burglary, murder, or the differences of the individual who commits these particular crimes. For example, a wino in the Bowery strikes his drinking buddy with a broom stick and steals his bottle of wine. He commits the crime of robbery in the first degree. A 16-year-old kid who has never been in trouble before threatens someone with brass knuckles in the park and steals a bike. He, too, commits the crime of robbery in the first degree. A hardened criminal with a lengthy record who holds up a bank with a sub-machine gun—shoots up the bank—and steals hundreds of thousands of dollars. He, too, commits the crime of robbery in the first degree. And no one in their right mind would advocate a similar sentence for each of these three robbers.[35]

Further, it is enlightening to examine the effectiveness of past attempts at fixed sentencing. Students of such laws are unanimous in their opinion that these measures have failed to contribute to crime control, been unworkably rigid in practice, and have been persistently resisted and evaded by court personnel. Radzinowicz and King are representative in their conclusion that "to exclude discretion from a substantial sector of our system is irrational, retrogressive and inhumane. Whether we attempted to effect such a change by detailed prescription or by mandatory sentences, we should find, as history has shown again and again, that it would not work."[36] Indeed, a noted example of this general principle is the statute passed in New York State under the Rockefeller administration that prescribed compulsory life sentences without parole for drug offenders. Significantly, this law was recently repealed because it failed to deter drug trafficking—but not before "hundreds of people convicted of selling and possessing small amounts of drugs" were given "mandatory prison terms that often were longer than those given to rapists and robbers."[37] Similarly, William Cook's analysis of the Nebraska Habitual Criminal Statute that mandates lengthy terms for third-time felons revealed that only three of eighty-two eligible offenders in Douglas County were actually sentenced under the law. This led Cook to the conclusion "that the 'mandatory' statute is being used with a great degree of arbitrariness or it is being consciously used as a threat to induce pleas of guilty from offenders." He further argued that the constitutionality of the act could be challenged on grounds of "discriminatory enforcement, coerced pleas of guilty or the cruel and unusual nature of the statute's application."[38] Finally, the potential for inhumanity under rigid, determinate sentencing codes is well illustrated by the recent, celebrated case of a Texas man sentenced under a state law requiring life imprisonment following a third conviction. The man's crimes included obtaining $120 under false pretenses, an $80 fraudulent credit card transaction, and forging a $28 check. Life imprisonment for $228 in stolen property—all in the name of just deserts.[39]

On a broader level, it is important to recognize that to turn to rigid sentencing in an attempt to eliminate the abuses of discretion is also to sacrifice the possibility that humane values, such as mercy, will also play a role in regulating sentencing decisions. As Judge David Bazelon has noted, the dangers of a movement that so readily abandons the concept of individualized justice are considerable: "I've heard nothing here about individualizing justice. Nowhere do I hear any word about understanding the individual. If we're giving up on that, then we're giving up on one of the most important concepts of democracy. The greatest inequality is equal treatment of unequals—and people are unequal."[40] And when we consider that we are in the midst of a period of conservative thinking about crime, we are left with the troubling prospect of a rigid sentencing system that aims to administer not simply uniform sanctions, but uniformly harsh sanctions.

One promising sign is that some of the recent determinate sentencing legislation has not substantially reduced the discretion exercised by judges. However, it is essential to note that this legislation gains its "promise" by retreating from or corrupting strict just deserts principles, and that they have the disadvantage of eliminating the ability of parole boards to review judicial sentences (see below). Moreover, the proclivity of legislators across the nation for passing severe mandatory, minimum prison terms for selected offenses shows no signs of waning.

SENTENCING DISPARITY AND THE EXPANSION OF PROSECUTORIAL POWER

Liberal reformers have argued that determinate sentencing will allow for greater equality before the law, particularly for the disadvantaged. Since sentencing would now be legislatively-prescribed and a function of crime seriousness, the social characteristics of an offender could not be utilized by court personnel to bias their decision-making. Again, however, we must question the viability of this liberal proposal and ask, will offenders really receive more equitable treatment?

To begin with, it appears that the present system is not as unruly as it is commonly portrayed. Certainly, there is excessive and at times outrageous unevenness in the administration of justice. Nevertheless, Silberman has reported that in any given jurisdiction "only seven to ten percent of the sentences involve real departure from court norms—instances in which sentences did seem to reflect arbitrary or idiosyncratic judicial behavior."[41] Similarly, there is research to suggest that social class and race are not overriding determinants of sentencing decisions by judges.[42] Alternatively, it is notable that social inequality is deeply reproduced in existing criminal codes that prescribe harsh sanctions for the crimes customarily committed by the poor but attach only meek penalties to the lawlessness of the rich. And this occurs despite the fact that the costs of white-collar crime—both in terms of money stolen and deaths and injuries sustained (e.g., from defective products like automobiles)—far surpass the harms engendered by the more familiar street-crimes.[43] Moreover, many socially injurious acts perpetrated by the advantaged are permitted to lie totally outside the reach of the criminal law and are either left uncontrolled or regulated only by civil and administrative agencies. Considerations of class and race thus appear to have a marked impact on the kinds of law and decisions politicians make, which again leads us to question the advisability of turning to a system of legislatively-fixed sentences. As Constance Motley has observed, "We do not hear, for example, any proposals for the imposition of severe mandatory prison terms upon those convicted of involvement in a two hundred million dollar securities fraud.... The present harsh proposals are designed to deal only with one segment of the criminal society."[44]

The quest by supporters of the justice model to achieve equality before the law in our nation's courts suffers as well from an inherent limitation: determinate sentencing proposals aim only at improving the consistency of punishing within single state boundaries. However, this in no way begins to remedy the more important problem of "significant disparities between states" and across the regions of the country (the South being the most punitive) in sentencing practices.[45] Importantly, these variations in sanctioning policies cannot be attributed to the differential nature of crime in particular states. William Nagel, for instance, has reported that there is a negligible correlation between a state's rate of crime and rate of incarceration.[46] In this regard, we find that states punish the same offenses quite distinctly. For robbery alone, the median time spent in prison ranges from 13 months in New Hampshire to 55 months in Tennessee.[47] More generally, a National Institute of Justice study concluded that "the links between crime and punishment are commonly assumed to be rigid, but our data show them to be strongly conditioned by local normative policy. Offenses which can cause imprisonment in one state may be treated with fines or probation in another, and may not be criminal at all in a third."[48]

But perhaps the most disturbing aspect of today's sentencing reform movement is that it seeks to dismantle parole boards. Daniel Glaser, as well as numerous other commentators, have observed that parole boards exercise the informal, imperfect, yet nonetheless invaluable function of first reviewing sentencing decisions and then equalizing the time inmates convicted of the same offense serve. As Glaser has commented, "I can assert with much confidence that the first concern of most parole boards with the vast majority of their cases is to reduce the disparity imposed by the courts."[49]

Now at the first glance, the absence of parole review of sentencing decisions would not seem to cause difficulties under a determinate sentencing format. After all, judicial behavior should be standardized by the constraints imposed by a legislatively-fixed code. However, this conception is misleading because it masks the important role played by the parole board (and judges) in reviewing decisions made earlier in the legal process by prosecutors. Briefly, under the current system, prosecutors exercise wide discretion, particularly in the negotiation of plea bargains. Ultimately, however, the actual sentence imposed remains a judicial function. Prosecutorial bargains for specific sentences must receive judicial approval, and even when the bargain is over what a defendant will be charged with, the judge typically retains the choice of either placing the offender on probation or assigning a prison term of varying length. In turn, parole boards are able to even out inconsistencies in judicial behavior that arise across the state.

It is notable that determinate sentencing threatens to upset the checks and balances built into this system. While legislatively-fixed terms eliminate discretion by dismantling parole boards and rigidly constraining judicial sentencing, they leave the discretion of prosecutors untouched and, most significantly, unreviewable by any personnel at a later stage in the legal process. Discretion thus does not disappear from the criminal justice system, but "merely descends to the prosecutors ... the system becomes inflexible at the top and rather free at other levels. That the criminal justice system works better with this shift of discretion is highly debatable."[50] Indeed, what would lead us to expect that the quality of the administration of justice will be improved by localizing discretion and hence power in the hands of prosecutors who are at once "uniformly far younger and less experienced" than judges,[51] often oriented toward utilizing their position as a stepping stone to a future political career, and whose daily workings are "invisible and invulnerable to externally imposed structure or control to an extent unknown in other sentencing agencies"?[52]

One immediate difficulty, just intimated, is that the expansion of unreviewable prosecutorial discretion also means the expansion of prosecutorial power. With 70 percent to 100 percent of all convictions now the result of plea bargaining,[53] the prosecutor is already the "king" of the criminal justice system. Yet, in the words of Anthony Travisano, fixed sentencing "will make him emperor."[54] With the punishment for a particular offense rigidly defined by the criminal code, bargaining for a charge also means bargaining for a specific sentence. And since the negotiation reached with the prosecutor will not be adjusted at a later stage, the prosecutor in essence is left with the sole power to sentence. It is true that defendants could choose to take their cases to trial. But to the extent that prosecutors threaten to enter serious charges, that legislators pass politically expedient harsh penal codes, and that the prospect of parole vanishes, such an option would prove attractive to few. The ACLU has warned that mandatory sentencing creates conditions conducive to coerced pleas, a practice that "unconstitutionally chills the Sixth Amendment right to trial by jury, and the Fifth Amendment right to plead not guilty, burdening the defendant's choice with heavy consequences if he should be convicted."[55]

Organizational demands for efficiency in processing cases may diminish the inclination of prosecutors to use this newly-found power to secure a harsher disposition of defendants; but little else will encourage such restraint. For one thing, the very nature of the position instructs prosecutors to assume an adversarial posture—far more than, for instance, judges and parole boards. Certainly, those who come before the court realize this. In a survey of defendants, Casper found that only 28 percent felt that prosecutors were more concerned with "doing justice" than "getting cases over with" and that prosecutors "do not want to see all defendants punished as heavily as possible," while just 19 percent agreed that their adversaries are "not out to get defendants." In contrast, judges were assessed far more favorably, with scores on each item of 68 percent, 59 percent and 62 percent.[56] For another thing, there are no economic constraints on local or county prosecutors against seeking harsh prison terms since offenders will serve these stays in state funded institutions. "In most systems," a National Institute of Justice report indicated, "there are few incentives for local ... prosecutors to view prison or jail capacity as a limited resource. ... Local decision-makers are not directly accountable for the cost consequences of their state commitment decisions."[57] Thus, when the Massachusetts corrections commissioner, faced with severe overcrowding in state institutions, asked prosecutors to "slow down prosecutions," his request was resoundingly refused.[58] Similarly, in an effort to limit spiraling inmate populations and related costs produced by the sentencing policies of county court personnel, California[59] and Minnesota[60] were forced to offer local jurisdictions financial incentives to keep offenders under community supervision in lieu of state commitment. In contrast, parole boards do not enjoy such immunity from the political pressures surrounding overcrowded penitentiaries, and they are often expected to use their power of parole-release to insure that prison populations do not exceed acceptable levels. Of course, this parole function would be lost under fixed-term sentencing.

Beyond these issues, the expansion of prosecutorial discretion would corrupt the liberals' quest to promote equality before the law through determinate sentencing reform. Again, the crux of the problem is that the prosecutors' decisions would be final and unreviewable. The inevitable idiosyncrasies in the processing of cases among individual prosecutors as well as the more patterned differences between, for example, hard pressed urban courts and rural jurisdictions would no longer be adjusted by judges and/or parole boards. As Silberman has concluded, "the result is likely to be a net increase in the amount of capaciousness and disparity in the sentences offenders serve."[61] Similarly, after an exhaustive study of proposed determinate sentencing legislation on the federal level, Schulhofer reported that "the prospects both for fairness in individual cases and for consistency overall seem appreciably worse than in the present system of vast judicial discretion, unsatisfactory as that system is."[62] And in words that liberals would do well to reread, he went on to caution, "If legislatures and reformers remain unwilling to attack sentencing disparities at their principle source, they should think twice about attractive, but piecemeal remedies like presumptive [determinate] sentencing, which—pursued in isolation—could well cause much more harm than good."[63]

Admittedly, plausible recommendations have been suggested as to how to structure prosecutorial discretion and thus attack the "principle source" of disparity. However, it seems equally implausible that such recommendations could be instituted.[64] We could expect prosecutors to lobby forcefully against any proposal that would curtail their "ability to do their jobs," and to systematically evade any restrictions imposed on their discretion.[65] Further, whether accurate or not, there is a widely-accepted image that tampering with the capacity of prosecutors to plea bargain effectively will inundate and paralyze the court with an endless flood of trials, and this would prove to be a potent deterrent to altering the current system. Finally, it is a telling reality that no determinate sentencing reform has yet to successfully structure prosecutorial discretion. As such, before determinate sentencing can be embraced as a liberal reform aimed at reducing the victimization of offenders, it seems incumbent upon reformers to demonstrate how the apparently insurmountable problem of prosecutorial discretion can be resolved not only theoretically but politically and pragmatically as well. Otherwise, as Albert Alschuler has warned, "this sort of reform is likely to produce its antithesis—to yield a system every bit as lawless as the current sentencing regime but one in which discretion is concentrated in an inappropriate agency and in which the benefits of this discretion are made available only to defendants who sacrifice constitutional rights."[66]

The movement toward fixed sentencing stands to exacerbate one additional source of disparity in the time inmates serve: institutional differences in the amount of good time revoked. The John Howard Association, for instance, has discovered that while the Menard (Illinois) maximum security prison is 19 percent larger, the number of good time days revoked at Stateville in 1979 was three and one-half times greater.[67] Such variations in the use of this control mechanism by correctional staffs with differing administrative styles and problems have long existed, but they assume new importance under determinate sentencing. Formerly, when an inmate lost good time days, it meant only that the date on which (s)he would become eligible for parole would be delayed. However, under fixed-term statutes where parole-release no longer occurs, when a day of good time is subtracted, it means that an inmate will actually spend an extra day in prison. A general consequence of determinacy, then, is that prison personnel in effect acquire sentencing powers. According to Paul Bigman of the John Howard Association, "Now your release date is not dependent on your parole board but on the guards and warden in your prison, because every time [they] take away a day of good time, what they are really doing is sentencing you to a day in prison."[68] In light of this new "sentencing power" at their disposal and the fact that staffs at the various state penitentiaries differ in their inclination to revoke good time, the institution to which an inmate is sentenced can now directly and significantly affect an inmate's tenure behind bars. Thus, in Illinois, offenders who suffer the misfortune of being sent to Stateville where good time days are liberally taken away are likely to serve longer sentences, regardless of the crime committed, than if they had been incarcerated at one of the state's other maximum security institutions.

The hard figures calculated by Bigman illuminate the substantial price that Stateville inmates must pay: "The average Stateville prisoner lost 38.9 days of good time in one year, while his counterpart . . . at Menard lost only 9.7 days. In effect, a prisoner at Stateville stays in prison one month longer for each year of his sentence than one at Menard with the same sentence." It might be objected that these statistics are to be anticipated because a more volatile population resides at Stateville. However true this assessment is, it does little to mitigate the injustices inherent in a system that engenders patterned differentials in the use of revocation. Hence, Bigman has raised the question, "Has the Department [of Corrections] established a secret policy of placing the prisoners most likely to violate regulations at Stateville? If so—and it seems unlikely—surely there should be established criteria to determine which prisoners should be subjected to the extra punishment of Stateville." A more probable explanation for the existing institutional variations, in Bigman's view, is that "either the disciplinary system is used in a harsher and more arbitrary manner at Stateville than at comparable Menard; or the conditions at Stateville, including the attitude of the staff, are so much worse that they create disciplinary problems." In the end, the difficulties surrounding good time revocation under determinate sentencing in Illinois have led Bigman to a disturbing conclusion that proponents of the justice model would do well to consider: "A prison disciplinary system does more than maintain order. It sets the tone for justice in the prisons. In the Illinois Department of Corrections, it is not surprising that many prisoners charge that 'there ain't no justice.'"[69]

"REHABILITATION DOESN'T WORK": IS PUNISHING REALLY BETTER?

By the mid-1970s, the rehabilitative ideal was wavering under a liberal attack that portrayed it as a "benevolent theory" that had ironically precipitated "ugly results." Yet the culminating and perhaps most devastating blow to the viability of criminal justice rehabilitation was delivered in 1974 by Robert Martinson and his associates. As discussed, Martinson's review of 231 empirical studies led him to the conclusion that treatment programs "so far have had no appreciable effect on recidivism." With the ineffectiveness of rehabilitation apparently exposed, it became prudent to explore an alternative correctional paradigm. In this context, the justice model seemed a promising replacement.

Yet it would be premature to accept Martinson's call for a requiem for rehabilitation. First, it is by no means clear that "rehabilitation doesn't work"; research findings are decidedly mixed. Palmer, for instance, has indicated that 48 percent of the outcomes reported in Martinson's survey "yielded positive results."[70] Similarly, there are a growing "number of programs which seem to work for certain types of individuals in certain situations."[71] Further, others have suggested that if treatment interventions do not fully halt recidivism, they nevertheless have the important salutary effect of suppressing the seriousness and/or amount of future criminality.[72] Most significant, however, is that Martinson himself eventually came to renounce the position that "nothing works." After completing a new study that extended his initial report by including both more recent evaluations of treatment programs (his previous work covered the years 1945-1967) and a broader range of research (555 studies vs. 231), he concluded that under certain circumstances rehabilitation is clearly effective in lowering recidivism rates. In his words, "contrary to my previous position, some treatment programs do have an appreciable effect on recidivism. Some programs are indeed beneficial. ... New evidence from our current study leads me to reject my original conclusion. ... I have hesitated up to now, but the evidence in our survey is simply too overwhelming to ignore."[73]

Now it should not prove surprising that criminal justice rehabilitation has been less than fully successful in reducing offender recidivism. The paucity of resources devoted to this difficult task is well illustrated by the fact that the New York Department of Correctional Services spends less than two percent of its annual budget of $130 million on educational and vocational rehabilitation.[74] More importantly, even those interventions which are instituted lack what is now being termed "program integrity." It is more the rule than the exception that the quality or integrity of current treatment programs can be questioned in one or more of the following respects:

> First, whether the intervention can be adequately conceptualized and whether that conceptualization has sufficient grounding in previous empirical evidence; second, whether service is actually delivered, whether it is sufficient in duration and intensity, and whether it is carried out as described; third, whether the personnel delivering the service are qualified, trained, and adequately supervised; and fourth, whether the treatment is actually appropriate for all those chosen to receive it.[75]

In this regard, Joan Petersilia has reported that a national survey conducted by Rand revealed that no more than 40 percent of the offenders in state prisons participate in a treatment program while incarcerated, and that only "one in four or five inmates with identified needs participates in prison treatment programs related to his needs."[76] Similarly, the Panel on Research on Rehabilitative Techniques has recently concluded that "When one looks at actual programs—at what has actually been tried—it turns out that much of what is called rehabilitation cannot reasonably be expected to effect real changes in behavior over time."[77] As such, if the current mix of findings does not permit unqualified support for the effectiveness of offender treatment, "neither could one say with justified confidence that rehabilitation cannot be achieved, and, therefore, no drastic cutbacks in the rehabilitative effort should be based on that proposition."[78]

But for liberals concerned with the welfare of offenders, particularly the incarcerated, the relevance of criminal justice rehabilitation does not end with the question of recidivism rates. Much of the thinking about rehabilitation has been dominated by this issue, at the price of overlooking the impact of treatment programs on other aspects of a criminal's life. This oversight assumes significance when we realize that nearly all offenders eventually pursue noncriminal roles in society, and that the recidivism rate among prison inmates is estimated to be less than 25 percent.[79] Apart from the issue of recidivism, then, does rehabilitation "work" in ways that improve the quality of an offender's life? Notably, Martinson's own research consistently demonstrates that different treatment modalities do indeed have positive effects in such areas as "institutional adjustment," "vocational adjustment," "educational achievement," and "personality and attitude change."[80] As he commented, "many treatments do indicate modest change on other dependent variables."[81]

In sum, we can again raise the question of whether a system that seeks to punish based on principles of desert will be more just and humane than one that seeks to temper punishment with the rehabilitative ideal. Thus far, we have proposed that determinate sentencing may not only result in sanctioning that is more severe, more rigid, and more unequal, but also would risk negating the potential benefits realizable through treatment interventions.

However, there is an additional issue to consider: the impact of sentencing reform on the quality of institutional conditions.

THE DETERIORATION OF PRISON CONDITIONS

For liberals, indeterminate sentencing has been corrupted into a coercive mechanism employed by the custodial regime to keep behaviorally and politically troublesome inmates in line. As such, release is contingent more on conformity than cure. Further, a constant strain for inmates is the uncertainty about the date of their return to society. Parole seems a lottery, and they are caught in the painful fluctuation between hope and despair. However accurate this critique is, would an inmate's lot be improved under determinate sentencing? If, as suggested, sentencing "reform" results in longer prison terms, then perhaps the debate should stop here. Nevertheless, to avoid any remaining uncertainty, there are four additional issues that deserve our attention.

First, in a 1976 ruling on the constitutionality of prison conditions in Alabama, Judge Frank M. Johnson found that "robbery, rape, extortion, theft and assault are everyday occurrences among the general inmate population."[82] It would be an exaggeration to claim that such conditions prevail in prisons in all states and at all levels of security. Yet neither are these events foreign to many of our penitentiaries. Rates of inmate victimization are rising[83] and the number of those seeking protective custody is keeping pace.[84] In the first six months of 1980 alone, nearly 150 prisoners died violently in state and federal prisons.[85] These realities raise the uneasy dilemma for liberals as to how best to control a difficult population in a difficult environment. It is generally agreed that indeterminate sentencing—"behave or you don't get out"—is "one of the most effective weapons for inmate control."[86] If the indeterminate sentence is not employed at least *in part* for this purpose, what will evolve to be used in its place—more or less coercive methods of prison discipline? And should the former alternative be followed, Gordon Hawkins has informed us that "past and present experience clearly indicates that the only result to be expected from the implementation of a more punitive policy in prisons would be greatly intensified unrest, turbulence, riot and revolt, and a substantial increase in death and injury for both staff and prisoners."[87]

Now proponents of determinate sentencing have suggested that good time be retained to handle the problem of institutional control. This strategy, however, has serious defects. Gresham Sykes observed long ago that good time is, in effect, "automatically subtracted from the prisoner's sentence when he begins his period of imprisonment." Consequently, it is "not defined as something to be earned but as an inalienable right—as the just due of the inmate which should not turn on the question of obedience or disobedience within the walls."[88] Taking away this "right" is thus likely to trigger resentment and create conditions conducive to inmate disorder.

In this light, the prospects for turmoil stemming from the revocation of good time appear to be substantially heightened under determinate sentencing. Since the loss of good time will now constitute the major control mechanism, we can anticipate that it will be utilized more frequently by the custodial staff. Significantly, in the year after fixed terms came into full usage in Illinois, the number of disciplinary cases at Stateville where good time was revoked increased 173 percent and the number of cases where 30 days or less were revoked increased 581 percent.[89] Further, as discussed, the loss of good time under determinate sentences means that extra days will have to be served. The stakes are thus upped and the emotions attached to revocations consequently intensified. According to the John Howard Association, "Revocation of good time is an emotionally charged issue and prisoners appear more threatened under the new determinate sentencing statute than under prior laws."[90] Moreover, inmate resentment for increased stays in prison will no longer be directed at a distant parole board. Instead, its new target will be more intimate and reachable: the guards that bring them before the prison disciplinary committee and who are "responsible" for in effect sentencing them to added days of imprisonment.[91] This situation is worsened by the fact that the rules governing the loss of good time are typically broadly and ambiguously stated, and hence allow nearly any behavior to be singled out as a disciplinary infraction. Speaking of Illinois' disciplinary prison code, Paul Bigman has observed, "They can take away years of good time for displaying gang insignia or swearing or showing disrespect to an officer or wearing a contraband hat."[92] As a result, inmates often experience revocation as an arbitrary and capricious punishment, and this again fuels their resentment toward the custodial staff. In sum, reliance on good time as the cornerstone of institutional control promises to exacerbate the problem of maintaining order. And it is the inmates and their keepers who will ultimately pay the price of living in more treacherous surroundings.

Second, the movement toward determinacy in sentencing will almost certainly contribute to the crisis of overcrowding plaguing our nation's penal institutions. With attitudes toward crime hardening, the population in state and federal prisons has surged to nearly 325,000,[93] and it is estimated that by 1983 this figure will have increased by as much as 20 to 30 percent in certain regions of the country.[94] While a number of states are undertaking prison construction programs, this is of little solace. A National Institute of Justice study has made the disturbing report that "where new space has been freely added, on the average it has been followed two years later by population increases of nearly equal size."[95]

As the number of inmates continues to spiral, fixed-term sentencing introduces a new and uncompromising danger. In the past, parole boards would employ their release prerogatives to keep the inmate populace at an organizationally manageable level. With determinacy in sentencing, however, there is no parole board to relieve the press of overcrowding and the tensions, idleness, and potential for disruption it induces. The prison will have lost its safety-valve. Admittedly, in the face of teeming penitentiaries, alternative release procedures could and undoubtedly will be evolved. Yet these adaptations are likely to be hastily instituted and to create new inefficiencies and inequities in the administration of justice.[96] At the very least, they will necessitate a corruption of fundamental principles espoused by supporters of determinacy: early release in response to population conditions undermines both the certainty of punishment (terms will now be "unfixed") and standards of strict equality (fluctuations in population levels and not simply the crime one commits will regulate the length of an inmate's sentence).

Further, to the extent that the current wave of determinate sentencing leads, as we have argued, to the increased usage of incarceration as a sanction as well as to expanded stays behind bars, this reform will help to inflate prison populations. In the absence of an appropriate release mechanism, this will compound the general problem of overcrowding which is already burdening institutions across the country. Moreover, lengthy fixed terms will add a troubling new dimension to the nature of the rising prison population: it will create an increasing pool of mostly youthful offenders who are facing prolonged sentences with no prospect of release. A dismayed David Fogel, the noted liberal justice model author and considered by many to be the "father of determinate sentencing" in Illinois, has thus offered a telling prediction that the actual fixed-term legislation ("Class X") that came to be passed in Illinois will result in "a very large number of people in prison at very young ages, with no place to go." He then continued, "You're going to get an irreducible minimum who are going to be more angry, more volatile, more dangerous, and they're going to be confined to mostly seven prisons. It's perfectly clear what this law is going to do. If you look far enough, by passing this law the General Assembly has just sentenced several white guards to death."[97] In the same vein as Fogel, Mike Midkiff, a corrections official in Indiana, is also troubled by the young offenders confronting long jail terms with little hope of parole—a group he has termed the "new lifers." "The old parole system had a lot of inequities," admits Midkiff, "but it still had a light at the end of the tunnel, however dim or faint.... Now when you tell a guy he doesn't have a chance until he serves half his term—it might be 40, or 50, or 60 years—what the hell. It's not going to take him long to get frustrated." A twelve-year veteran of Indiana corrections, Midkiff cannot recall "any period during that time when the conditions were more ripe" for a prison disturbance.[98]

Third, what will be the future of the current rehabilitation programs once just deserts becomes the dominant correctional paradigm? Liberals propose that treatment will now become voluntary. Yet it is difficult to see why there would be a continuing impetus for the state to provide such programs. As prison populations expand and the fiscal crisis of American corrections heightens, there would remain little ideological justification for maintaining costly rehabilitation services which have been proven by liberal social scientists to be "unworkable." "Now with the new policy of punishment," Henry Glick has warned, "we may see the legitimate dismantling of whatever meager services that were provided.... If rehabilitation had little chance for success in the past due to lack of resources and genuine commitment, then it has practically none in the foreseeable future since it rapidly is becoming legitimate to explicitly opt for retribution."[99] It must also be remembered that the majority of America's incarcerated are drawn from minority groups and can be easily portrayed by the state, if the need occurs, as a "dangerous class" who are deserving of little sympathy and are unlikely candidates for reformation and subsequent reintegration into the dominant social order. Francis Allen has thus explicitly linked the current decline in the potency of the rehabilitative ideal directly to "rising percentages of non-caucasian inmates in prisons," and he has proceded to observe that "optimism about the possibilities of reform flourishes when strong bonds of identity are perceived between the reformers and those to be reformed. Conversely, confidence in rehabilitative effort dwindles when a sense of difference and social distance separates the promoters from the subjects of reform."[100] The abandonment of correctional rehabilitation thus potentially reinforces the notion that the disadvantaged in our penitentiaries are incurably criminal, beyond our good intentions and saving, and deserving only of our punishment and ill-treatment.

These comments bring us directly to a fourth and final issue: the very real risk that a just deserts or retributive philosophy will "give a new legitimacy to neglect."[101] Implicit in the philosophy of basing punishment strictly on the crime and not the criminal is the assumption that the state not only has no right but also *no obligation* to do anything about the condition or needs of an offender. Moreover, "by labeling the offender as untreatable, we make it apparent to one and all that we cannot be held accountable for his improvement or his deterioration."[102] Yet we may ask, is a philosophy that supports state neglect of individual needs likely to be more benevolent than one that mandates, however imperfectly, state concern? One Indiana inmate serving a life sentence has provided an answer to this question:

> The indeterminate sentence at least recognizes that a man, no matter how evil or misguided, has the potential for change. A determinate sentence denies this potential and, therefore, denies the humanity of the individual.... Determinate sentencing, in effect, says "We fail to live up to our ideals; therefore, we will cease to strive for them. Instead, we will lower them so low that we will be assured of achieving them." It seems to me to be a cop-out, and should not be accepted.[103]

In this same regard, available evidence calls into question the broad claims of the liberal proponents of the justice model that society's captives seek to abandon the rehabilitative ideal due to the coercion inherent in a treatment ideology. It appears instead that inmates recognize that rehabilitation programs are one of the few features of prison life that hold the potential to mitigate the boredom and harshness of idleness, create possibilities of self-improvement, and foster hope and not despair. Thus, recent data collected on a sample of inmates at a minimum-medium security prison in Illinois showed strong support for rehabilitation. Sixty-four percent of the inmates rejected the conclusion that "the rehabilitation of adults just does not work," three-fourths concurred that rehabilitation is "the only effective and humane cure to the crime problem in America," and over 80 percent favored "expanding rehabilitation programs that are now being undertaken in our prisons."[104] These results are consistent with the research reported by Hans Toch. Drawing on a survey of offenders incarcerated at all levels of security in the New York State prison system, Toch discovered that the most important need identified by inmates during imprisonment was "support—a concern about reliable tangible assistance from persons and settings, and about services that facilitate self-advancement and self-improvement."[105] Instructive as well is Gordon Hawkins' observation, based on an examination of inmate riot demands, that "it is ironic that, at a time when authorities and experts throughout America are repudiating the rehabilitative ideal, some of the most 'radical' prisoners should be in effect endorsing it so forcefully."[106]

Now even more disturbing than the denial of the state's obligation to do more than punish adult offenders, this same sense of neglect is currently creeping into the juvenile justice system. A sponsor of recent just deserts legislation in Washington remarked that "we are not sending [juveniles to institutions] to do them any good. We're sending them there because their behavior has demonstrated that they are a menace to society."[107] In such a context, "can we rely on authorities to be more humane toward juveniles," LaMar Empey questions, "when their primary mandate is to respond not to the personal characteristics of those juveniles, but only to the acts they commit?"[108] Similarly, David Rothman recorded that "it was Willard Gaylin who commented, with all sarcasm intended, that he finally understood the motive impulse of the adversarial moment: to substitute for the hardnosed, belligerent, tough-minded psychiatrist the attention of the gentle, understanding, empathetic lawyer!"[109]

In sum, neither the administration of justice nor the quality of an inmate's life will be improved by the current wave of sentencing reform; indeed, all evidence points to the increased victimization of the offender. The poverty of the liberals' justice model thus seems complete. However, it is still necessary to consider briefly the conservatives' claim that the social benefit of reduced crime rates will be reaped through determinate sentencing.

DETERMINATE SENTENCING AND CONTROLLING CRIME: ASSESSING THE CONSERVATIVES' POSITION

It is the fundamental premise of conservative theorizing that abandoning rehabilitation in favor of fixed-term sentencing will eventuate in greater social protection by increasing the deterrent and incapacitative powers of the criminal law. On closer inspection, however, the claim that just deserts or retributive sentencing will improve crime control *above and beyond that already provided by the current system* seems problematical at best. It must be remembered that judges are already sending one out of every two convicted felons to prison, and that those who persist in breaking the law rarely escape incarceration at some point in their criminal careers.[110] In this respect, Charles Silberman has asserted that our courts are "fulfilling their crime-control function remarkably well: they are punishing most of those who should be punished."[111] Moreover, the sanctions currently imposed on offenders are more severe than those employed both in our own past and in other nations. After discovering that the rate of incarceration climbed from 138 per 100,000 citizens in 1880 to over 200 by the 1970s (and prison populations have risen another 40 percent since this time),[112] Margaret Cahalan observed that "the United States has demonstrated a willingness to rely more and more upon incarceration."[113] Similarly, Eugene Doleschal's analysis of cross-cultural variations in criminal sanctioning revealed that "with the possible exception of political prisoners in totalitarian states, prisoners in American penitentiaries serve the harshest sentences in the world."[114]

The argument for greater deterrence rests primarily on the assumption that determinate sentencing will fortify the certainty of punishment. People will be reluctant to begin or return to crime if they know that a conviction will invariably mean suffering the penalty listed in the criminal code. Yet this thinking has only surface appeal. Sentencing reform does little to change the largest source of uncertainty in the criminal justice system: policing that is reactive in nature and unable to attain high clearance rates for nearly all offense categories. In raw numbers, the police are able to make arrests in fewer than 20 percent of the offenses listed on the FBI Crime Index.[115] In addition, the certainty that legislatively-prescribed penalties will actually be imposed is further undermined by the fact that such reform not only does not touch but also will expand prosecutorial discretion. Bargain justice, not certain justice, will continue to be the rule.

As intimated, determinate sentencing may very well increase the severity of criminal punishments, and some might allege that this will supplement the deterrent powers of the state. This proposition can be objected to on the moral grounds that sanctions are already too harsh. Yet it can also be opposed on the empirical grounds that severity is only minimally related to criminal participation. As Harry Elmer Barnes' look into the past revealed, "history shows that severe punishments have never reduced criminality to any marked degree."[116] Moreover, recent empirical research is far from clear that criminal punishment can in fact deter either specifically or generally. William Nagel, as mentioned earlier, has found that rates of crime and incarceration are essentially unrelated; some states that punish harshly nevertheless have high crime rates while others have low rates, and vice versa.[117] Similarly, deterrence theory may rest on the faulty assumption that the most crucial ingredient in the decision to violate the law is the potential "costs" that might be incurred. However, a survey of prison inmates indicated that "individual offense rates are related only to offenders' perceptions of the benefits to be derived from crime," and not to the risks of being caught and punished.[118] Perhaps most notable, however, is the conclusion reached by the Panel on Research on Deterrent and Incapacitative Effects. After an exhaustive review of available research, the Panel reported that "we cannot yet assert that the evidence proves the existence of deterrent effects."[119]

The other half of the conservatives' crime control package is the mandating of lengthy fixed prison terms in order to achieve greater incapacitative effects. "Lock 'em up and throw away the keys, so at least they can't harm anybody anymore," is the conservative cry. Putting aside the question of the morality of calling for the increased use of incarceration and the fact that this policy completely ignores the considerable amount of crime that occurs in and is precipitated by the unnatural environment of the penitentiary, the pragmatics of incapacitation are shaky at best. A large inflation of the prison population would be required to secure even a modest reduction in the crime rate. One study in New York estimated that it would be necessary to increase the state's prison population by 264 percent to reduce FBI Index crimes by ten percent. The costs of pursuing such a policy, as Diana Gordon of the National Council on Crime and Delinquency has noted, "would be staggering. It would cost $3 billion just to construct the additional cells necessary and probably another $1 billion each year, in 1980 dollars, to operate them (not counting financing costs)."[120] Another computation completed by Schrag placed the cost to the American public for each crime prevented by caging criminals at $34,675.[121] Consistent with these assessments, Steve van Dine and his associates asserted that the economic costs "are so great that we must conclude that incapacitation is not a reasonable course to adopt for the achievement of a reduction of violent crime,"[122] while Stevens Clarke has added, "considering the problems involved, the benefit is not worth the cost."[123]

Alternative proposals have been made by conservatives to mandate lengthy determinate sentences exclusively for the small group of predatory criminals who are responsible for a large proportion of the serious crime rate. Even here, however, there is doubt that this policy would be effective unless we are willing to tolerate substantial increases in inmate populations. More significantly, we simply do not have the technology to selectively quarantine the predatory without also incarcerating anywhere from six to fifteen times as many "false positives."[124] That is, our ability to predict who will be the dangerous recidivist is so inexact that it would be necessary to imprison many other offenders who share similar characteristics with the real predators but would not actually become involved in serious crimes in the future. As Gordon has remarked, "if we assume that some convicted offenders will commit further crimes in the community, but we don't know which ones, incapacitating the future criminals will require locking up all others too."[125] These difficulties suggest, in David Greenberg's words, "the unfeasibility of a policy of selective quarantine."[126]

In sum, there is little reason to have confidence in the conservative stance that determinate sentencing will enhance crime control. Yet to the extent that this view is popularized and unwittingly permitted by liberals through their general support of sentencing reform, we can expect much human misery to result.

CONCLUSION

LaMar Empey has cautioned that "just deserts proponents have worried about the abuse of discretion and power in a treatment-oriented system, but have said surprisingly little about the possible abuses that might be associated with a justice model. If abuses were associated with a system whose ostensible principles were mercy, love, and understanding, what will happen in a system whose goals are due process and punishment?"[127] Indeed, it appears that the potential for abuse is considerable. Building on the insights of a growing number of analysts who are now suggesting that the merits of the justice model should be reconsidered, it has been proposed that the current sentencing reform movement will do little to attain the liberals' goal of the more equitable and humane treatment of offenders. Determinate sentencing is in its essence a conservative reform aimed at crime control, and thus promises to increase the length, rigidity, and disparity of sentences, as well as to result in the atrophy of beneficial rehabilitation programs and the degeneration of prison conditions. In the end, it is difficult to escape the conclusion that we are better off with the system we now have.

This is not to suggest that we should embrace and not seek reform of the current criminal justice system; its vices clearly outweigh its virtues. However, it is to argue that it is illusory to believe that progress in the administration of justice can be secured—particularly in a conservative social climate—through such easy remedies as determinate sentencing. The intimate link between crime, punishment, and society means that true criminal justice ultimately awaits true social justice, and that meaningful improvements in a criminal justice system located in an inequitable society are only attained through concerted efforts that guard carefully against the corrupting influences of prevailing interests. This might strike some as a pessimistic thought, but it is also an appropriately sobering one.

NOTES

[1]Quoted in Torsten Eriksson, *The Reformers: An Historical Survey of Pioneer Experiments in the Treatment of Criminals.* (New York: Elsevier, 1976), p. 30.

[2]Francis A. Allen, *The Decline of the Rehabilitative Ideal: Penal Policy and Social Purpose.* (New Haven: Yale University Press, 1981), p. 87.

[3]For works critical of current determinate sentencing reform, see Seymour L. Halleck and Anne D. Witte, "Is rehabilitation dead?" *Crime and Delinquency* 25 (October 1977), pp. 372–383; Sue Titus Reid, "A rebuttal to the attack on the indeterminate sentence." *Washington Law Review* 51 (1976), pp. 565–606; Franklin E. Zimring, "Making the punishment fit the crime." *Hastings Center Report* 6 (December 1976), pp. 13–17; Brooke E. Spiro, "The future course of corrections." *Social Work* 23 (July 1978), pp. 315–320; Arthur G. LaFrancois, "An examination of a desert-based presumptive sentence schedule." *Journal of Criminal Justice* 6 (1978), pp. 35–46; David F. Greenberg and Drew Humphries, "The cooptation of fixed sentencing reform." *Crime and Delinquency* 26 (April 1980), pp. 206–225; Sol Rubin, "New sentencing proposals and laws in the 1970's." *Federal Probation* 43 (June 1979), pp. 3–8; Henry D. Glick, "Mandatory sentencing: the politics of the new criminal justice." *Federal Probation* 43 (March 1979), pp. 3–9; Frederick Hussey, "Just deserts and determinate sentencing: impact on the rehabilitative ideal." *The Prison Journal* 59 (Autumn-Winter 1979), pp. 36–47; Susette M. Talarico, "What do we expect of criminal justice? Critical questions of sanction policy, sentencing purpose, and the politics of reform." *Criminal Justice* Review 4 (Spring 1979) pp. 55–72; "Put them in jail: the conversion of Marvin Wolfgang." *Institutions Etc.* 2 (January 1979), pp. 1–4; Gray Cavender, "The philosophical justifications of determinate sentencing." *American Journal of Jurisprudence* 26 (Fall 1981); Donald R. Cressey, "Criminological theory, social science, and the repression of crime." *Criminology* 16 (August 1978), pp. 171–191, and his "Sentencing: legislative rule versus judicial discretion. Pp. 52–69 in Brian A. Grosman (ed.), *New Directions in Sentencing.* (Toronto: Butterworths, 1980). See more generally the special September 1977 issue of *Corrections Magazine*, "Determinate sentencing: making the punishment fit the crime"; Wingspread Conference, *Criminal Justice Alternatives.* (Racine, Wisconsin: Johnson Foundation, 1977); and National Institute of Law Enforcement and Criminal Justice, *Determinate Sentencing: Regression or Reform?* (Washington, D.C.: U.S. Government Printing Office, 1978).

[4]For instance, see Marvin Zalman, "A commission model of sentencing." *Notre Dame Lawyer* 53 (December 1977), pp. 266–290 and, more generally, Patrick D. McAnany, "Doing justice to the justice model: an exorcism of some persistent myths." Paper presented at the 1980 meeting of the American Society of Criminology.

[5]Andrew von Hirsch, *Doing Justice: The Choice of Punishments.* (New York: Hill and Wang, 1971), p. 139.

[6]Quoted in Donald R. Cressey, "Criminological theory, social science, and the repression of crime," p. 81.

[7]Greenberg and Humphries, "The cooptation of fixed sentencing reform," p. 220.

[8]National Committee Against Repressive Legislation, "1984: It comes from the old Nixon/Mitchell S. 1 . . . only they call it S. 1722." Pamphlet. (Washington, D.C.: NCARL, 1980).

[9]John P. Conrad, "In my opinion." *Corrections Magazine* 3 (September 1977), p. i; Todd R. Clear, John D. Hewitt, and Robert M. Regoli, "Discretion and the determinate sentence:

its distribution, control and effect on time served." *Crime and Delinquency* 24 (October 1978), p. 443.

[10]New York State Bar Association, *Report of Subcommittee of Criminal Justice on the Correctional System.* (New York: New York State Bar Association, 1978), pp. 50–64.

[11]Richard Singer, *Just Deserts: Sentencing Based on Equality and Desert.* (Cambridge, Ma.: Ballinger, 1979), p. 193.

[12]Greenberg and Humphries, "The cooptation of fixed sentencing reform," p. 214.

[13]Quoted in Edgar May, "Officials fear long flat term proposals." *Corrections Magazine* 3 (September 1977), p. 43.

[14]Conrad, "In my opinion," p. i.

[15]Michael J. Hindelang, "Public opinion regarding crime, criminal justice, and related topics." *Journal of Research in Crime and Delinquency* 11 (July 1974), p. 107.

[16]"Opinion roundup." Public Opinion 4 (April/May 1981), p. 40.

[17]Arthur L. Stinchcombe, Rebecca Adams, Carol A. Heimer, Kim Lance Scheppele, Tom W. Smith, and D. Garth Taylor, *Crime and Punishment: Changing Attitudes in America.* (San Francisco: Jossey-Bass, 1980); Joseph H. Rankin, "Changing attitudes toward capital punishment." *Social Forces* 58 (September 1979), pp. 194–211; Francis T. Cullen, John B. Cullen, Nellie Ann Sims, and Steven G. Hunter, "The punishment – rehabilitation controversy: insider and outsider perspectives." Paper presented at the 1981 meeting of the American Society of Criminology. See also James O. Finckenauer, "Crime as a national political issue: 1964–76, from law and order to domestic tranquility." *Crime and Delinquency* 24 (January 1978), pp. 13–27.

[18]Richard A. Berk and Peter H. Rossi, *Prison Reform and State Elites.* (Cambridge, Ma.: Ballinger, 1977), p. 83; Pamela Johnson Riley and Vicki McNickle Rose, "Public and elite opinion on correctional reform: implications for social policy." *Journal of Criminal Justice* (No. 6, 1976), pp. 345–356.

[19]Zimring, "Making the punishment fit the crime," p. 14.

[20]Jeffrey H. Reiman and Sue Headlee, "Marxism and criminal justice policy." *Crime and Delinquency* 27 (January 1981), pp. 44–47 and compare with Greenberg and Humphries, "The cooptation of fixed sentencing reform," pp. 215, 224.

[21]Harry Elmer Barnes, *The Story of Punishment: A Record of Man's Inhumanity to Man.* (Montclair, N.J.: Patterson-Smith, 1972).

[22]"The history of justice is replete with violence and fear. Ever since the concept of law came into being, the authorities have been convinced that respect for the law mainly depends on the severity of the punishment. Many people, perhaps the majority, hold this conviction, even though history provides ample evidence to the contrary." Torsten Eriksson, *The Reformers: An Historical Survey of Pioneer Experiments in the Treatment of Criminals*, p. 1.

[23]Zimring, "Making the punishment fit the crime," p. 17.

[24]See David L. Bazelon, "Street crime and correctional potholes." *Federal Probation* 41 (March 1977), pp. 3–9; Greenberg and Humphries, "The cooptation of fixed sentencing reform," pp. 215–216.

[25]Talarico "What do we expect of criminal justice?" pp. 62–63. As discussed in Chapter 6, this has already occurred in Pennsylvania. See Stephen P. Lagoy, "The politics of punishment and the future of sentencing reform: the Pennsylvania experience." Paper presented at the 1981 meeting of the American Society of Criminology.

[26]S. David Hicks, *The Corrections Yearbook.* (New York: Criminal Justice Institute, Inc.), p. 27.

[27]"Just the Facts." Pamphlet. (Philadelphia: American Institute of Criminal Justice, n.d.), p. 5; Joan Mullen and Bradford Smith, *American Prisons and Jails, Volume III: Conditions and Costs of Confinement.* (Washington, D.C.: National Institute of Justice, 1980), p. 119.

[28]Greenberg and Humphries, "The cooptation of fixed sentencing reform," p. 225.

[29]David Sudnow, "Normal crimes: sociological features of the penal code in a public defender's office." *Social Problems* 12 (December 1965), pp. 255–276.

[30]"When a system is confronted with legislative changes in procedures, capability or sanction, the behavior of key actors probably changes as little as necessary to comply and as much as possible to mediate the perceived disruption of the change." Joan Mullen with Kenneth Carlson and Bradford Smith, *American Prisons and Jails, Volume I: Summary Findings and Policy Implications of a National Survey.* (Washington, D.C.: National Institute of Justice, 1980), p. 108.

[31]Clarence Schrag, "Rediscovering punitive justice." Pp. 463–467 in Barry Krisberg and James Austin (eds.), *The Children of Ishmael: Critical Perspectives on Juvenile Justice.* (Palo Alto, Ca.: Mayfield, 1978), p. 467.

[32]Gresham M. Sykes and Stephen R. West, "The seriousness of crime: a study of popular morality." Paper presented at the 1978 meeting of the Eastern Sociological Society; Stephen D. Gottfredson, Kathy L. Young, and William S. Laufer, "Additivity and interactions in offense seriousness scales." *Journal of Research in Crime and Delinquency* 17 (January 1980), pp. 26–41.

[33]Zimring, "Making the punishment fit the crime," p. 16.

[34]Quoted in Joanne D'Alcomo, "Mandatory terms opposed by prosecutors." *Brockton Enterprise* (January 2, 1979), p. 1.

[35]Quoted in Sam Rosensohn, "Top judge slams D.A.'s call to scrap parole board for fixed jail terms." *New York Post* (January 5, 1979), p. 4.

[36]Sir Leon Radzinowicz and Joan King, *The Growth of Crime: The International Experience.* (New York: Basic Books, 1977), p. 327.

[37]"Gov. Carey repeals tough N.Y. drug law." *Washington Post* (July 8, 1979), p. A2. A similar fate befell a previous New York "habitual felon" act (Baumes Law). See Barnes, *The Story of Punishment,* p. 170.

[38]William J. Cook, "The 'bitch' threatens, but seldom bites: a study of habitual criminal sentencing in Douglas County." *Creighton Law Review* 8 (July 1975), p. 918.

[39]Joe Kolman, "Crime and punishment in Illinois: the Class X question." *Reader* 9 (August 15, 1980), p. 30. The Supreme Court ruled 5–4 that this sentence did not constitute cruel and unusual punishment. See "'Les miserables,' Texas-style." *Chicago Tribune* (March 24, 1980).

[40]Judge David Bazelon, "Discussion." Pp. 78–79 in *Determinate Sentencing: Reform or Regression?* (Washington, D.C.: U.S. Government Printing Office, 1978), p. 78. Of further interest here, Martin A. Levin's study of urban courts found that Pittsburgh judges who were less legalistic than their Minneapolis counterparts were also more lenient in their sentencing practices. "By contrast, whereas the decision-making of the Pittsburgh judges tends not to satisfy the values of equality and consistency, it does tend to be benevolent and to satisfy those of individuality and desert. Not constrained or guided by general standards, it instead places its emphasis on kindness and expediency, rather than equality, and it operates with a considered inconsistency." See *Urban Politics and the Criminal Courts.* (Chicago: University of Chicago Press, 1977), p. 203.

[41]Charles E. Silberman, *Criminal Violence, Criminal Justice.* (New York: Pantheon, 1978), p. 292.

[42]See, for example, Theodore G. Chiricos and Gordon P. Waldo, "Socioeconomic status and criminal sentencing: an empirical assessment of a conflict proposition." *American Sociological Review* 40 (December 1975), pp. 753–772.

[43]It is estimated that the economic costs of white-collar crime exceed those of the offenses listed on the FBI Crime Index by at least ten times. See John E. Conklin, *"Illegal But Not Criminal": Business Crime in America.* (Englewood Cliffs, N.J.: Prentice Hall, 1977), p. 4. Similarly, the physical costs (injuries, deaths, diseases) of one brand of upperworld lawlessness alone, corporate crime, exceeds the toll exacted by more conventional street-crimes. Marshall Clinard and his associates have thus concluded that "far more persons are killed through corporate criminal activities than by individual criminal homicides," and Gilbert Geis has observed that "there is no doubt that commercial fraud kills more people than are murdered by acts that come to be listed as criminal homicide on the Uniform Crime Reports tabulated by the FBI." See Marshall B. Clinard, Peter C. Yeager, Jeanne Brissette, David Petrashek, and Elizabeth Harries, *Illegal Corporate Behavior.* (Washington, D.C.: U.S. Government Printing Office, 1979), p. xvi; Gilbert Geis, "Victimization patterns in white-collar crime." Pp. 89–105 in I. Drapkin and E. Viano (eds.), *Victimology: A New Focus, Volume V, Exploiters and Exploited.* (Lexington, Ma.: Lexington Books), p. 93.

[44]Constance Baker Motley, "'Law and order' and the criminal justice system." *Journal of Criminal Law and Criminology* 64 (September 1973), p. 260.

[45]Stephen Gettinger, "Fixed sentencing becomes law in 3 states; other legislatures wary." *Corrections Magazine* 3 (September 1977), p. 21; "Sentences vary widely from state to state." *Corrections Magazine* 7 (April 1981), p. 2. Similarly, Mullen and Smith, *American Prisons and Jails, Volume* III, p. 143, have noted that "The rate of incarceration per 100,000 civilian population (for state and local prisoners combined) was 273 in the South, followed by 195 in the West, 153 in the North Central region and 132 in the Northeast. Even within regions, the disparities were often wide: Louisiana's rate was 290 while neighboring Mississippi incarcerated 172 persons per 100,000 members of the general population" (for 1978).

[46]William G. Nagel, "On behalf of a moratorium on prison construction." *Crime and Delinquency* 23 (April 1977), pp. 154–172.

[47]Gettinger, "Fixed sentencing becomes law," p. 20.

[48]Kenneth Carlson, *American Prisons and Jails, Volume II: Population Trends and Projections.* (Washington, D.C.: National Institute of Justice, 1980), p. 3.

[49]Daniel Glaser, "The counterproductivity of conservative thinking about crime." *Criminology* 16 (August 1978), p. 219.

[50]Caroline K. Simon, "Needed: a new look at punishment." *American Bar Association Journal* 62 (October 1976), p. 1299.

[51]Stephen J. Schulhofer, *Prosecutorial Discretion and Federal Sentencing Reform.* (Washington, D.C.: Federal Judicial Center, 1979), p. 3.

[52]Steven P. Lagoy, Frederick A. Hussey, and John H. Kramer, "The prosecutorial function and its relation to determinate sentencing structures." Pp. 204–237 in William F. McDonald (ed.), *The Prosecutor.* (Beverly Hills, Ca.: Sage, 1979), p. 211.

[53]Kathleen Brosi, *A Cross City Comparison of Felony Case Processing.* (Washington, D.C.: U.S. Government Printing Office, 1979), p. 35.

[54]Quoted in the New York State Bar Association, *Report of Subcommittee of Criminal Justice Section Committee on the Correctional System,* p. 49.

[55]American Civil Liberties Union, "Is expanded use of mandatory prison sentences a sound approach to reducing crime—con." *Congressional Digest* 55 (August-September, 1976), p. 217.

[56]Jonathan D. Casper, *Criminal Courts: The Defendant's Perspective—Executive Summary.* (Washington, D.C.: U.S. Government Printing Office, 1978), p. 6.

[57]Mullen, *American Prisons and Jails, Volume I,* p. 130.

[58]Timothy Dwyer, "Prosecutors get plea: slow down." *Boston Globe* (July 17, 1980), pp. 1, 17.

[59]Andrew T. Scull, *Decarceration: Community Treatment and the Deviant—A Radical View.* (Englewood Cliffs, N.J.: Prentice Hall, 1977), pp. 53–56.

[60]Mullen, *American Prisons and Jails, Volume I,* p. 133.

[61]Silberman, *Criminal Violence, Criminal Justice,* p. 295.

[62]Stephen J. Schulhofer, "Will presumptive sentencing legislation backfire?—The problem of prosecutorial discretion." Paper presented at the 1979 meeting of the American Society of Criminology, p. 10.

[63]Ibid., p. 13.

[64]See, for example, the recommendations of Schulhofer, *Prosecutorial Discretion and Federal Sentencing Reform.*

[65]Milton Heumann and Colin Loftin, "Mandatory sentencing and the abolition of plea bargaining: the Michigan felony firearm statute." *Law and Society Review* 13 (Winter 1979), pp. 393–430.

[66]Albert Alschuler, "Sentencing reform and prosecutorial power: a critique of recent proposals for 'fixed' and 'presumptive' sentencing." Pp. 59–88 in *Determinate Sentencing: Reform or Regression?* (Washington, D.C.: U.S. Government Printing Office, 1978), p. 59.

[67]John Howard Association, "Stateville revisited: 'Shakedown/shakeup—one year later.'" Mimeograph (February 25, 1980), p. 12.

[68]Quoted in Kolman, "Crime and punishment in Illinois," p. 31.

[69]Paul Bigman, "Good time, hard times." *Prison Law and Advocacy* 2 (November 1980), p. 4. Bigman has also noted that a Prisoner Review Board exists that reviews the Department of Corrections' requests for revocation of good time. While the possibility for balancing institutional disparities thus exists, this does not occur since the Board approves nearly all—96.3%—of the Department's requests.

[70]Ted Palmer, "Martinson revisited." Pp. 41–62 in R. Martinson, T. Palmer, and S. Adams, *Rehabilitation, Recidivism, and Research.* (Hackensack, N.J.: National Council on Crime and Delinquency, 1976), p. 42. See also Paul Gendreau and Bob Ross, "Effective correctional treatment: bibliotherapy for cynics." *Crime and Delinquency* 25 (October 1979), pp. 463–489; Halleck and Witte, "Is rehabilitation dead?"; Michael R. Gottfredson, "Treatment destruction techniques." *Journal of Research in Crime and Delinquency* 16 (January 1979), pp. 39–54; Robert R. Ross and H. Bryan McKay, "Behavioral approaches to treatment in corrections: requiem for a panacea." Pp. 694–710 in Sheldon L. Messinger and Egon Bittner (eds.), *Criminology Review Yearbook, Volume I.* (Beverly Hills: Sage, 1979); Roger Hood and Richard Sparks, *Key Issues in Criminology.* (New York World University Library, 1970), p. 191; Carl Klockars, "The true limits of *The Effectiveness of Correctional Treatment.*" *Prison Journal* 55 (Spring-Summer 1975), pp. 53–64.

[71]Halleck and Witte, "Is rehabilitation dead?, p. 376; Lois Shawver and Bruce Sanders, "A look at four critical premises in correctional views." *Crime and Delinquency* 23 (October 1977), p. 432; Leonard J. Hippchen, "Can corrections correct?" Pp. 405–421 in R. G. Iacovetta and Dae H. Chang (eds.), *Critical Issues in Criminal Justice.* (Durham, N.C.: Carolina Academic Press, 1979), pp. 408–409.

[72]Charles A. Murray and Louis A. Cox, Jr., *Beyond Probation: Juvenile Corrections and the Chronic Delinquent.* (Beverly Hills: Sage, 1979); Halleck and Witte, "Is rehabilitation dead?" pp. 375–376; Panel on Research on Rehabilitative Techniques, *The Rehabilitation of Criminal Offenders: Problems and Prospects.* (Washington, D.C.: National Academy of Sciences, 1979), p. 32.

[73]Robert Martinson, "New findings, new views: a note of caution regarding sentencing reform." *Hofstra Law Review* 7 (Winter 1979), pp. 244, 252. See also Paul Gendreau and Robert Ross, "Offender rehabilitation: the appeal of success." *Federal Probation* 45 (December 1981), pp. 45–48.

[74]Ernest N. Steels, Jr. and Jerry Evans, "The thin line: retribution or rehabilitation?" Pamphlet. (New York: Prison Advisory Board, 1977), pp. 10–11.

[75]Panel on Research on Rehabilitative Techniques, *The Rehabilitation of Criminal Offenders*, p. 40. See also Gendreau and Ross, "Effective correctional treatment," p. 467; Reid, "A rebuttal to the attack on the indeterminate sentence," pp. 604–605; David A. Ward, "Evaluative research for corrections." Pp. 184–206 in Lloyd E. Ohlin (ed.), *Prisoners in America.* (Englewood Cliffs, N.J.: Prentice Hall, 1973), p. 187.

[76]Joan Petersilia, "Which inmates participate in prison treatment programs?" *Journal of Offender Counseling, Services and Rehabilitation* 4 (Winter 1980), p. 121.

[77]*The Rehabilitation of Criminal Offenders*, p. 35.

[78]Ibid., pp. 102−103.

[79]Further, a large percentage of those who "recidivate" are returned to prison not for new violations but for violations of their parole. See David Greenberg, "The incapacitative effect of imprisonment: some estimates." Pp. 362−372 in Peter Wickman and Phillip Whitten (eds.), *Readings in Criminology*. (Lexington, Ma.: D.C. Heath, 1978); Robert Martinson, "In my opinion." *Corrections Magazine* 2 (December 1976), p. i and "New findings, new views: a note of caution regarding sentencing reform," p. 252; Clarence Schrag, "Rediscovering punitive justice," pp. 465−466.

[80]Douglas Lipton, Robert Martinson, and Judith Wilks, *The Effectiveness of Correctional Treatment: A Survey of Treatment Evaluation Studies*. (New York: Praeger, 1975), pp. 532−558.

[81]Robert Martinson, "Evaluation in crisis—a postscript." Pp. 93−96 in Martinson et al., *Rehabilitation, Recidivism, and Research*, p. 94.

[82]Quoted in Silberman, *Criminal Violence, Criminal Justice*, p. 380.

[83]As Silberman, ibid., p. 380 has noted, "According to estimates for the country as a whole, intra-inmate homicides more than tripled in a decade, from an annual average of 40 in 1964−65 to 120−130 in 1974−75." See also, Hans Toch, *Living in Prison: The Ecology of Survival*. (New York: The Free Press, 1977), pp. 141−178; Lee H. Bowker, *Prison Victimization*. (New York: Elsevier, 1980); Daniel Lockwood, *Prison Sexual Violence*. (New York: Elsevier, 1980); Clemens Bartollas, Stuart J. Miller, and Simon Dinitz, *Juvenile Victimization: The Institutional Paradox*. (New York: John Wiley, 1976).

[84]Silberman, *Criminal Violence, Criminal Justice*, pp. 380−381; David C. Anderson, "The price of safety: 'I can't go back out there.'" *Corrections Magazine* 4 (August 1980), pp. 7−15.

[85]Hicks, *The Corrections Yearbook*, p. 32.

[86]New York State Bar Association, *Report of Subcommittee of Criminal Justice Section Committee on the Correctional System*, p. 13.

[87]Gordon Hawkins, *The Prison: Policy and Practice*. (Chicago: University of Chicago Press, 1976), p. 46.

[88]Gresham M. Sykes, *Society of Captives: A Study of a Maximum Security Prison*. (Princeton, N.J.: Princeton University Press 1958), pp. 51−52.

[89]John Howard Association, "Stateville revisited," p. 12.

[90]Ibid., p. 12.

[91]Patrick D. McAnany, Frank S. Merritt, and Edward Tromanhauser, "Illinois reconsiders 'flat time': an analysis of the impact of the justice model." *Chicago-Kent Law Review* 52 (No. 3, 1976), pp. 655−656.

[92]Quoted in Kolman, "Crime and punishment in Illinois," p. 31.

[93]Carol B. Kalish, "Prisoners at midyear 1981." *Bureau of Justice Statistics Bulletin*. (Washington, D.C.: Bureau of Justice Statistics, 1981). See also and compare with Jerrold

K. Footlick, "Lock 'em up—but where?" *Newsweek* (March 23, 1981), p. 54; Krajick, "The boom resumes."

[94]Mullen, *American Prisons and Jails, Volume I*, pp. 98−99.

[95]Mullen and Smith, *American Prisons and Jails, Volume III*, p. 146.

[96]For instance, see our discussion in Chapter 6 of the problems surrounding the "early release" program developed in Illinois to deal with severe overcrowding in the state's prisons.

[97]Quoted in Kolman, "Crime and punishment in Illinois," p. 31.

[98]Davis S. Robinson, "Tough sentencing straining prisons here . . . and in Indiana, where the 'new lifers' are taking over." *Chicago Sun Times* (July 19, 1981), p. 4, section 2— "Views."

[99]Glick, "Mandatory sentencing," pp. 3, 8.

[100]Allen, *The Decline of the Rehabilitative Ideal*, pp. 30−31.

[101]David J. Rothman, "The state as parent: social policy in the Progressive era." Pp. 67−96 in W. Gaylin, I. Glasser, S. Marcus, and D. Rothman, *Doing Good: The Limits of Benevolence.* (New York: Pantheon Books, 1978), p. 94.

[102]Gendreau and Ross, "Effective correctional treatment," pp. 488−489.

[103]John R. Lee, "Letter from an inmate." *Corrections Magazine* 3 (September 1977), p. 24.

[104]Cullen, et al., "The punishment-rehabilitation controversy: insider and outsider perspectives."

[105]Hans Toch, *Living In Prison: The Ecology of Survival.* (New York: The Free Press, 1977), pp. 4, 243—see Table 12−5).

[106]Hawkins, *The Prison*, p. 77.

[107]Quoted in Michael S. Serrill, "Washington's new juvenile code." *Corrections Magazine* 6 (February 1980), p. 41.

[108]LaMar Empey, "Foreword—from optimism to despair: new doctrines in juvenile justice." Pp. 9−26 in Charles A. Murray and Louis A. Cox, Jr., *Beyond Probation: Juvenile Corrections and the Chronic Delinquent* (Beverly Hills, Ca.: Sage, 1979), p. 24.

[109]Rothman, "The state as parent," p. 94.

[110]Silberman, *Criminal Violence, Criminal Justice*, p. 261 and, more generally, pp. 253−308. See also Daniel Glaser's discussion of "does crime pay?" in which he has concluded that "although their high success rates mean that property offenders 'get away with' most of their crimes, the notion that this permits most of them to support themselves for years with impunity is an illusion . . . The small net income to criminals from separate index offenses, however, makes much repetition of a crime necessary for self-support . . . Thus, those who expect to live by these crimes are usually not long free." *Crime in Our Changing Society.* (New York: Holt, Rinehart and Winston, 1978), p. 97.

[111]Silberman, *Criminal Violence, Criminal Justice*, p. 285.

[112]Krajick, "The boom resumes," p. 16.

[113]Margaret Cahalan. "Trends in incarceration in the United States since 1880: a summary of reported rates and the distribution of offenses." *Crime and Delinquency* 25 (January 1979), p. 21.

[114]Eugene Doleschal, "Crime—some popular beliefs." *Crime and Delinquency* 25 (January 1979), p. 4. See also Doleschal's "Rate and length of imprisonment: how does the United States compare with The Netherlands, Denmark, and Sweden?" *Crime and Delinquency* 23 (January 1977), pp. 51−56. Also, see "Proportion of prisoners per 10,000 population." *Corrections Compendium* 7 (February-March 1978), p. 12.

[115]FBI, *Uniform Crime Reports: Crime in the United States, 1979.* (Washington, D.C.: U.S. Government Printing Office, 1980), p. 179. See also the early work of Courtlandt C. Van Vechten, "Differential criminal case mortality in selected jurisdictions." *American Sociological Review* 7 (December 1942), pp. 833−839. Also of note is the observation of George Bernard Shaw in *The Crime of Imprisonment.* (New York: The Philosophical Library, 1946), p. 36, that "there is no better established rule of criminology than that it is not the severity of punishment that deters but its certainty. And the flaw . . . is that it is impossible to obtain enough certainty to deter. The police are compelled to confess each year, when they publish their statistics, that against the list of crimes reported to them they can set only a percentage of detections and convictions."

[116]Barnes, *The Story of Punishment*, p. 6.

[117]Nagel, "On behalf of a moratorium on prison construction."

[118]Mark A. Peterson, Harriet B. Braiker with Suzanne M. Polich, *Doing Crime: A Survey of California Prison Inmates.* (Santa Monica, Ca.: Rand, 1980). p. xii.

[119]Panel on Research on Deterrent and Incapacitative Effects, *Deterrence and Incapacitation: Estimating the Effects of Criminal Sanctions and Crime Rates.* (Washington, D.C.: National Academy of Sciences, 1978), p. 47.

[120]Diana R. Gordon, "Being tough doesn't work because . . . being lenient was never the problem." *Fortune News* (April-May, 1981), p. 7.

[121]Schrag, "Rediscovering punitive justice," pp. 465−466.

[122]Steve van Dine, John P. Conrad, and Simon Dinitz, "The incapacitation of the chronic thug." *Journal of Criminal Law and Criminology* 70 (Spring 1979), p. 135.

[123]Stevens H. Clarke, "Getting 'em out of circulation: does incarceration of juvenile offenders reduce crime?" *Journal of Criminal Law and Criminology* 65 (December 1974), p. 535.

[124]David F. Greenberg, "The incapacitative effect of imprisonment: some estimates." Pp. 363−372 in Peter Wickman and Phillip Whitten (eds.), *Readings in Criminology.* (Lexington, Ma.: D.C. Heath, 1978), p. 364.

[125]Gordon, "Getting tough doesn't work . . . because being lenient was never the problem," p. 7.

[126]Greenberg, "The incapacitative effect of imprisonment," p. 369.

[127]Empey, "Foreword—from optimism to despair," pp. 23−24.

Implementing the Justice Model: Problems and Prospects

Perhaps the most significant indicator of the waning faith in the rehabilitative model has been the shift toward determinate sentencing in a number of states. The current skepticism about our ability to effectively treat the criminal offender, as we have seen, is shared by conservatives and liberals alike. Thus, the movement to abandon the indeterminate sentence (a sentencing system which has been intimately associated with the rehabilitative model) and to focus instead on punishment and retribution as the primary ends of the criminal sanction has received broad-based support across the political spectrum. The speed with which determinate sentencing has taken hold across the country is surely not unrelated to this widespread political support, and to the relative absence of defenders of the rehabilitative ideal on the other hand.

Given the almost universally-perceived need for criminal justice reform, determinate sentencing would seem to offer something for everyone. However, this initial appeal has masked the more specific and mutually exclusive ends espoused by liberal and conservative champions of sentencing reform. Liberal justice model supporters, for example, have sought to curb the state's control over its offenders by reducing and regulating the unbridled discretion within the criminal justice system and by equalizing the sanctions meted out for similar offenses. Conversely, conservatives have looked upon the determinate penalty structure as a means of ensuring greater societal protection by increasing the certainty of punishment and by curtailing the power of judges and parole boards to release offenders prematurely. Moreover, justice model proponents have strongly advocated short sentences and the proliferation of alternatives to imprisonment, whereas conservatives have been convinced that longer prison terms are integral to the reduction of the crime problem. In the end, one reality has thus become clear: the "bare bones" of determinacy and desert are as easily adaptable to a program of "getting tough on crime" as to one of "doing justice."

In this light, it can again be noted that the crucial issue to be resolved is whether determinate sentencing reform will ultimately take on a conservative or liberal flavor. That is, can liberals realistically anticipate that their justice model will emerge from the political arena unscathed and serve as the blueprint for a new era of American criminal justice? Or, after battling with conservative forces in state legislatures, is it more likely that the left will suffer, at the very least, partial defeat and see only portions of its paradigm for justice

Reaffirming Rehabilitation. DOI: http://dx.doi.org/10.1016/B978-1-4557-3130-5.00006-4

written into law? This latter consideration assumes much significance when one realizes that justice model proponents have presented their strategies for reform as a comprehensive, internally consistent program which cannot readily be implemented on a piecemeal basis. Doing justice requires, in short, that the whole of the model be put into place. Thus, the Working Party of the American Friends Service Committee has stated that:

> The point bears emphasizing that the components of an alternative system tend to be of a piece. They cannot easily be implemented piecemeal. Fixed and uniform sentences imposed by the legislature, for example, would contribute little toward the elimination of discrimination and inequity unless the discretionary powers of police and prosecutors were curbed at the same time. The capacity of one part of the criminal justice system to negate reforms affecting only other parts of the system is considerable.[1]

In a similar plea for comprehensive and integrated reforms, Gaylin and Rothman have warned that "to abandon the rehabilitative model without a simultaneous gradation downward in prison sentences would be an unthinkable cruelty and a dangerous act."[2]

In the previous chapter, we endeavored to illuminate a variety of areas in which the benevolent intentions of justice model advocates are particularly vulnerable to corruption should determinate sentencing become the reform agenda of the left in the years ahead. Below, an effort is undertaken to investigate whether the hopes of the liberal proponents of just deserts have been realized in the fixed-term legislation that has appeared in recent times. The major conclusion derived from this review is that liberal support for retribution-based determinate sentencing systems has resulted not only in sentencing reforms which have fallen far short of justice model goals, but also in laws which typically afford little more if not less "justice" than those laws they have replaced. In many states, processes of legislative compromise among the various advocates of determinacy have fundamentally subverted justice model principles and have helped to bring about the very sort of piecemeal reform so decried by the proponents of the justice model. With Greenberg and Humphries, we argue as well that the "vocabulary of just deserts" has been utilized by conservatives to support their own legislative agenda.[3] Further, the conservative message has had a particularly forceful appeal in the "nothing works" and "get tough on crime" climate of the 1970s and 1980s. It now seems difficult to dispute, we believe, that the new sentencing legislation is typically far more conservative than liberal in its central features.

The strategy to be employed in this chapter will be to examine the content of determinate sentencing laws in a number of states in relation to the major tenets of the liberals' justice model. This will allow us to determine the extent to which justice model principles are reflected in the structure of the new sentencing statutes. Also, we will trace the legislative history of the determinate sentencing bill in one state (Illinois) to illustrate the political processes which may undermine liberal efforts to operationalize "justice." Further, we will seek to assess the functioning and impact of these laws on such crucial variables as type and length of sentences given and served, size of prison populations, sentence disparity, and patterns of discretion within the criminal justice and correctional systems.

In order to facilitate this task, it would perhaps prove helpful to review the core parameters of the justice model. First, punishment is for the purpose of retribution and is based on considerations of desert. Desert, in turn, is determined by the harmfulness of the criminal act as well as offender culpability. An individual's prospects for rehabilitation should not control his/her punishment, nor should participation in prison treatment programs affect length of sentence. Such goals of punishment as deterrence and incapacitation clearly play only a secondary role (if any) in sentencing. Second, prison sentences should be determinate in nature. If a range of sentences is provided for each offense or category of offenses, this range should be a narrow one. Possible circumstances in aggravation and mitigation of the penalties should be spelled out in the law; these circumstances should normally reflect conditions affecting desert. The amount of acceptable departure from the usual sentence should also be specified. Thus, the penalty is fixed at the time of sentencing; parole boards lose their power to determine duration of sentence. Third, prison sentences should generally be short, and are to be employed only for the most serious offenses. Alternatives to incarceration should be utilized for less serious offenses/offenders. Penalties are to be proportionate to the social harm engendered by the offense. Fourth, similar punishments should be given for similar offenses. Conversely, crimes of differing levels of seriousness should receive different penalties. Hence, more serious offenses will ordinarily receive heavier penalties than will less serious offenses. Fifth, discretion in the criminal justice and correctional systems should be reduced, made visible, and regulated. This includes that of the prosecutor, judge, institutional officials, and parole board. Sixth, voluntary involvement in rehabilitative programs is acceptable. Prisons should provide treatment programs for those who wish to utilize them, but inmates should neither be rewarded for participation nor punished for non-participation. Seventh, the granting of good time as a means of encouraging conforming behavior in prison is approved. Clear criteria and procedures should be established for the awarding and revocation of good time credit. Good time, once earned, should "vest" on a regular basis. And finally, the rights of inmates should be protected from abuse in prison. Programs of inmate self-governance are to be encouraged as well.

It must also be emphasized at the outset of this analysis of current state sentencing laws that the forms determinate sentencing may take are diverse.

For example, Cavender and Musheno have categorized determinate sentencing laws into four general varieties:

1. *Presumptive*, in which the legislature establishes a specific term to be given for each offense, but also specifies an acceptable range from which a term may be selected given the presence of aggravating or mitigating factors.

2. *Definite*, in which the legislature provides a range of sentences for each offense from which the judge selects a particular fixed penalty.

3. *Guidelines*, in which some agency other than the legislature (usually a sentencing commission or parole board) establishes specific offender and offense criteria to determine appropriate sentence length. In the case of sentencing guidelines employing a determinate model, the guidelines could theoretically reflect either a presumptive or definite format; however, these guidelines are usually defined as advisory in nature. Parole guidelines, on the other hand, retain for the parole board its traditional role in determining sentence

length; but criteria for this decision are detailed and specific, and the offender learns his planned release date early in his term.

4. *Mandatory sentences*, in which the legislature establishes fixed penalties or mandatory minimum penalties for a given offense or category of offense.[4]

Each of these types will be discussed in the course of our analysis. By the same token, important and striking variations can be found in the intent and specific features of state sentencing laws of the same general variety (e.g., presumptive). Moreover, political processes surrounding the development and modification of determinate sentencing laws within a given state may produce significant differences in the characteristics of earlier and later versions of the law, often in the direction of more severity. It is in order to illustrate this last point that we now turn to a brief discussion of the evolution of the determinate sentencing law in Illinois.

THE PROCESS OF SENTENCING REFORM IN ILLINOIS

It is interesting to note that the original proposal for sentencing reform in Illinois was drafted by David Fogel, then the director of the Illinois Law Enforcement Commission under Governor Walker's administration.[5] This proposed legislation attempted to put a number of "justice model" principles into effect. It featured flat sentences (with relatively small ranges of flexibility to allow for aggravating and mitigating circumstances) as a replacement for the wide ranges and indeterminacy of the law then in effect. The flat sentences were intended to represent actual average time then served by offenders in Illinois, rather than to constitute a radical departure from past sentence lengths. Another important aspect of the proposal was the notion of day-for-day good time, thereby in effect halving the sentence of the conforming inmate. Fogel's proposal was introduced in the Illinois Senate in April, 1976 where it never emerged from committee.

At the same time, a subcommittee of the Illinois House Judiciary Committee II was reviewing current sentencing practices. A report by the subcommittee set forth a proposal of its own for sentencing reform, and a number of its conclusions paralleled Fogel's. The disparity and arbitrariness of the current sentencing system were decried, and determinate sentencing was proposed as an alternative. The recommendations of the subcommittee featured a range of years for each class of crimes within which a specific number of years was to be selected (the ranges in this proposal were similar to Fogel's, although somewhat wider for Class 1—the most serious—felonies, and slightly wider for Class 2 and 3 felonies). Following committee hearings, modifications were made in the proposal: the ranges of terms for murder and Class 1 felonies were substantially expanded and in the direction of more severity while the ranges of terms for Class 2 and Class 3 felonies were reduced by raising the minimum terms by one year. This amended proposal ultimately was introduced into the Illinois House as HB 1500 in March of 1977.

Meanwhile James Thompson, the newly-elected governor of Illinois, lent his support to a bill introduced in the Illinois Senate in April of 1977 which became identified as "Class X." The intent of Class X was to "get tough on crime" by singling out certain former Class 1 crimes (now to be called Class X crimes) for particularly severe terms without possibility of probation. The Class X proposal in its original form was not a determinate sentencing measure; in fact, most of its major propositions had little in common with the justice model.

Ultimately, the HB 1500 and the "Class X" forces struck a compromise in which a number of the Class X provisions was grafted on to HB 1500. Thus, the new law that took effect on February 1, 1978 was an uneasy juxtaposition of determinacy and attempts to reduce sentence disparity with a crackdown on crime featuring wide ranges of terms for the most serious crimes and the potential for increased punishment for these crimes. Table 6.1 points up the important differences in penalties between the original Fogel proposal and the penalties which were enacted as part of the new sentencing law. It is clear that Fogel's hopes for a code that would be characterized by moderation in penalties and severely constrained judicial discretion have not been realized. Getting tough, more than dealing offenders a fair hand, was the agenda in Illinois.

Even once passed, determinate sentencing laws are, of course, far from immune from a kind of "eraser justice,"[6] in which legislators simply scratch out the sentences set forth in the first version of the criminal code and pencil in more stringent prison terms. California presents an instructive illustration of this disquieting possibility. Since the original determinate sentencing law was passed in California in 1976, it has experienced several modifications, all instituted under the auspices of "getting tough" with crime. The passage of SB 42 (the initial determinate sentencing bill) was supported by liberal prison reform groups as an alternative to the injustices involved in indeterminacy; a major objective was to curtail the discretion of judges and parole boards to determine sentence lengths. However, subsequent revisions of the law have had the effect of increasing both discretion and the severity of the penalty structure. Thus, AB 476 (the Boatwright Amendment) passed just prior to the July 1, 1977 implementation of determinate sentencing in California, among its other provisions, had the effect of expanding the amount of time which could be added on to the

Table 6.1 Comparison Between Fogel's Justice Model Proposals and Illinois' New Sentencing Law

Class of Crime	Justice Model	New Law
Murder	25 years or life (20-30 years)	20-40 years or natural life
Class X felonies	[no Class X Crimes—these would be Class 1 in Fogel's model]	6-30 years
Class 1 felonies	8 years (6-10 years)	4-15 years
Class 2 felonies	5 years (3-7 years)	3-7 years
Class 3 felonies	3 years (2-4 years)	2-5 years
Class 4 felonies	2 years (1-3 years)	1-3 years

Note: Fogel's proposal featured flat terms; however, any definite sentence within the permissible range could be chosen to reflect the weight of aggravating or mitigating factors. The new Illinois law lists only the appropriate range from which a determinate term is to be selected, and gives no specific "point of departure" for choosing a particular sentence within the range.

base terms as "enhancements" for many offenses. It is important to note that the support for AB 476 came largely from judges, prosecutors, and correctional officials. SB 709, passed in 1978 as an amendment to the determinate sentencing law with the backing of law enforcement groups, increased the middle and upper base penalties for a number of violent crimes. Also passed in 1978 was SB 1057, which raised the period of parole from one to three years in most cases; this change was strongly advocated by correctional authorities. Legislative changes in the 1979 session included measures to heighten penalties for rape, other sex offenses, and arson. The net effect of these legislative changes has been in the opposite direction from the original bill, which sought to reduce unwarranted discretion and to hold penalties at the levels then prevalent under the indeterminate structure. These later amendments have moved in the direction of enhanced discretion for prosecutors and judges as well as harsher penalties for crimes.[7]

To understand more fully the structure and dynamics of determinate sentencing laws, however, it is necessary to investigate the goals behind these reforms. It is to this task that we next turn.

THE GOALS OF SENTENCING REFORM

Analysts of the sentencing reforms of the last few years have generally argued that punishment has supplanted rehabilitation as the primary goal of criminal sentencing.[8] Retributive justifications for sentencing may be particularly attractive to state legislatures in that, first, retributive systems are less subject to charges of ineffectiveness than are utilitarian goals such as rehabilitation, deterrence, and incapacitation—in a sense, a retribution-based system legitimates promising (and getting) less from our criminal justice system. Second, systems designed to punish may raise (or lower) the amounts of punishment without violating the assumptions of the retributive model, in that the "social harm" of an act or acts is socially defined. The issue becomes not whether or not punishment is appropriate as the guiding principle of sentencing, but merely a matter of degree.

At the same time, however, it would seem that the utilitarian goals of sanctioning have not been completely abandoned in many of the new laws. For example, Illinois cites as one of the goals of its Code of Corrections to "forbid and prevent the commission of offenses." Similarly, the New Jersey Code of Criminal Justice cites deterrence and "public protection" among its purposes. And criticism of the efficacy of rehabilitation notwithstanding, both codes cite rehabilitation as an aim of sanctioning.[9]

So it is that the stated goals of proportionate punishment, individualized handling, deterrence, incapacitation, and rehabilitation continue to co-exist in many states. Given that these diverse aims are not integrated into any logical and coherent scheme which distinguishes priorities among goals, we should not be surprised that determinate sentencing seems on its face to promise "something for everyone."

It is instructive to look at the ways in which these utilitarian goals are manifested in the new laws.

UTILITARIAN CONSIDERATIONS IN SENTENCING

It is not always possible to distinguish the intended deterrent features of the new laws from the incapacitative ones. "Common sense" notions of deterrence usually involve increasing penalties for offenses (it is not clear whether or not most legislators adopt the common sense view), although since the days of the utilitarians it has been contended that certainty is more crucial than severity of punishment to a deterrent effect.[10] However, it cannot be assumed that greater certainty of punishment is achieved by the new reforms, in light of the lack of input into prosecutorial decision-making, relative absence of standards to guide the probation versus prison decision, and wide ranges of possible sentences that are characteristic of many of the new state laws.

The new statutes take diverse approaches to the overall severity of the law. For example, the original sentencing proposal for California built its determinate penalty system around the average terms served for each class of crime under the former indeterminate law[11] (although, as we have noted, subsequent amendments to the law have moved in the direction of somewhat more severity for certain crimes). Illinois's early legislative proposals also focused on average terms served under the indeterminate law of that state, although the law as passed featured more severe penalties for the most serious crimes.[12] The Indiana law, on the other hand, had the goal of stepping up penalties for serious crimes from previous levels.[13] Thus, states like Illinois, Indiana, and New Mexico feature extremely high maximum terms for the most serious categories of crimes.

Further, a number of the new laws include the possibility of stiff enhancements in penalties for violent criminals or repeat offenders. The application of some of these enhancements is discretionary with the sentencing judge; others are mandatory. For example, mandatory enhancements of various lengths are prescribed in New Mexico for such circumstances as use of a firearm in the commission of a felony, intentional injury to a person 60 or over during commission of a felony, and for repeat offenders.[14] In Indiana, conviction on a third (unrelated) felony mandates an addition of thirty years to the term given for the third offense; similarly, in Illinois, upon conviction of a third Class 2 or above felony sentencing as a Class X offender is mandated, and a sentence of natural life must follow a third conviction for a Class X crime.[15] Colorado mandates a 25-year minimum term upon a third felony conviction, and life imprisonment following a fourth felony conviction.[16]

Other enhanced or extended terms may be imposed at the sentencing judge's discretion. For example, both Arizona and Illinois allow substantial enhancements for a second (or subsequent) felony conviction within ten years of the first.[17] A number of determinate states also allow enhanced terms for such situations as use of a firearm or an exceptionally brutal crime.

Mandatory sentences are an increasingly frequent feature of state codes in both determinate and indeterminate states. In 1979 alone, eighteen states passed some form of mandatory sentencing legislation.[18] This legislation can take a variety of forms: requiring at least a minimum term of imprisonment for certain serious offenses, requiring a specific term added on to a base term for a violent or repeat offender, or dictating mandatory life terms for habitual, serious offenders. Mandatory sentencing can be viewed as primarily a deterrent and incapacitative strategy (although not without elements of desert), particularly when mandatory enhancements represent large increases over the base penalties. However, the value of incapacitation in reducing crime in these instances may be less than expected because of the application of these statutes to limited categories of offenders; further, large increases in prison populations (already bursting at the seams) are likely to bring about only modest incapacitative effects.[19]

The utilitarian ends of the new sentencing laws are also readily apparent in the aggravating and mitigating factors which are specified in these codes. The presence of aggravating or mitigating factors usually allows the judge to sentence at the higher or lower end of the sentencing range respectively. While many of the factors listed in state statutes are related to considerations of desert (e.g., nature of the offense, prior record of the offender, harm to the victim, provocation by the victim) a number of others are related to other ends of punishment. For example, the need for deterring others is mentioned as an aggravating factor in the Illinois and New Jersey codes. Further, the New Jersey statutes list the risk of the offender committing another offense as an aggravating factor, while the Colorado code expressly states that the potential for future criminality of the offender (unless this determination is based on prior criminal conduct) should not be a consideration in setting the length of sentence.[20] On the other hand, the Illinois, New Jersey, and Indiana laws all include the unlikelihood of further criminality of the offender as a factor in mitigation of the penalty. In addition, New Jersey and Indiana each included a rehabilitation-related factor in their codes: New Jersey law mentions the potential for success on probation as a mitigating factor whereas Indiana lists an individual's need for rehabilitation which can best be given in a prison environment as a factor in aggravation.[21] It is also noteworthy that a number of determinate sentencing states list no specific aggravating or mitigating factors at all, thereby leaving judges relatively free to employ their own set of factors in the sentencing decision. Even in states which do specify important factors, judges may be free to consider "any other such factors ... that are consistent with the purposes and principles of sentencing"[22] as stated in the code; thus, concerns other than desert may affect judicial decisions.

Interestingly, the awarding of institutional "good time" in several states is in part dependent on participation in treatment programs, despite the tenet of the justice model that length of sentence should be unrelated to participation (or non-participation) in prison programs of rehabilitation. For example, both California and Colorado, while awarding the largest amount of their good time for good behavior in prison, reserve an additional amount which can be earned by involvement in prison programs. In addition, California law specifies that some good time can also be lost for "failure to participate."[23] And in Arizona, good time can only be earned by those in Class 1 parole eligibility: that is, those individuals who observe prison rules and "voluntarily" participate in prison programs.[24]

In sum, it is apparent that the liberal goal of doing justice has been at best a subsidiary concern for legislators fashioning determinate sentencing codes. Instead, lawmakers have brought about sentencing reforms which evidence little ideological integrity. Thus, determinate sentencing becomes a way of reassuring the public that something is indeed being done about crime as much as a method of reducing unfairness in sentencing. High maximum penalties and substantial increases in penalties for repeat offenders in many states clearly violate justice model principles regarding desert as the major determinant of punishment. The significant role of utilitarian considerations in these laws is all the more ominous because they are nested within reforms which have as stated goals "justice" and "fairness."

EFFECTS ON DISCRETION AND DISPARITY

As we have seen, one of the central goals of the justice model is the equalization of penalties for individuals committing similar offenses. To this end, discretion throughout the criminal justice system is to be both narrowed and made subject to regulation. Thus, the wide ranges of possible penalties for a given offense that were characteristic of indeterminate sentencing statutes should be substantially reduced. Judges should be provided with a set of appropriate criteria which are to be considered in the selection of a particular sentence within the narrow range; other factors such as race, gender, and social class should not affect the sentencing decision. The sentence set by the judge should be the sentence served (less good time, if any). Hence, parole boards no longer determine the actual length of sentence, as was the case in indeterminate models. The need for regulation of prosecutorial discretion is also stressed by a number of justice model proponents; however, specific plans for accomplishing this task are conspicuous by their absence in "just deserts" tracts. The discretion of institutional officials is also to be curtailed. Prison disciplinary actions and revocation of good time credits should be subject to clear rules and procedures which allow a fair hearing for inmates.

In order to evaluate the impact of determinate sentencing laws on discretion and disparity throughout the criminal justice and correctional systems, we will look at the effects of the laws on the general areas of sentencing, parole and institutional decision-making, and prosecutorial discretion in the light of the objectives discussed above. If the new determinate sentencing laws are to qualify from a liberal perspective as true reforms, we should expect dramatic improvements in the direction of less arbitrary and more equitable handling of offenders.

DISCRETION IN SENTENCING

The potential for sentence disparity is increased, first of all, if the range of possible sentences for a given category of offenses is wide. A number of state statutes include wide ranges from which a determinate term is to be selected; an extreme example is Maine, where only the maximum term for each offense is set in the statute.[25] Illinois features a 24-year range for Class X felonies and an 11-year range for Class 1 felonies, and these ranges can be increased substantially under the "extended term" provisions of the law.[26] Similarly, the Indiana code provides 30-year ranges for murder and Class A (the most serious) felonies, as well as a 14-year range for Class B felonies.[27] On the opposite extreme, California specifies a range of three years for some offense categories.[28] It is important to note as well that the Illinois and Maine codes in particular are also characterized by substantial overlaps of range across different offense categories. These overlaps are a violation of the principle of proportionality in that more serious offenses can conceivably receive penalties that are equal to or even less than those given for less serious offenses in these schemes.

States also vary with respect to the amount of discretion the judge possesses to locate a sentence within a particular range. In states such as California, New Jersey, Indiana, and Arizona a presumptive term is specified, whereas in states like Maine and Illinois judges are given no such point of reference. While most determinate-sentencing states specify aggravating and mitigating factors which are to aid the judge in sentencing within the permissible range (Maine is a prominent exception), most of these laws do not provide specific guidance as to how much to depart from the presumptive term or the midpoint of the range when certain factors are present. Further, factors in aggravation and mitigation are typically not limited to those spelled out in the code, thereby allowing the judge to consider virtually any factors which (s)he considers to be important.

A number of the determinate sentencing states afford judges the opportunity to sentence outside the normal range. Thus, whether or not to sentence an offender to an enhanced or extended term is a decision which frequently rests with the judiciary. In addition, Colorado allows the judge to impose a sentence outside the presumptive range for "extraordinary" aggravating or mitigating circumstances; this sentence can be up to twice the maximum or as low as one-half the minimum term in the presumptive range.[29] And both New Jersey and Indiana permit the judge to sentence an offender to a penalty one class lower than the actual offense under certain conditions.[30]

Another prominent source of potential disparity is the prison-nonprison decision. Generally, determinate sentencing laws to date have provided few clear guidelines to judges to regulate this in-out decision. Most of these states do list certain offenses for which probation is not to be given; a number of others rule out probation for certain violent or repeat offenders. Illinois, after excepting certain offenses, states that a presumption of probation shall obtain unless imprisonment is necessary for protection of the public, or unless probation would deprecate the seriousness of the crime.[31] New Jersey, on the other hand, includes a presumption of imprisonment for crimes of the first or second degree, and a presumption of non-imprisonment for first offenders in the other offense categories.[32] The aggravating and mitigating factors listed in most state codes are to be used not only to determine sentence length but also to determine whether or not to imprison. However, the codes are generally silent as to how these factors should be weighed in the in-out decision.

In light of the potential for disparity evident in a number of the determinate sentencing states, it is important that there be available some mechanism for appellate review of sentencing decisions. Illinois and New Jersey both provide for sentence appeals in all cases, although Illinois applies a rebuttable presumption that the sentence is appropriate, and the sentence can be either raised or lowered on appeal.[33] Colorado allows for appeal of a sentence which is outside the normal presumptive range.[34] A number of other state codes are silent on the topic of sentence appeals, although Maine and California do provide for review by state administrative boards;[35] however, it is unclear as to how much power these boards have in obtaining a revision of the penalty from the sentencing court.

A crucial test of the new statutes with respect to the issue of sentencing parity is to assess whether or not the determinate sentencing laws substantially have reduced disparity over the indeterminate systems they replaced. While evaluative studies on the impact of determinate sentencing laws are scarce, some preliminary information on a limited number of states is available.

Hussey and Lagoy compared the statutory sentencing ranges of the indeterminate and determinate codes in the states of Maine, California, Indiana, Illinois, and Arizona for selected offenses. They found determinate sentencing ranges to be narrower than previous indeterminate ranges in 73% of the offense comparisons, whereas ranges were wider in 24% of the comparisons.[36] But it should be noted that the basis of comparison here was the statutory ranges and not the ranges of sentences actually imposed; it must be remembered that disparity in practice may vary substantially from disparity in theory. Also, Hussey and Lagoy only studied statutory sentencing ranges for first offenders, thereby omitting one of the greatest possible sources of disparity in the new codes: the stiff increases in penalties generally available for repeat offenders.

Preliminary analyses of the impact of determinate sentencing laws in California[37] and Indiana[38] (based on estimates of time to be served rather than time actually served under determinate sentencing) indicate that disparity of sentences may be reduced somewhat under the new codes in these states. In the case of California this should not be particularly surprising, as that state moved from a very highly indeterminate system with extremely broad statutory ranges to a narrow range of determinate terms. And to the extent that the assumptions concerning the amount of good time credit likely to be gained may be erroneous, estimates of time served may not be a reliable indicator of actual sentence lengths.

PAROLE BOARD AND INSTITUTIONAL DISCRETION

Determinate sentencing states vary greatly with respect to the role of the parole board in sentencing. In states like Arizona and Oregon, for example, the parole board still, in effect, determines the actual length of sentence to be served. In a number of other states like California, Illinois, Indiana, and Colorado, parole boards no longer determine the duration of imprisonment, but a period of supervision in the community follows the prison term. Maine, on the other hand, has abolished parole entirely.[39]

Since parole boards have, for the most part, lost their sentencing role in determinate states, institutional officials have gained increased power through their discretion over "good time." In states with good time, the rate at which it can be accumulated, provisions for "vesting" of good time (if any), and the maximum amount which can be taken away per offense or per period are frequently set by statute. Often, institutional officials are left free to establish rules and procedures for revocation, and, of course, to carry out policy on a continuing basis.

Although the impact of determinate sentencing laws on disparity at the institutional stage has barely begun to be evaluated, some insights may be gained from an overview of the Illinois experience.

Illinois, as was previously noted, no longer relies on a state parole board to fix the duration of prison sentence. Inmates are no longer subject to parole; however, a term of supervised release (more or less indistinguishable from parole supervision, except that the supervised release term is not defined as part of the sentence but rather an addition to it) must be served.[40] Even though supervised release is defined as separate from the prison sentence, violation of the conditions of supervised release (including technical violations) can result in re-incarceration.[41]

Illinois has a system of day-for-day good time, which does not vest. Up to ninety days additional good time can be earned for "meritorious service in specific instances" at the discretion of the director of corrections.[42] Up to one year of good time may be taken away for a single infraction. If the good time at issue represents more than thirty days the State Prisoner Review Board must review the case; otherwise, institutional officials have relatively unfettered discretion to revoke or to restore good time.[43]

These features of the Illinois law can be criticized on a number of grounds.

1. A period of mandatory supervised release grafted on to a prison term violates the spirit of determinacy and extends punishment beyond what is deserved. The repressive potential of the law is further apparent in that noncriminal ("technical") violations can result in criminal penalties.[44]

2. There is no built-in "safety valve" mechanism to reduce prison overcrowding. In order to alleviate overcrowding the state recently turned to the "meritorious good time" provision of the law and released several thousand inmates up to ninety days early.[45] This was an ill-conceived, stopgap measure which will do little to resolve the long-term problems of overcrowding.

3. Large amounts of good time are taken away from inmates, and disparities in revocation patterns are apparent. A John Howard Association report indicated that during fiscal 1980, the Department of Corrections added a total of over 486 years to prisoners' sentences as a result of revocation of good time.[46] Further, striking inter-institutional differences in revocation rates are apparent, even for institutions at the same security level.[47]

4. Since good time is not vested, and institutional decisions to revoke good time are seldom reversed, inmate protections against arbitrary outcomes are minimal.

The experience of Illinois indicates that the institution may be the area into which justice model principles have penetrated least. But as long as arbitrariness and disparity exist there, "just deserts" cannot prevail.

PROSECUTORIAL DISCRETION

One of the central criticisms of determinate sentencing has been that it leaves prosecutorial discretion virtually untouched.[48] In fact, the power of the prosecutor may actually increase in that, first of all, bargaining over charges has a more direct effect on the eventual sentence in determinate systems than in indeterminate ones. Second, to the extent that determinate sentencing laws contain particularly harsh components, pressures for circumvention of these components may well arise—and one likely mechanism for circumvention is the plea- and charge-bargaining process.

While the effect of determinate sentencing statutes on the functioning of the prosecutor has yet to be fully assessed, preliminary indications from Indiana and California are that the prosecutor has indeed become more powerful in influencing criminal justice system outcomes. In California, a Rand study of the determinate sentencing law there reported that judges and trial attorneys interviewed agreed that prosecutors have more power under the new law because of the availability of enhancements as a bargaining tool. Especially likely to be filed are those enhancements concerning injury to the victim and use of a weapon. The interviewees also expressed concern that prosecutorial bargaining patterns under the new code might give rise to sentence disparities among different areas of the state, or between those who plead guilty and those who go to trial, or to convictions based on weak evidence.[49]

In Indiana, we can reasonably expect even greater opportunity for exercise of prosecutorial power. Given the wide and severe sentencing ranges in the law, together with the lack of provisions governing amount of time to be added or subtracted from presumptive terms in the presence of aggravating and mitigating factors, prosecutors may find themselves with more "leverage" and accused persons with more "incentive" to bargain. Another impetus for bargaining in Indiana may be mandatory imprisonment provisions. For example, any nonsuspendable offense may also be charged as an "attempt," which *is* a suspendable offense. That is, a charge of "robbery" would preclude the granting of probation, but if bargained to "attempted robbery" probation would become a possibility. Similar pressures to charge-bargain will likely be brought to bear on second-time felony offenders (whose sentences are ostensibly not suspendable) and three-time offenders (who face the possibility of stiff habitual offender enhancements).[50]

EFFECTS ON TYPE AND LENGTH OF SENTENCES

As we have seen, justice model proponents argue that prison sentences for most crimes should be short in duration. They contend as well that imprisonment is not appropriate for every offense, and thus encourage the proliferation and utilization of alternatives to incarceration. Clear guidelines should, in their eyes, govern the in-out decision.

We have already pointed out a number of components of the new determinate sentencing codes which may undermine these goals. The high and wide sentencing ranges as well as the stiff enhancements and repeat offender provisions which are characteristic of many determinate statutes hold out the promise of long sentences rather than short ones. Particular crimes may be singled out for especially severe treatment as a result of piecemeal amendments to determinate sentencing codes. Vague or nonexistent guidelines for structuring the in-out decision, combined with a "get tough" political climate, may bring about increased use of prison and decreased use of alternative sanctions. The presence of any or all of these factors in a state may contribute substantially to rising prison populations and, ultimately, to prison overcrowding.

A number of critics of determinacy have maintained that longer sentences and higher prison populations are likely to constitute the legacy of the sentencing reforms on the late 1970s. In order to attempt to evaluate this claim, we will look briefly at the "early returns" from three determinate sentencing states.

CALIFORNIA

Three studies have recently been conducted which assess the impact of the determinate sentencing law (DSL) in California.[51] One of the major findings of this research is that the average estimated time served under DSL tends to be lower than the average actual length of sentence under the former indeterminate sentencing law (ISL) for most offenses. However, it cannot be automatically concluded that this is attributable to greater leniency under the DSL. First, in computing the anticipated prison terms of offenders now incarcerated, these researchers proceed on the unrealistic assumption that offenders would be granted the *maximum* number of days of good time credit. Second, the "early return" studies on California utilize data primarily from 1977 and 1978, prior to the time the legislature enacted SB 709 which increased terms for violent offenses. Third and perhaps most importantly, there is evidence to suggest that judges are making greater use of prison sentences under the new law. There seems to be a "lower threshold of seriousness" for prison under DSL; that is, a number of offenders who once might have spent up to a year in the local jail are now more likely to be sent to prison, thereby altering the "offense mix" in prison. As a consequence, the average term served by the entire prison population would be reduced not because serious offenders are now receiving shorter sentences, but rather because a greater number of less serious offenders who previously escaped a prison sentence are now being sent to the state penitentiary.[52] Of further note, the use of probation seems to be decreasing, while dispositions of probation with jail are increasing.[53] Finally, the number and rate of prison commitments have increased under the new law. This probably cannot be attributed solely to the effects of DSL, as this trend was under way in California (as well as throughout the United States) prior to the implementation of the DSL. Nevertheless, DSL has done little to stem the increase, and indeed may have aggravated the problem.[54]

INDIANA

A study comparing actual time served under the former indeterminate law with estimated time to be served (allowing for maximum good time and jail credit provisions) by offenders sentenced determinately in the period from October 1977 to August 1978 reveals a varied pattern. Thus, projected time served under DSL is shorter for robbery, longer for burglary, and approximately equal for all felonies combined.[55] Data from Marion County, Indiana revealed no significant differences pre-and post-determinate sentencing in relative use of alternative dispositions.[56] It was pointed out by the researchers that the statewide cases represented in the study were the earliest under determinate sentencing in Indiana, and may have represented the most easily bargained. Therefore, their projected terms may have been shorter than those who waited for trial and consequently were not included in the sample. Also, Indiana's relatively severe repeat offender provisions were not studied in the research, as additional time is needed to assess the full impact of these provisions.[57]

ILLINOIS

An Illinois Department of Corrections report provides preliminary data on the first year of determinate sentencing in that state. The data indicate that the average estimated time served under determinate sentencing (assuming the full complement of earned good time— not a reality in Illinois as we have seen) for all offenses is lower than the average time served under the old indeterminate law. This was particularly true for Classes 2, 3, and 4, which include the more frequently committed offenses. On the other hand, average time served under determinate sentencing has increased for both murder and rape. Most notably, longer determinate sentences were imposed during the *second* six months of determinate sentencing than in the first six months.[58] These conclusions must be taken as tentative, however, in that the authors report "some problems with regard to the accuracy of some of the data" gathered from the Department of Corrections' Information System. Moreover, the determinate sentencing group included both individuals in the transition period who chose determinate over indeterminate terms, and those who received a determinate sentence with no choice; these groups could not be separated for purposes of the analysis.[59]

In summary, it is clear that analysis of the effects of determinate sentencing laws has barely begun. Early results suggest that average terms served under determinate sentencing laws may be marginally lower than those under indeterminate sentencing. But again, these findings have typically assumed that all good time will be granted, have been conducted prior to the passage of more stringent amendments to original laws, and have not taken into account the impact of repeat offender provisions. Moreover, there is no evidence to suggest that determinate sentencing laws have been accompanied by greater utilization of probation or other alternatives to imprisonment. Thus, there is little in the empirical results to date which is indicative of the sweeping changes from past sentencing patterns envisioned by justice model advocates.

Up to now, we have given our attention primarily to the legislatively-based determinate laws, as they have constituted the predominant model of determinacy. Next, however, we will look briefly at two alternative models: sentencing and parole release guidelines.

A NOTE ON GUIDELINES

Both sentencing guidelines and parole release guidelines have been suggested as alternatives to legislatively-determined presumptive or flat sentencing strategies. Such guidelines, set by a panel of judges or a statewide sentencing commission (in the case of sentencing guidelines), or by the state parole board (in the instance of parole release guidelines), seek to reduce sentence disparity by structuring the discretion of judges and parole boards.[60] Proponents contend that the development of guidelines by agencies other than the legislature may provide some insulation from the "get tough" pressures to which state legislatures can be subjected; thus, the escalation of penalties which has been a feature of a number of legislatively-designed penalty systems may be avoided.[61] Given the claims of advocates that such systems of guidelines may represent a better means of "doing justice" than penalties set by state legislators,[62] it seems appropriate to consider these claims in light of current programs of sentencing and parole guidelines.

SENTENCING GUIDELINES

Guidelines for sentencing can be formulated either by judges themselves or by a sentencing commission. The starting point for their development is usually an analysis of past sentencing practices in a jurisdiction. The purpose of reviewing these past decisions is to distill a set of the most important factors explaining the variation in sentences. These factors, usually sorted into the categories of offense and offender considerations, become the basis for a two-dimensional grid which allows a judge to locate the appropriate sentence (or sentence range) at the intersection of the offense seriousness and offender characteristics scores. Typically, if aggravating or mitigating factors are present in a given case the judge may sentence outside the recommended range, but the judge is expected to state in writing the reasons for such departures. For an illustration of a sentencing grid, see Table 6.2.

Minnesota offers an example of a state which has instituted guidelines set by a nine-member sentencing commission comprised of judges, attorneys, corrections officials, and public members. The commission analyzed past sentencing practices in the state, but constructed their guidelines to reflect a desert-oriented model rather than merely formalizing past sentencing patterns.[63] The appropriate presumptive sentence is determined by a sentencing judge by locating the offender in the grid with respect to the seriousness of the offense and the offender's criminal history score.[64] A range of years around the presumptive term is also provided for those offense/offender categories for which a prison sentence is presumed; this range represents acceptable variations from the presumptive sentence.[65] Judges may sentence outside the indicated range, but must state the reasons for their decisions in such cases; the guidelines list both appropriate and inappropriate reasons for deviation from the recommended sentence. Further, sentences may be appealed by either the prosecution or the defense.

Table 6.2 Hypothetical Sentencing Matrix

Offense Seriousness	Offender History			
	No Past Criminal Record 1	2	3	Long Criminal Record 4
Level 1 (Least Serious)	Probation	Probation	1-2 yrs.	3-5 yrs.
2	Probation	1-2 yrs.	3-5 yrs.	6-9 yrs.
3	1-2 yrs.	3-5 yrs.	6-9 yrs.	10-13 yrs.
4	3-5 yrs.	6-9 yrs.	10-13 yrs.	14-17 yrs.
5	6-9 yrs.	10-12 yrs.	14-17 yrs.	18-20 yrs.
Level 6 (Most Serious)	10-13 yrs.	13-17 yrs.	18-22 yrs.	21-25 yrs.

The Minnesota guidelines have only recently been implemented; therefore, assessment of their impact is not possible at present. Nevertheless, the guidelines have been commended as an example of a thoughtful and promising attempt to implement determinate sentencing. It has been argued that this system may have avoided some of the significant pitfalls of legislatively-based sentencing systems: lack of a coherent ideological framework upon which to structure penalties, and insufficient attention to the effects of sentencing reform on the size of state prison populations.[66] Thus, the Minnesota guidelines were structured expressly to avoid the rapid expansion of inmate populations that is occurring in a number of the "get tough on crime" states.[67]

Although it seems possible that the sentencing guidelines system in Minnesota may escape some of the excesses of legislatively-set penalties, it is important to note certain characteristics of the Minnesota system which suggest caution.

First, although the guidelines provide input concerning the prison-nonprison decision, judges receive no guidance as to whether to assign probation versus a stay in the local jail for those for whom a term in the state penitentiary is deemed inappropriate.[68]

Second, the guidelines are essentially voluntary. That is, the judge can depart from the guidelines and give an offender virtually any sentence he/she feels is warranted. Even though reasons for departure from the guidelines must be stated in writing, it remains to be seen whether the right of appeal will represent an adequate curb on this judicial option.

Third, since rehabilitation is now viewed as voluntary, inmates have no means by which to challenge the number and type of treatment programs in prison. Thus, the selection and implementation of such programs is deemed to be the sole prerogative of the commissioner of corrections, and "no action challenging the level of expenditures for programs authorized under this section, nor any action challenging the selection, design or implementation of these programs, may be maintained by any inmate in any court in this state."[69] Inmates, therefore, must trust in the good will of the state to provide programs which represent, at best, only secondary goals of the system.

Fourth, Minnesota, as von Hirsch and Hanrahan point out, is a state which has a history of moderation in sentencing; perhaps, then, we should not be surprised that the penalty structure reflected in the guidelines manages to avoid the more draconian overtones of other determinate sentencing states. Nevertheless, it cannot be assumed that other states which adopt the strategy of sentencing guidelines set by a sentencing commission will be similarly temperate, especially since it is normally state legislatures which must approve or reject a commission's proposed sentencing structure. A case in point is the recent attempt of Pennsylvania to develop sentencing guidelines. In 1979, a bipartisan sentencing commission representing a broad spectrum of criminal justice perspectives was created to develop guidelines. The commission was charged to reduce disparity in sentencing, to develop criteria both for the probation vs. prison decision and for the minimum sentence lengths offenders are to receive (sentence maximums are set by judges with a ceiling determined by state statute). Beyond these instructions, little input was provided by the legislature as to the form or content of the guidelines; the commission was to be given a relatively free hand to determine appropriate sentencing policy. The original guidelines created by the commission were published in October of 1980. After public hearings, they were revised and sent to the legislature in January of 1981. The Pennsylvania legislature rejected the guidelines in April of 1981 on the grounds that they were too lenient. The sentencing commission was instructed to substantially revise the guidelines in the direction of increasing sentence lengths and broadening judicial discretion. The reworked guidelines, released in October of 1981, are substantially more severe than the first version, reflecting the crime-control orientation of the lawmakers. Although Pennsylvania (unlike Minnesota) utilizes the indeterminate sentence, the lesson is clear nonetheless: sentencing reform in the direction of greater determinacy, even under the seemingly optimum circumstances of an apolitical, broad-based sentencing commission, is not immune from current political pressures to "get tough."[70]

Given that the Minnesota system of guidelines has only recently been established, it is instructive to look at the experience of several other jurisdictions throughout the country with voluntary sentencing guidelines. Wilkins et al.[71] attempted to develop guidelines in Denver and Vermont which included the important factors (and weights given to these factors) actually used by judges in sentencing. It was the conclusion of these researchers that a limited number of offense and offender-related variables were used to reach sentencing decisions; therefore, guidelines constructed using these factors would allow judges to see how their colleagues would be likely to sentence an individual with a particular combination of these offense and offender characteristics. The researchers concluded as a result of their experience that sentencing guidelines offered both a feasible and promising means for structuring discretion. Subsequently, similarly-constructed guidelines were introduced in Philadelphia, Newark, Phoenix, and Chicago.

However, both the empirical adequacy and the practical efficacy of the guidelines in these jurisdictions have been seriously questioned on several grounds.[72] It has been argued, for example, that the predictor variables contained in the guidelines only account for a small percentage of the variance in sentence lengths. Further, several significant predictor variables were omitted from the guidelines. In other words, the factors included in the guidelines explain only a small portion of the variation in judicial sentencing practices. Also, the guidelines used a single set of variables for both the in-out and length of sentence determinations, although it is contended that different factors influenced each type of decision. The guidelines, then, cannot claim to be merely descriptive of judges' sentencing patterns; instead, they are reflective of policy-making decisions by the researchers.

In addition, critics have argued that the voluntary guidelines were ineffective in a number of sites in that compliance rates by judges were low, or judges used the guidelines inappropriately.[73] To the extent that their usage is attenuated, of course, the hoped-for reductions in sentencing disparity will not materialize.

PAROLE RELEASE GUIDELINES

The idea for parole guidelines originated with the United States Parole Commission as a means of sentencing federal offenders. A number of states are also becoming interested in the potential of such guidelines for reducing disparity in sentencing.

It has been contended that retaining the sentencing function in the parole board under a guideline system has several distinct advantages over an exclusively judicial model of sentencing. Greater understanding and support of the guidelines are likely in that the drafters of the guidelines are also their implementers on a day-to-day basis.[74] Moreover, sentences are meted out by a panel rather than by an individual, and the total number of sentencers is small, thereby enhancing the chances for consistency and avoidance of extremes in sentencing.[75]

One of the states which operates under a parole release guideline system is Oregon. In that state, the guidelines were developed by an eleven-member Advisory Commission comprised of both judges and parole board members. Intended to reflect a "modified desert" philosophy, the guidelines consist of a matrix which combines both offense severity and offender criminal history/risk variables; a range of terms which is within the maximum terms set by statute for each class of offense is available for each offense and offender combination on the matrix. The actual term is set within six months of an inmate's arrival in prison by a "hearing panel," comprised of at least two members of the parole board. If a preponderance of the evidence indicates the presence of aggravating or mitigating factors, the panel may depart from the normal range by a limited amount; the reasons for the departure must be stated on the record.[76]

Although Oregon retains the parole board as an important sentencing agency, the system has been categorized as determinate in that it seeks to promote equity in sentencing and in that the release date of offenders is known early (but obviously not at the judicial sentencing stage) in their term.[77] Nevertheless, there are certain important features of the Oregon guidelines which may interfere with these goals. First of all, in order to bring about a sentence higher than that specified by the matrix, judges may set a minimum term of up to one-half the maximum term they have specified. Preliminary data indicate that this option is used only infrequently at present,[78] but its availability opens the door for possible inequities. Second, the parole guidelines only govern the length of prison sentence, leaving the judicial in-out decision untouched.[79] Third, the parole board may elect not to set parole dates for particularly violent or dangerous criminal behavior, for certain three-time offenders, or for an offender whose record contains a diagnosis of severe emotional disturbance. In addition, a set parole date can be postponed for "serious misconduct during confinement."[80] Fourth, certain offender variables used to determine sentence length seem to be based more on predictive criteria than on desert, notably: age at first commitment, escapes or failures on probation or parole, and drug or alcohol problems. Together, these three items make up five of eleven possible points in the offender category.[81] And while ranges for any given offense/offender *combination* are relatively narrow (especially at the lower levels of offense severity), the spans across a given level of offense severity are substantially wider. It is thus possible that the longest terms given for a particular level of offense severity may be several times longer than the shortest terms given for the same level of offense seriousness. To the degree that variations within this wide span are based on offender factors unrelated or only marginally related to desert, justice model principles are violated. When permissible departure from the ranges for aggravating and mitigating circumstances are included, the possible variations in sentencing become even more pronounced.

The actual effects of the Oregon parole guidelines on sentencing patterns are only now being studied.[82] A complete assessment of the impact of the guidelines must await the results of such empirical analysis.

GENERAL CONSIDERATIONS

In our discussion of sentencing and parole guidelines, we have focused on two states which have sought to give primary consideration to "just deserts" and determinacy as goals of sentencing reform. Nevertheless, there is no necessary relationship between guidelines and determinacy (e.g., Pennsylvania) or between guidelines and a primary emphasis on desert (e.g., Georgia). The two state systems which we have described in detail are generally thought to be among the most carefully conceived and moderate reforms of their kind although even they, as we have shown, contain weaknesses which may subvert justice model aims.

We cannot assume, however, that future systems of guidelines will necessarily take similar forms or practice similar moderation. State guidelines will approach the goals of the justice model only insofar as they:

- begin with a desert rationale and bring the system of penalties into line with this goal, rather than merely codifying present sentencing practices
- exclude or greatly minimize the use of offender characteristics involving predictive criteria to determine sentence lengths
- provide guidelines for the in-out decision as well as for sentence lengths
- provide narrow ranges for each category and specify appropriate and inappropriate aggravating and mitigating circumstances to guide sentencing decisions
- limit the extent to which and conditions under which judges or parole boards are free to depart from the guidelines
- allow for appeal of sentence by the offender
- include clearly articulated and regulated procedures for modifying the guidelines
- minimize the population of offenders not covered by the guidelines
- are linked to a structured means of reducing prosecutorial discretion.

Whether or not current or future systems of sentencing or parole guidelines are capable of meeting these criteria is at present an open question.

CONCLUSION

The determinate sentencing systems we have examined in this chapter hold, for the most part, little promise for achieving justice model objectives. We have seen that many of the so-called reforms have no underlying, unifying philosophy or purpose to aid in structuring penalties in a consistent and cohesive manner. Moreover, while some previously-existing types of discretion and disparity have been curtailed under determinate sentencing, other areas have remained untouched and new sources of disparity have arisen as well. Further, the overall level of penalties has not been dramatically reduced under determinacy, and the potential for harsh punishments remains.

Thus, most of the determinate sentencing laws cannot qualify as liberal reforms. However, liberal abandonment of rehabilitation and support of punishment as the primary goal of the criminal justice system, together with liberal advocacy of the determinate sentence, has perhaps accomplished an unintended goal: it has presented conservatives with a vocabulary and a sentencing structure which can be as easily molded to conservative as to liberal ends. By rejecting the goal of rehabilitation as a guiding principle of corrections, liberal proponents of the justice model have inadvertently left themselves without any forceful rationale for opposing a conservative agenda that calls for more and longer punishments. In effect, liberal resistance to harsh penalty structures degenerates into a disagreement over numbers—how long should sentences be—hardly a solid ideological base from which to counteract conservative pressure to "get tough" on crime.

Some might counter that "law and order" policies are being instituted not only in determinate sentencing states but also in jurisdictions that have retained indeterminacy. It must be admitted that repression is emerging as a favorite tactic to respond to crime across the nation. While conclusive evidence will not be available until the new sentencing structures have an opportunity to settle fully into place, our analysis nevertheless suggests that the justice outcomes will be worse in those states that have actively undertaken sentencing reform based on punitive principles in the midst of a conservative climate. Yet to the extent that sentencing practices in indeterminate states do assume a more stringent character, it is imperative that we begin to assess what is responsible for this occurrence. As pervasive attacks, including those leveled by liberals, have made it less fashionable to invoke rehabilitation as a justification for handing down a particular sentence, it is clear that judges in these states are not sending offenders to prison for longer terms on the ostensible grounds of effecting their treatment. Instead, it seems reasonable to conclude that the discrediting of treatment ideology has robbed rehabilitation of an important portion of its legitimacy and in turn has permitted punitive concerns to flourish even in these states that possess the trappings of indeterminacy. In this light, the movement toward determinacy and just deserts—again, a movement which has received much of its impetus from liberal sources—may have repressive consequences that extend well beyond the boundaries of those states that have actually transformed their criminal codes in recent times. This is certainly a disturbing prospect to entertain.

Given the foregoing considerations, it is difficult to avoid the conclusion that liberals may have prematurely and dangerously rejected the rehabilitative ideal, a paradigm that sought to sustain the link between indeterminacy and treatment. We are thus led to question the current dominance of justice principles and policies as the focus for liberal energies. Our general dissatisfaction with the justice model further prompts us to ask: What should be the direction of liberal reform efforts in the years ahead? As we endeavor to explain in the next and final chapter, we believe that the wisest path for liberals to choose is to reaffirm rehabilitation.

NOTES

[1]American Friends Service Committee, *Struggle for Justice*. (New York: Hill and Wang, 1971), pp. 158–159.

[2]Willard Gaylin and David J. Rothman, "Introduction." Pp. xxi–xli in Andrew von Hirsch, *Doing Justice: The Choice of Punishments.* (New York: Hill and Wang, 1976), p. xl.

[3]David F. Greenberg and Drew Humphries, "The cooptation of fixed sentencing reform." *Crime and Delinquency* 26 (April 1980), pp. 206–225.

[4]Gray Cavender and Michael C. Musheno, "The adoption and implementation of determinate-based sentencing policies: a critical perspective." Paper presented at the 1981 meeting of the American Society of Criminology.

[5]Our discussion of the history of determinate sentencing legislation is based on the following sources: Marvin E. Aspen, "New Class X sentencing law: an analysis." *Illinois Bar Journal* 66 (February 1978), pp. 344–351; James J. Bagley, "Why Illinois adopted determinate sentencing." *Judicature* 62 (March 1979), pp. 390–397; Patrick D. McAnany, Frank S. Merritt, and Edward Tromanhauser, "Illinois reconsiders 'flat time': an analysis of the impact of the justice model." *Chicago-Kent Law Review* 52 (No. 3, 1976), pp. 621–662.

[6]This term is based on Franklin Zimring's assertion that as a legislature is considering determinate sentencing "it takes only an eraser and pencil to make a one-year 'presumptive sentence' into a six-year sentence for the same offense." Franklin E. Zimring, "Making the punishment fit the crime." *Hastings Center Report* 6 (December 1976), p. 17.

[7]Joan Galler, "Determinate sentencing legislation in California." Paper presented at the 1981 meeting of the American Society of Criminology; and Albert J. Lipson and Mark A. Peterson, *California Justice Under Determinate Sentencing: A Review and Agenda for Research.* (Santa Monica, California: Rand Corporation, 1980), pp. 10–15. For background on the determinate sentencing law in California, see also Sheldon L. Messinger and Phillip D. Johnson, "California's determinate sentencing statute: history and issues." Pp. 13–58 in National Institute of Law Enforcement and Criminal Justice, *Determinate Sentencing: Reform or Regression?* (Washington, D.C.: U.S. Government Printing Office, 1978). It is worth noting that the version of the sentencing law that eventually took effect in Indiana also moved in the direction of greater severity as compared to earlier forms of the bill. For a summary of the background of the Indiana law see Richard Ku, *American Prisons and Jails, Volume IV: Supplemental Report—Case Studies of New Legislation Governing Sentencing and Release.* (Washington, D.C.: National Institute of Justice, 1980), p. 77.

[8]For example, see Ku, *American Prisons and Jails, Volume IV*, pp. 17–18 and Richard G. Singer, *Just Deserts: Sentencing Based on Equality and Desert.* (Cambridge, Massachusetts: Ballinger, 1979), ch. 10.

[9]*Illinois Revised Statutes* Chapter 38, section 1001-1-2; and *New Jersey Statutes Annotated* Title 2C, section 2C:1-2. Given the features of the laws of both states, the goal of rehabilitation clearly plays a secondary role.

[10]Cesare Beccaria, *On Crimes and Punishments.* (Indianapolis: Bobbs-Merrill, 1963), p. 58.

[11]Messinger and Johnson, "California's determinate sentence statute: history and issues," p. 30.

[12]James J. Bagley, "Why Illinois adopted determinate sentencing," pp. 393–394.

[13]Todd R. Clear, John D. Hewitt, and Robert M. Regoli, "Discretion and the determinate sentence: its distribution, control, and effect on time served." *Crime and Delinquency* 24 (October 1978), pp. 428−445.

[14]Stephen P. Lagoy and John H. Kramer, "The second generation of sentencing reform: a comparative assessment of recent sentencing legislation." Paper presented at the 1980 meeting of the American Society of Criminology.

[15]Stephen P. Lagoy, Frederick A. Hussey, and John H. Kramer, "A comparative assessment of determinate sentencing in the four pioneer states." *Crime and Delinquency* 24 (October 1978), p. 393; *Illinois Revised Statutes* Chapter 38, sections 33B-1 and 1005-5-3.

[16]*Colorado Revised Statutes*, section 16-13-101.

[17]*Arizona Revised Statutes*, section 13-604; *Illinois Revised Statutes* Chapter 38, section 1005-8-2.

[18]*Justice Assistance News* 1 (April 1980), p. 9.

[19]Joan Petersilia and Peter W. Greenwood, "Mandatory prison sentences: their projected effects on crime and prison populations." *Journal of Criminal Law and Criminology* 69 (Winter 1978), pp. 604−615.

[20]*Illinois Revised Statutes* Chapter 38, section 1005-5-3.2; *New Jersey Statutes Annotated* Title 2C, section 2C:44-1; *Colorado Revised Statutes*, section 18-1-105.

[21]*Illinois Revised Statutes* Chapter 38, section 1005-5-3.1; *New Jersey Statutes Annotated* Title 2C, section 2C:44-1; Ku, *American Prisons and Jails, Volume IV*, p. 79.

[22]*Illinois Revised Statutes* Chapter 38, section 1005-8-1(b).

[23]*California Penal Code*, section 2931(b) and (c).

[24]Lagoy and Kramer, "The second generation of sentencing reform," pp. 5−6.

[25]Lagoy, et al., "A comparative assessment of determinate sentencing in the four pioneer states," p. 387.

[26]*Illinois Revised Statutes* Chapter 38, sections 1005-8-1 and 1005-8-2.

[27]Ku, *American Prisons and Jails, Volume IV*, p. 80.

[28]*California Penal Code*, section 1170.

[29]*Colorado Revised Statutes*, section 18-1-105.

[30]*New Jersey Statutes Annotated*, section 2C:44-1(f); Ku, *American Prisons and Jails, Volume IV*, p. 80.

[31]*Illinois Revised Statutes*, Chapter 38, section 1005-6-1.

[32]*New Jersey Statutes Annotated*, section 2C:44-1(d) and (e).

[33]*Illinois Revised Statutes*, Chapter 38, section 1005-5-4.1.

[34]*Colorado Revised Statutes*, section 18-1-105.

[35]Lagoy et al., "A comparative assessment of determinate sentencing in the four pioneer states," pp. 388 and 390.

[36]Frederick A. Hussey and Stephen P. Lagoy, "The impact of determinate sentencing structures." *Criminal Law Bulletin* 17 (May-June 1981); pp. 197−225.

[37]Ku, *American Prisons and Jails, Volume IV*, pp. 53−76; Lipson and Peterson, *California Justice Under Determinate Sentencing: A Review and Agenda for Research*. These evaluations

of the California law predate the enactment of SB 709, which increased penalties for a number of violent crimes and which took effect on January 1, 1979.

[38]Ku, *American Prisons and Jails, Volume IV*, pp. 77–105.

[39]Lagoy et al., "A comparative assessment of determinate sentencing in the four pioneer states," p. 388.

[40]Paul Bigman, *Discretion, Determinate Sentencing and the Illinois Prisoner Review Board: A Shotgun Wedding.* (Chicago: Chicago Law Enforcement Study Group, 1979), pp. 14–15.

[41]*Illinois Revised Statutes* Chapter 38, section 1003-3-9.

[42]*Ibid.*, section 1003-6-3(a).

[43]*Ibid.*, section 1003-6-3(b).

[44]Bigman, *Discretion, Determinate Sentencing and the Illinois Prisoner Review Board: A Shotgun Wedding*, p. 15.

[45]Michael Sneed and Lynn Emmerman, "Release plan isn't working: parole aide." *Chicago Tribune*, April 6, 1981. It is contended that in the flood of early releases, parole officers can "lose track" of large numbers of releasees.

[46]John Howard Association, "Against the walls: the John Howard Association's policy statement on prison overcrowding in Illinois," September 3, 1981, p. 4.

[47]Paul Bigman, "Good time, hard times." *Prison Law and Advocacy* 2 (1981), p. 4. Bigman indicates that "the average Stateville prisoner lost 38.9 days of good time in one year, while his counterpart at Pontiac lost only 14 days, and at Menard only 9.7 days. In effect, a prisoner at Stateville stays in prison one month longer for each year of his sentence than one at Menard with the same sentence."

[48]See, for example: Albert W. Alschuler, "Sentencing reform and prosecutorial power: a critique of recent proposals for 'fixed' and 'presumptive' sentencing." Pp. 59–79 in National Institute of Law Enforcement and Criminal Justice, *Determinate Sentencing: Reform or Regression?* (Washington, D.C.: U.S. Government Printing Office, 1978); and Leonard Orland, "From vengeance to vengeance: sentencing reform and the demise of rehabilitation." *Hofstra Law Review* 7 (Fall 1978), pp. 29–56.

[49]Lipson and Peterson, *California Justice Under Determinate Sentencing: A Review and Agenda for Research*, pp. 16–17.

[50]Clear et al., "Discretion and the determinate sentence: its distribution, control, and effect on time served," pp. 435–436; and Ku, *American Prisons and Jails, Volume IV*, pp. 81–82.

[51]David Brewer, Gerald E. Beckett, and Norman Holt, "Determinate sentencing in California: the first year's experience." *Journal of Research in Crime and Delinquency* 18 (July 1981), pp. 200–231; Ku, *American Prisons and Jails, Volume IV*, pp. 53–76; and Lipson and Peterson, *California Justice Under Determinate Sentencing: A Review and Agenda for Research*.

[52]Ku, *American Prisons and Jails, Volume IV*, p. 62; Lipson and Peterson, *California Justice Under Determinate Sentencing: A Review and Agenda for Research*, p. 29.

[53]Brewer et al., "Determinate sentencing in California: the first year's experience," p. 211.

[54]Lipson and Peterson, *California Justice Under Determinate Sentencing: A Review and Agenda for Research*, p. vi.

[55]Ku, *American Prisons and Jails, Volume IV*, p. 87.

[56]*Ibid.*, p. 85.

[57]*Ibid.*, pp. 85 and 87.

[58]Illinois Department of Corrections, *Determinate Sentencing Impact*, Draft copy (1979), pp. 28–29.

[59]*Ibid.*, pp. 9–10.

[60]Leslie T. Wilkins, "Sentencing guidelines to reduce disparity?" *Criminal Law Review* (April 1980), pp. 201–214.

[61]Andrew von Hirsch and Kathleen Hanrahan, "Determinate penalty systems in America: an overview." *Crime and Delinquency* 27 (July 1981), pp. 289–316.

[62]See also Richard G. Singer, *Just Deserts: Sentencing Based on Equality and Desert.* (Cambridge, Massachusetts: Ballinger, 1979), pp. 62–66.

[63]von Hirsch and Hanrahan, "Determinate penalty systems in America: an overview," p. 305.

[64]Minnesota's guideline matrix provides guidance to the judge not only for length of sentence, but also for the prison-nonprison (in-out) decision as well.

[65]Minnesota Sentencing Guidelines Commission, *Report to the Legislature* (1980), p. 38.

[66]von Hirsch and Hanrahan, "Determinate penalty systems in America: an overview," pp. 305–306.

[67]*Ibid.*, p. 306.

[68]*Ibid.*, p. 307.

[69]*Minnesota Statutes Annotated*, Volume 16, section 244.03.

[70]This discussion on the history of the Pennsylvania guidelines draws heavily from Stephen P. Lagoy, "The politics of punishment and the future of sentencing reform: the Pennsylvania experience." Paper presented at the 1981 meeting of the American Society of Criminology.

[71]Leslie Wilkins, Jack M. Kress, Don M. Gottfredson, Joseph C. Calpin, and Arthur M. Gelman, *Sentencing Guidelines: Structuring Judicial Discretion.* (Washington, D.C.: National Institute of Law Enforcement and Criminal Justice, 1980).

[72]William D. Rich, L. Paul Sutton, Todd R. Clear, and Michael J. Saks, *Sentencing Guidelines: Their Operation and Impact on the Courts.* (Williamsburg, Virginia: National Center for State Courts, 1980); and John D. Hewitt and Bert Little, "Examining the research underlying the sentencing guidelines in Denver, Colorado: A partial replication of a reform effort." *Journal of Criminal Justice* 9 (1981), pp. 51–62.

[73]Rich et al., *Sentencing Guidelines: Their Operation and Impact on the Courts*, pp. 28–29, 48.

[74]von Hirsch and Hanrahan, "Determinate penalty systems in America: an overview," p. 310.

[75]Peter B. Hoffman and Michael A. Stover, "Reform in the determination of prison terms: equity, determinacy, and the parole release function." *Hofstra Law Review* 7 (Fall 1978), p. 113.

[76]Ku, *American Prisons and Jails, Volume IV*, p. 113.

[77]von Hirsch and Hanrahan, "Determinate penalty systems in America: an overview," p. 295.

[78]Ku, *American Prisons and Jails, Volume IV*, p. 113.

[79]von Hirsch and Hanrahan, "Determinate penalty systems in America: an overview," p. 310.

[80]*Oregon Revised Statutes*, Title 14, sections 144.120(4) and 144.125(2).

[81]Ku, *American Prisons and Jails, Volume IV*, pp. 111–112.

[82]Sheldon Messinger, Richard Sparks, and Andrew von Hirsch, Project on Strategies for Determinate Sentencing (National Institute of Justice, forthcoming).

Reaffirming Rehabilitation

"Today, optimism has turned to pessimism, fervent hopes to despair."[1] In these brief but telling words, LaMar Empey has captured the mood that pervades the writings of those arguing that desert and determinacy rather than state enforced rehabilitation should be the reform agenda embraced by those on the left. Such proponents of the justice model assert that the grand design of past liberals to save society's outcasts and unfortunates from a life in crime must be abandoned, the impossibility of doing good in the coercive environment of custodial institutions admitted. In their view, the paternalism of the state has proven to be abusive, not kindly, and hence the state cannot be trusted to care in a humane fashion for the needs or welfare of offenders. As a consequence, the priority of liberal reform, they argue, should no longer be the lofty goal of compelling the state to "do good" for its captives. Rather, liberal efforts should be devoted to severely reducing state intervention and the inevitable harms that result by compelling the state to "do justice" and no more. Indeed, while all would have rejoiced at the creation of a benevolent system that corrects, experience demands that this idealistic and unrealistic hope be forfeited—however reluctantly. In the face of the ruthless exercise of state power under the guise of rehabilitation, liberals would do better to pursue less noble but more needed policies—such as the expansion of due process protections and equal justice before the law—that constrain the discretion and hence power of the state's criminal justice agents and thereby minimize the harms that have so often been engendered by the disorderly administration of criminal punishments in our society.

In their introduction to von Hirsch's *Doing Justice*, Willard Gaylin and David Rothman thus embrace the concept of just deserts but then continue on to admit that "still we are not happy. Our solution is one of despair, not hope." It would have been preferable to have saved offenders in a merciful way, but "under the rehabilitative model we have been able to abuse our charges, the prisoners, without disturbing our consciences. Beneath this cloak of benevolence, hypocrisy has flourished, and each new exploitation of the prisoner has inevitably been introduced as an act of grace." Despite being "trained in humanistic traditions," they have thus found it necessary to reject rehabilitation and to explore a path that holds out not the fragile and perhaps illusory promise of doing good but the real prospect of doing less harm:

Permeating this report is a determination to do less rather than more—an insistence on not doing harm. The quality of heady optimism and confidence of reformers in the past, and their belief that they could solve the problem of crime and eradicate the presence of deviancy, will not be found in this document. Instead, we have here a crucial shift in perspective from a commitment to do good to a commitment to do as little mischief as possible. ... Thus, however modest these new proposals, they *are intended to generate less disastrous consequences than the programs we now administer.* (emphasis added)[2]

In short, proponents of the justice model now contend, in the words of Ira Glasser, that the "principle of least harm" should guide liberal reform objectives: "Every program designed to help the dependent ought to be evaluated, not on the basis of the good it might do, but rather on the basis of the harm it might do."[3] Yet if the "principle of least harm" is to be the criterion used to assess the relative merits of competing reform agendas, our analysis has furnished little confidence that the justice model is a wise path to follow. While its supporters, like Gaylin and Rothman, intend the justice alternative to "generate less disastrous consequences than the programs we now administer," the opposite appears the more certain outcome—more injustice, not less, more inhumanity not less. When the dreary pragmatics of what the institution of the justice model would entail are thus considered, it is clear that liberal despair would only become more profound should this "reform" be pursued in earnest. Indeed, there is every reason to surmise that we are better off with the criminal justice system, however inadequate, that we now have.

If nothing else, the current system that has partially embraced and perhaps more fully corrupted the rehabilitative ideal appears less despairing—and dangerous—than the alternative image of a system that selectively utilizes justice model principles to legitimate the more stringent repression of crime. While this is sufficient reason to insist that liberals mute their call that desert and determinacy form the underpinnings of the nation's courts and correctional facilities, it provides little instruction as to where liberals should go from here. If we have good reason to suspect that the harms produced by attempts to "do justice" will surpass those presently endured, this does not erase the knowledge that intolerable harms nevertheless continue despite, if not because of, liberal efforts to force the state to "do good." In the end, liberals must face the disillusioning prospect that their two major agendas for reform—state enforced rehabilitation and the justice model—have been substantially (though we believe unequally) discredited. According to Steven Marcus, liberals have learned that "we can degrade people by caring for them;" yet as our analysis of the justice model suggests, "we can degrade them by not caring for them" as well. And as Marcus has followed, "in matters such as these there are neither simple answers nor simple solutions."[4]

In a very real sense, then, it can be said that liberal thinking about criminal justice is in a state of crisis. Where should reform efforts be directed when all paths seem corrupted and no enlightening solutions are apparent? Should we accept as inevitable that all reforms will fail and aggravate rather than mitigate the pains of imprisonment? For those of us schooled in the past two decades, it is difficult to expect that either the state or the structure of interests in the criminal justice system will permit any benevolent intentions to remain untainted. Yet despite these fears and reservations, it is our firm belief that the most promising option for liberal reform is to reaffirm and not to reject the ideology of criminal justice rehabilitation. Again, it can be maintained that the principle of least harm would guide us to favor a treatment rather than a justice paradigm because it is the lesser of two evils. However, we would like to argue more for rehabilitation than this: that rehabilitation is not simply an evil but a source of actual and potential good that can be abandoned only at considerable risk. At the same time, it will be proposed that the poverty of state *enforced* rehabilitation should be recognized and this concept attacked. Instead, liberal interest groups should embark on efforts to transform enforced therapy into a program of state *obligated* rehabilitation that takes seriously the betterment of inmates but legitimates neither coercion in the name of treatment nor neglect in the name of justice. Finally, we will close with a discussion of why liberal reform should be pursued rather than more conservative or radical alternatives.

THE VALUE OF REHABILITATION

There can be little dispute that the rehabilitative ideal has been conveniently employed as a mask for inequities in the administration of criminal penalties and for brutality behind the walls of our penal institutions. Yet as our analysis of the realities of the current swing toward determinate sentencing has revealed, the existence of inhumanity and injustice in the arena of crime control does not depend on the vitality of rehabilitation. Indeed, a punitive "just deserts" philosophy would serve the purposes of repressive forces equally well, if not with greater facility. It would thus seem prudent to exercise caution before concluding that the failure of the criminal justice system to sanction effectively and benevolently is intimately linked to the rehabilitative ideal and that the ills of the system will vanish as the influence of rehabilitation diminishes. As Francis Allen has recently observed, "the contributions of the rehabilitative ideal to these failures has been peripheral."[5]

This line of reasoning is liberating in the sense that it prompts us to consider that the state's machinery of justice might well have been *more* and not less repressive had history not encouraged the evolution of the rehabilitative ideal. This suggests in turn that preoccupation with the misuses and limitations of treatment programs has perhaps blinded many current-day liberals to the important benefits that have been or can be derived from popular belief in the notion that offenders should be saved and not simply punished. In this respect, the persistence of a strong rehabilitative ideology can be seen to function as a valuable resource for those seeking to move toward the liberal goal of introducing greater benevolence into the criminal justice system. Alternatively, we can begin to question whether the reform movement sponsored by the left will not be undermined should liberal faith in rehabilitation reach a complete demise. In this context, four major reasons are offered below for why we believe that liberals should reaffirm and not reject the correctional ideology of rehabilitation.

1. *Rehabilitation is the only justification of criminal sanctioning that obligates the state to care for an offender's needs or welfare.* Admittedly, rehabilitation promises a payoff to society in

the form of offenders transformed into law-abiding, productive citizens who no longer desire to victimize the public. Yet treatment ideology also conveys the strong message that this utilitarian outcome can only be achieved if society is willing to punish its captives humanely and to compensate offenders for the social disadvantages that have constrained them to undertake a life in crime. In contrast, the three competing justifications of criminal sanctioning—deterrence, incapacitation, and retribution (or just deserts)—contain not even the pretense that the state has an obligation to do good for its charges. The only responsibility of the state is to inflict the pains that accompany the deprivation of liberty or of material resources (e.g., fines); whatever utility such practices engender flows only to society and not to its captives. Thus, deterrence aims to protect the social order by making offenders suffer sufficiently to dissuade them as well as onlookers entertaining similar criminal notions from venturing outside the law on future occasions. Incapacitation also seeks to preserve the social order but through a surer means; by caging criminals—"locking 'em up and throwing away the keys"—inmates will no longer be at liberty to prey on law-abiding members of society. The philosophy of retribution, on the other hand, manifests a disinterest in questions of crime control, instead justifying punishment on the grounds that it presumably provides society and crime victims with the psychic satisfaction that justice has been accomplished by harming offenders in doses commensurate with the harms their transgressions have caused. The following comments by Nicholas Kittrie are instructive here:

> At the very least, the therapeutic programs help set a humanizing climate of new social expectations and aims. . . . Under the traditional criminal formula, society is the wronged party. It owes nothing to the guilty party, and his rehabilitation remains an incidental accomplishment of the penal sanction. Under the *parens patriae* formula [rehabilitative ideal], the concept of personal guilt is bypassed, if not totally discarded, and much more weight is given the offender's shortcomings and needs. Society accordingly cannot shrug off its responsibility for treatment, since it is inherent in the very exercise of this social sanction.[6]

These considerations lead us to ask whether it is strategically wise for liberals wishing to mitigate existing inhumanities in the criminal justice system to forsake the only prevailing correctional ideology that is expressly benevolent toward offenders. It is difficult to imagine that reform efforts will be more humanizing if liberals willingly accept the premise that the state has no responsibility to do good, only to inflict pain. Notably, Gaylin and Rothman, proponents of the justice model, recognized the dangers of such a choice when they remarked that "in giving up the rehabilitative model, we abandon not just our innocence but perhaps more. The concept of deserts is intellectual and moralistic; in its devotion to principle, it turns back on such compromising considerations as generosity and charity, compassion and love."[7] They may have shown even greater hesitation in rejecting rehabilitation and affirming just deserts had they had an opportunity to dwell on the more recent insights of radical thinkers Herman and Julia Schwendinger:

> Nevertheless, whatever the expressed qualifications, the justice model now also justifies objectively retrogressive outcomes because of its insistence that social

policies give priority to punishment rather than rehabilitation. Punishment, as we have seen, is classically associated with deprivation of living standards. Rehabilitation, on the other hand, has served as the master symbol in bourgeois ideology that legitimated innumerable reformist struggles against this deprivation. By discrediting rehabilitation as a basic principle of penal practice, the justice modelers have undermined their own support for better standards of living in penal institutions.[8]

Now it might be objected by liberal critics of rehabilitation that favoring desert as the rationale for criminal sanctioning does not mean adopting an uncaring orientation toward the welfare of offenders. The reform agenda of the justice model not only suggests that punishment be fitted to the crime and not the criminal, but also that those sent to prison be accorded an array of rights that will humanize their existence. The rehabilitative ideal, it is countered, justifies the benevolent treatment of the incarcerated but only as a means to achieving another end—the transformation of the criminal into the conforming. In contrast, the justice perspective argues for humanity as an end in and of itself, something that should not in any way be made to seem conditional on accomplishing the difficult task of changing the deep-seated criminogenic inclinations of offenders. As such, liberals should not rely on state enforced rehabilitation to somehow lessen the rigors of imprisonment, but instead should campaign to win legal rights for convicts that directly bind the state to provide its captives with decent living conditions. Contending that "a free people can make justice live—even in the stark environment of the American prison," John Conrad has thus called for reforms that will grant inmates the essentials of "citizenship," including the "right to personal safety, to care, to personal dignity, to work, to self-improvement, to vote, and to a future."[9]

It is not with ease that those of us on the political left can stop short of completely and publically embracing the concept that "humanity for humanity's sake" is sufficient reason for combatting the brutalizing effects of prison life. This value-stance is, after all, fundamental to the logic that informs liberal policies on criminal justice issues. In this light, it should be clear that we applaud attempts to earn inmates the human rights innumerated by Conrad among others, and urge their continuance. However, we must stand firm against efforts to promote the position that the justice model with its emphasis on rights should replace the rehabilitative ideal with its emphasis on caring as the major avenue of liberal reform. Already, we have illustrated in past chapters that support for the principles of just deserts and determinacy has only exacerbated the plight of offenders both before and after their incarceration. But there are additional dangers to undertaking a reform program that abandons rehabilitation and seeks *exclusively* to broaden prisoner rights. Most importantly, the realities of the day furnish little optimism that such a campaign would enjoy success. In February of 1981, Chief Justice Warren Burger voiced his opinion to the American Bar Association that "too much concern for the rights of criminal defendants may be nourishing American's growing crime rate."[10] In June of the same year, the United States Supreme Court voted a resounding 8-1 that it is not unconstitutional to house two inmates in a cell that measures 10 1/2 by 6 1/2 feet. "The Constitution does not mandate comfortable prisons," wrote Justice Lewis A. Powell. Indeed, "discomfort" is justly deserved:

"To the extent that such conditions are restrictive and even harsh, they are part of the penalty that criminal offenders pay for their offenses against society."[11] In this context, it is not surprising that one social commentator has observed that the prisoners' rights movement is in "disarray," a fact that is evident in the disturbing "ease with which the courts now rebuff efforts of prison reformers to win more humane living conditions for a growing prison population."[12] Even justice model advocate David Fogel is aware that "the courts continue to draw narrow issues around prisoner complaints until large stacks are amassed. The Supreme Court then levels them one at a time. Not much," he concludes, "may be expected in the way of enduring correctional change through the drama of litigation when the central actors are reluctant judges and resistant prison administrators."[13]

Further, the promise of the rights perspective is based on the shaky assumption that more benevolence will occur if the relationship of the state to its deviants is fully adversarial and purged of its paternalistic dimensions. Instead of the government being entrusted to reform its charges through care, now offenders will have the comfort of being equipped with a new weapon—"rights"—that will serve them well in their battle against the state for a humane and justly administered correctional system. Yet this imagery contains only surface appeal. As David Rothman has warned, "an adversarial model, setting interest off against interest, does seem to run the clear risk of creating a kind of ultimate shoot-out in which, by definition, the powerless lose and the powerful win. How absurd to push for confrontation when all the advantages are on the other side."[14] In this regard, Illinois inmates under determinate sentencing have won the "right" to challenge the revocation of their good time before the Prisoner Review Board. But the achievement of justice here is more illusory than real: the Board rarely reverses—in fewer than five cases in one hundred—the Department of Corrections' revocation decisions. "A reversal rate that low for a judge," Paul Bigman has observed, "might merit national recognition for extraordinary capability. In the prisons, however, the judge and jury are the co-workers of the accuser."[15]

Moreover, the rights perspective is a two-edged sword. While rights ideally bind the state to abide by standards insuring a certain level of due process protection and acceptable penal living conditions, rights also establish the limits of the good that the state can be expected or obligated to provide. A rehabilitative ideology, in contrast, constantly pricks the conscience of the state with its assertion that the useful and moral goal of offender reformation can only be affected in a truly humane environment. Should treatment ideology be stripped away by liberal activists and the ascendancy of the rights model secured, it would thus create a situation in which criminal justice officials would remain largely immune from criticism as long as they "gave inmates their rights"—however few they may be at the time. With the movement for prisoner rights now suffering significant defeats in the courts, this constitutes a troubling prospect.

Even more perversely, the very extension of new rights can also be utilized to legitimate the profound neglect of the welfare of those under state control. The tragic handling of mental patients in recent years is instructive in this regard. As it became apparent that many in our asylums were being either unlawfully abused or deprived of their liberty, the "mentally ill" won the right to be released to or remain in the community if it could be proven that they were of no danger to themselves or others. With the population in mental hospitals declining precipitously over the past two decades from 420,000 to fewer than 145,000, many can now feel confident that we are well beyond the days of the "Cuckoo's Nest." Yet, what has been the actual result of this "right" to avoid state enforced therapy? It brought forth not a new era in the humane treatment of the troubled but a new era of state neglect. Instead of brutalizing people within institutional structures, the state now permits the personally disturbed to be brutalized on the streets of our cities. While it previously cost between $25,000 and $30,000 annually to hospitalize each patient, the state currently allots ex-patients (through Supplemental Security Income) merely $3,000 on which to survive. Homeless, many of the mentally ill end up in one of the many decrepit boarding houses— "large psychiatric ghettos"—that have sprung up to exploit their vulnerability. Their lives are "hellish at best. They live totally alone, and people don't even know their names or come by and ask them how they feel. They are looked upon as a paycheck and nothing more."[16] In this context, we would do well to keep in mind Charles Marske and Steven Vargo's broader observation regarding the effects of the due process or rights movement in various sectors of our society in recent years: "Unfortunately, the darker side of legalization is its implication in depersonalization.... A curious irony emerges: the very groups that called for expanded legalism to establish and protect their individual rights now suffer its consequences."[17]

 2. *The ideology of rehabilitation provides an important rationale for opposing the conservative's assumption that increased repression will reduce crime.* Those embracing the conservatives' call for "law and order" place immense faith in the premise that tough rather than humane justice is the answer to society's crime problem. In the political right's view, unlawful acts occur only when individuals have calculated that they are advantageous, and thus the public's victimization will only subside if criminal choices are made more costly. This can be best accomplished by sending more offenders away to prison for more extended and uncomfortable stays. Indeed, the very existence of high crime rates is prima-facie evidence that greater repression is required to insure that lawlessness in our nation no longer pays.

 Liberals have traditionally attacked this logic on the grounds that repressive tactics do not touch upon the real social roots of crime and hence rarely succeed in even marginally reducing criminal involvement. Campaigns to heighten the harshness of existing criminal penalties—already notable for their severity—will only serve to fuel the problem of burgeoning prison populations and result in a further deterioration of penal living standards. The strategy of "getting tough" thus promises to have substantial costs, both in terms of the money wasted on the excessive use of incarceration and in terms of the inhumanity it shamefully introduces.

 It is clear that proponents of the justice model share these intense liberal concerns over the appealing but illusory claims of those preaching law and order. However, their opposition to repressive crime control policies encounters difficulties because core assumptions of the justice model converge closely with those found in the paradigm for crime control espoused by conservatives. Both perspectives, for instance, argue that (1) offenders are responsible beings who freely choose to engage in crime; (2) regardless of the social injustices that may have prompted an individual to breach the law, the nature of the crime and not the nature of the circumstances surrounding a crime should regulate the severity of the sanction meted out; and (3) the punishment of offenders is deserved—that is, the state's infliction of pain for pain's sake is a positive good to be encouraged and not a likely evil to be discouraged. Admittedly, those wishing to "do justice" would contend that current sanctions are too harsh and that prison conditions should be made less rigorous. But having already agreed with conservatives that punishing criminals is the fully legitimate purpose of the criminal justice system, they are left with little basis on which to challenge the logic or moral justification of proposals to get tough. Instead, their opposition to such measures is reduced to a debate with conservatives over the exact amount of deprivation of liberty and of living conditions during incarceration that each criminal act "justly deserves." Significantly, this debate is settled not in academic forums where ideal conceptions of "justice" can be formulated and discussed, but in legislative sessions where it is known that the majority of the electorate want sanctions increased and believe that "conditions in this country's prisons are not harsh enough."[18]

In contrast, the ideology of rehabilitation disputes every facet of the conclusion that the constant escalation of punishment will mitigate the spectre of crime. To say that offenders are in need of rehabilitation is to reject the conservatives' notion that individuals, regardless of their position in the social order—whether black or white, rich or poor—exercise equal freedom in deciding whether to commit a crime. Instead, it is to reason that social and personal circumstances often constrain, if not compel, people to violate the law; and unless efforts are made to enable offenders to escape these criminogenic constraints, little relief in the crime rate can be anticipated. Policies that insist on ignoring these realities by assuming a vengeful posture toward offenders promise to succeed only in fostering hardships that will, if anything, deepen the resentment that many inmates find difficult to suppress upon their release back into society. As Judge David Bazelon has poignantly commented, "Most disturbing, all these proposals fail to consider the social injustices that breed crime.... I do not understand how these academicians and politicians can have a clear conscience preaching repression as the solution to crime, unless of course they believe that despite the accident of birth everyone in this country is equally endowed, mentally and physically, and has the same opportunities they have had to get ahead."[19]

A rehabilitative stance thus allows us to begin to speak about, in Karl Menninger's words, not the "punishment of crime" but the "crime of punishment."[20] The conservatives' plea for repression is exposed as a "crime" because it both needlessly dehumanizes society's captives and falsely deceives the public that strict crime control measures will afford citizens greater safety. Drawing on the logic of the Positivist School of criminology while casting aside the classical image of the lawbreaker, the concept of rehabilitation reveals that fundamental changes in offenders will not be realized as long as inflicting deprivation remains the legitimate goal of our system of criminal "injustice." As Menninger has observed, "the more fiercely, the more ruthlessly, the more inhumanely the offender is treated—however legally—the more certain we are to have more victims."[21] Alternatively, a treatment ideology prompts us first to appreciate the troubles and disadvantages that drive many into crime and then to reach out and assist offenders to deal with the conditions and needs that have moved them to break the law. The demand is made, in short, that caring rather than hurting be the guiding principle of the correctional process. Moreover, in sensitizing us to the fact that much of the illegality that plagues society is intimately linked to existing social inequalities and injustices, rehabilitative ideology makes clear that a true solution to the crime problem ultimately rests in the support of reform programs that will bring about a more equitable distribution of resources through a broad structural transformation of the social order. This is in notable contrast to the philosophy of just deserts that assumes full individual responsibility, focuses on the culpability of the single perpetrator, and therefore "acquits the existing social order of any charge of injustice."[22]

It is apparent, then, that the ideology of rehabilitation is fully oppositional to the conservatives' agenda for the repression of crime. Importantly, it thus furnishes liberals seeking to effect criminal justice reform with a coherent framework with which to argue that benevolence and not brutality should inform society's attempts to control crime. Sharing no assumptions with the right's paradigm of law and order, it does not, as in the case of the justice model, easily give legitimacy to either repressive punishment policies or the neglect of offender well-being. Instead, it remains a distinctly liberal ideology that can be utilized as a resource in the left's quest to illustrate the futility of policies that increase pain but accomplish little else.

3. Rehabilitation still receives considerable support as a major goal of the correctional system. With prison populations exploding and punitive legislation being passed across the nation, it is of little surprise to find opinion polls indicating a hardening of public attitudes toward crime control.[23] For instance one recent national survey discovered that 53 percent of the respondents felt that present prison conditions were not harsh enough, 18 percent just about right, 13 percent too harsh, and 16 percent not sure.[24] In this light, it can be imagined that public opinion would constitute a serious and perhaps insurmountable obstacle to any proposals advocating the treatment rather than the mere punishment of offenders. The viability of liberal reform strategies aimed at reaffirming rehabilitation would thus seem questionable at best.

But this is not the case. While the average citizen clearly wants criminals to be severely sanctioned—in particular, sent to prison for longer stays—survey research consistently reveals that the American public also believes that offenders should be rehabilitated.[25] In the national survey cited above which reported that the majority of Americans in July of 1981 judged prisons to be too soft, the respondents were also asked: "What do you think should be the primary purpose of putting criminals in prison?" Notably, 37 percent answered "to rehabilitate them," compared with 31 percent who favored the alternative "to punish them" and 25 percent that favored "to remove them from society" (7 percent were "not sure").[26] A similar portrait of public opinion is indicated by a 1979 survey of Springfield, Illinois residents. The results of this poll are presented in Table 7.1.[27] By examining the second column in the table (labeled "Public"), it is readily apparent that large percentages of the residents agreed that punishment is deserved (93.2 percent) and that stiffer sanctions will reduce crime (80.6 percent). Nevertheless, over three-fourths of the public also expressed the belief that inmates should be "given the chance to be rehabilitated" and almost 60 percent concurred that rehabilitation is "just as important as making a criminal pay for his or her crime." Further, less than 40 percent felt that adult criminals could not be reformed, while nearly half of the residents said that they would

Table 7.1 Percentage Agreeing with Punishment and Rehabilitation Philosophy, by Item and Group (1979)

Items	Sample total	Public	Prison Guards	Legislators	Judges	Lawyers	Correctional Administrators	Prison Inmates
1. Criminals deserve to be punished because they have harmed society.	87.9	93.2	93.5	96.9	94.2	86.8	91.7	68.6
2. Stiffer jail sentences will help reduce the amount of crime by showing criminals that crime doesn't pay.	62.9	80.6	77.4	69.8	64.0	48.1	50.0	22.4
3. While I believe that criminals deserve to be punished and sent to jail, I also believe that criminals should be given the chance to be rehabilitated.	90.4	76.7	93.5	95.1	98.9	90.5	100.0	87.2
4. Rehabilitating a criminal is just as important as making a criminal pay for his or her crime.	75.6	58.3	74.2	79.7	77.3	81.8	91.7	78.8
5. The rehabilitation of adult criminals just does not work.	26.8	38.8	26.6	26.6	34.1	17.1	25.0	27.9
6. I would support expanding the rehabilitation programs that are now being undertaken in our prisons.	67.5	47.8	58.1	65.1	65.2	74.0	91.7	82.6
Sample Size (N) =	434	74	31	65	89	77	12	86

"support expanding the rehabilitation programs that are now being undertaken in our prisons."

Significantly, support for rehabilitation was discovered to be even more pronounced when groups associated with the Illinois criminal justice system were asked to respond to the items listed in Table 7.1.[28] As can be seen by reviewing this table, substantial proportions of the state's legislature, members of the legal profession, and correctional participants agreed that the system should reform as well as punish, rejected the idea that rehabilitation is a failure, and supported the expansion of existing treatment programs.[29] These findings are of particular interest in that they occurred in a state that had just previously passed determinate sentencing legislation called "Class X" to reflect its "get tough" orientation. Moreover, as discussed previously in Chapter 5, it is revealing that the objects of the wisdom of liberal reform—prison inmates—continue to express a firm faith in the rehabilitative ideal. There is little support for the position voiced by advocates of the justice model that treatment is more hurtful than helpful, a finding that should give pause to those of the left before they proceed to announce the demise of rehabilitation.[30] Thus, over 80 percent of the inmates sampled desired to see an increase in treatment services. Similarly, in response to items not included in Table 7.1, fewer than 10 percent agreed that such "rehabilitation programs often violate the rights of prisoners and therefore should be abolished," and only two inmates in five would say rehabilitation has "resulted in prisoners being punished more severely than if they had just been left alone and allowed to serve their time in jail."

In sum, existing survey data suggest that rehabilitation persists as a prevailing ideology within the arena of criminal justice. This does not mean that treatment programs in our prisons are flourishing and remain unthreatened by the pragmatics and punitiveness of our day. But it is to assert that the rehabilitative ideal and the benevolent potential it holds are deeply anchored within our correctional and broader cultural heritage. That is, rehabilitation constitutes an ongoing rationale that is accepted by or "makes sense to" the electorate as well as to criminal justice interest groups and policy-makers. Consequently, it provides reformers with a valuable vocabulary with which to justify changes in policy and practice aimed at mitigating the harshness of criminal sanctions—such as the diversion of offenders into the community for "treatment" or the humanization of the prison to develop a more effective "therapeutic environment." Unlike direct appeals for inmate rights to humane and just living conditions that can be quickly dismissed as the mere coddling of the dangerous ("Why should we care about their rights when they certainly didn't care about the rights of their innocent victims?"), liberal reforms undertaken in the name of rehabilitation have the advantage of resonating with accepted ideology and hence of retaining an air of legitimacy. And should the confidence of citizens about specific proposals waver, it is always possible to impress upon the public that, despite overflowing penitentiaries, the average prisoner is back on the streets within two years and that fewer than 9 percent of the inmate population is serving a life sentence.[31] If the public is not willing to pay now to facilitate the betterment of those held in captivity, it can be made clear to them that they will be forced to pay in more bothersome, if not tragic, ways at a later date.

Our message here is simple but, in light of the advent of the justice model, telling in its implications: for liberals to argue vehemently against the ideology of rehabilitation—to say that treatment cannot work because the rehabilitative ideal is inherently flawed—is to undermine the potency of one of the few resources that can be mobilized in the left's pursuit of less repression in the administration of criminal punishments.

4. *Rehabilitation has historically been an important motive underlying reform efforts that have increased the humanity of the correctional system.* Liberal critics have supplied ample evidence to confirm their suspicions that state enforced therapy has too frequently encouraged the unconscionable exploitation of society's captives. Their chilling accounts of the inhumanities completed under the guise of "treatment" call forth the compelling conclusion that far greater benevolence would grace the criminal justice system had notions of rehabilitation never taken hold.

However, while the damages permitted by the corruption of the rehabilitative ideal should neither be denied nor casually swept aside, it would be misleading to idealize the "curious" but brutal punishments of "bygone days" and to ignore that reforms undertaken in the name of rehabilitation have been a crucial humanizing influence in the darker regions of the sanctioning process. Gaylin and Rothman have thus noted that "while rehabilitation may have been used as an excuse for heaping punishment upon punishment, it was also a limiting factor, and was a rationalization and justification for what few comforts were introduced into the lives of the prisoners."[32] Similarly, Francis A. Allen has recently commented that "it is a historical fact that the great reforms in the physical and moral conditions of institutional life have been accomplished largely by persons whose humanitarian impulses were joined with rehabilitative aspirations."[33] It is instructive as well to contemplate fully the thoughtful observations of Graeme Newman:

> Yet it would seem that to throw out the whole idea of good intentions, because most of the time they do not reach the lofty heights they were supposed to achieve, may be to throw out many other values that have often accompanied them: human values, the wish, at least, to treat people humanely. Some argue that we do not need the medical [rehabilitative model] as an "excuse" to treat offenders humanely, that we ought to do it for the sake of being humane in and of itself. But this argument, although admirably principled, does not recognize the great cultural difficulties (largely unconscious) that we have had, and continue to have, in acting humanely to those who are society's outcasts. Surely this is the lesson of history. It is only a couple of hundred years since we gave up mutilating, disemboweling, and chopping up criminals, and we still cannot make up our minds whether to stop killing them. It would seem to me, therefore, that while the medical [rehabilitative] model has its own drawbacks, it has brought along with it a useful baggage of humane values that might never have entered the darkness of criminal justice otherwise.[34]

Those who have traditionally sought to treat offenders have thus also sought to lessen the discomforts convicts are made to suffer. In part, this occurs, as Allen has remarked, because "the objectives both of fundamental decency in the prisons and the rehabilitation of prisoners... appears to require the same measures."[35] Yet the studies of Torsten Eriksson suggest that it is the case as well that those endeavoring to pioneer "the more effective treatment of criminals" have commonly been united in their "indomitable will to help their erring brother." They stand out as "beacons in the history of mankind, the part that deals with compassion with one's fellow man."[36] In this context, we can again question the wisdom of liberal attempts to unmask the rehabilitative ideal as at best a "noble lie" and at worst an inevitably coercive fraud. For in discrediting rehabilitation, liberal critics may succeed in deterring a generation of potential reformers from attempting to do good in the correctional system by teaching that it is a futile enterprise to show care for offenders by offering to help these people lead less destructive lives. And should rehabilitation be forfeited as the prevailing liberal ideology, what will remain as the medium through which benevolent sentiments will be expressed and instituted into meaningful policy? Will the medium be a justice model that is rooted in despair and not optimism, that embraces punishment and not betterment, that disdains inmate needs and disadvantages in favor of a concern for sterile and limited legal rights, and whose guiding principle of reform is to have the state do less for its captives rather than more? Or will, as we fear, this vacuum remain unfilled and the liberal camp be left without an ideology that possesses the vitality—as has rehabilitation over the past 150 years—to serve as a rallying cry for or motivating force behind reforms that will engender lasting humanizing changes?

STATE OBLIGATED REHABILITATION

During a recent educational workshop at the Iowa State Penitentiary sponsored by the prisoners' Progressive Black Culture Organization, we witnessed an inmate rise to the podium and declare, "They call this a correctional institution, but they don't do any correcting." This offender's remarks sensitized us to two realities: first, the inmates present that day were clear in their call for more rather than less rehabilitative services that would facilitate their self-improvement and enable them to achieve a reasonable stake in conforming upon their re-entry into society. And second, despite the fact that their parole-release was to be an important degree contingent on their capacity to demonstrate their reformation, insufficient pressure was being exerted on the state to supply these inmates with meaningful opportunities to become rehabilitated.

These insights provide the point of departure for our assessment of why treatment practices have been so often flawed and in turn of the strategies that we believe liberals should employ to reaffirm rehabilitation. Now the thrust of our analysis has been that the inequities and inhumanities of the criminal justice system that liberals find so intolerable will be exacerbated and not diminished should the left embrace the justice model as its dominant avenue of reform. Fostering the principles of desert and determinacy runs the grave risk of adding legitimacy to the conservatives' efforts to affect a new wave of repressive legislation and incarcerative practices, and of condoning the neglect of inmate needs. We have argued as well that rehabilitation is an ideology of benevolence that not only has precipitated reform movements that have tempered the harshness of punishments but also, as a persisting rationale for criminal sanctioning, retains the potential to be mobilized to justify future ameliorations of the correctional system.

Yet in illustrating the dangers of attacking and rejecting rehabilitation, we are not insensitive to the abuse inherent in a system that links liberty to self-improvement but furnishes few means to secure this end. Under the practice of enforced therapy, the state ideally institutes comprehensive treatment programs and in return demands that offenders take advantage of these opportunities and show signs of their willingness to conform. However, as the inmate at the Iowa State Penitentiary was painfully aware, the state cannot be trusted to keep its half of the bargain: "it doesn't correct." While control officials are willing to base release decisions on an offender's "progress," they provide only minimal services that inmates can use to better equip themselves to negotiate the constraints of the wider society.

Liberal advocates of the justice model have thus argued that this link between being cured and being set free is coercive and must be broken. In place of enforced therapy which compels offenders to seek reform on the threat of longer stays behind bars, they assert that rehabilitation must become "voluntary"—that is, that both entry into and subsequent performance in a treatment program will have no impact whatsoever on when an inmate will be released from jail. With the coerciveness surrounding treatment fully dissipated, only those inmates who really desire to improve themselves will take advantage of the limited services currently available. Prison programs will, as a consequence, become more meaningful for those who choose to participate, and their effects on reducing recidivism will be commensurately enhanced.

The logic that we should "help only those who want to be helped" is attractive but it avoids some rather sticky considerations. For one thing, if the state has been lax in its provision of rehabilitative resources when it has struck a public bargain to do so, how diligent will its commitment to this task be when rehabilitation becomes voluntary and the state's obligation to treat its captives is no longer strictly mandated? More importantly, if we conclude that rehabilitation should be left voluntary and hence that an inmate's prospect for cure is not to be a standard regulating length of incarceration (or if incarceration is appropriate at all), then what criterion will be substituted? Of course, the answer to this question is retribution or, as liberals prefer, just deserts. This brings us back to the original controversy of whether reforms that abandon notions of rehabilitation and promote the principles of the justice model will mitigate or aggravate the proclivity of the correctional machinery to victimize its charges. And as we have suggested throughout, there is good reason to surmise that a criminal justice system that seeks exclusively to inflict punishment in the name of justice will be substantially worse than one that punishes but endeavors as well to rehabilitate society's wayward members.

Yet in again rejecting the justice model as violating the "principle of least harm," we do not mean to imply that liberals should simply become resigned to accept state enforced therapy as it is currently practiced—however despairing this alternative might seem—because it is the lesser of two evils. While we have argued for the advantages of trumpeting treatment ideology, we believe that it is equally important that liberal reform seeks to reaffirm rehabilitation in ways that negate its more abusive features. In this regard, the remarks of the Iowa inmate remind us that a crucial flaw of state enforced therapy is that it is imbalanced: the inmate has the obligation to be reformed in order to win release, but in the absence of sufficient pressure, the state has no real obligation to rehabilitate. It is thus incumbent upon liberals to attack this imbalance by exerting pressure on the state to fulfill more adequately its half of the bargain. This would involve undertaking a persistent campaign to expose the state's failure to meet its responsibilities and to institute policies that obligate correctional officials to supply inmates with the educational, occupational, and psychological services as well as the community programs it has so long promised to deliver.

In short, we are proposing that liberals discard state enforced therapy and embrace *state obligated therapy* as an avenue of criminal justice reform. Since it has been tragically and repeatedly demonstrated that the state cannot be trusted through appeals to its good will to create uniformly meaningful treatment programs, reforms aimed at obligating the state to rehabilitate must be sensitive to the need to restructure the prevailing interests in the correctional system that have long undermined the provision of treatment services to offenders. There can be no illusions that this task will be easily accomplished. Nevertheless, we can suggest three beginning strategies that can be pursued by liberals endeavoring to intensify the state's interest in and hence obligation to rehabilitate.

CORRECTIONAL OFFICIAL ACCOUNTABILITY

Few would disagree with the thrust of our Iowa inmate's observations that we call our prisons "correctional institutions, but they don't correct"—despite the fact that many offenders voice a desire for self-improvement and the chance for conformity. Yet, why is this the case? To be sure, partial answers to this query can be found in such factors as low budgets for rehabilitation programs, the problems that inhere in changing people, the non-therapeutic nature of imprisonment, and the lack of an adequate theory of crime that can direct us to prescribe the scientifically appropriate intervention for each offender. However, it is instructive as well to take notice that correctional administrators have achieved greater success in accomplishing an equally, if not more difficult task: maintaining order in the prison. Although faced with the burdens of volatile inmate populations, severe overcrowding, racial conflicts, inmate victimizations of one another, the profound tensions incarceration inevitably produces, and a poorly educated and trained custodial staff, only on rare occasions do we find the equilibrium of the prison disturbed by either mass inmate insurgency or escape. Admittedly, penitentiaries are frequently dangerous and whatever peace that is attained is an uneasy one; nevertheless, officials have become adept at insuring that "all hell doesn't break loose" in the institutions they manage.

Why, then, have administrators done a better job at securing institutional order than at correcting their charges? Indeed, why have they even gone so far as to typically look upon prison rehabilitation not as an opportunity to treat but rather as another mechanism that can be used to facilitate order by keeping inmates in line (e.g., to tell inmates "behave or you don't get out")? Perhaps the simplest but most truthful answer is that while both tasks are complex and not easily accomplished, correctional officials *get paid to maintain order and not to rehabilitate*. David Rothman's analysis of the evolution of corrections in America thus led him to conclude that "In effect, the state and the prison had struck a mutually agreeable bargain: As long as the warden ran a secure institution which did not attract adverse publicity . . .he would have a free hand to administer his prison as he liked. . . . In the end, it was security that counted, not rehabilitation and the prison administrators knew it, fashioned their routine accordingly, and survived in power."[37] Similarly, the writers of *Institutions, Etc.* have commented that "It is an unspoken axiom in correctional administration that in order to gain tenure there are three principles that must be followed: 1) keep within your budget, 2) keep your staff happy, and 3) keep your institutions free from incidents." Significantly, "none of these need relate to the more mundane goals of your agency—for example, whether one is lowering recidivism rates or treating inmates decently."[38]

In light of these pragmatics, it is not surprising that administrators have sacrificed genuine concern for treatment to enhance institutional control. This is not to portray correctional officials as a particularly self-serving and uncaring bunch; indeed, surveys indicate that these officials strongly support the idea that offenders should be afforded the chance to be reformed.[39] But it is to say that their decisions have been constrained by the prevailing realities of their occupational position that discourage them from placing a high priority on providing truly substantive treatment services. In turn, the policy implications of this insight are clear: if liberals want prisons not only to remain orderly but to rehabilitate as well, they must attempt to restructure these "realities" and make it distinctly in the interest of administrators to cure their charges. At its most fundamental level, this means paying officials to rehabilitate and firing them if they don't.

One liberal reform strategy is thus to obligate the state to rehabilitate by holding its agents, correctional administrators, accountable if this task is not effectively undertaken. A first step in this strategy is to reaffirm that offender rehabilitation is a legitimate and attainable correctional goal. This could be accomplished by mobilizing the widespread support for treatment ideology that still exists among both legislators and the electorate. Second, it can be argued openly that the reason that rehabilitation programs are in a shambles is that no one is ever held responsible for their quality. Few other organizations would tolerate such ineptitude, and most would ultimately lay the blame for continued mismanagement at the feet of its executives. As such, correctional officials must be told that it is their obligation to insure that treatment programs are run in an acceptable fashion, and that if they are not equal to this task, then replacements can be found. Third, reasonable measures of an administrator's "effectiveness"—that is, of what an official can be expected to accomplish—should be developed. It would seem wise to argue against the use of recidivism rates because they are often difficult to assess accurately and can be made to fluctuate by factors that administrators have little control over (e.g., a worsening economy, changes in judicial attitudes toward parole revocation). Instead, the effectiveness of an official's performance should be tapped by evaluating his or her ability to establish viable programs that facilitate the acquisition of interpersonal and occupational skills by inmates. For instance, each institution should be monitored and compared on such measures as the percentage of inmates participating in treatment programs, the average number of hours each week that an inmate spends in a rehabilitation program, what is done during this time ("program integrity"), the number of educational degrees earned, the number of former inmates placed in jobs related to the training they received in prison, and the size of work-release populations.

In sum, we are proposing that by making correctional administrators accountable for the quality of rehabilitation programs, our prisons will see the emergence of more and better treatment services, reduced inmate idleness, increased inmate self-improvement, and ultimately more productive and less criminogenic offenders released back into society. In taking this stance, we are not oblivious to the many obstacles that officials would have to confront in order to create meaningful therapeutic environments. Yet such obstacles will never be overcome until they are not permitted to constitute "insurmountable" excuses. For years, the executives of American automobile corporations claimed they could not produce fuel efficient vehicles, yet moved rapidly to do so once the profit structure of the industry was threatened. Cars and criminals are obviously not the same, but the lesson to be learned is: organizations have the potential to achieve new and difficult goals—whether it is building smaller autos or rehabilitating rather than simply controlling inmates—if the fortunes of those at or near the top depend on it.

PAROLE CONTRACTS

By instituting standards of administrative accountability, it is intended that correctional officials will coalesce into a potentially powerful interest group having a stake in actively campaigning for the allocation of increased resources to treatment programs. Yet it can be anticipated as well that the current corps of correctional administrators would offer stiff resistance to any efforts to impose standards that jeopardize their employment security. Thus, while we believe that notions of "accountability" embodying sentiments of bureaucratic rationality and utilitarianism make good sense to the public and politicians alike and hence can be used eventually to win support for policy changes, it is apparent that the battle to make administrators formally responsible for program quality will be an arduous and precarious one. As a consequence, it is important that liberals simultaneously explore alternative strategies that can obligate the state and its agents to rehabilitate.

One promising avenue of reform is to establish a system of "parole (or rehabilitation) contracts." Under this concept, inmates agree to complete certain rehabilitation programs and in exchange are given the exact date on which they will be paroled. For instance, after negotiations with the parole board, an inmate may be accorded a release date contingent on his (her) completing a treatment program that includes graduating from high school, finishing a trade training course, and regularly attending Alcoholics Anonymous meetings. These negotiations ideally occur during the first weeks of incarceration, and the specifics of the bargain are written into a legally binding contract.

The feasibility of pursuing reforms constructed along these lines is indicated by the fact that over ten states have experimented with the use of such contracts with varying degrees of success.[40] One evaluation of three pilot programs revealed that recidivism rates for offenders participating in the program remained unaffected. However, this study also reported that prison terms were not lengthened and that inmates were clearly favorable to the idea of contracting for their release.[41] In addition, advocates have suggested that in the long run the very existence of a contract system will exert pressure on correctional officials to improve treatment services. Leon Leiberg, the leading proponent of this reform, has thus asserted that contracts have the advantage of fostering accountability: "a contract forces an institution to account for the availability and effectiveness of its programs."[42] Similarly, John Conrad has predicted that as the number of inmates contracting for parole expand, "prison officials in turn will be motivated to use a combination of initiative and ingenuity to create genuine work assignments which can qualify for contract programming."[43] On a more general note, Daniel Glaser has termed this innovation "a great thing. It reduces the indeterminacy of sentences, gives the client a role [in programming], and leads to more realistic and adequate [job] training."[44]

Significantly, the policy of parole contracts also has the decided advantage of being perhaps the only reform that could garner support both from liberals favoring the justice model and from those on the left who have not forsaken the rehabilitative ideal. Adherents to the justice model can take comfort in the knowledge that (1) sentence lengths will be determined shortly after incarceration and hence that inmates will not be kept in torturous suspense regarding their release dates, and (2) that the written contract will constitute a statement of the rights of offenders and afford them protection against the abusive use of the unfettered discretion traditionally exercised by the correctional regime.[45] On the other hand, supporters of treatment can embrace the concept of parole contracts because it denies the advisability of legislatively-fixed terms, reaffirms the importance of rehabilitation as a correctional goal, and retains elements of individualized treatment. In this light, contract programming has the potential to "offer a middle ground between conflicting correctional philosophies... halfway between the 'medical model' and the Fogel model of 'justice.'"[46] In turn, this creates the refreshing possibility that liberals can once again undertake a unified rather than a divisive reform effort which, as a result, would enjoy a heightened probability of success.

While the broad notion of contracting for treatment services and parole-release is appealing, the specific dimensions of such a reform would be crucial in determining its ability to promote rehabilitation and mitigate the severity of penal sanctions. In this regard, we suggest the following considerations. First, in programs currently in operation, both the inmate and the state enter into the contract on a voluntary basis. Some might prefer this policy since it means that inmates are not coerced to participate in the program, but instead are free to choose to be paroled under present regulations. However, a voluntary approach also means that the state has the discretion to deny inmates the opportunity to contract. Now as long as the pool of offenders wishing to contract does not outstrip an institution's treatment resources, correction officials can be expected to exercise this option infrequently. Moreover, as suggested above by Leiberg and Conrad, even voluntary contracts promise to motivate officials to improve the quality and perhaps quantity of existing programs. Nevertheless, under a voluntary system, what will occur should the concept of contracting for parole flourish and a large proportion of inmates express a desire to bargain for rehabilitative services and a release date? There is a very real and troubling prospect, particularly with prison populations steadily rising, that correctional officials will conclude that their only choice is to exercise their discretion and limit the number of inmates given contracts according to the number of slots available in the existing rehabilitation programs in their institutions. Despite the existence of a contract system, then, correctional officials would ultimately be under no obligation to expand treatment services to meet inmate needs. Consequently, a substantial segment of the inmate populace could potentially be denied access to the rehabilitation they desire. In this context, we propose that the participation by each inmate and the state in the formulation of parole contracts be made universally mandatory.[47] This clearly implies that every offender has a responsibility to make a genuine effort for self-improvement while imprisoned. Yet it also binds the state and its agents, correctional officials, to develop a comprehensive treatment program for every offender. Of import is that this might well place correctional administrators in the awkward position of having insufficient resources to uphold the state's half of the bargains made with inmates. As such, we could expect that officials would be under pressure to mobilize their political power in order to secure the increased treatment facilities that would allow them "to do their jobs."

In short, mandatory contracts permit us to move in the direction of obligating the state to rehabilitate, while voluntary contracts risk subverting this goal. However, there is an additional problem that must be addressed: what is to prevent the state from making contracts with inmates and then turning around and not providing the treatment services it promised? One potent deterrent is the threat of a flood of civil suits launched by inmates seeking to recover damages from the state. Another possibility is that contracts will tend to make specific officials manifestly responsible for supplying services and in turn open the way for appeals for administrative accountability, preferably to the point of firing those who persist in disregarding contracts. Further, attempts could be made to introduce a system of penalties that would be levied against the state in the event of contractual violations, and hence would function to bolster the state's interest in rehabilitating its charges. These penalties would be in the form of reduced sentences for inmates who suffer broken agreements; if the state fails to abide by its obligation to rehabilitate, then the offender gets out early. Ideally, the penalty schedule, with exact time reductions stated for each service not provided, would be written directly into the contract. This would parallel business contracts that delineate sanctions when services are not supplied or completed on time (e.g., contract states that a company will be assessed a set monetary loss for every day it takes past a deadline to deliver promised materials).

Finally, every effort should be expended to minimize the coercive potential that inheres in contract parole. To begin with, the initial contract talks between the offender and correctional officials (most likely the parole board) is a negotiation between unequals. Offenders thus have little choice but to accept the release date and rehabilitative conditions put forth by state officials. "As the Mafia is reputed to do," Norval Morris has observed, "the state here makes him an offer he cannot refuse."[48] This is not desirable, but it must be remembered that apart from plea bargaining, current parole-release policies as well as determinate sentencing schemes afford offenders no role whatsoever in the sentencing process. At the very least, a contract system creates a bargaining opportunity for some inmate input into the length and conditions of incarceration. Given this inroad, liberal reformers could then argue for increased inmate participation in defining the specifics of a contract on two grounds. First, there is evidence that "involving offenders in planning and implementing their own treatment" will lower recidivism rates.[49] Second, fairly bargained contracts will militate against the emergence of inmate feelings of resentment and injustice that could precipitate prison turmoil. In David Fogel's words, "Men who negotiate their fates do not have to turn to violence as a method of achieving change."[50]

As a further protection for inmates, attempts should also be undertaken to establish an appeal process for offenders who are dissatisfied with the contracts they are offered. It would be best to have members of the judiciary, who have no direct occupational interests at stake, arbitrate all disputes. If this is not feasible, then another, perhaps more attainable option would be to create the position of an "ombudsman" in the correctional system. This person would be answerable only to the governor's office, not to the department of corrections, and would have the responsibility to endeavor to resolve all controversies stemming from contract negotiations.[51]

Similarly, it can be anticipated that disagreements will arise over whether inmates have fulfilled their contractual obligations. Most of these difficulties can be avoided if the parole contracts designate in unambiguous terms the exact treatment goals that an offender must achieve to be released on the specified date.[52] In the same vein, the contracts should set forth the exact time an inmate's sentence will be extended in the event an inmate does not live up to any condition agreed upon. This practice will mirror the penalty schedule the state will suffer should it violate the contract, and will ultimately give offenders the right to reject their responsibility to be rehabilitated at the price of a longer tenure in captivity. However, in instances where contractual transgressions are not clear and disputes remain—such as if the claim were made that treatment personnel were punishing an inmate by preventing his/her progress in a rehabilitation program—an arbitration system would be essential. Again, judges or an ombudsman could perform this function. Yet a more likely candidate, given its existence, is the parole board. This alternative possesses its dangers, because of the proclivity of parole boards to believe the correctional officials' version of any story. Consequently, reformers would have to serve as watchdogs who pressure boards to be equitable by publicizing both the percentage of cases decided in the state's favor and any miscarriages of justices that may occur.

CAMPAIGN IN FAVOR OF REHABILITATION

Recently, Tony Platt and Paul Takagi offered these poignant and disturbing remarks:

> The current "law and order" campaign, orchestrated at the highest levels of federal, state and local governments, is well under way to eliminate the minimal reforms in criminal justice and corrections that were won in the 1970's. *The justification for this shift to tougher punishments*—deterrence, incapacitation, mandatory sentences, restitution, etc.—*is that "rehabilitation" has failed to reduce crime or reform prisoners* [emphasis added].[53]

Platt and Takagi's observations reveal the urgency for those on the left to combat forcefully the right's call for repressive law and order policies by reaffirming both the vitality of the rehabilitative ideal and the state's obligation not simply to punish but also to treat. Already, we have proposed two avenues of liberal reform oriented in this direction: administrative accountability and parole contracts. Yet these reforms would both necessitate securing legislative approval for what would constitute a rather broad transformation of existing correctional policy. In either case, this will not be easily nor, importantly, immediately accomplished. While more ambitious and fundamental structural reforms of the correctional system are being sought, then, what posture should liberals assume at this moment in the face of the current swing in criminal justice toward conservatism and punitiveness? We can suggest one present-oriented strategy that liberals can employ on a continuing basis and with the expectation of short-range but potentially significant benefits: campaign in favor of rehabilitation. This tactic is dual-pronged, emphasizing the need for liberals both to publicly advocate rehabilitative ideology and to use this ideology to pressure correctional officials to fulfill their obligation to supply offenders with more adequate treatment services. Let us be more specific.

With Platt and Takagi's warning in mind, it seems crucial that liberals bind together and actively seek to bolster the legitimacy of rehabilitation while simultaneously illuminating the irrationality of repressive crime control measures. This campaign should be undertaken through the media and, most generally, should endeavor to capitalize on and to strengthen existing public sentiments that persist in accepting rehabilitation as an appropriate, if not preferred, correctional goal. Some important parameters of this campaign would include: first, highlight the successes of rehabilitation. This would involve publicizing treatment programs that lower recidivism rates or that supply useful community services.[54] Equally important, however, is to facilitate the reporting of news stories on individual offenders who have become "rehabilitated" and are now "upstanding" members of their communities. These human interest accounts are valuable in deflating the myth that inmate self-advancement is not possible. Second, keep stressing that rehabilitation is not, even today, really being tried. Liberals must constantly reveal the paucity of resources typically committed to offender treatment, and assert that this is why society often fails to reform its criminals. Third, remind the public and politicians that all but a few offenders will eventually return to their own or bordering communities. It should be maintained that a lack of meaningful rehabilitation programs simply means that ex-cons will be released unchanged if not more resentful, and hence more likely to victimize the public than had previously been the case. It can be further argued that without the benefit of treatment, even those offenders who do manage to stay straight promise to be less economically productive, more personally troubled, and therefore potential burdens on society. Fourth, communicate the age-old prison wisdom that harsh sanctions that offer inmates little hope of improvement and freedom are almost certain to generate prison riots that will be expensive in terms of property damaged and lives lost—of both the kept and their keepers. Finally, inform the public of the fact that not only do "get tough" policies not reduce the crime rate but also that they inflate prison populations beyond capacity and what sound reasoning would dictate. Warehousing offenders, it should be shown, will cost the tax payers over $10,000 annually for each inmate but accomplish little else.

The second dimension of the campaign should involve liberals actually getting out into the field and pressuring correctional officials to do a better job at rehabilitating. Efforts should be made to rely on existing reform groups to secure constant visits to and public inspections of the penitentiaries. Reformers should enter each "correctional" setting voicing the assumption that rehabilitation is still a legitimate function of penal sanctioning, and then proceed on to ask administrators why their institutions are not making a concerted attempt to "correct." If rebuffed and institutional treatment programs and living conditions do not improve, reform groups should stage demonstrations and sit-ins protesting the failures of specific wardens or upper-level officials, precipitate investigative news stories that publicly unmask bureaucratic obstacles to offender rehabilitation, and ask friendly legislators to overtly or covertly press correctional officials to get their house in order.

The thrust of the strategy is thus to repeatedly reaffirm rehabilitation as a task that administrators have an obligation to perform and in turn to expose those who are unequal to the task. It is expected that when confronted with sufficient turmoil and pressure, particularly if this public controversy reaches the point of challenging their job security, it will be in the interest of officials to improve existing treatment programs. Admittedly, sustaining such intense pressure on correctional officials over a prolonged period would be difficult. As a result, unless more permanent policy changes could be won that restructure prevailing interests in the correctional system in a manner that makes providing treatment a rational option for administrators, the state's willingness to abide by its obligation to rehabilitate will prove momentary and will eventually wane. Nevertheless, a campaign at this time to reaffirm rehabilitation would have the invaluable functions of providing a needed forum for liberal resistance to the right's get tough stance, and of challenging the troubling notion that offenders are a dangerous class who cannot and do not want to be reformed. Further, it has the advantage of provoking beginning changes in the correctional system that can be utilized by liberal activists to pave the way for more lasting and far-reaching reforms that will mandate the state's obligation to rehabilitate on a continuing basis.

WHY LIBERAL REFORM?

Our evaluation of the ideology and pragmatics of the current determinate sentencing movement is clear in its conclusion that this "reform" promises to be a major impediment to liberal efforts to introduce greater benevolence into the criminal justice system. As a consequence, we have urged that those on the ideological left abandon the justice model as an avenue of correctional reform and devote their energies instead to investigating strategies that will reaffirm rehabilitative ideology and in turn obligate the state to treat its charges more humanely and justly.

Yet returning to our warning at the end of Chapter I, this policy recommendation must be understood in the political context from which it emerges. Throughout our entire analysis, we have assumed that the liberal reform goals of greater justice and humanity in the processing of offenders are worthy of pursuit and are the standards against which any criminal justice policy or practice—including determinate sentencing—ought to be evaluated. It is certainly legitimate to question, however, why liberal reform is preferable to the agenda set forth by those on the right and by those further to the left. In the pages that remain, we will thus endeavor to detail the case for undertaking liberal as opposed to conservative or radical criminal justice reform.

The central thrust of the conservatives' crime control package is to "get tough" with offenders in order to afford greater protection to the social order. Stricter fixed terms will inform lawbreakers that crime does not pay or, at the very least, will keep the dangerous caged up where they cannot harm anyone. In short, more punishment and more incarceration—not more rehabilitation and more benevolence—is held up as the cure to the problem of crime plaguing society.

Yet as discussed in Chapter 5, there is little reason to believe that the panacea being offered by the conservatives contains much substance. A look to our past can furnish scant evidence that "wars on crime" or repressive control strategies have ever been successful in reducing the public's victimization; neither, it must be added, can we anticipate a better record for such measures in the future. While the call to "get tough" with crime seems to make sense on the surface, the logic underlying this approach is fundamentally flawed. For one thing, the right's punishment policy implicitly embraces a classical image of the offender, thus assuming that criminal acts are the direct manifestation of the rational calculation of costs and benefits by those pondering a legal violation. This image disregards the insights of positivist criminology and treats the many personal and social circumstances in which people find themselves as incidental to the origin of crime. Whether it is the pressures of poverty or of corporate life, hanging around with a delinquent gang or growing up in a troubled home, being emotionally disturbed or suffering a drug addiction, none of these conditions are seen as relevant to our understanding of why crime occurs and what should be done about it. Experience teaches most of us that such a conclusion just is not warranted. People commit crimes for a variety of complex reasons, and the knowledge that offenders often escape harsh sanctions is only one of these many contributing factors.[55] A system that exercised more rigorous punishments thus may possibly deter some prospective offenders, but only at the price of continuing to leave the real root causes of the vast majority of offenders untouched and flourishing.

For another thing, it must be remembered that America already sends more offenders to prison per 100,000 population and for longer stays than any other free society. Notably, this includes nations with much lower crime rates than ours. Now an immediate reaction by many readers to this revelation might be, "Of course, if America has a higher crime rate, we are going to have more people in jail than countries that don't have as many criminals running around as we do." But it is crucial to be clear that the logic of the conservatives' "get tough" position is not that our prisons are full because we are burdened with a high crime rate, but rather that crime is flourishing in the United States because we do not punish strictly enough—that is, because lenient judges are not sending people away to prison in sufficient numbers to insure that crime in America no longer pays. As such, the existence of nations that punish less harshly than we do yet also have markedly lower crime rates presents a significant challenge to the conservatives' theory of crime by suggesting that "coddling" criminals does not lead inescapably to high offense rates and, conversely, that repressive justice is not required to prevent criminal behavior.

Further, even if it were granted that the classical image of the lawbreaker is sound, would getting tougher on offenders really have an impact on the crime rate? As explained previously, we think not. According to the principles of the classical school, the most important ingredient in deterrence (making crime not pay) is the certainty and not the severity of sanctions. However, the get tough policies proposed by conservatives, such as determinate sentencing, invariably lead only to the imposition of harsher penalties. Certainty is not enhanced by these crime control measures because they neither heighten the police's ability to catch offenders nor eliminate the discretionary powers exercised by prosecutors. Whether either of these obstacles is surmountable, given the nature of police and prosecutorial work, is quite problematic. Moreover, efforts to decrease crime by caging up large numbers of criminals are similarly destined to fail. While incapacitation might possibly bring about marginal reductions in the crime rate, this could only be achieved if the public would be willing to shoulder the exorbitant cost of substantially expanding a prison system that is already filled to the brim.

Yet it is important to realize that the appeal of the conservatives' get tough stance perhaps has less to do with its pragmatic effects on crime and far more to do with the sentiment it embodies: "Criminals are evil people who have done mean things to good innocent citizens. If conditions are miserable in prison, that's just too bad; they should have thought about that before they went around hurting people. As far as I'm concerned, they deserve to rot in jail for a long time." Indeed, each semester our lectures in favor of doing good in the criminal justice system inevitably elicit the widespread reaction among students, "Why should we treat criminals kindly? How would you feel if it were your brother or sister who had been mugged or killed? I bet you wouldn't be such a liberal then!"

Admittedly, only the most saintly would not have the immediate, if not long lasting impulse to see an offender who harmed a loved one be forced to suffer. And this is what makes the repressive practices so seductive: they resonate with our basest feelings of vengeance and hatred. Yet we can begin to reconsider the wisdom of rooting our criminal justice policies in these feelings by asking ourselves to reverse the question our students so often pose: How would you feel if it were your brother or sister who had mugged or killed? Would you be so willing to demand that your loved one be tossed in jail and the keys thrown away? Could you sit by serenely as (s)he, year after year, lived without the means or hope of reform, endured the excessive heat of summer and cold of winter, ate tasteless food and received inadequate medical treatment, survived in a small cage located within a society of fear? And whether one claims to be a religious person, a humanist or both, we all must then ask, should we treat those in our prisons any differently than we would have our own brothers and sisters treated?

Further, should those close to us be victimized by crime, what benefits are reaped by casting the offender into inhumane surroundings for a decade or two? It will not, as we have repeatedly shown, make our homes or streets more secure. It will not bring back life, limb, or property. It will not obviate the tragedy or sorrow that the crime might have evoked. At most, it provides a fleeting moment of satisfaction as one's thirst for vengeance is quenched. And this is a small reward when we consider the price of tolerating inhumanity in our midst.

This line of reasoning sensitizes us as well to the real poverty of the conservatives' call to get tough. Those on the political right often stand before us and proclaim that punishing more criminals more harshly reflects a concern for the innocent victim. However, this proves, in the end, to be a shallow concern—one which seldom produces real relief for the crime victim. For in the conservatives' world view, the state ultimately fulfills its obligation to the victim once a criminal is caught and placed in a degrading penal institution for a lengthy stay. Just as the state has no obligation to care for the needs of those who break the law, neither is it seen to have an obligation to care in any fundamental way for the needs of those having the misfortune to be victimized by a criminal act. The values underlying the conservatives' crime control package thus limit their ability to reach out and do good for anyone—whether it be those victimized by crime or by a life in crime. Their concern is of such a nature that it can lead only to the passage of harsh fixed terms that produce greater injustices in our system of criminal "justice." Meanwhile, thoughts of systematically providing social services to victims and their families—for instance, psychological counseling, financial assistance, or job retraining necessitated by disability—remain notably absent from the rhetoric of conservative writers and speakers.

> Admittedly, liberals have also been remiss in championing a movement to extend services in a meaningful way to victims. But two caveats can be noted here. First, in contrast to today's conservatives, liberals do not now come before the public and assert that they are guardians of the social order and of the innocent victim. And second, again unlike those on the right, liberal values are fully consistent with any reform program that would seek to obligate the state to care in a benevolent fashion for the welfare of any needy group—whether it is the aged, the sick, the poor, the criminal, or the victim. In this regard, we would urge that the liberal inclination to do good should prompt reformers to endeavor to bind the state to make a therapeutic response not only to offenders but to their victims as well.

Taken together, these considerations point to the final and most far-reaching reason why liberals believe that benevolence and not the punitiveness advocated by the right should be the guiding principle of the criminal justice system. Now it must be realized that liberals do not have a romanticized vision of society's criminals nor do they believe that criminal acts should go unpunished and the dangerous permitted to prey on the public. However, they do believe that inequities in wealth and power should not influence the administration of justice, that the deprivation of liberty in a free society is a severe sanction that should be used parsimoniously, that only the most incorrigible should be incarcerated, that all of society's captives should reside in decent and humane living conditions, and that all inmates should be afforded a meaningful opportunity to become productive citizens with a true stake in the social order. To a very real degree, liberals hold to these positions because they wish to better offenders and save them from the irrational sufferings imposed by repressive control policies. But there is a more fundamental reason for rejecting practices that brutalize offenders that is rooted not in a paternalistic sentiment but in stark self-interest: we should treat society's wayward justly and humanely not simply so we do not degrade them but so that we do not degrade ourselves.

It is here that we are reminded of Dostoevsky's famous dictum, "The degree of civilization in a society can be judged by entering its prisons." This is a message that deserves serious consideration. For to the extent that we are willing to construct and tolerate repressive "correctional" institutions that are in Leonard Orland's words, "houses of darkness," we make a very grave statement about what our society is about. It is to have us choose inhumanity over humanity, injustice over justice, cruelty over kindness, vengeance over mercy, insensitivity over caring, despair over hope.

It is, in short, to affirm our worst values, not our best. Unwilling to reinforce this vision of society, liberals thus reject any policy that would exacerbate the already shameful state of our correctional system. In the end, they argue for benevolence not because offenders who have acted with malice are worthy of it but because we as a people would be unworthy to live by any other standards. Swedish Minister of Justice Herman Kling has eloquently captured the essence of why we as liberals oppose the harsh proposals of the conservatives and continue to work for reforms of the criminal justice system:

> We must practice humanity without expecting anything in return. Humanitarianism should be regarded as a fundamental obligation to mankind, no matter where it leads. It is particularly important that we be steadfast in our allegiance to this principle in criminal policy, a prejudice-riddled area in which vengeful feelings are so easily aroused. The treatment of a criminal should not be designed according to what appears to be worthy of the individual in question. It should be worthy of society itself. I fear that we in Sweden, as in all other parts of the world, have to admit that our methods in this field are still not entirely worthy of society.[56]

While the doctrines of conservatives and liberals diverge at nearly every point, this is not true of liberals and radicals. Located on the political left, both groups agree that social inequalities and injustices engender crime and are reproduced in the administration of American criminal justice. Yet despite sharing this general orientation, a core disagreement remains and creates a deep chasm between the two camps. Liberals, as we have seen, embrace the assumption that efforts to reform the criminal justice system can bring about tangible gains for those subject to state control and are indispensable in the fight to resist the repressive forces on the right. In contrast, radicals traditionally assert that such limited reform agendas are either destined to fail or will be used by ruling elites to solidify their power by pacifying those on the brink of insurgency. Within the context of an exploitive capitalist system, the radicals proclaim, it is thus futile to seek improvements of our courts and prisons. Only through a larger structural transformation that eradicates existing class differences in wealth and power will the administration of justice become possible. Consequently, those wishing to introduce benevolence into our correctional system should abandon ill-fated, piecemeal liberal reform and devote their energies to the revolutionary struggle for a socialist society that will eliminate injustice and inhumanity throughout the entire social fabric.[57]

Now few liberals would dispute the radicals' conclusion that true criminal justice awaits true social or distributive justice. Yet to take this principle to the extreme and to contend that only revolutionary action is warranted constitutes a dangerous path to follow. For such a profound disinterest by radicals in the happenings of the criminal justice system legitimates the complete neglect of the welfare of those currently held captive by the state. While the long battle to establish a new socialist order is in progress, the fate of those caught up in the correctional system is casually given over to the repressive forces in society and the misery in our prisons is accepted as inevitable and permitted to deepen. For liberals, this alternative is clearly unacceptable. The call for a more equitable society cannot be used to excuse us from confronting inhumanity where it now exists or to allow us to comfortably turn our backs on those suffering its consequences. To be sure, liberal reform efforts are only on occasion rewarded with full success. Nevertheless, they are largely responsible for the advances in legal protections and in penal living standards that have been won both in recent and past times. Further, these efforts persist in pricking society's conscience and thus in counteracting the constant demands from the right that the punitiveness of criminal sanctions be escalated.

Again, radicals are typically suspicious of any liberal reforms that prove to mitigate the human damage arising from the more poignant injustices of the correctional system. These improvements are envisaged as mere opiates that defuse the anger of those under the domination of the state's social control apparatus and hence rob them of the motive to rebel. By ameliorating the worst burdens of penal life, liberals inadvertently perpetuate a system that may become more tolerable but at its core remains brutalizing. It would be better, radicals maintain, to allow the inhumanity of our prisons to intensify to the point where it fuels a militancy among society's captives that will ultimately contribute to the general working class struggle for a socialist society. Yet it must be realized that this policy rests on a difficult, if not indefensible, ethical choice. For in the future hope of bringing about a more just regime, radicals in effect sacrifice those presently enduring the hardships of imprisonment. Radicals thus make the decision to allow inmates to suffer more than they otherwise might have—and without their consent—on the prospect that a larger good will result. Whether it is wise or moral to exchange humane concerns in the present for uncertain revolutionary gains in the future is not easily resolved.

The radicals' policy of heightening the woes of the correctional system becomes all the more problematic when we consider that it may simply be strategically misguided. First, by the radicals' own logic, any movement with hopes of fundamentally restructuring the existing distribution of wealth and power will have to involve the widespread participation of the members of the working class in a general social upheaval. The significance of the incarcerated in such a process is not readily foreseeable. They are comparatively small in number, often not closely identified with labor, and extremely vulnerable to state repression in the event of any attempted insurgency. Their contribution to a socialist struggle would thus seem marginal at best. Consequently, the utility of standing in the way of reforms that lessen the pains inmates must confront in their daily lives does not, on balance, appear to be substantial. Second, and more importantly, the radicals' policy may be based on an incorrect theory of how revolutions occur. As socialist criminologist David Greenberg has observed:

> Some radicals have feared that successful campaigns to achieve short-run goals might make a socialist revolution harder to achieve.... If some concessions are won, this argument goes, militant opposition to the state will dry up. Behind this concern lies an implicit "big bang" model of how revolutions are made: conditions get worse and worse until the oppressed can't stand it anymore and one day explode. In the industrialized capitalist world such a model seems farfetched. In fact, it is a pernicious model, since it encourages socialists to sit back and do nothing while social conditions deteriorate. In an alternative view, a socialist movement is built through socialists' participation in concrete struggles, struggles that win real, though necessarily partial victories. After all, people join movements that show some possibility of improving their lives. What would be the point of joining a movement that only loses?[58]

Similar to Greenberg, other radical thinkers have begun to accept the notion that reforms of the existing correctional system should be undertaken.[59] Even here, however, we must question the pragmatics of their vision. The thrust of their proposals is generally threefold: create linkages between inmates and the working class, raise the socialist consciousness of inmates, and seek ways to empower inmates so that they will play a larger role in the governance of the prison. From our vantage, none of these avenues of reform holds much promise of success. At present, it is difficult to imagine that criminals and members of the proletariat could soon find a common ground on which to join together in the struggle for a socialist order. For one thing, false-consciousness remains rampant among working people and prevents a clear perception of the interests they share with the incarcerated. For another, the criminal offenses committed by the less advantaged, particularly those of interpersonal violence, involve extensive intra-class victimization. These acts serve to intensify the antagonism of the working class toward offenders and in turn reinforce their belief that inmates deserve longer and less comfortable stays behind bars.

Problems also surround attempts to heighten the revolutionary consciousness of convicts. On the positive side, exposure to socialist ideas could allow offenders to situate their individual plights within a wider structural context, understand their commonalities with their fellow inmates, and create a basis for concerted inmate action for reform. But there is a bleaker side to this picture as well. Experience teaches us that radicalized inmates who attempt to prompt their compatriots to action live a precarious existence. They are invariably defined as "troublemakers" and quickly whisked off to "protective" custody or transferred to another correctional facility. In the same vein, we can expect that state officials will move rapidly to neutralize radical reformers who preach socialist doctrines and who endeavor to empower inmates at the expense of prison administrators. Not wishing to tolerate their interference, officials will discredit them as "communists" trying to "incite unrest" and will soon deny them access to the correctional arena. Consequently, the radicals' reform efforts will founder and their influence on the system will ultimately recede to the point where they can effect no meaningful or lasting improvements that better an inmate's life.[60]

This final consideration is a telling one. As we find punitive determinate sentencing legislation emerging across the nation, prison populations burgeoning, public attitudes toward crime hardening, and a prominent federal task force urging the harsher treatment of criminals, the need to resist repression is now manifestly paramount. It is thus crucial that those on the left not find themselves in a position where they unwittingly abandon the criminal justice system to conservative forces. Yet, as suggested, this is exactly what the pursuit of radical reform promises. Regardless of their firm and genuine resolve to do good or of the intellectual merits of their analysis of state control, the ideology espoused by radicals makes them immediate dangers to the state and leads to their exclusion from the making of criminal policy. It is instructive that instances of criminal justice reforms by radicals have been episodic at best and, with rare exception, ineffectual in their outcome.

In contrast, liberals have enjoyed a long and established dialogue with both politicians and criminal justice bureaucrats. And whatever their failings, liberals have used their access to the system to improve the plight of those imprisoned in our penitentiaries. Now if the influence of liberals has become attenuated in recent times, it is not fully dissipated. Their linkages to the system remain and must be exploited. Indeed, unless liberals persist in their quest to see benevolence prevail over brutality, we can anticipate that little, except perhaps financial worries, will be left to deter the mounting campaign by the right to "get tough" in the name of imposing social order. Again, we believe that the strategy informing liberal resistance must remain true to its own ideological heritage. That is, we believe that liberal reformers should seek both to combat the irrationalities and repression inherent in the conservatives' agenda and to resolve the current crisis in criminal justice policy by reaffirming rehabilitation.

NOTES

[1] LeMar T. Empey, "Foreword—from optimism to despair: new doctrines in juvenile justice." Pp. 9–26 in Charles A. Murray and Louis A. Cox, Jr., *Beyond Probation: Juvenile Corrections and the Chronic Delinquent.* (Beverly Hills, Ca.: Sage, 1979), p. 10. Similarly, see George I. Diffenbaucher, "Settling for 'humanization': evidence of despair or of facing reality?" *Federal Probation* 40 (March 1976), pp. 25–28.

[2] Willard Gaylin and David J. Rothman, "Introduction." Pp. xxi-xli in Andrew von Hirsch, *Doing Justice: The Choice of Punishments.* (New York: Hill and Wang, 1976), pp. xxxiv, xxxviii, xxxix.

[3] Ira Glasser, "Prisoners of benevolence: power versus liberty in the welfare state." Pp. 97–170 in Willard Gaylin, Ira Glasser, Steven Marcus, and David Rothman, *Doing Good: The Limits of Benevolence.* (New York: Pantheon Books, 1978), pp. 145–146.

[4] Steven Marcus, "Their brothers' keepers: an episode from English history." Pp. 39–66 in Gaylin et al., *Doing Good,* pp. 65–66.

[5] Francis A. Allen, *The Decline of the Rehabilitative Ideal: Penal Policy and Social Purpose.* (New Haven: Yale University Press, 1981), p. 60.

[6] Nicholas N. Kittrie, *The Right to be Different: Deviance and Enforced Therapy.* (Baltimore: Penguin Books, 1971), p. 396.

[7] Gaylin and Rothman, "Introduction," p. xxxix.

[8]Herman and Julia Schwendinger, "The new idealism and penal living standards." Pp. 185–191 in Tony Platt and Paul Takagi (eds.), *Punishment and Penal Discipline: Essays on the Prison and the Prisoners' Movement.* (Berkeley, Ca.: Crime and Social Justice Associates, 1980), p. 187.

[9]John P. Conrad, "Where there's hope there's life." Pp. 3–21 in David Fogel and Joe Hudson, *Justice As Fairness: Perspectives on the Justice Model.* (Cincinnati: Anderson Publishing Co., 1981), pp. 18–21. See also Hans Toch, "In my opinion: in the era of 'just deserts,' prisons still need programs." *Corrections Magazine* 6 (August 1980), pp. 22–23. Similarly, Diffenbaucher, "Settling for 'humanization,'" p. 28 has commented "that we recognize that what I have called 'settling for humanization,' rather than opting for more 'lofty goals' of 'rehabilitation,' is at second glance after all not really having to 'settle' for anything. Moving further toward humanization is a reasonable, worthy, and 'lofty' enough direction in which to move and is completely in keeping with the significant changes that have already been made in corrections."

[10]Reported in "Too much concern for criminals causing U.S. crime increase?" *Peoria Journal Star* (February 9, 1981), p. A-2.

[11]"Rhodes v. Chapman: two men, one cell." *Institutions Etc.* 4 (July 1981), p. 1.

[12]Dan Siegel, "The movement for prisoners' rights: the 1970's have left it in disarray." *The Progressive* 43 (December 1979), p. 22.

[13]David Fogel, *"We Are the Living Proof": The Justice Model for Corrections.* Second edition. (Cincinnati: Anderson Publishing Co., 1979), p. 180.

[14]David J. Rothman, "The state as parent: social policy in the Progressive era." Pp. 67–95 in Gaylin et al., *Doing Good*, p. 94.

[15]Paul Bigman, "Good time, hard times." *Prison Law and Advocacy* 2 (November 1980), p.4.

[16]"Boarding homes: recurring nightmare and a national disgrace." *Institutions Etc.* 4 (March 1981), pp. 1–3. See also Marjorie Mendel, "Ousted mental patients find streets a cruel home." *St. Louis Post-Dispatch* (March 8, 1981), pp. 1, 8, and, more generally, Andrew T. Scull, *Decarceration: Community Treatment and the Deviant—A Radical View.* (Englewood Cliffs, N.J.: Prentice Hall, 1971).

[17]Charles E. Marske and Steven Vargo, "Law and dispute processing in the academic community." *Judicature* 64 (October 1980), p. 175.

[18]"Prisons too soft, most in poll say." *St. Louis Globe* (July 22, 1981).

[19]David L. Bazelon, "Street crime and correctional potholes." *Federal Probation* 41 (March 1977), p. 6.

[20]Karl Menninger, *The Crime of Punishment.* (New York: Penguin Books, 1966).

[21]*Ibid.*, p. 10.

[22]Jeffrey H. Reiman, *The Rich Get Richer and the Poor Get Prison: Ideology, Class, and Criminal Justice.* (New York: John Wiley, 1979), p. 144. See also the comments of David F. Greenberg and Drew Humphries, "The cooptation of fixed sentencing reform." *Crime and Delinquency* 26 (April 1980), pp. 215–216: " a just deserts philosophy focuses attention on the individual perpetrator alone ...in placing ...culpability and punishment ...at the

center of attention, other topics are pushed to the periphery: the dynamics of the capitalist economy; the manner in which it allocates benefits and injuries among classes, races, and sexes—and in so doing generates the structural conditions to which members of the society respond when they violate the law. ... All these are neglected in favor of an abstract moral preoccupation with the conduct of the individual offender."

[23]Arthur L. Stinchcombe, Rebecca Adams, Carol A. Heimer, Kim Lance Scheppele, Tom W. Smith, and D. Garth Taylor, *Crime and Punishment: Changing Attitudes in America.* (San Francisco: Jossey-Bass, 1980); Joseph H. Rankin, "Changing attitudes toward capital punishment." *Social Forces* 58 (September 1979), pp. 194—211.

[24]"Prisons too soft, most in poll say."

[25]See, for instance, David Duffee and R. Richard Ritti, "Correctional policy and public values." *Criminology* 14 (February 1977), pp. 449—459; John T. Gandy, *Community Attitudes Toward Creative Restitution and Punishment.* (Unpublished Ph.D. dissertation, University of Denver, 1975); Market Opinion Research Co., *Crime in Michigan: A Report from Residents and Employers.* Sixth edition. (Detroit: Market Opinion Research Co., 1978); Pamela Johnson Riley and Vicki McNickle Rose, "Public and elite opinion on correctional reform: implications for social policy." *Journal of Criminal Justice* 8 (No. 6, 1980), pp. 345—356.

[26]"Prisons too soft, most in poll say."

[27]The items included in Table 7.1 were drawn from a more general survey instrument that contained 55 items assessing attitudes toward various aspects of criminal sanctioning. Each respondent was instructed to use a 7-point Likert scale ranging from 1 = very strongly agree to 7 = very strongly disagree to "state the extent to which you either agree or disagree with each statement listed below." In all, questionnaires were sent to 200 Springfield residents, of which 74 usable surveys were returned. A more comprehensive discussion of the results of this study is reported in Francis T. Cullen, John B. Cullen, Nellie Ann Sims, and Steven G. Hunter, "The punishment-rehabilitation controversy: insider and outsider perspectives." Paper presented at the 1981 meeting of the American Society of Criminology.

[28]Again, see Cullen et al., "The punishment-rehabilitation controversy" for a more complete analysis of these results. It can be noted here, however, that the sample of criminal justice "insiders" included circuit court judges and administrators of correctional institutions across the state, lawyers from the Springfield area, both Illinois senators and representatives (all were sampled), and guards and inmates from the minimum-medium security prison at Sheridan. Also, to minimize response difficulties, only inmates with the equivalence of an eighth grade education or above were given a survey to complete. While the nature of the inmate sample may bias the results and lead us to overestimate prisoner support for rehabilitation, it is also notable that the conclusions we draw from these inmate data are not inconsistent with existing research in the field.

[29]Similar findings have been reported by Frank O. Mathis and Martin B. Rayman, "The ins and outs of crime and corrections." *Criminology* 10 (November 1972), pp. 366—373; James B. Jacobs, "What prison guards think: a profile of the Illinois force." *Crime and Delinquency* 24 (April 1978), pp. 185—196; Michael S. Serrill, "Is rehabilitation dead?" *Correctional Magazine* 1 (May-June 1975), pp. 3—12, 21—32. Also of interest is that the support for juvenile rehabilitation evidenced by those in our sample associated with the

criminal justice system was especially high. See Kathryn M. Golden, Francis T. Cullen, and John B. Cullen, "Is child saving dead?" Paper presented at the 1981 meeting of the Midwest Association of Criminal Justice Educators.

[30]Instructive in this regard is T. J. Juliani's warning that "The need for soliciting attitudes of convicted adult criminals toward the public system of criminal justice remains a neglected area of study.... It certainly cannot be suggested that the majority of ills confronting the criminal justice system are due to the nonrecognition of the prisoner; however, unilateral and archaic policy construction and continued bypassing of the 'prisoner perspective' can serve only to harden the apparent resentment and contempt for a criminal justice system predicated on brass-bound policy ideals." See "The prisoner's perspective: a needed view in policy formulation." *International Journal of Comparative and Applied Criminal Justice* 5 (Spring 1981), p. 119.

[31]S. David Hicks, *The Corrections Yearbook.* (New York: Criminal Justice Institute, Inc., 1981), pp. 30–31.

[32]Gaylin and Rothman, "Introduction," p. xxxix. Similarly, E. R. East, "Is reformation possible in prison today?" *Journal of Criminal Law and Criminology* 38 (1947), pp. 130–131 has commented that "The idea of reformation, although over-stressed as a function to be fulfilled by a prison, must not be abandoned. It is this principle which has effected so many progressive and commendable changes in prison life and administration tending toward the improvement of the general welfare and happiness of the men confined."

[33]Allen, *The Decline of the Rehabilitative Ideal*, pp. 80–81.

[34]Graeme Newman, "*Book Review of Conscience and Convenience: The Asylum and Its Alternatives in Progressive America*, David J. Rothman." *Crime and Delinquency* 27 (July 1981), p. 426. In the same vein, Barbara Wootton in Social Science and Social Pathology (London: George Allen and Unwin, 1959), p. 334 has noted that "Whatever may be thought of the scientific pretentions of psychiatry, there can be no question as to its humanizing effect upon the treatment of socially refractory persons and particularly of offenders against the criminal law."

[35]Allen, *The Decline of the Rehabilitative Ideal*, p. 81.

[36]Torsten Eriksson, *The Reformers: An Historical Survey of Pioneer Experiments in the Treatment of Criminals.* (New York: Elsevier, 1976), p. 252.

[37]David J. Rothman, *Conscience and Convenience: The Asylum and Its Alternatives in Progressive America.* (Boston: Little, Brown, 1980), p. 157.

[38]"Amos and the beanstalk." *Institutions Etc.* 4 (January 1981), p. 5.

[39]As can be seen in Table 7.1 reported earlier in this chapter, correctional administrators express near unanimous support for both the concept of rehabilitation and for its expanded use. See also Serrill, "Is rehabilitation dead?"

[40]Michael Kannensohn, *A National Survey of Parole-Related Legislation Enacted During the 1979 Legislative Session.* (Washington, D.C.: U.S. Department of Justice, 1979). See also American Correctional Association, "Mutual agreement programming." Pp. 342–347 in Robert M. Carter, Daniel Glaser, and Leslie T. Wilkins (eds.), *Correctional Institutions.* Second edition. (Philadelphia: J.B. Lipincott, 1977).

[41]The results of this survey were reported in Steven Gettinger, "Parole contracts: a new way out." *Correctional Magazine* 2 (September-October 1975), p. 8.

[42]*Ibid.*, p. 5.

[43]John P. Conrad, "The law and its promises: flat terms, good time, and flexible incarceration." Pp. 89−109 in *Determinate Sentencing: Reform or Regression?* (Washington, D.C.: U.S. Department of Justice, 1978), p. 96.

[44]Quoted in Gettinger, "Parole contracts: a new way out," p. 5.

[45]For a proponent of the justice model sympathetic to the idea of parole contracts, see Conrad, "The law and its promises: flat terms, good time, and flexible incarceration," pp. 95−97. Compare with Norval Morris, *The Future of Imprisonment.* (Chicago: University of Chicago Press, 1974), pp. 44−45.

[46]Gettinger, "Parole contracts: a new way out," p. 5.

[47]Of course, those serving life sentences without chance of parole would not be issued a contract with a release date. Even here, however, it would be feasible to negotiate contracts that link the achievement of rehabilitation goals with certain privileges or freedoms within the correctional system. For instance, in exchange for progress toward treatment goals, lifers could be given a date at which they would be transferred to a medium or minimum security institution and eventually permitted to participate in a work-release program.

[48]Morris, *The Future of Imprisonment*, p. 45.

[49]Paul Gendreau and Bob Ross, "Effective correctional treatment: bibliotherapy for cynics." *Crime and Delinquency* 25 (October 1979), p. 474.

[50]David Fogel, *"We Are the Living Proof": The Justice Model for Corrections*, p. 206.

[51]In this regard, see Stanley Anderson, "The corrections ombudsman." Pp. 252−269 in *Justice As Fairness*.

[52]For an example of a parole contract with very specific and objective conditions, see the illustration presented in Gettinger, "Parole contracts: a new way out," p. 3.

[53]Tony Platt and Paul Takagi, "Law and order in the 1980's." *Crime and Social Justice* 15 (Summer 1981), p. 2.

[54]In this latter regard, see Charles Silberman's account of how inmates at the Vienna Correctional Center in Illinois provide emergency ambulance medical care as well as other services to the local community. As Silberman has observed, when the new warden "took over in 1968, he redirected public relations effort away from the value of a prison as such, and toward the desirability of making it an open, progressive institution. By using VCC to provide a wide variety of services, he has given citizens a stake in the continuation of its programs and open style of government." *Criminal Violence, Criminal Justice.* (New York: Random House, 1978), pp. 416−423.

[55]Survey evidence thus indicates that the public, criminal justice employees, and criminals themselves attribute the etiology of crime to an array of social, psychological, and legal conditions. See Hazel Erskine, "The polls: causes of crime." *Public Opinion Quarterly* 38 (Summer 1974), pp. 288−298; Louis Harris, *The Public Looks at Crime and Corrections.* (Washington, D.C.: Joint Commission on Correctional Manpower and Training, 1968),

p. 5; Louis Harris, *Corrections 1968: A Climate for Change.* (Washington, D.C.: Joint Commission on Correctional Manpower and Training, 1968), p. 16; Joan Petersilia, "Developing programs for the habitual offender: new directions in research." Pp. 104—123 in C. Ronald Huff, *Contemporary Corrections: Social Control and Conflict.* (Beverly Hills, Ca.: Sage, 1977), p. 118; Francis T. Cullen, Gregory A. Clark, and John B. Cullen, "Attribution, crime salience, and attitudes toward criminal sanctioning." Unpublished paper, Western Illinois University, 1982; Market Opinion Research Co., *Crime in Michigan: A Report from Residents and Employees*, p. 30.

[56]Quoted in Eriksson, *The Reformers*, p. 249. See also Menninger, *The Crime of Punishment*; Bazelon, "Street crime and correctional potholes"; and William Nagel, "Crimes, corrections and justice challenges for human values." *Fortune News* (August-September 1981), pp. 7—8. It is appropriate as well to consider these words expressed by Seymour L. Halleck, "A society can be judged by the manner in which it treats its deviant citizens. If it treats them as lesser beings who are to be systematically degraded and abused, it is not a great society. It is not even a decent society." See *Psychiatry and the Dilemmas of Crime: A Study of Causes, Punishment and Treatment.* (New York: Harper and Row, 1967), p. 349.

[57]Commenting on the distinction between liberal and radical perspectives of criminal justice, Erik Olin Wright, *The Politics of Punishment: A Critical Analysis of Prisons in America.* (New York: Harper and Row, 1973), pp. 313—314, has noted that "Stated simply, the liberal perspective on reform is that fundamental changes in the prison system are possible without changes in the rest of the society, while the radical perspective is that fundamental change in prisons can come about only through radical change in the society itself."

[58]David F. Greenberg, (ed.), *Crime and Capitalism: Readings in Marxist Criminology.* (Palo Alto, Ca.: Mayfield Publishing Company, 1981), p. 489.

[59]See, for example, Herman and Julia Schwendinger, "The new idealism and penal living standards"; James Garofolo, "Radical criminology and criminal justice: points of divergence and contact." *Crime and Social Justice* 10 (Fall-Winter 1978), pp. 17—27.

[60]See in this regard Bob Martin, "The Massachusetts correctional system: treatment as an ideology of control." Pp. 156—164 in Platt and Takagi (eds.), *Punishment and Penal Discipline.*

The Future of Rehabilitation: From Nothing Works to What Works (An Epilogue)

The history of American correctional policy is marked by long periods of continuity that are suddenly punctuated by times in which sharp change occurs. One of these moments arose in the 1970s when offender therapy was attacked. Up until that time, the rehabilitative ideal had guided correctional policy for much of the previous century. Academic and cultural elites, as well as much of the public, had increasingly advocated the view that the nation's march toward progress—toward a truly civilized society—entailed the rejection of vengeful, barbaric punishments and the embrace of a system based on therapeutic principles rooted in the science of criminology. But the ideal's unquestioned dominance was shattered when not only conservatives but also liberals questioned its legitimacy. By 1982, when the first edition of this book was published, correctional rehabilitation had fallen from grace. It was widely believed that "nothing works" to reform offenders, and that the discretion inherent in individualized treatment had led to injustice and recidivism. Defenders of offender treatment were in short supply. A correctional turning point had transpired.

But if not rehabilitation, what should guide correctional policy and practice? In 1982, which road American corrections might take was still in dispute. As discussed previously, two options existed. One road was to create a justice model whose main focus was ensuring that sentencing and other correctional processes were based on a commitment to equal justice, fair legal principles, and the judicious, if not sparing, use of imprisonment. A second road was what might be termed the "punishment model." This paradigm had three core features, all of which endorsed getting tough on crime. First, punishments should be harsher to exact much-deserved retribution, to teach that crime does not pay, and to remove predators from the streets. Second, mass imprisonment was the key to crime control. The more offenders who were in prison and serving lengthy sentences, the more retribution, deterrence, and incapacitation would be achieved. Third, rehabilitation programs and services that address the welfare of offenders are unimportant. They are costly and, more importantly, they increase crime by making the correctional experience less painful. The more noxious the sanction—especially doing hard time for years in prison warehouses—the more likely it is that offenders will avoid recidivating so as to avoid the pains of imprisonment.

Back in 1982, we presented a strong case that the justice model would be corrupted and that the turn away from rehabilitation would usher in a period of law and order policies

Reaffirming Rehabilitation. DOI: http://dx.doi.org/10.1016/B978-1-4557-3130-5.00008-8

favored by conservatives. Our prognostication proved to be correct. Even so, we could not have imagined how far correctional policy would move in a get tough direction. As time progressed, politicians showed virtually no restraint in their advocacy for inflicting pain on offenders. Todd Clear describes what occurred as the "penal harm movement."[1] We refer to it as a "mean season" in corrections, characterized by stringent sentencing reform, a great experiment in mass imprisonment, and punitively oriented intervention programs. Many of these policies were accompanied by nasty rhetoric. Elected officials had descended to the point where expressing enmity toward offenders was sported as a political badge of honor.

Today, however, American corrections stands at another turning point. It is now clear that the punishment model is bankrupt. Criminologists have evaluated its policy components and found them wanting. To be sure, a meaningful amount of crime is saved by locking up more than two million offenders. But these reductions are achieved only by diverting monies from a host of other correctional and social programs that, if well funded, might have achieved even more crime savings and, in so doing, improved people's lives. Beyond this issue, little evidence exists that inflicting pain on offenders—including sending them to prison—makes them less likely to return to crime.

The punishment model also is bankrupt in a more literal sense. The financial crisis that struck the United States in 2008 created enormous financial pressures on state governments, many of which were or came to be headed shortly thereafter by fiscally conservative Republican governors. Elected on a pledge not to raise taxes, it soon became clear that the pressure to balance budgets would be eased by decreasing prison expenditures. In 2009, for the first time in 38 years, the state prison population declined.[2] Since that time, governors across the nation have been seeking ways to reduce prison populations, calling current levels of incarceration "unsustainable."[3] Prisoner reentry programs are being trumpeted and more emphasis is being placed on community-based interventions.[4]

The failure of the punishment model does not mean that, by default, rehabilitation will once again dominate correctional policy and practice. Thirty years of punitiveness and neglect of offenders will not be reversed quickly. Many bad laws, bad practices, and bad people remain in place and their influence will have to be overcome. Still, a clear opportunity now exists to develop another "new penology"—one rooted in the traditional rehabilitative ideal but that promises as well to be more effective, accountable, and professional.

In this chapter, we begin by evaluating the mean season in corrections that has, like a tsunami, swept over the correctional landscape and left wreckage in its wake. We then discuss the most important development in offender treatment—the production of empirical and theoretical knowledge that has allowed rehabilitation to move from a "nothing works" to a "what works" era. Finally, we end by setting forth four recommendations for guiding the future of rehabilitation.

THE MEAN SEASON IN CORRECTIONS

When the anti-rehabilitation sentencing reform movement emerged in the 1970s, the works carried such titles as *Doing Justice* and *Struggle for Justice*.[5] These titles reflected the reformers' hopes to renovate the correctional system so that offenders' rights would be taken seriously and the worst forms of injustice—many permitted by the unfettered discretion given to judges, parole boards, and other officials—would be rooted out. By contrast, the bookshelves of today's criminologists are populated by volumes of a very different sort, including: *Harsh Justice, The Culture of Control, Governing Through Crime, Addicted to Incarceration,* and *American Furies: Crime, Punishment, and Vengeance in the Age of Mass Incarceration.*[6] Taken together, these titles signify the nature of American crime control policy for more than three decades. Concerns about justice have receded as policymakers in virtually every state took steps to get tough on crime—year after year, decade after decade. Some of these policies made sense; none of us would welcome predatory criminals as our neighbors. But many of these initiatives were crass efforts at one-upmanship—of elected officials trying to show voters who could do the most to inflict pain on offenders.

As noted, the result was a mean season in corrections. The adjective "mean" is used purposefully. Policymakers during this era did not judiciously assess criminal statues and, in a careful, empirically informed fashion, increase penalties where needed. Rather, a virtual feeding frenzy too often prevailed, with officials fully intending, if not taking pleasure in, proposing laws to be tough on crime. Thus, the meanness of the correctional system was a clear choice. This decision to be mean-spirited is seen both in the fate of sentencing reform and in the embrace of mass imprisonment as the linchpin of American crime control policy. We turn to these issues next.

THE CORRUPTION OF SENTENCING REFORM

The advocates of the justice model were not foolish. They were convinced that the rehabilitative ideal, as then practiced in the correctional system, was a failure. As Garland notes, this "failure model" had three core components that combined to offer a stinging critique. First, the "perversity thesis" argued that rehabilitation "makes offenders worse not better. … '*Everything backfires.*'" Second, the "futility thesis" argued that treatment programs were ineffective and wasteful. '*Nothing works.*'" Third, the "jeopardy thesis" argued that rehabilitation "undermines fundamental values such as moral autonomy, the rights of the individual, due process, and the rule of law. … '*Justice is in jeopardy.*'"[7]

Strongly held, coherent beliefs, however, can have a blinding effect. It is not sufficient to recognize what is wrong with the existing system—in this case, corrections based on the rehabilitative ideal. It also is necessary to be capable of implementing the proposed reforms as intended—in this case the reforms specified by the justice model. The critical challenge was that reformers were taking power away from judges and correctional officials and relocating it in the hands of prosecutors and, in particular, legislators. The United States was at the tail end of an era of inordinate liberal reform. Legislatures had enacted unprecedented civil rights legislation, and the U.S. Supreme Court had expanded due process rights. Reformers thus had some reason for optimism that their vision for a more just system would be realized.

Still, by 1982, it was apparent that betting on politicians' good will was risky. Get tough rhetoric already was a staple of conservatives' political campaigns.[8] More disquieting, it also was apparent that racial politics infused much of this discourse. When right-wing officials promised to reestablish law and order, they were largely telling white voters that they would crack down on urban violence perpetrated by young, African American males. Whites were socially constructed as "innocent victims," whereas blacks were socially constructed as the "criminal other." This juxtaposition was often done implicitly and with a wink of the eye. But other times, the fear of the black man was expressed so forthrightly as to leave nothing to the imagination. Take these comments by moderate Republican Gerald Ford:

> The war at home—the war against crime—is being lost. ...The homes and the streets of America are no longer safe for our people. This is a frightful situation. ...When a Rap Brown or a Stokely Carmichael are allowed to run loose, to threaten law-abiding Americans with injury and death, it's time to slam the door shut on them and any like them—and slam it hard![9]

In this context, justice model advocates tragically underestimated the willingness of legislators to take control of crime policy and to enact a host of harsh statutes that were devoted to curbing lawlessness and not injustice. Under rehabilitation, the fate of offenders was determined by several factors—by the penalties written into law, by judicial decisions at sentencing, and by parole boards with the power to release inmates. But as discretion was taken away from judges and parole officials, the fate of offenders was increasingly concentrated in the hands of elected officials—controlled by the penalties they wrote into criminal codes. And, as we have noted, politicians moved swiftly to side with victims over predators and thus to author laws aimed at locking up as many offenders as possible.[10]

Michael Tonry provides a clear evaluation of the justice model's quest to improve the correctional system. "The irony of 'just deserts,'" he observes, "is that it backfired."[11] In his view, "the result has been both to make punishment more severe and to create disparities as extreme as any that existed under indeterminate sentencing."[12] David Rothman, a prominent advocate of abandoning the rehabilitative ideal, offers a similar appraisal, lamenting that "the reformers proved wrong on all counts. ...Fixed sentences" have had "relatively little effect on disparity in sentences" and have "promoted prison overcrowding." Meanwhile, the "distaste for rehabilitation has also contributed to making prisons into human warehouses."[13]

In retrospect, the political and social forces that fueled the get tough movement for the past several decades might have been so convergent and powerful as to have been irresistible. That is, even if justice model liberals had not existed and helped to sponsor determinate sentencing laws, the United States' swing away from social welfare policies might have eroded the legitimacy of rehabilitation as the dominant correctional ideology.[14] David Garland argues, however, that this might not have occurred—or had such a devastating effect. The key issue is that virtually nobody remained to defend rehabilitation. As Garland notes:

> And in any case, if the penal-welfare system was fairing badly in this respect there was no evidence that alternative approaches would do a better job. Had these defenses been fully mobilized, one might have expected them to prevail, at least to the extent of warding off radical change. It is, after all, notoriously difficult to overcome

the inertia of an institutional system once it has become established. But these defenses were not widely adopted, and where they were adopted, they were not widely successful.[15]

As time passed, justice model liberals were aghast at what transpired, but what alternative could they suggest? Once they declared that treatment was a failed enterprise, they had no competing ideology to put forth. They had agreed with conservatives that punishment should be the goal of the system, and now the two parties were simply debating how much punishment there should be and what purpose it should serve. They favored leniency and justice, whereas the conservatives promised toughness and public safety—a far more persuasive policy package.

When sentencing reform first appeared, the debate was clearly stated: would determinate sentencing produce more justice (less sentencing disparity, shorter sentences) than indeterminate sentencing? The evidence on this narrow question is mixed and limited.[16] But here is the critical point: this key question of the early 1980s became moot. The reason is that regardless of whether a sentencing system moved heavily in a determinacy direction or retained indeterminacy and parole, every state in America and the federal system experienced legislative control over sentencing. Elected officials used a particular strategy to ensure that some kinds of criminals—and, in some states, many kinds of criminals—would go to prison: mandatory minimum prison sentences.[17] Written into law, these sentences were intended to stop judges from placing offenders on probation by requiring that they impose a prison term for a minimum period of time.

"Between 1975 and 1996," notes Tonry, "mandatory minimums were America's most frequently enacted sentencing law changes."[18] A study found that by 1994, 20 states had some form of determinate sentencing. Notably, however, every state had mandatory sentencing.[19] Many of these state laws focused on repeat felony offenders, drunk driving, violent crimes, and use of a firearm in the commission of a crime. By 1991, the U.S. Congress enacted statues that mandated prison terms for over 100 offenses; by 2008, the figure stood at 171 mandatory minimum provisions.[20] The offenses covered by these mandates are expansive, including, for example, refusing to testify before Congress, illegal food stamp activity, immigration violations, identity theft, commodities price fixing, obstruction of justice, piracy, and the sexual exploitation of children.[21] Importantly, many of these statutes were enacted without, as then-U.S. Supreme Court Chief Justice Rehnquist noted, "any careful consideration"; rather, such laws were "frequently the result of floor amendments to demonstrate emphatically that legislators want to 'get tough' on crime."[22]

One additional point needs to be made: at both the state and federal levels, a special target for mandatory penalties were drug offenses. Elected officials declared a war on drugs and decided to use the threat of imprisonment as their principal weapon. Between 1980 and 1997, drug arrests rose from 581,000 to 1.58 million[23] Draconian mandatory penalties were implemented. According to Beckett and Sasson, between 1985 and 1996, the proportion of state inmates serving time for drug offenses rose from 9 percent to 23 percent. In federal prisons, the results were even more dramatic, with drug offenders now constituting 59.9 percent of the inmate population, up from one-third.[24] In 2010, drug offenders comprised two-thirds of convictions for federal crimes carrying a mandatory minimum sentence. About half of these drug offenders had minimum penalties of 10-year sentences.[25]

In 1994, the federal government took the added step of pressuring state legislators to have felony offenders serve at least 85 percent of their sentences through the passage of so-called truth-in-sentencing-laws. Traditionally, the sentence given in court was not intended to be served in full. Earlier release from prison could be earned through parole or through "good time" for inmates' cooperative behavior. In the Violent Crime Control and Law Enforcement Act of 1994, however, the U.S. Congress offered funding to states wishing to construct or expand prison capacity. To receive funds, the states had to implement policies mandating that violent offenders serve at least 85 percent of their sentences.[26] Incentive grants were allocated to 27 states. In addition to the federal government, by 1999, another 13 states had adopted truth-in-sentencing statutes for at least some categories of offenders.[27]

The mid-1990s saw yet another get tough sentencing initiative, this one aimed at locking away habitual criminals for life: "three strikes and you're out" legislation. Using the baseball metaphor of a strikeout, these laws mandated that offenders convicted of three offenses—typically violent felonies—would receive a life sentence. In practice, some states counted non-violent crimes as "strikes," and some mandated life imprisonment after only two strikes. Some states also set the sentencing range at 25 years to life. The first three-strikes statute was enacted in 1993 in the state of Washington. The most celebrated law, however, was passed the following year in California through a referendum approved by 72 percent of the voters. This initiative received national attention because of the statute's support from the family of Polly Klaas, a 12-year-old girl kidnapped from her bedroom during a slumber party and murdered in 1993 by Richard Allen Davis, who had a lengthy record of violent offenses, had been paroled three months before after serving only half of a 16-year sentence.[28] Three-strikes fever then swept the nation. By 1995, 15 states had enacted versions of three-strikes laws, and legislation was pending in 16 other states.[29] By 1996, laws had been established in "no fewer than 26 criminal justice jurisdictions in the United States."[30]

Importantly, get tough provisions also extended into the juvenile justice system. Barry Feld and Donna Bishop refer to the 1980s and 1990s as the "get tough era" in juvenile justice.[31] Rising youth gun violence in urban areas, which began in the mid-1980s and peaked in 1994 (falling rapidly since then), fueled a spate of legislation to make juveniles who "commit adult crimes do adult time." Once seen as immature, malleable wayward youths to be saved from a life in crime, now they were depicted as stone-cold "super-predators" that needed to be caged.[32] Once again, legislators moved to take discretion away from juvenile court judges so as to ensure that these nascent career criminals would be punished harshly. Feld and Bishop describe the sweeping nature of these get tough efforts:

> Legislators in nearly half the states adopted offense-based sentencing provisions to restrict juvenile court judges' discretion. ...In fifteen states, lawmakers shifted to prosecutors authority to choose the forum—juvenile or criminal court—in which a case would be tried and allowed them to direct file—transfer a case—without any hearing

or judicial review. Most states statutorily excluded some serious or violent crimes from juvenile court jurisdiction, often without regard to the offender's age. In some states, children as young as ten may be tried as adults....Many states adopted "once an adult, always an adult" provisions that amplified the impact of these other provisions. Some states lowered their juvenile courts' maximum age of jurisdiction and converted all youths above the new, lower-age threshold into criminals.[33]

In practical terms, it is estimated that 250,000 youths are processed annually in adult courts—"many of whom," as Feld and Bishop observe, are "neither serious nor chronic offenders."[34]

Finally, the punitiveness of lawmakers is vividly displayed in one other area: the imposition of collateral consequences on those convicted of a crime. Sometimes called "invisible punishments," collateral consequences are all the rights and privileges that are denied to offenders due to a conviction. These disabilities, most of which are often unknown to offenders and their lawyers at the time of sentencing, are not clearly spelled out in the criminal code where penalties are listed. Rather, they are embedded in a vast array of statutes, often passed without any deliberation and attached as riders to other legislation. Still, beyond the sanction imposed at sentencing (e.g., probation, prison), they constitute significant penalties and are often cited as impediments to offenders' reentry and avoidance of recidivism.[35]

When the rehabilitation ideal was dominant, it was recognized that collateral consequences would interfere with offender reintegration. But in the mid-1980s, as the punishment model was raging forward, many efforts were undertaken to enlarge the disabilities that a felony conviction would bring. Already, a conviction could cause a loss of voting rights, forfeiture of parental rights, and the inability to work in a host of occupations—from teaching to being a barber. In the 1980s, many states adopted or expanded restrictions in these areas. Along with the federal government, they also moved to exclude offenders from supports offered by the welfare state, such as public assistance, public housing, and financial support for education.[36] These disabilities, moreover, were tied not just to convictions for violent crimes but to drug crimes as well. They had a particularly disparate impact on minority offenders—so much so that Michelle Alexander refers to these penalties as "the new Jim Crow."[37]

To be sure, some restrictions make sense—such as excluding those convicted of sexual predation from working with children or barring from public housing those who used an apartment to sell drugs. Still, the movement to expand collateral consequences had a gratuitously punitive quality to it—the sense that elected officials were mainly just heaping as much punishment on offenders as possible. They did not seem to worry that socially excluding offenders—reducing their capacity to earn a living, find a home, reattach to their families, attend college, and participate in the political process—might sever the very conventional social bonds that pull offenders out of crime.[38] Fortunately, states are now recognizing that collateral consequences that have no direct tie to public safety are difficult to defend and need to be reconsidered.[39] [Still, much harm was done and many irrational restrictions on offenders remain to be repealed.

In sum, when taken together, the roster of punitive policies is disquieting: general mandatory minimum penalties, truth-in-sentencing laws, three strikes and you're out laws, the harsh treatment of juvenile offenders, and collateral consequences laws. Indeed, these policies are antithetical to the principles of the justice model. Thus, there is little doubt that the justice model advocates' vision for sentencing reform was fundamentally corrupted by the dominance of the conservatives' punishment paradigm.

Conservatives, of course, might offer the rejoinder that their punishment agenda was needed to make citizens safer—to restore law and order in a society robbed by liberal welfare thinking of a much-needed commitment to individual responsibility and discipline. We cannot dismiss the possibility that placing offenders behind bars for long periods achieved some reductions in lawlessness. But it remains highly unlikely that mandating a host of severe punishments achieved substantial crime savings. From his review of extant studies, Tonry concludes poignantly that there "is little basis for believing that mandatory penalties have any significant effects on rates of serious crime."[40] Three reasons explain this dismal finding. First, these laws had nothing to do with whether offenders were arrested and sanctioned; rather they sought to increase the harshness of the penalties imposed on lawbreakers. In terms of recidivism, however, offenders appear to respond, if at all, more to the certainty than to the severity of punishment. Second, due to plea bargaining, the penalties are inconsistently applied, thus undermining their mandatory quality. And third and most important, punitive sanctions do not change the underlying risk factors that create a stable propensity to offend. Punishment, in short, is the wrong medicine for what ails most offenders—an issue we return to below.

The larger concern is that in devising the get tough legislation of the 1980s and beyond, conservative policymakers rarely consulted the science of criminology, which would have cautioned about the limited effects of legal sanctions to prevent illegal conduct. David Garland has captured the quality of these initiatives and why their impact was, in some ways, beside the point:

> Other legislative measures might be described as a form of *acting out*—which is to say that they engage in a form of impulsive and unreflective action, avoiding realistic recognition of underlying problems, the very fact of acting providing its own form of gratification. Many of the laws passed in the 1980s—Megan's Law, Three Strikes, sexual predator statutes, the reintroduction of children's prisons, paedophile registers, and mandatory sentences—take this form and might be understood in these terms. Such measures are designed to be expressive, cathartic actions, undertaken to denounce crime and reassure the public. Their capacity to control future crime, though always loudly asserted, is often doubted and in any case is less important than their immediate ability to enact public sentiment, to provide an instant response, to function as a retaliatory measure that can stand as an achievement in and of itself.[41]

THE GREAT AMERICAN PRISON EXPERIMENT

Writing in 1985, not long after *Reaffirming Rehabilitation* appeared, Elliott Currie lamented the over-reliance on imprisonment as a means of reducing criminal conduct. In his classic book, *Confronting Crime: An American Challenge*, he showed how the roots of crime were tied to core social domains, such as the family, work, and community. He brilliantly illuminated the central propositions of the conservatives' criminological model and why the linchpin of their model—incarceration—would have only limited effects on the nation's crime rate. He admitted that substantial rises in imprisonment could keep crime a bit lower. "But the experience of the past decade," he observed, "leads us to the inescapable conclusion that the impact is small, relative to the investment it requires; that although imprisonment is all too often an unavoidable necessity, it is not an effective way to prevent crime."[42]

How large was this investment in prisons? From 1930 to 1970, the incarceration rate (those serving time in state and federal prisons) manifested an amazing stability, averaging about 110 per 100,000 Americans. In 1970, this rate stood below 100, and state and federal prisons housed fewer than 200,000 inmates—a count that had declined almost 24,000 since 1961.[43] By 1984, however, Currie was chagrined to report "huge increases" in imprisonment. The incarceration rate had more than doubled to 195 per 100,000 Americans, and the inmate population had shot up to more than 450,000.[44] [Given prisons' staggering costs and small impact on crime rates, Currie questioned the rationality of continuing this policy agenda. He cautioned that "much greater increases in incarceration would turn the American penal system, already swollen out of proportion, into a home-grown Gulag of dreadful proportions."[45] Currie proved prescient.

Let us move ahead to Todd Clear's publication of *Harm in American Penology* in 1994. It was time to be shocked again. Clear noted that "prisoners increased by 332% between 1973 and 1992"—figures that he called "astounding."[46] By this time, more than 850,000 inmates were housed in state and federal prisons—almost double the 1984 statistic that had worried Currie.[47] Surely, the nation would come to its senses and halt this seemingly intractable escalation in prison populations. But this did not occur for nearly two decades, when financial crises and a deep recession depleted state treasuries and made reining in correctional spending integral to balancing budgets. As noted, 2009 was the first time in 38 years that state prison populations declined (although increases in the federal system ensured that the overall inmate count would still rise).[48]

But despite this promising development, the time to rejoice is far from at hand. The statistics on the United States' correctional population are disquieting—and the nation's prison system now approaches the swollen Gulag that Currie had feared. As Table 8.1 reveals, between 1982 (the publication date of *Reaffirming Rehabilitation*) and 2009, the state and federal prison population rose from just over 400,000 to more than 1.5 million—almost a four-fold increase. When jail populations are included, the jump was from 610,767 to nearly 2.3 million. The last column in Table 8.1 shows the true reach of the correctional system. In 1982, about 2.2 million Americans were under some form of correctional supervision. Now, that number stands at over 7.2 million.

These statistics on mass imprisonment have been cited so often and for so long that they have a certain banality to them. But the true scale of the American Gulag—to use Currie's term—might be appreciated more if these broad figures are translated into a more concrete form. Thus, on any given day in the United States, 1 in every 100 adults is behind bars. The figure for minorities is especially troubling. For African American men 18 and older, the

Table 8.1 The Growth of Incarceration and Correctional Control in the United States[*]

Year	Prison	Jail	Probation	Parole	Total[**]
1982	402,914	207,853	1,357,264	224,604	2,197,600
1992	850,566	441,780	2,811,611	658,601	4,762,000
2002	1,367,547	658,228	4,024,067	750,934	6,750,500
2009	1,524,513	760,400	4,203,967	819,308	7,225,800

*Data from the Bureau of Justice Statistics, U.S. Department of Justice (see http://bjs.ojp.usdoj.gov/content/glance/tables/corr2tab.cfm).
**Total rounded to the nearest hundred.

statistic is 1 in 15; for black males ages 20 to 34, 1 in 9 sits in a cell.[49] In terms of correctional control, 1 in 31 adults is either in an institution or under community supervision. The number for African Americans, males and females, is 1 in 11.[50] And one more consideration: the annual price tag for corrections is $21.18 billion—$18.65 billion of which is spent on prisons.[51]

Importantly, the United States is not participating in a worldwide prison boom; rather, America's embrace of mass imprisonment is exceptional among advanced Western democracies. In 2009, the nation's imprisonment rate per 100,000 stood at 760—a statistic that gave the U.S. the dubious honor of being the "number 1" incarcerator on the globe. Russia was not too far behind (620 per 100,000), but no other Western nation was close. To understand just how exceptional America is, let us list the incarceration rates for a few additional countries—rates all dwarfed by that of the U.S.: England and Wales, 154; China, 119; Canada, 116; France, 96; Germany, 90; Japan, 63. And just to add one final startling figure: America comprises 5 percent of the world's population, but accounts for 25 percent of the inmate population.[52]

Over the past thirty years, then, commentators in every decade have been stunned by the continued growth in imprisonment. At some point, it did not seem possible that the U.S. could add another 400,000 or so new inmates each decade, but until now the nation did. Still, as worrisome as this ineluctable upward swing in mass imprisonment has been, there is another quality to correctional policy that is equally disturbing: the desire to inflict pain—penal harm—on offenders. Thus, gaining force in the mid-1990s, a movement emerged to strip inmates of a range of amenities. Get tough politicians characterized prisons as "resorts" and "hotels," and took steps to deprive offenders of "luxuries" and make their stay behind bars more noxious. In 1996, the U.S. Congress enacted the "No Frills Prison Act," which banned "in-cell televisions, unmonitored phone calls, the viewing of R-, X-, and NC-17-rated movies, and the possession of pornographic materials, electronic instruments, computers, in-cell coffee pots, and hot plates in all federal prisons."[53] A number of states and counties followed suit either through legislation or administrative policies, with popular targets including the prohibition of weightlifting and charging offenders for services (e.g., medical tests and procedures).[54]

Clearly, the notion that inflicting more discomfort on inmates could have beneficial effects is antithetical to the rehabilitative ideal. Effective therapeutic communities do not require luxurious surroundings. But they are fully inconsistent with the application of gratuitously punitive policies that communicate to offenders that they are disliked and are worthy only of even more pain. No-frills prisons were, to use David Garland's words again, another case of politicians "acting out" in a symbolic attempt to be the toughest politician in town, so to speak. It is patently ridiculous, however, to claim that making harsh environments even harsher will deter offenders from recidivating. In fact, the available scientific evidence shows that more painful prison conditions are, if anything, associated with higher rates of reoffending.[55]

This last observation brings us to the issue of the impact of mass incarceration on crime in America. A number of commentators have characterized the nation's commitment to locking up Americans as a "prison experiment."[56] We have added the adjective "great" to capture the experiment's inordinate scope, both in terms of its length (four decades) and its size (over 2.2 million behind bars on a given day). The term "experiment" is used because launching this war on crime, with prison as its linchpin, represents a huge bet that imprisonment is the key to ensuring public safety. Ironically, conservatives frequently castigate liberals for relying on big government to solve complex problems; alas, it appears that the war on crime waged via wide-reaching correctional control is a stunning exception to this principle. Regardless, to choose our correctional future, it is crucial to assess whether the Great American Prison Experiment has been a success—or a failure.

Too many criminologists give the knee-jerk reaction that prisons do not reduce crime and thus that they should be used sparingly. The issue is far more complex than this. For one thing, the United States is in the midst of a historic decline in crime.[57] On the surface, this would suggest that mass imprisonment has done its job. This conclusion would conveniently ignore the many times over the past forty years when lawlessness and prison populations have risen together. It also ignores cross-cultural examples where nations with stable or falling incarceration rates have experienced crime reductions.[58] Obviously, examining the bivariate correlation between imprisonment and crime rates is nonsensical because the world is multivariate. That is, many factors are involved in whether crime rates go up or down—of which incarceration is only one.[59]

The fairest reading of the evidence yields three conclusions.[60] First, if prison populations are quadrupled, crime rates certainly will be reduced. There is a meaningful "incapacitation effect"—the concept used to describe the amount of crime saved from offenders being caged and not free to victimize innocent citizens. In perhaps the most sophisticated analysis of the incapacitation effect, William Spelman estimated that doubling the prison population lowers crime between 16 percent and 31 percent.[61] He also estimated that in the 1990s, the "crime drop would have been 27 percent smaller than it actually was, had the prison buildup never taken place."[62] Other research places the effect at a lower level, and there is good evidence that imprisonment is a matter of diminishing returns—the more offenders who are incarcerated, the less crime is saved (presumably because an expanding pool of offenders increasingly includes more and more low-risk criminals).[63] Still, offenders behind bars are less likely to offend than those not behind bars.

Second, despite this common-sense reality, estimates of the incapacitation effect are based on a fundamental flaw. They assume that the alternative to incapacitating offenders is allowing them to roam free on the streets to carry out their crimes. So, of course, if offenders are behind bars they will commit fewer crimes than those who receive no intervention. But in experimental language, this is a phony control group. The real policy issue is whether more crime was saved by spending nearly $20 billion a year on imprisonment or whether that money might have been better spent to supervise and provide quality rehabilitation programs to offenders in community-based settings. If so, billions would have been left over to fund early intervention and other prevention programs—as well as social interventions to improve at-risk families' quality of life. As Spelman notes, the "$20 billion could provide child care for every family that cannot afford it, or a college education for every high school graduate, or a living-wage job to every unemployed youth."[64]

To make this point perfectly clear, let us use a medical analogy. Will hospitalizing the sick reduce illness? Well, overall, the answer has to be "yes." But the real question is this: compared to what? Many sick people do not require a long hospitalization or do not require any hospital stay to regain their health. In fact, they might receive better care from their family doctors who know them and have appropriate treatments right at hand. Placing mildly ill individuals in hospitals also may expose them to infections or unnecessary treatments that could make them sicker—so-called iatrogenic effects. Further, because hospitals are expensive, money spent on them takes away money that might be allocated to more effective preventative care. The message, of course, is that institutionalizing people—whether the sick or the criminal—makes sense only for high-risk cases. Many others may receive an equally, if not more, effective intervention in the community.[65]

Third, and most critically, prisons do not specifically deter. If offenders are sent to prison versus being given a non-custodial sanction, they are equally likely to recidivate. If anything, the research suggests that compared to community-based penalties, imprisonment is slightly criminogenic.[66] This finding is of enormous importance. It means that across inmates, the average effect on recidivism is, at best, null. It means that the prison experience, however painful, does not teach offenders that crime does not pay. In fact, if incarceration were an effective teaching tool, inmates' recidivism rates would not remain so high. They would learn their lesson and choose never to break the law again. But this frequently does not occur. Thus, after examining the "state of recidivism," the Pew Center on the States decried the "revolving door of American prisons."[67] The Center noted that between 1994 and 2007, recidivism rates "consistently remained around 40 percent."[68]

Not long ago, Mark Kleiman published *When Brute Force Fails: How to Have Less Crime and Less Punishment*.[69] In many ways, the book's title sums up what the most judicious criminologists have concluded about the Great American Prison Experiment. There are many dangerous offenders, and they may well warrant lengthy stays in prison. But the nation's almost mindless embrace of mass imprisonment was a mistake. Prisons are not *the* answer to crime, but only part of the answer. Even if driven by financial exigency, elected officials finally seem to have come to their senses. Our approach to crime needs to be smarter, multifaceted, and informed by the best science.

The Great American Prison Experiment was a partial success in that locking over two million people for lengthier sentences will prevent some crime. How could it not? But better options were available, including a crime-control agenda that strategically employs imprisonment for high-risk and heinous offenders, community-based sanctions for low-risk offenders, and effective rehabilitation to address the sources of recidivism. Instead, states employed a one-size-fits-all sanction, placing diverse offenders behind bars. They did so even though not a scintilla of evidence existed that prisons specifically deter offenders—the very reason why inmates' recidivism rates remained stubbornly high. Worse, the swollen American Gulag has proven to be extraordinarily expensive and now to have no future—it has exhausted its possibilities. More of the same will not do. And perhaps most disturbing, the growth of prisons was often trumpeted out of bad faith (politicians exploiting populist passions) or out of hatred toward offenders.

Does use of the word "hatred" make us guilty of hyperbole? We do not believe so—especially after listening to thirty years of nasty rhetoric. The mean season in corrections was only possible if policymakers advancing one get tough initiative after another—from three-strikes laws to no-frills prisons—truly denied offenders' humanity by transforming them into "the other," a category of citizens undeserving of any compassion or assistance. To be sure, it is equally risky to ignore the pathology of many criminals, which is precisely why rehabilitation is needed—to cure their problems. Still, at a very fundamental level, intense enmity toward offenders has brought corrections into the dark side of the force where evil thoughts and actions are experienced as mere banality. *Reaffirming Rehabilitation* is, in the end, a stand against such thinking and policy. This phrase, "reaffirming rehabilitation," had been and remains a call for us to be at once pragmatic and noble, to fashion a corrections that is a source of national pride, not shame.

THE CALIFORNIA EXPERIENCE

Just to be clear: our central message is that a correctional system that forfeits the rehabilitative ideal risks opening a Pandora's Box and unleashing a host of negative unanticipated consequences. Too often, crime control policy flows from the correctional "id" within us—a sense of anger triggered by a senseless, heinous act that leads us to seek vengeance against all offenders in the pursuit of collective gratification. Rehabilitation, however, functions much as a superego in reminding us not to lose our decency by becoming too mean-spirited, and it functions much as an ego in reminding us that extreme punitive policies often are not rooted in empirical criminological reality. The point is that with rehabilitation "out of the way," not much remains to restrain the punitive id that seeks personal catharsis or political advantage.

This thesis can be demonstrated one final way—by examining corrections in California over the past half century or so. As discussed in Chapter 4, California was among the first states to implement determinate sentencing legislation, passing the Uniform Determinate Sentencing Act in 1976. The act repudiated rehabilitation as the guiding correctional theory, stating that "The Legislature finds and declares that the purpose of imprisonment for crime is punishment."[70] As Joshua Page observes, the act "broke the cornerstone of rehabilitation in California: the indeterminate sentence."[71]

Again, the indeterminate sentence in California was seen as the culprit for what ailed corrections by those on both ends of the political spectrum. By the mid-1970s in California, the arguments against enforced rehabilitation and indeterminacy were widely known. Inmates had come to see treatment as a sham and to see discretionary parole as a means of control (i.e., be obedient or remain in prison). Many offenders claimed to be "oppressed," and the state even enacted an Inmate Bill of Rights.[72] At the same time, law and order rhetoric had become a staple of conservative commentary on crime and corrections. One politician accused fellow legislators of "coddling criminals" and, in response to negotiations to establish a Prisoners' Union in 1976, said: "We're talking about Bolsheviks, inside and outside the prisons who want to foment as much internal strife in this country as they can."[73] As inmate protests and disorder increased, more restrictive policies were installed (e.g., segregation of gang members, rectal and body searches, extended lock-downs of prisons). Officials also "eliminated convict self-help groups and rehabilitative programs, hired more officers, terminated treatment staff, and divided cellblocks into smaller, more manageable units."[74] The idea of a therapeutic corrections no longer seemed tenable.

California's decisive embrace of determinate sentencing was so striking because the state had been the most advanced in its support of offender treatment. "In the 1950s and 1960s," notes Jonathan Simon, "California went the furthest in attempting to build a scientifically informed and rehabilitative penal system along the lines of the Progressive vision."[75] There was widespread belief in the malleability of offenders—that interventions could save the wayward. The indeterminate sentence, and thus parole, were seen as essential components of the treatment enterprise.

In 1944, Republican Governor Earl Warren, later to be a famous Chief Justice of the U.S. Supreme Court, appointed Richard A. McGee to head up California corrections. McGee introduced what would become an exemplar for modern correctional practice—or, in Joan Petersilia's words, "the nation's premier corrections system from the 1940s to the 1960s."[76] California led the way in "developing the nation's first inmate classification system, the first recidivism prediction scoring system, and an array of model prison and parole programs, including today's well-regarded therapeutic communities."[77] As Blake McKelvey notes, this "ambitious program...prompted the migration to California of many of the most talented professionals. They found support for their innovative treatment programs and for protracted tests of their performance."[78] The corrections department at one time had 80 researchers on staff and had wardens who wrote books and held social work degrees.[79] One of McGee's first hires was Stanford sociologist Norman Fenton, who was persuaded to become director of classification and treatment. Other academics were recruited as well.[80] The commitment to rehabilitation can be seen in McGee and Fenton's implementation of group counseling across the correctional system, sessions that met for an about an hour twice a week. In 1956, over 5,000 inmates were participating in these treatment groups—at a time, we might add, when California's prison population stood at only 15,532.[81]

To use Francis Allen's words, California corrections was imbued with a "social purpose."[82] Through rehabilitation, it seemed possible to improve offenders' lives and thereby protect public safety. The Department of Corrections realized that convicts needed to be "securely" confined and that "some offenders...are considered so great a threat to society they are never released."[83] But despite this reality, the department's leaders embraced their obligation to "discern each inmate's basic problems and needs" and to place offenders "in appropriate correctional programs."[84] Thus, inmates were not to be devalued and portrayed as super-predators beyond redemption. Rather, the correctional enterprise was, in the end, fundamentally about correcting offenders.

In their study of women's prisons in the "Golden State," Candace Kruttschnitt and Rosemary Gartner capture the social purpose that informed California's lone women's prison in the early 1960s—the California Institute for Women (CIW).[85] The CIW was constructed in a rural area of the state (Corona) so that there would be no need for "concrete walls, barred windows, or guard towers." The inmates, called "residents," were housed in six living units or cottages "arranged around a central lawn and flower beds planted with roses."[86] The units were staffed by "women's correctional supervisors (WCSs)"—many with college degrees—who provided both custody and treatment. They also were expected "to present themselves as role models and confidants for prisoners and like the ideal mother, they supervised prisoners' training in homemaking, deportment, dress, and grooming."[87] The inmates were allowed to wear their own clothes and had much freedom of movement. They were required to work four hours a day and to participate in "twice weekly 'living group' problem-solving sessions in their cottages."[88] Other treatment programs were available, although the demand outstripped the availability. Most instructive, those in charge viewed the female offenders as meriting assistance. "We deal with people who have been buffeted by fate, the rejected, the unwanted, the inadequate, the insecure," observed Superintendent Alma Holzschuh in 1957. "Unless our relationship is one of generous professional interest, seasoned with warmth and friendliness, it has no value."[89]

Thus, the orientation of this time was to see these women convicts as wayward souls to be saved and not as evil-doers to be condemned to a correctional hell. The case of Diane Feinstein, now a U.S. Senator from California, is further instructive. In the early 1960s, she served on the parole authority for female prisoners, described at the time as a "bright young housewife from San Francisco who looks more like a fashion model."[90] Feinstein took her role seriously and was said to use "every free moment to stroll around the grounds and chat informally with the girls," gaining special insights into their lives.[91] "And," as it was said in the gendered language of the early 1960s, "just seeing Dianne Feinstein—smartly but simply dressed, a poised, friendly, obviously successful young woman—serves as inspiration to those who have been less fortunate."[92] Notably, Feinstein translated her apparent concern into action. During her time on the parole board, time served for CIW inmates "dropped substantially," and she supported "community-based halfway houses, rehabilitative responses to convicted offenders, and paroling convicted murderers after a few years in prison."[93]

But this story has one final twist. As Feinstein's political career advanced, her views on crime control would change. In an unsuccessful 1990 bid for the state's governorship, she endorsed the death penalty and increased prison terms for felons. In becoming California's first female senator two years later, she termed her lenient parole decisions many years before as "'mistakes back then and counterpunched with forceful calls for cracking down on crime and strengthening criminal justice responses to illegal immigration."[94] These policy shifts are not necessarily evidence of pure political expediency; officials can revise views in response to changed circumstances. Still, by the 1980s and 1990s, as Kruttschnitt and Gartner note, "California's politicians were masters at feeding off of and reinforcing the public's anxieties."[95] In the post-rehabilitation era, even progressive politicians in California were scurrying to show that they, too, were tough on crime.

Again, the 1976 determinate sentencing law marked a sea change in California; rehabilitation was officially discredited and punishment was officially legitimized. As Franklin Zimring and his colleagues note, determinacy in sentencing was a direct attack on the expertise of judges and parole boards to make sentencing and release decisions that could be trusted. To remove or constrain their discretion, these powers had to be usurped by someone. In California and elsewhere, the powers were shifted to politicians. "The 1976 reform," observe Zimring et al., "made the state legislature into the central bank of just deserts, with institutional authority over judges in determining the particular prison term for each felony in the penal code."[96] No longer would "criminal punishment in California" be separated from "democratic power."[97] Elected officials, rather than correctional experts, would decide who went to prison and for how long. Others have used the phrase "penal populism" to describe this situation.[98]

Politicizing crime control, however, can have untoward effects. Once elected officials believe that they can gain political capital by passing get tough laws, little exists to restrain their punitive impulses. Inmates have no constituency, and there is no immediate cost to laws whose effects may be felt in some other politician's term in office. Not surprisingly, Petersilia reports that from "1984 to 1991, the legislature passed over 1,000 crime bills, with almost none of them reducing sentences and many imposing sentence enhancements....Media-driven add-ons and enhancements ratcheted up penalties, and therefore the size of the prison population."[99] As discussed previously, California's three-strikes law would be passed in 1994.

But how much could prison populations increase? When Ronald Reagan became California's governor in 1967, the state's prison population stood at 28,000. At his instruction, the parole board used its release powers under indeterminate sentencing to reduce this number to less than 18,000.[100] As of December 31, 1976, California still incarcerated only 21,088 offenders.[101] At this juncture, the state slowly and then vigorously embraced mass imprisonment. Indeed, California went on a spending and construction spree, paying to build and run 22 new prisons between 1984 and 1997 (they also added "40 camps, 12 community correctional facilities, 5 prisoner-mother facilities, and 6 youth correctional facilities").[102] Then, the state proceeded to fill these newer institutions and their existing counterparts to nearly twice beyond their planned capacity. When *Reaffirming Rehabilitation* was published in 1982, the state housed 34,640 inmates, an increase of over 13,000 since the passage of determinate sentencing. A quarter century later, the state's inmate count had risen, quite astonishingly, to more than 174,000. As of 2007, one in every seven inmates in a state prison in the United States was housed in a California facility.[103]

But it was not just what California corrections added that is important but also what it lost: any sense of optimism and of higher social purpose. "California's prison system is in crisis," observes Joan Petersilia. "It has deteriorated from being one of the best systems in the country to being dysfunctional."[104] In 2011, because crowding conditions so endangered inmate health and physical safety and thus violated constitutional protections against cruel and unusual punishment, the conservative-leaning U.S. Supreme Court ordered the state to release 37,000 inmates.[105] According to Page, life inside prisons had become "increasingly stark, depressing, and punitive," with offenders having "few genuine opportunities to change their lives."[106] Indeed, as of 2006, half of the inmates essentially sat idle during their entire prison terms, receiving no work assignments or treatment programs.[107] Despite spending over $34,000 per inmate annually, most offenders' treatment needs were unmet, causing Petersilia to assert that "no other state spends more on its corrections system and gets back less."[108] [With rehabilitation devalued and programs cut back, research showed that California offered fewer treatment programs than comparable states. For example, only 2.5 percent of inmates received professionally run drug treatment, even though 56 percent of the population was judged to be in "high need" of these services.[109]

With no higher social purpose to restrain the prevailing mean season, California corrections descended into what Jonathan Simon, a scholar known more for his judiciousness than hyperbole, calls a "waste management system."[110] Toxic waste cannot be changed but rather must be segregated from society and contained securely. The toxic waste prison thus starts with the premise that offenders are intractably toxic and beyond redemption. Resources should not be devoted to their rehabilitation. Rather, the task is to determine the level of toxicity or "risk" posed by each inmate. The truly dangerous are to be placed in super-max prisons where their capacity to damage is fully limited. Other offenders are to be segregated into facilities that can securely contain their risk. Similar to other pollutants, the risks posed by offenders are to be managed—since transforming them into something healthy and contributing is beyond our technology and, for that matter, concern. In Simon's words,

> The waste management model no longer works through broad efforts at shaping the personalities and personal relations of inmates....The primary mandate of the prison has been to sort inmates by the danger they pose to the order of the prison and then sort them into prisons designed primarily to deal with risk of a certain level....Unlike the big-house or the correctional institution, the waste management prison needs to make few promises about its ability to penetrate and influence the mentality or will of criminal offenders. Indeed, the state can produce more security on this theory simply by building more prisons and filling them, no matter what happens inside those walls.[111]

Metaphors have their limits, of course, but this general approach to corrections is reflected in the operation of a second-generation prison constructed for women in California—Valley State Prison for Women (VSPW) opened in April 1995. Recall the discussion above about the California Institution for Women (CIW) in the 1960s. As Kruttschnitt and Gartner discovered from their qualitative study in the late 1990s, VSPW sports no cottage living arrangements, no women's correctional supervisors who help offenders explore their feelings in group therapy sessions, no freedom of clothing choice or movement around the grounds, and no future U.S.-senators-to-be who stroll around the institution, hold encouraging chats with the "girls," and advocate for their early release. Instead, consistent with the waste management model, priority is given to maintaining custody and not to curing criminogenic needs.

Kruttschnitt and Gartner discovered that unlike CIW, Valley State Prison for Women would never be mistaken for a "high school campus."[112] Rather than cottage-style living, the female inmates were housed in a facility with the same design as a typical men's prison, replete with "multiple perimeter walls and fences (some electrified), thousands of yards of coiled razor wire, foot and vehicle patrols by armed perimeter guards, and multi-sensory stadium light standards and guard towers."[113] Four gray concrete housing units, separated by fences, faced "onto a featureless dirt and concrete open space."[114] These "physical markers of control and containment" were matched by the prison's internal workings.[115] Thus, correctional officers, which included males, carried batons, pepper spray, and handcuffs. Inmates were frequently searched and prohibited from traveling to other prison yards or housing units. VSPW's "pessimistic and austere approach to imprisonment" made it "a much stricter and bleaker place to do time" than CIW.[116] The male warden was concerned that many of his charges' needs were not being met during their incarceration, which heightened their risk of recidivating. But he also understood that his institution had too few resources to deal with these needs, and that he confronted a bureaucracy unreceptive to program innovation. In line with his mission, he assumed a "no-nonsense attitude about the importance of safety and security."[117] In an interview with Kruttschnitt and Gartner, "he did not mention rehabilitation, and when questioned about the biggest challenge facing corrections for women in California he quickly replied 'Finding places to put all of them.'"[118]

The final chapter in this story about post-rehabilitation California pertains to the system's ineffectiveness in advancing public safety. What has the state's rejection of rehabilitation in favor of "waste management" achieved? In recent years, as Petersilia notes, about 120,000 California inmates reenter their communities annually—most of whom "do not get the help they need."[119] Even though determinate sentencing abolished parole release for nearly all offenders, "virtually all are assigned to postprison parole supervision in which services are limited."[120] According to Petersilia, "the outcome is predictable: two-thirds of parolees return to prison within 3 years—nearly twice the national average."[121] So much for the effectiveness of ignoring offenders' criminogenic needs and using penal harm to scare them straight.

In short, meanness has consequences, few of which are good or defensible. Whether one is an evangelical Christian or a secular humanist, or whether one holds some other set of beliefs, ethics mandates doing more than processing tens of thousands of offenders through a waste management system. It is difficult to believe that when the rejection of rehabilitation took place in 1976 under determinate sentencing, anyone could have anticipated that the state's prison apparatus would become unconstitutionally crowded, increasing eight-fold to over 170,000 inmates. And few would have anticipated how a system once concerned with the welfare of offenders could become inured to widespread inmate idleness, hopelessness, and misery. But, as with the banality of other evils, all this occurred without any sustained political will to reverse course. The task of opposing this evil was made all the more difficult because the superego of corrections, rehabilitation, had been stripped away. Punitive sentiments had no constraints and were allowed to run amok.

Some hopeful signs have surfaced. In 2005, then-Governor Arnold Schwarzenegger expanded the Department of Corrections' title to include "and Rehabilitation." The department's mission statement now reads: "We protect the public by safely and securely supervising adult and juvenile offenders, providing effective rehabilitation and treatment, and integrating offenders successfully into the community."[122] And even if under the mandate of a court order, California's prison population is being reduced substantially, with some thoughts of not simply dumping inmates onto the street but placing them in programs. But whether these developments will result in a new era of scientifically informed progressive corrections in California—one that can reject penal harm and reaffirm rehabilitation in a meaningful way—remains to be seen.[123]

FROM NOTHING WORKS TO WHAT WORKS

Showing the limits of a punishment model of corrections is not the equivalent of demonstrating the effectiveness of rehabilitation. In fact, if both punishment and rehabilitation are unable to change offender behavior, then the only remaining option would seem to be incapacitating offenders. Since the publication of *Reaffirming Rehabilitation*, however, scholars have compiled a substantial body of evidence showing "what works" to lower offender recidivism. In this section, we discuss how, ironically, strident attacks on rehabilitation helped to inspire concerted efforts to uncover the principles of effective correctional intervention. Today, we know a great deal about how to rehabilitate offenders.[124]

NOTHING WORKS: MARTINSON AND BEYOND

As we have explained, *Reaffirming Rehabilitation* was not simply an assessment of the narrow issue of whether treatment programs reduce recidivism. Rather, the debate hinged on the larger question of whether a correctional system that was based on social welfare-therapeutic principles would be more humane to offenders and more protective of public safety than a system that was based on some amalgamation of the justice model and get tough principles. Liberals cited the ineffectiveness of treatment in their critiques, but they were far more concerned about discretionary power being exercised over offenders by judges, correctional officials, and parole boards. Whether used ineptly or in bad faith, they feared that such unfettered power resulted in the convicted being treated inequitably and coercively. The constraint of discretion, not improving the effectiveness of correctional programming, was their main concern.

Robert Martinson's 1974 article in which he asked whether "nothing works" in offender treatment was discussed in Chapters 4 and 5. As a reminder, Martinson reported the results of a project, conducted with Douglas Lipton and Judith Wilks, that examined 231 treatment studies and reached the following now-famous conclusion: "With few and isolated exceptions, the rehabilitative efforts that have been reported so far have had no appreciable effect on recidivism."[125] This rather technical language was interpreted to mean that "nothing works" in corrections to change offender behavior—a conclusion that treatment's critics were pleased to cite repeatedly. But something more transformative occurred. As the years progressed, the case against rehabilitation shifted from a debate over what principles should guide the correctional system to the much narrower question of program effectiveness. That is, critiques of the therapeutic state, once so prominent in the literature, virtually vanished from sight. Rather, those hostile to rehabilitation now would simply say, "Well, it doesn't work."

Why did this transformation transpire? Two reasons seem most relevant. First, liberals soon discovered that the least of their problems was too much welfare and too much treatment—or even too much discretion. Rather, they had to face the harsh reality that the absence of rehabilitation did not lead to a system based on just deserts and the judicious use of imprisonment but to the rise of the punitive state and a mean season in corrections. Their focus thus shifted from unmasking how the benevolent ideology of the rehabilitative ideal allowed for coercion to showing how the malign ideology of the "get tough ideal" encouraged the purposeful infliction of pain on offenders. Their particular worry was the intractable rise of inmate populations, which eventually became known as the movement for "mass imprisonment." Of course, it is precisely this outcome that we had warned about in 1982.

Second, chanting the nothing works doctrine was a parsimonious way of silencing treatment advocates. If Martinson was right, then it made little sense to continue any conversation about the value of rehabilitation. When something does not work, it is time to move in a different direction. Phrased differently, the discussion did not have to involve the complex, larger issues raised in *Reaffirming Rehabilitation* about the problems that arise when treatment is severed from corrections. Rather, the debate was ended by holding up Martinson's article as proof that rehabilitation was a failed and thus indefensible enterprise.

Notably, Martinson's nothing works finding quickly became accepted as a criminological fact—both within academia and among policy makers. To a large extent, this occurred because Martinson's essay was read by a receptive audience. His findings did not change minds but merely confirmed what people already believed—that rehabilitation was fatally flawed. At this point, Martinson's empirical conclusion left the realm of science (i.e., as evidence to be scrutinized) and became part of the field's professional ideology (i.e., incontrovertible truth).[126] The hallmark of science is organized skepticism, a normative prescription mandating that claims of fact be subjected to rigorous scrutiny and empirical replication.[127] But ideological views are articles of faith. Once something is "known," there is no need for further reconsideration. Skepticism is reserved for scholars who continue to challenge the new disciplinary faith. Indeed, as Michael Gottfredson demonstrated, researchers who presented positive treatment results were subjected to a withering critique marked by the use of special, unfair evaluative standards—what he famously called "treatment destruction techniques."[128] As Galileo discovered, heretics should anticipate such attacks!

Let us be clear. Martinson's assessment of treatment studies was exemplary. Along with his colleagues, he was fair and rigorous in his reading of the program evaluations. But rarely can a single piece of research, let alone a review of other studies, render the final word on something as complex as whether offenders' recidivism can be lowered. For one thing,

Martinson's review of studies ended in 1967. Might advances in treatment be made after this point? Thus, due to a lack of available studies, his review did not contain a category for behavioral interventions. Subsequently, cognitive-behavioral programs would be found to be particularly effective in reducing reoffending.[129] As noted in Chapter 5, in 1979, Martinson published an updated review of the evaluation literature that covered 555 studies and revised his nothing works position.[130] Of course, this subsequent article was widely ignored and did not lead scholars or policy makers to retract their belief that nothing works to save the wayward.

Make no mistake about it. Belief in the nothing works doctrine did much to damage correctional practice. It put those seeking to assist offenders on the defensive, always having to overcome the snickers that they were engaged in a utopian effort at best and a foolish effort at worst. Ironically, however, Martinson's nothing works critique was pregnant with an important opportunity for rejoinder. If the status of offender treatment now depended on demonstrating its effectiveness, then there was one way to restore rehabilitation's credibility: show that it worked! That is, the nothing works doctrine gave treatment proponents a clear target. To knock the target down, so to speak, they had to accumulate enough empirical evidence to make the case that interventions with offenders were capable of reducing recidivism.

The silver lining to Martinson's work is that it was an early call for corrections to be what is now termed "evidence-based."[131] He was correct in pointing out that many treatment interventions were flawed and should not be used with offenders. The challenge for treatment advocates is to show that programs exist that can reduce recidivism. It has taken several decades, but the evidence in favor of rehabilitation is now quite solid.[132]

As discussed in Chapter 5, Ted Palmer offered perhaps the most prompt and poignant rebuttal to the nothing works position. Palmer reanalyzed 82 studies cited in Martinson's 1974 article. He discovered that 39 of these studies—or 48 percent—actually reported positive or partially positive results.[133] If so many programs were effective, how could Martinson say that nothing worked? This is a point that almost nobody understands. Thus, Palmer pointed out that when Martinson concluded that nothing works, what he really meant was that the studies in any given *treatment category* (e.g., individual counseling, milieu therapy) did not always find that this modality lessened recidivism. Sometimes they did, but sometimes they did not. One possibility would have been to explore whether the programs that worked differed from the programs that did not. It then might have then been possible to derive some principles of effective treatment (a strategy we will discuss in the next section). But Martinson did not probe his data in this way. Rather, in the face of conflicting evidence, he decided that he could not give clear advice as to which specific intervention should be used with offenders. We can quibble over whether his strict, if not idiosyncratic, reading of the evidence was reasonable. Still, unlike Palmer, few scholars or policy makers read the fine print in Martinson's work. They simply assumed that with "isolated exceptions," to use Martinson's words, none of the programs diminished criminal involvement. Even though Palmer demonstrated that this was not the case, they embraced and trumpeted the mistaken view that "nothing works."[134]

Other scholars provided thorough reviews of the treatment literature that also showed that numerous programs reduced recidivism.[135] Remember, however, that the nothing works doctrine was deeply ingrained in criminologists' professional ideology. Just because reviews of research appeared did not mean that they would change anyone's mind. One way of rebuffing findings one does not like is to accuse the authors of bias. Especially if they are proponents of rehabilitation, their presentation of positive results can be dismissed as lacking "objectivity." But a more complex issue is that the literature on most social science topics includes positive, negative, and null effects. Interpreting what these studies mean often involves a *qualitative* judgment. And this leads to the age-old question: is the glass half full or half empty? Rehabilitation advocates would see the glass as half full ("look at all the positive results"), whereas skeptics would see the glass as half empty ("look at all the negative results."). In a way, this is what occurred between Martinson ("negative results can be found in all treatment categories") and Palmer ("but half of the studies showed positive results").

In the late 1980s and 1990s, however, a new technique for quantitatively synthesizing the results of treatment evaluation studies appeared: the meta-analysis. A meta-analysis is like computing a treatment batting average. For each study, the researcher records the strength of the relationship between the treatment condition, such as a cognitive-behavioral program, and recidivism, such as rearrest within three years (the effect would range from minus-one to plus-one). Once the size of this effect is coded for every study, then it is possible to calculate the average impact of the treatment on recidivism across all studies. This is called the "mean effect size." It is also possible to take into account the size of the sample in each study, giving more credit to studies with more participants. This number is called the "weighted mean effect size." If researchers wish to be rigorous, it is further possible to conduct multivariate analyses to see whether the mean effect size varies by methodological or substantive factors. Finally, if someone disputes the results, it would be possible to replicate the study by taking the researcher's coding instrument and reanalyzing the evaluations. This replication is rarely done (it would take a lot of effort), but it provides a rebuttal to those who would criticize the results: "go analyze the data yourself!"

An important feature of a meta-analysis is that it yields a number that shows whether the treatment condition reduces recidivism. This quantitative result is not the same as a qualitative judgment. It is not simply one person's interpretation of the literature. If the number comes out in the "wrong direction," an advocate of rehabilitation cannot say that the glass is half full. Negative results are negative results. Consequently, rehabilitation's credibility hinged decidedly on whether the mean effect size for treatment would be positive (reduce recidivism) or either null (no effect on recidivism) or negative (increase recidivism).

Importantly, meta-analyses conducted by diverse scholars appeared—including several by a particularly well-respected researcher, Mark Lipsey.[136] It is instructive that they tended to reach similar conclusions: across all types of interventions, treatment reduced recidivism by about 10 to 12 percent.[137] This rather technical statement had enormous implications. Reliable quantitative data now existed that falsified the claim that nothing works to reform offenders. Those who had long relished the apparent ineffectiveness of rehabilitation were now on the wrong side of science. The evidence was incontrovertible. As a result, it gave treatment advocates a critical weapon in the battle against those who dismissed rehabilitation as "coddling criminals" and preached instead punitive correctional policies.

Further investigation, however, yielded a second finding that was even better news for supporters of rehabilitation: treatment effects were *heterogeneous*. It is a trite observation, but this meant that the impact of different types of programs were not *homogenous*. Meta-analysts might have discovered that all treatment modalities work about the same—that they all produce a modest reduction in recidivism (such as 10 percent across the board). In a way, this was Martinson's position—that different categories of treatment all worked about the same (only, in his view, not too well). But the opposite was found to be true. Again, the effects were heterogeneous. Thus, some interventions reduced recidivism a lot (20 to 30 percent), whereas others had no effect on or even increased recidivism. Scholars have sought to detail the components of these effective programs, and we will explore this issue in the next section.[138]

Here is the final piece of good news for rehabilitation's advocates. Guess which correctional programs turned out not to work? Punishment-oriented interventions—such as scared straight sessions, boot camps, or intensive supervision programs—were found to be ineffective or even criminogenic.[139] Law-and-order policy makers who sneered at traditional treatment displayed amazing hubris in assuming that they could use threats, discipline, and punishment to reduce recidivism. This confidence was based on the mistaken belief that people go into crime mainly because the price tag for breaking the law is so low. In this view, when punishments are weak, crime pays and only the irrational will pass up this bargain. Of course, this thinking ignores two realities. First, it fails to explain why, if crime is so rational, most of us do not take to the streets each day to rob and burglarize. Perceptions of the chances of getting caught and punished severely are only one thing that we consider in making our daily decisions, and, as it turns out, this consideration is only a weak to modest predictor of criminal involvement.[140] Second, it ignores a century of criminological research that has shown that crime is caused by diverse factors. As noted earlier, unless these risk factors are targeted for change by correctional interventions, offenders' behavior will persist.

The fate of control-oriented intensive supervision programs (ISPs) is particularly instructive. In the 1980s, ISPs were introduced with much fanfare as a promising intermediate sanction—a punishment that was harsher than mere probation and less expensive than prison.[141] But would not ISPs be just another way of coddling probationers or parolees released early from prison? To make these sanctions credible—to make the case that they would have the same capacity to deter as prison—they had to be "tough." Thus, the supervision of offenders would be both "intensive" and oriented toward "control," not treatment. Essentially, probation and parole officers would be correctional police whose job was to watch offenders so closely so that the risk of getting caught for violating supervision conditions would be high. Offenders also had to know that violations would trigger the no-nonsense response of revocation and a stay behind bars.

This offered a wonderful opportunity to test the theory of specific deterrence. Resources were devoted to having officers place offenders under close surveillance and to threaten them with punishment for breaking the rules. The threat should be credible because officers had small case loads that allowed them to have the time to supervise their probationers or parolees intensively. But as noted above, control-oriented ISPs proved to be ineffective. Joan Petersilia and Susan Turner's classic study, while they were researchers for RAND, provided a poignant rebuff of this punitive correctional intervention. In an experimental design, they assessed the impact on recidivism of control-oriented ISPs across 14 sites. "At no site," reported Petersilia and Turner, "did ISP participants experience arrest less often, have a longer time to failure, or experience arrests for less serious offenses than did offenders under routine supervision."[142] In fact, the ISP participants' recidivism rate was higher than the control group (37 percent to 33 percent).[143] Further, in a supplementary analysis on programs in California and Texas, they examined what occurred when some offenders received treatment services while in their ISPs. Notably, they discovered that rehabilitation worked. Thus, "higher levels of program participation were associated with a 10-20 percent reduction in recidivism."[144]

In short, the research now is clear. To make offenders less likely to recidivate, it is essential to take seriously the *quality* of the criminal sanction.[145] The effects of punishment have been wildly over-sold; they are, in fact, limited. Thus, behavioral change—whether one is talking about criminals or spouses!—is not achieved through suspicious surveillance, harshly worded threats, inconsistently applied sanctions, or efforts to make living conditions noxious. Treating others badly risks making them angry and defiant—and, in our case, more criminal.[146] For high-risk offenders, who tend not to consider consequences and who have often been yelled at, whacked, expelled, and rejected by authority figures, punitive reactions have lost their sting. The key to inspiring offenders to go straight thus is to devote time not to inventing new scare tactics but to investing human services that address their criminogenic needs.

The reason for taking this action is obvious: reforming offenders will improve their lives and is essential to advancing public safety. Why would we ever forego the opportunity to rehabilitate an offender when doing so might create a productive citizen and prevent the public from suffering a needless victimization? For this reason, it becomes important to know how best to save the wayward and to make sure that best practices are used in the correctional enterprise. We turn to this important issue next.

WHAT WORKS: PRINCIPLES OF EFFECTIVE CORRECTIONAL TREATMENT

Literature reviews and meta-analyses thus were instrumental in demonstrating empirically that treatment programs can be effective. Importantly, this hard work boosted treatment's legitimacy and largely relegated the nothing works doctrine to the dustbin of criminology. Still, for many practitioners, knowing broadly that rehabilitation programs tend to reduce recidivism and even knowing that certain types work better than others (e.g., cognitive-behavioral programs) are not enough actually to implement an efficacious intervention. Too many questions remain, such as who and what should be targeted for change and what tools can be used to implement the program with therapeutic integrity.

In this context, one of the most important developments in the past two decades has been the efforts of several Canadian scholars—most notably the late Don Andrews, James Bonta, and Paul Gendreau—to create a coherent treatment paradigm. To give clear guidance, they derived a set of fifteen principles, three of which form the core of their model: the principles of risk (R), need (N), and responsivity (R). Because of the significance of the three principles, the Canadians' correctional theory is known widely by its acronym—the "RNR model."[147] Let us briefly review these principles.

First, the *risk principle* states that interventions should be directed to high-risk (in particular) and medium-risk offenders, but not to low-risk offenders. Even when treatment is involved, bringing low-risk individuals into the criminal justice system potentially increases their risk of recidivating. If given a minimal penalty or diverted from the system, they are likely to never break the law again. By contrast, unless treated efficaciously, higher risk offenders will persist in their criminal conduct. The risk principle thus involves prediction (the idea that those assessed to be of higher risk will recidivate) and matching (the idea that interventions should be determined by the risk level of offenders).

How is a practitioner to determine the risk level of offenders? One way is to exercise clinical judgment. Based on their experience, officials might try to intuit who is more likely to recidivate. Clinical judgments, however, are notoriously prone to error, and they do not perform as well as actuarial judgments—that is, decisions based on a prediction instrument validated empirically for its accuracy.[148] Fortunately, Andrews and colleagues have developed a well-validated instrument that practitioners can use to assess the risk of offenders—the Level of Service Inventory or the "LSI."[149] Now revised, the LSI-R includes 54 items, scored on a zero-one format. The items were selected because previous research showed that they are related to criminal conduct. Importantly, Andrews, Bonta, and Gendreau realized that to deliver effective treatment, practitioners must be equipped with the technology to do so. This is a valuable lesson for those wishing to set forth rival treatment approaches.

Second, the *need principle* states that to reduce recidivism, it is necessary to target for change the known risk factors that predict recidivism. In a way, this is common sense. What should one target for change—factors unrelated to crime? In fact, this misguided focus is precisely what most failed correctional interventions do. They try to change factors—whether perceptions that crime pays or low self-esteem—that are either unrelated or only weakly related to criminal involvement. Phrased differently, they misdiagnose offenders' problems and thus prescribe the wrong correctional cure for them.

Andrews and his Canadian colleagues understood that sound knowledge is the key to sound intervention. Part of this knowledge was drawn from their home discipline, psychology, and their adherence to a well-supported model of human behavior—cognitive-social learning theory. This perspective essentially argues that what we think and what we have learned is what shapes our behavior. It follows that criminogenic cognitions and learning should contribute to why people offend. Part of their knowledge also came from reviewing the data on risk factors, including the use of meta-analysis to see which predictors of recidivism rank the highest.[150]

Importantly, they also saw the need to distinguish between two types of predictors or "risk factors": those that cannot be changed (e.g., gender), which they called "static risk factors," and those that can be changed (e.g., antisocial attitudes), which they called "dynamic risk factors." Dynamic risk factors are especially crucial because they are precisely what interventions must target during treatment (as opposed to static factors that are, by definition, unchangeable). For example, if holding antisocial attitudes predicts offending (which it does), then treatment can reduce recidivism if it is capable of erasing such criminal thinking and replacing it with prosocial attitudes.

Andrews and Bonta use the term the "Big Four" to describe the four strongest dynamic risk factors—ones that should be prime targets in any intervention. They also use the term "criminogenic needs" to describe these predictors because they represent deficits that require treatment. This is where the "N" comes from in the RNR model. These Big Four criminogenic needs include: antisocial cognitions, antisocial associates, an antisocial personality pattern (e.g., impulsive, aggressive), and a history of antisocial behavior. This final factor might be seen as a static risk factor. Andrews and Bonta note, however, that although "a history cannot be changed," it is still possible to focus on related "appropriate intermediate targets of change" such as "building up new noncriminal behaviors in high-risk situations, and building self-efficacy beliefs supporting reform ('I know what to do to avoid criminal activity and I know that I can do what is required')."[151] Further, in addition to the Big Four needs, Andrews and Bonta identify four additional risk factors that, when added in, comprise the "Central Eight" criminogenic needs These secondary, but still salient, risk factors include: family/marital circumstances (e.g., conflict), school/work (e.g., low performance and satisfaction), leisure/recreation (e.g., low involvement and rewards), and substance abuse.[152]

Third, the *responsivity principle* states that for recidivism to be reduced, a treatment must be used that is capable of changing offenders' criminogenic needs. Again, a medical analogy is appropriate. Even if a physician correctly diagnoses a patient's illness, this person will not get better if prescribed the wrong medicine. Similarly, for a correctional treatment to work, it must deliver the right "medicine" to offenders. One reason why punitive programs such as boot camps and ISPs are ineffective is that they are not responsive to the dynamic risk factors that underlie recidivism. Will watching probationers closely really change their antisocial thinking or teach them how to overcome the habits established in a life-long history of antisocial conduct? When phrased this way, the absurdity of punitive programs becomes manifest. By contrast, and consistent with their preferred brand of psychology, Andrews et al. are clear in what they suggest should be used with offenders:

> Offenders are human beings, and the most powerful influence strategies available are cognitive-behavioral and cognitive social learning strategies. It matters little whether the problem is antisocial behavior, depression, smoking, overeating, or poor study habits—cognitive-behavioral treatments are often more effective than other forms of intervention. ...These powerful influence strategies include modeling, reinforcement, role playing, skill building, modification of thoughts and emotions through cognitive restructuring, and practicing new, low-risk alternative behaviors over and over again in a variety of high-risk situations until one gets very good at it.[153]

We would be remiss if we did not also note that Andrews, Bonta, and Gendreau have developed another crucial piece of technology to ensure that the RNR model is implemented with integrity: the Correctional Program Assessment Inventory, known by its acronym of the "CPAI." Many agencies, observe Andrews and Bonta, "do what they do because that is what they have always done, or because that is what they were told to do."[154] However, if an agency wishes to create an appropriate therapeutic context that is capable of delivering RNR programming, the CPAI can direct these efforts. This inventory consists of eight scales and 141 items that measure organizational culture, program implementation/maintenance, management/staff characteristics, client risk/need practices, program characteristics, core correctional practice, inter-agency communication, and evaluation.[155] [According to Andrews and Bonta, the CPAI is completed by trained on-site visitors who "(1) interview staff, managers, and clients, (2) review agency documents and case files, (3) complete casual observations of ongoing activity, and (4) conduct systematic observations of staff relationship and structuring skills in their interactions with clients."[156] Notably, scores on the CPAI are predictive of offender recidivism; agencies with higher scores produce lower rates of offending.[157] Accordingly, the CPAI can provide practitioners with a means of diagnosing and fixing ineffective practices so as to improve service delivery.

In sum, the RNR model states that treatments should focus on higher risk offenders, target the strongest dynamic risk factors (or criminogenic needs) for change, and use modalities that are capable of changing or are responsive to the factors underlying offenders' criminality. Taken together, the RNR principles make a great deal of sense. Consider the alternative prescription: focus on low-risk offenders, ignore the known predictors of recidivism, and use treatment modalities that cannot fix what you are trying to change. Sadly, many correctional interventions violate one or more of the RNR principles and, as a result, are incapable of reducing recidivism. Again, beyond the three core guidelines, Andrews et al. have spelled out a series of other principles that should be followed so as to deliver appropriate treatment. Therefore, we encourage those interested in more complete statements of the model to consult the writings of Andrews, Bonta, and Gendreau.[158] For our purposes, we will end by sharing two considerations.

First, the RNR model should not be viewed as sacrosanct. Rather, it should be subjected to the field's organized skepticism, and efforts should be undertaken to improve it.[159] Further, if another treatment model can be developed to rival the RNR approach, then corrections would be enriched. Multiple "cures" are preferable to a single antidote to crime. With these caveats in mind, it nonetheless holds that Andrews et al. have invented a ground-breaking treatment model. They have spent more than three decades marshalling empirical data to support every facet of their approach.[160] The evidence in favor of the RNR model is now extensive.[161] For this reason, it is perhaps not surprising that the Canadians' paradigm is now the "dominant model" in offender rehabilitation and is used across the United States and across the globe. According to Devon Polaschek, "the RNR model remains the only empirically validated guide for criminal justice interventions that aim to help offenders depart from that system."[162]

The broader point is that the know-how exists to treat offenders successfully. Again, the RNR model provides specific advice as to which offenders to treat, what to target for change, and how to make reform occur. That is, we now can show not only *that* rehabilitation works but *how* to make it work in real-world settings.

Second, Andrews and his colleagues' three decades of sustained scholarship have led them to highlight the importance of what they call the "principle of human service." In fact, they see this as a core principle, ranking alongside the risk, need, and responsivity principles. From having worked in correctional settings, they know that mean-spirited practices are of questionable ethical and pragmatic value. For this reason, their human service principle asserts that the "typical legal and judicial principles of deterrence, restoration, just deserts, and due process have little to do with the major risk/need factors." As a result, it is only "through human, clinical, and social services that the major causes of crime may be addressed."[163] This is wise advice that we fail to follow at our peril.

THE FUTURE OF CORRECTIONS: FOUR GUIDING PRINCIPLES

Over the past three decades, many of the gloomy prognostications set forth in *Reaffirming Rehabilitation* have, unfortunately, come to fruition. The correctional enterprise simply is not viable when the rehabilitative ideal is stripped away and mocked. To be sure, offenders commit foolish, nasty, and at times heinous acts. At the moment of their crimes, they are not typically sympathetic figures. Victims merit our concern and assistance. They also deserve a measure of justice; offenders should be punished. But these observations should not be taken to the extreme. Concern for victims should not mean complete disregard for offenders. Exacting a measure of justice should not mean erecting a penal system that is crowded, mean-spirited, and ineffective.

Rehabilitation is not a panacea for all that ails the correctional system. Such a view would be naïve and empirically suspect. Still, the rehabilitative ideal is a powerful cultural resource whose influence should not be taken lightly. When a system is committed to saving the wayward, our better selves are called on to recognize the humanity of those under our control. We are no longer comfortable depicting offenders as "scum" to be punished and as the "wicked" to be caged. We must take responsibility for their futures, because not doing so is to consign them to a life in crime and to consign community members to needless victimization.

In a very real way, spouting get tough rhetoric and incarcerating loads of offenders in spartan conditions is the easy way out of a complex policy issue. But once criminals are locked up and the proverbial key thrown away, then what? As the saying goes, some politicians' concern with life ends at birth; in the same way, their concern with crime and criminals ends at offenders' admission to prison. We deserve better. Elected officials now have no excuse not to read the evidence (or have their staff do so) that shows that all sorts of punitive practices—from prisons to intensive supervision—do not specifically deter and do not enhance public safety. Again, we now have a mountain of evidence—not available in 1982—revealing that rehabilitation is our best option if we wish to reduce recidivism.

Thirty years of the punishment paradigm since the publication of *Reaffirming Rehabilitation* has left American corrections in a disquieting state. We have engaged in a punitive orgy that has diminished our societal health. In too many places, we have a correctional system that is bloated and far less effective than it should be. But we worry as well about the corrosive effect of this punitive era. It has encouraged us not to value our fellow citizens—even those who have offended—but to see them as objects for scorn and meanness. Is this really the avenue to a good society? Such punitive practices are often justified in the name of encouraging personal responsibility by teaching that bad acts have consequences. Yet are we not concerned about our own personal responsibility—the need to fulfill the obligation to do more than inflict pain on others, especially when it offers little more than catharsis?

We need, more than ever, to reaffirm rehabilitation. The daunting challenge, however, is how to do so. Just because punitive policies have been found so wanting is not grounds for over-confidence. The failure of punishment does not guarantee the success of rehabilitation. Indeed, humility, not hubris, should inform our efforts.

In this context, we wish to end by setting forth four principles that might guide efforts to revitalize American corrections. These principles are, in many ways, very pragmatic. They seek to outline strategies for bridging the gap between research findings and real-world performance. Much is at stake. If we do not succeed in implementing effective treatment programs, a nothing works era could once again take hold. We do not want our recent past to be our distant future.

PRACTICE EVIDENCE-BASED CORRECTIONS

Many Americans recently became introduced to evidence-based decision making when they either read Michael Lewis's best-selling book *Moneyball* or saw the movie by the same title starring Brad Pitt as the Oakland A's general manager, Billy Beane. The purpose of *Moneyball* was to unravel how a low-budget team, the Athletics, could win over 90 games a year when its big-market competitors, such as the New York Yankees, had seemingly unlimited resources. The answer was that Beane made personnel decisions not on intuition (so-called gut feelings) or on a player's imposing physical appearance but rather on performance-based statistics, especially things called on-base percentage and slugging percentage. Across a whole team, these data predicted runs scored and, when balanced against runs given up, predicted the team's total number of wins. In short, Beane employed "sabermetrics," made famous by the long-ignored Bill James, or what we prefer to call "evidence-based baseball."[164]

The gist of *Moneyball* thus is that decision-making is improved by paying attention to the evidence. As noted previously, clinical judgments—decisions based on experience and intuition—often are flawed. This is not to say that clinical or experiential-based knowledge is of no value and does not have a role to play in trying to figure out the complexities of life. In fact, some very talented people might make very skilled decisions using their clinical expertise. But across the rest of us, gut-level insights tend to be unreliable. This is one reason why a variety of fields, starting with medicine, are demanding that decisions involving other people's lives be evidence-based.[165]

In this context, we have entered the era of "Moneyball corrections."[166] As noted, since the early part of the 2000s, increasing calls have been made to base interventions with offenders on data and not opinion. Corrections cannot be like the Yankees or Red Sox; we do not have money to waste and our mistakes lead not to lost ball games but to lost lives—whether offenders or victims. The point, of course, is that we simply cannot afford to make bad decisions. We must be like Billy Beane in his heyday. Resources are limited, so let's maximize their use.

Unfortunately, the history of corrections is littered with failed interventions—some based on noble ideas and some based on mean-spirited ideas. Intent is no insulation to folly. The difficulty is that at any given time, a proposed intervention can strike us as eminently plausible—even if, later on, we will wonder what in the world we could have been thinking. For example, in the so-called Greatest Generation many men went off to World War II and felt that their military service was a maturing experience that contributed to their success in life. If boot camp and service instilled discipline in them, would it not have a similar effect on wayward young adults? Would it not make sense to subject them to a military-style boot camp so as to "break them down and build them back up"? Such tough love would inculcate the moral fiber and self-control needed to pursue a straight and narrow path. Of course, nobody bothered to review the evidence on whether military service, let alone boot camps, reduces crime or to ask why the military no longer recruits those with criminal records. And nobody reviewed the criminological literature to see what predicted recidivism and whether a boot camp regimen would change or be responsive to such factors. Instead, equipped with rhetoric and hubris, policy makers pushed ahead and implemented numerous boot camps. As is now known, this intervention proved to be a dismal failure. Millions of dollars were wasted, and the opportunity was forfeited to save youngsters from a life in crime and to prevent the harms they would visit on their future victims.[167]

The point is that *correctional quackery* is normative, not the exception, when dealing with offenders.[168] If physicians used medicines that were unproven and regularly had iatrogenic effects, they would be sued to the point of poverty in civil court and driven out of their profession. Quackery, however, is permitted in corrections. Part of the reason for using foolish, if not counterproductive, interventions is that offenders have harmed others. Accordingly, the criminal sanction must have some sting to it so as to achieve a measure of just deserts. But much of the bad practice in corrections occurs because there is no requirement, when intervening with offenders, to know anything about crime and how to treat it. Ignorance is no barrier to working with correctional clientele; in fact, at times, anti-intellectualism is celebrated.

This claim might seem exaggerated, but it is not. Sadly, those charged with supervising offenders might receive training in how to fill out forms, obey work rules, and give priority to security when watching offenders, but they are typically not trained in the "Big Four," the RNR principles, and how to deliver a cognitive-behavioral treatment. Admittedly, some very important advances have been made over the past decade. The use of risk assessment instruments with offenders increasingly is becoming a standard practice, and professional organizations—such as the International Community Corrections Association—regularly hold conferences on "what works" in offender treatment. Knowledge is spreading. Still, on a fundamental level, corrections as a field has yet to make a concerted stand against quackery. If a correctional agency places offenders in ineffective programs—or, for that matter, in no programs at all—nobody gets sued for malpractice and nobody gets fired.

The challenge is how to transform corrections from a field where quackery is standard to a field that demands evidence-based practice. Part of the answer is increased accountability—an issue addressed in the next section. But part of the answer also must be that those working with offenders come to see themselves not as employees who punch a clock but as professionals with a calling. This calling is daunting for it involves trying to save the lives of offenders who are at times difficult, if not dangerous. Still, tough tasks demand the best, not the worst, of us. In this case, correctional staff must, as members of any profession do, approach their challenges ethically and with expertise. Only by using the best knowledge available will they meet their obligation to improve offenders' lives and thereby protect the public.[169]

INCREASE CORRECTIONAL ACCOUNTABILITY

Thirty years ago, another nothing works doctrine had arisen in the field: nothing that the police do reduces crime.[170] The traditional model of officers using police vehicles to patrol communities and then rushing to a crime scene with sirens blaring and lights flashing did little to prevent crime or catch offenders. Importantly, however, many prominent law-enforcement officials accepted this disappointing evidence and refused to engage in police quackery. Instead, the field of policing took stock of its failures and embarked on an unprecedented era of innovation.[171]

Not all of these initiatives were successful, but some likely contributed to the substantial reductions in street crime achieved in major cities across the United States.[172] Further, although they differed in specifics, the best innovations have tended to share two qualities. First, they have been receptive to criminological data and insights. To deploy police resources more effectively, they have relied on statistics that map crime "hot spots," and they have sought to devise "problem-oriented" strategies that block the sources of crime in specific places. Second, the initiatives have used performance measures to assess effectiveness. With such standards in place, it has been possible to hold police managers accountable for deploying resources in a sensible way and for reducing crime. The Compstat program, first developed by the New York City Police Department in 1994, is perhaps the most prominent example of police officials being required to practice evidence-based policing and then to participate in regular meetings where the efficacy of their solutions is assessed. As described by Eli Silverman:

> Compstat is most frequently understood by its most visible elements today. These include: up-to-date computerized crime data, crime analysis, and advanced crime mapping as the bases for regularized, interactive crime strategy meetings which hold managers accountable for specific crime strategies and solutions in their areas. ...The rapid redesign of the department's organizational architecture was based on the concept of continuous performance improvement characterized by clearly delineated objective standards, benchmarking, sharing of "best practices," and the development and analysis of timely and accurate information to manage change.[173]

In Chapter 7, we made a strong case for "correctional official accountability." What we stated thirty years ago is no less true today: *correctional officials get paid to maintain order and not to rehabilitate.* Indeed, in contrast to their police counterparts, correctional managers are not held accountable for their performance when it comes to *reducing crime.* In Chapter 7, we mainly focused on making sure that officials provided treatment services. Our logic was that were quality programs to be instituted, then reoffending would be diminished. In retrospect, we are not sure that this strategy would be effective—and certainly it has not come to pass. A better approach would seem to be to start with a desired performance outcome—*reduced recidivism*—and hold managers responsible for meeting this goal. In this situation, they would then have a powerful incentive to find those interventions that allow them to satisfy this standard.

To be sure, some correctional officials might experiment with punitive programs. But the ineffectiveness of these interventions would lead to unmet performance standards. Instead, we suspect that managers—whether wardens in prisons or those administering probation and parole agencies—would realize that their best bet for success would involve adopting evidence-based treatments based on RNR principles. Phrased differently, the most compelling way to create incentives to use quality programs is to make it in the interest correctional officials to do so.

Just to be clear, the intent is not to find an excuse to fire a bunch of correctional managers—though especially recalcitrant personnel might have to be replaced. Rather, the goal is to change how they conceive their jobs and to enlist them as active contributors in the rehabilitation enterprise. We want to encourage these officials to be thinking all the time about how they might reduce offenders' recidivism. In performance meetings, the task should not be to castigate but to educate—to induce officials to use best practices to prevent reoffending and protect public safety. Innovating, being on the cutting edge of something new and consequential, can be exciting.

Of course, managers might well claim that they cannot be held accountable for something they do not control. For example, wardens might assert that reentering offenders recidivate because of what occurs in the community, not in prison. Or they might argue that they cannot treat offenders if resources to support programming are cut from their budgets. All this might be true, but if so, then wardens had better find ways to partner with community corrections agencies to improve reentry or lobby politicians for treatment dollars. They must see themselves as a constituency for offender rehabilitation and recidivism reduction.

Is all this naïve? Perhaps so. But the lessons from policing are stunning. Three decades ago, we could not have imagined that police officials would perceive a need to change and then experiment with a variety of innovations. Every excuse that correctional officials might muster could have been spouted by their police counterparts—and probably were. But now is a time not for timidity but for boldness. As the United States turns away from mass incarceration, the opportunity exists for new ideas and initiatives. Doing more of the same is no longer good enough. Corrections needs to be a system not designed for failure but for success. Making this transformation will require that correctional managers become leaders, not resisting better performance but meeting this challenge.[174]

IT'S NEVER TOO EARLY, IT'S NEVER TOO LATE

Recent advances in criminology, notes Friedrich Lösel, "suggest an intervention policy that is both evidence-led and humane: 'It's never too early and never too late.'"[175] We have seen how research over the past decades has created the capability to intervene with high-risk offenders deep into their criminal careers. Although some law-breakers might eventually prove unredeemable, many chronic offenders are capable of change.[176] Accordingly, assuming that "it's never too late" to intervene with the criminally wayward is a prudent policy.

In this section, however, we are concerned with the other half of Lösel's advice: "it's never too early" to intervene. This prescription flows from the findings of a perspective known as developmental or life-course criminology.[177] Especially over the past two decades, criminologists have shown that, for serious offenders, the origins of crime tend to start early in life, including in the pre-natal period. Most hard-core criminals do not wake up at age 16 and decide to forego college in favor of a career in crime. Rather, they manifest difficult temperaments and other deficits in the toddler years and antisocial behavior during childhood. These conduct disorders are a prelude to the early onset of delinquent activities, which in turn lead to a life of serious offending. Childhood is thus much like a train depot. If a youngster boards a train destined for crime and prison, jumping off this speeding locomotive and into a prosocial life will be challenging.[178]

These criminological realities, however disquieting, offer hope. A stable antisocial trajectory begins in the first stages of life. But it will progress to a later criminal career only if it is neglected and allowed to unfold. Unfortunately, research suggests that most high-risk youngsters receive little quality intervention prior to entering the juvenile court.[179] Accordingly, it appears that the failure to intervene early in life is a glaring missed opportunity. Many troubled youngsters and their future victims could be spared the harms of crime if only a systematic effort were made to curtail their criminal development.

The promising news, however, is that a growing body of research identifies a range of early intervention programs that work. These focus on minimizing neuropsychological deficits during pregnancy, improving early intellectual enrichment, training parents in child management stills, fostering school social bonds, and targeting problems across a youngster's multiple social systems.[180] A close examination of these interventions shows that they adhere to the RNR principles in that they focus on high-risk cases, target for change risk factors (or needs) shown empirically to lead to antisocial conduct, and use responsive treatments that typically fall within the cognitive-behavioral and social learning modality.[181] From a policy perspective, it also is relevant that early intervention programs are cost effective and are strongly supported by the American public.[182]

The future of rehabilitation thus must involve the use of treatment not only in the correctional system but also prior to or during the initial development of criminal careers. Developmental/life-course criminology teaches us that the line between serious antisocial behavior and crime is meaningful only in the sense that legal sanctions are reserved for the latter category. But from a behavioral standpoint, antisocial and criminal conduct exist on the same developmental continuum. This is a criminological fact that we ignore at our peril.

Finally, when a predatory young adult stands before the court, we often castigate this offender for making bad choices and for a lack of personal responsibility. But we also often forget that a decade before, this same individual would likely have been the object of our sympathy. Observing an eight- or ten-year-old manifesting conduct disorders, we would have lamented that he (or she) was burdened with an impulsive temperament, language deficits, school failure, rejection by other kids, a young mother lacking parenting skills, residence in an impoverished high-crime area, and so on. We might have felt a tug at our heart, fearing that this child, having lost the birth lottery, was facing a life of personal troubles, social failure, and bad behavior. Knowing that the past is the prelude to the future—that sympathetic at-risk youngsters are tomorrow's predators—cannot be conveniently ignored. We, as well, must take responsibility for our choices, good and bad. With lives clearly at stake, inaction—the failure to intervene—is no longer excusable.

CONTINUE TO REAFFIRM REHABILITATION

Thirty years ago, we were writing in the midst of a crisis. The rehabilitative ideal had lost much credibility, and a vital competition had emerged over what correctional theory would shape the field's future. Again, our main concern was that the embrace of punishment, whether on grounds of advancing a kindly version of just deserts or of advancing get tough crime control policies, would be misguided. Based on what we knew about criminology and politics, we were convinced that neither justice nor public safety would be enhanced by what treatment's critics were proposing. We also feared that extracting rehabilitation from corrections would result in an enterprise that was prone to punitive excess. In most respects, our concerns were not misplaced.

But now we are writing at a very different historical junction. The punitive model has had its day and has been found wanting. Mass imprisonment has finally proven unsustainable, and politicians of both parties are seeking to find ways to lower inmate populations. There finally is a genuine recognition, we believe, that punishment has limits and that the troubles that lead people into crime must be addressed. No longer is it viable to pretend that we can scare everyone straight or, failing that, lock everyone up.

If we are to reaffirm rehabilitation, however, it must be done responsibly. In embracing offender treatment, the temptation exists to think of oneself as one of the "good guys." But as critics of the rehabilitative ideal so poignantly illuminated three decades ago, benevolent intentions can still have negative consequences. As we have noted above, a more sober, responsible corrections must be evidence-based and move toward performance-based accountability. Such corrections also must find ways to extend its reach into the early years of life so as prevent the needless development of criminal careers.

It is a privilege to have the opportunity to revisit a work that we authored three decades ago. We are heartened that over the years, this volume has served an important purpose. In the face of doubts and dismissal, it advanced a belief that, even in our more mature years, we still firmly embrace: that rehabilitation should be reaffirmed. This abiding faith in the treatment enterprise is based on three compelling considerations. We will end by sharing these reasons for continuing to reaffirm rehabilitation.

First, reaffirming rehabilitation makes the correctional system more effective. An exclusive focus on punishment has two fundamental problems. First, it ignores the criminological reality that people offend for diverse reasons—or risk factors—that are not changed by threats and the application of sanctions. As we have discussed, these criminogenic propensities often arise in childhood and stabilize over time. It is conceivable that fear of punishment might restrain unlawful action for a period, but the underlying propensity is not altered. And as with any problem, if the "medicine" is not appropriate, the problem will continue.

Second, punishment is prone to overdose. Its very logic makes it virtually limitless. Failure—that is, offender recidivism—is taken as evidence that the price of crime was not high enough, which leads to efforts to punish more harshly. This tendency constantly to up the ante is particularly attractive to elected officials who rely on common sense to make policy. They do not consider that the failure of punishment to deter might indicate a need not to get even tougher (as common sense would suggest) but rather to declare punishment a failure (as criminology would suggest).

By contrast, rehabilitation is rooted in the science of criminology. People make choices, but these choices are shaped intimately by their past, their personalities, and their social circumstances. By targeting these risk factors for change, it is possible to diminish criminogenic propensities and to replace them with prosocial cognitions and behaviors. The evidence is now indisputable that treatment works and punishment does not. To punish and not treat is a luxury we can no longer afford.

Second, reaffirming rehabilitation is what the public supports. In Chapter 7 (see Table 7.1), we presented evidence that the public continued to endorse rehabilitation as a core correctional goal. This finding, based on a 1979 survey of Springfield, Illinois, residents, was surprising. The law-and-order era was gaining strength and the nothing works doctrine with regard to offender treatment was widely believed, at least among criminologists and policy makers. In fact, when we conducted this study, we expected to discover that the rehabilitative ideal had fallen from favor. But we did not. To be sure, plenty of support for punishment existed. However, Americans did not believe that their only policy choice was to select either punishment *or* rehabilitation. Rather, they favored a diversified correctional response, one that both punished *and* treated offenders.[183]

Were these findings idiosyncratic—the product of a small survey conducted in Illinois many years ago? As it turns out, they were not. In fact, a voluminous amount of survey evidence now exists that has replicated these results. Virtually every reputable survey conducted in the past three decades has found that citizens believe that offenders deserve to be punished but also want the correctional system to "correct."[184] In the face of years of get tough rhetoric and a mass imprisonment movement disdainful of offender change, it is a remarkable criminological fact that the embrace of treatment has remained unshakable.[185] This reality suggests that rehabilitation is not an ephemeral belief but rather deeply embedded in American culture. Giving people a second chance, trying to save the wayward, appears to be, to use Alexis de Tocqueville's concept, a "habit of the heart."[186]

The extent of continued public support can be seen in a 2001 national survey, which contained items similar to those reported in Table 7.1.[187] Again, these results are similar to more recent polls. To give just one example, a 2010 poll found that 78 percent of Americans "agree" with the following statement: "I think trying to rehabilitate people who have committed crimes is an important part of preventing crime."[188] Now, in the 2001 National Crime Policy Survey, the respondents were asked what should be the "main emphasis" of prison. In a forced-choice response (i.e., only one option could be selected), 55 percent of the sample selected "rehabilitation." By contrast, the percent agree for "protect society" was 25 percent, for "punishment" was 14 percent, and for "not sure" was 6 percent.[189] We also can list the responses to the statements that approximate those in the 1979 survey. We have selected four statements for illustrative purposes. The percentage of the respondents agreeing with items is listed:

- It is a good idea to provide treatment to offenders who are in prison. (Agree = 92 percent)
- Rehabilitation programs should be available even for offenders who have been involved in a lot of crime in their lives. (Agree = 69 percent)
- It is important to try to rehabilitate adults who have committed crimes and are now in the correctional system. (Agree = 88 percent)
- It is important to rehabilitate juveniles who have committed crimes and are now in the correctional system. (Agree = 98 percent)[190]

The most important lesson to draw from these survey results is that the American public is not a barrier to revitalizing the nation's correctional system so that it takes rehabilitation seriously. Considerable ideological space exists for policy makers to initiate bold reforms that include not only reducing prison populations judiciously but also developing evidence-based, accountable treatment programs. Again, we are the nation that called our first institutions not prisons but "penitentiaries" and that now calls our correctional agencies not the Ministry of Justice but the Department of Corrections. We are a nation that has long reaffirmed rehabilitation; the democratic will of the public would favor our continuing to do so.

Third, reaffirming rehabilitation is the right thing to do. In making this claim, we admittedly run the risk of appearing excessively moralistic. Were we or those close to us victimized in a serious way, we likely would have the same feelings of anger and thirst for vengeance as anyone else. So, yes, we understand why exacting a measure of justice is appropriate. But we also understand that an exclusively punitive system runs another sort of risk. To see offenders only as objects to inflict pain upon, we must view them as "the other"—as so far apart from us, the "good people," as to warrant nothing but our worst sentiments. By contrast, the very process of diagnosing and treating offenders reminds us of their humanity. Although their pathology, if not dangerousness, is not ignored, we see the need for someone to do the hard work to give them a chance to have a better life. It is this sense of connection, of decency, that makes us intolerant of policies and practices that are gratuitously mean-spirited. It is what calls us to be a better people.

In the end, futures—including correctional futures—are chosen. Too often over the past three decades, advocates of a more humane corrections have spoken in opposition to the punishment paradigm—or what Sasha Abramsky has called "American furies."[191] These critical analyses have been important, but being against bad practices and policies is not sufficient. It also is essential to articulate a different, persuasive vision for corrections to pursue. At its core, this vision must be hopeful, but realistic—it must appeal to our sense of goodness, but also be sober enough to address the harmfulness of crime. As we argued thirty years ago, rehabilitation offers this future. Fortunately, in the intervening period, our confidence in this advice has only grown—both due to the disheartening effects produced by the mean season in corrections and to the exciting emergence of effective evidence-based interventions. Accordingly, we are able to conclude, as we did before, that the more promising future for corrections will be realized by reaffirming rehabilitation.

NOTES

[1]Todd R. Clear, *Harm in American Penology: Offenders, Victims, and Their Communities.* (Albany: State University of New York Press, 1994).

[2]Pew Center on the States, *Prison Count 2010: State Population Declines for the First Time in 38 Years.* (Washington, D.C.: Pew Charitable Trusts, 2010).

[3]Nicole D. Porter, *The State of Sentencing 2010: Developments in Policy and Practice.* (Washington, D.C.: The Sentencing Project).

[4]Joan Petersilia, "Parole and prisoner re-entry." Pp. 925-952 in Michael Tonry (ed.), *The Oxford Handbook of Crime and Criminal Justice.* (New York: Oxford University Press, 2011); Edward E. Rhine and Anthony C. Thompson, "The reentry movement in corrections: resiliency, fragility, and prospects." *Criminal Law Bulletin* 47 (No. 2, 2011), pp. 177-209.

[5]Andrew von Hirsch, *Doing Justice: The Choice of Punishments.* (New York: Hill and Wang, 1976); American Friends Service Committee Working Party, *Struggle for Justice: A Report on Crime and Punishment in America.* (New York: Hill and Wang, 1971).

[6]James Q. Whitman, *Harsh Justice: Criminal Punishment and the Widening Divide between America and Europe.* (New York: Oxford University Press, 2003); David Garland, *The Culture of Control: Crime and Social Order in Contemporary Society.* (Chicago: University of Chicago Press, 2001); Jonathan Simon, *Governing Through Crime: How the War on Crime Transformed American Democracy and Created a Culture of Fear.* (New York: Oxford University Press, 2007); Travis C. Pratt, *Addicted to Incarceration: Corrections Policy and the Politics of Misinformation in the United States.* (Thousand Oaks, Calif.: Sage Publications, 2009); Sasha Abramsky, *American Furies: Crime, Punishment, and Vengeance in the Age of Mass Imprisonment.* (Boston: Beacon Press, 2007).

[7]Garland, *The Culture of Control*, p. 70, emphasis in the original.

[8]See Chapter 4. See also Katherine Beckett, *Making Crime Pay: Law and Order in Contemporary American Politics.* (New York: Oxford University Press, 1997); Katherine Beckett and Theodore Sasson, *The Politics of Injustice: Crime and Punishment in America.* (Thousand Oaks, Calif.: Pine Forge Press, 2000); John Hagan, *Who Are the Criminals? The Politics of Crime Policy in the Age of Roosevelt to the Age of Reagan.* (Princeton, N.J.: Princeton University Press, 2010).

[9]Cited in Hagan, *Who Are the Criminals?*, pp. 152-153. See also Michael Tonry, *Punishing Race: A Continuing American Dilemma.* (New York: Oxford University Press, 2011); Löic Wacquant, "Class, race and hyperincarceration." *Daedelus* 139 (Summer 2010), pp. 74-90. For an assessment of the connections between racial animus and punitiveness, see James D. Unnever, Francis T. Cullen, and Cheryl Lero Jonson, "Race, racism, and support for

capital punishment." Pp. 45-96 in Michael Tonry (ed.), *Crime and Justice: A Review of Research, Volume 37*. (Chicago: University of Chicago Press, 2008).

[10]Marie Gottschalk, *The Prison and the Gallows: The Politics of Mass Incarceration in America*. (New York, Cambridge University Press, 2006), pp. 77-114; Joshua Page, *The Toughest Beat: Politics, Punishment, and the Prison Officers in California*. (New York: Oxford University Press, 2011).

[11]Michael Tonry, *Sentencing Matters*. (New York: Oxford University Press, 1996), pp. 13-14.

[12]*Ibid.*, p. 14.

[13]David J. Rothman, *Conscience and Convenience: The Asylum and Its Alternatives in Progressive America*, revised edition. (New York: Aldine de Gruyter, 2002), pp. 429-430.

[14]A number of analyses have been published that illuminate the complex factors that might have contributed to the growth of the punitive policy model in the United States. For an assessment of the main explanations, see Michael Tonry, *Thinking About Crime: Sense and Sensibility in American Penal Culture*. (New York: Oxford University Press, 2004). See also Michael Tonry, "Determinants of penal policies." Pp. 1-48 in Michael Tonry (ed.), *Crime, Punishment, and Politics in Comparative Perspective—Crime and Justice: A Review of Research, Volume 36*. (Chicago: University of Chicago Press, 2007).

[15]Garland, *The Culture of Control*, p. 65.

[16]Brian D. Johnson, "Sentencing." Pp. 696-729 in Michael Tonry (ed.), *The Oxford Handbook of Crime and Criminal Justice*. (New York: Oxford University Press, 2011), pp. 715-717; compare Pamela L. Griset, *Determinate Sentencing: The Promise and the Reality of Retributive Justice*. (Albany: State University of New York Press, 1991), with Richard S. Frase, "Sentencing guidelines in Minnesota, 1978-2003." Pp. 131-219 Michael Tonry (ed.), *Crime and Justice: A Review of Research, Volume 32*. (Chicago: University of Chicago Press, 2005).

[17]Beckett and Sassoon, *The Politics of Injustice*, p. 176.

[18]Michael Tonry, "Mandatory penalties." Pp. 730-756 in Michael Tonry (ed.), *The Oxford Handbook of Crime and Criminal Justice*. (New York: Oxford University Press, 2011), p. 736.

[19]James Austin, Charles Jones, John Kramer, and Phil Renninger, *National Assessment of Structured Sentencing*. (Washington, D.C.: Bureau of Justice Assistance, U.S. Department of Justice, 1996), pp. 19-21.

[20]Tonry, *Sentencing Matters*, p. 146; United States Sentencing Commission, *Overview of Statutory Mandatory Minimum Sentencing*. (Washington, D.C.: Author, 2009), p. 1.

[21]United States Sentencing Commission, *Overview of Statutory Minimum Sentencing*, Appendix A, Statutory Provisions Requiring Mandatory Minimum Terms of Imprisonment; United States Sentencing Commission, *Report to Congress: Mandatory Minimum Penalties in the Federal Criminal Justice System*. (Washington, D.C.: Author, 2011).

[22]Quoted in Christopher Mascharka, "Mandatory minimum sentences: exemplifying the law of unintended consequences." *Florida State University Law Review* 28 (Summer, 2001), pp. 974-975.

[23]Rothman, *Discovery of the Asylum*, pp. 432-433. See also Elliott Currie, *Reckoning: Drugs, the Cities, and the American Future*. (New York: Hill and Wang, 1993); Diana R. Gordon, *The Return of the Dangerous Classes: Drug Prohibition and Policy Politics*. (New York: W. W. Norton and Company, 1994).

[24]Beckett and Sassoon, *The Politics of Injustice*, p. 178.

[25]United States Sentencing Commission, *Report to Congress: Mandatory Minimum Penalties in the Federal Criminal Justice System*, p. xxxii.

[26]William J. Sabol, Katherine Rosich, Kamala Mallik Kane, David P. Kirk, and Glenn Dubin, *The Influences of Truth-in-Sentencing on Changes in States' Sentencing Practices and Prison Populations*. (Washington, D.C.: Justice Policy Center, Urban Institute, 2002).

[27]Paula M. Ditton and Doris James Wilson, *Truth in Sentencing in State Prisons*. (Washington, D.C.: Bureau of Justice Statistics, U.S. Department of Justice, 1999), p. 1.

[28]Page, *The Toughest Beat*, p. 95.

[29]Michael G. Turner, Jody L. Sundt, Brandon K. Applegate, and Francis T. Cullen, "'Three strikes and you're out' legislation: a national assessment." *Federal Probation* 59 (September 1995), pp. 16-35.

[30]Franklin E. Zimring, Gordon Hawkins, and Sam Kamin, *Punishment and Democracy: Three Strikes and You're Out in California*. (New York: Oxford University Press, 2001), p. 17.

[31]Barry C. Feld and Donna M. Bishop, "Juvenile justice." Pp. 627-659 in Michael Tonry (ed.), *The Oxford Handbook of Crime and Criminal Justice*. (New York: Oxford University Press, 2011), p. 635. See also Barry C. Feld, *Bad Kids: Race and the Transformation of the Juvenile Court*. (New York: Oxford University Press, 1999).

[32]John J. DiIulio, Jr., "The coming of the super-predators." *The Weekly Standard* (November 27, 1995), pp. 23-28. See also William J. Bennett, John J. DiIulio, Jr., and John P. Walters. *Body Count: Moral Poverty and How to Win America's War Against Crime and Drugs*. (New York: Simon and Shuster, 1996).

[33]Feld and Bishop, "Juvenile justice," p. 636.

[34]*Ibid.*

[35]Jeremy Travis, "Invisible punishment: an instrument of social exclusion." Pp. 15-36 in Marc Mauer and Meda Chesney-Lind (eds.), *Invisible Punishment: The Collateral Consequences of Mass Imprisonment*. (New York: The New Press, 2002). pp. 15-17.

[36]*Ibid.*, pp. 18-25. See also Velmer S. Burton, Jr., Francis T. Cullen, and Lawrence F. Travis, III, "The collateral consequences of a felony conviction: A national study of state statutes." *Federal Probation* 51 (September 1987), pp. 52-60; Kathleen M. Olivares, Velmer S. Burton, Jr., and Francis T. Cullen, "The collateral consequences of a felony conviction: A national study of state legal codes ten years later." *Federal Probation* 60 (September 1996). pp.10-17; Jeff Manza and Christopher Uggen, *Locked Out: Felon Disenfranchisement and American Democracy*. (New York: Oxford University Press, 2006).

[37]Michelle Alexander, *The New Jim Crow: Mass Incarceration in the Age of Colorblindness*. (New York: The New Press, 2010).

[38]See Robert J. Sampson and John H. Laub, *Crime in the Making: Pathways and Turning Points Through Life*. (Cambridge, Mass.: Harvard University Press, 1993); John Braithwaite,

Crime, Shame and Reintegration. (Cambridge, United Kingdom: Cambridge University Press, 1989).

[39]See, for example, Gary C. Mohr, *Addressing Collateral Consequences in Ohio*. (Columbus, Oh.: The Ohio Department of Rehabilitation and Correction, 2012); State of Colorado, *Senate Bill 12-105: Concerning Provisions That Improve the Reintegration Opportunities for Persons Involved in the Criminal Justice System*. (Denver: Sixty-Eighth General Assembly, 2012).

[40]Tonry, "Mandatory penalties," p. 749. See also Michael Tonry, "The mostly unintended effects of mandatory penalties: two centuries of consistent findings." Pp. 65-114 in Michael Tonry (ed.), *Crime and Justice: A Review of Research, Volume 38*. (Chicago: University of Chicago Press, 2009).

[41]Garland, *The Culture of Control*, pp. 132-133.

[42]Elliott Currie, *Confronting Crime: An American Challenge*. (New York: Pantheon Books, 1985), p.52.

[43]Alfred Blumstein and Jacqueline Cohen, "A theory of the stability of punishment." *Journal of Criminal Law and Criminology* 64 (No. 2, 1973), pp. 198-206.

[44]Currie, *Confronting Crime*, p. 32.

[45]*Ibid.*, p. 91.

[46]Clear, *Harm in American Penology*, p. 43.

[47]Bureau of Justice Statistics, *Key Facts at a Glance: Correctional Populations*. (Washington, D. C.: Bureau of Justice Statistics, U.S. Department of Justice). Retrieved June 10, 2012 from http://bjs.ojp.usdoj.gov/content/glance/tables/corr2tab.cfm.

[48]Pew Center on the States, *Prison Count 2010*, p. 1.

[49]Pew Charitable Trusts, *One in 100: Behind Bars in America 2008*. (Washington, D.C.: Author, 2008), pp. 5-6.

[50]Pew Center on the States. *One in 31: The Long Reach of American Corrections*. (Washington, D.C.: Pew Charitable Trusts, 2009).

[51]*Ibid.*, p. 11.

[52]Francis T. Cullen and Cheryl Lero Jonson, *Correctional Theory: Context and Consequences*. (Thousand Oaks, Calif.: Sage Publications, 2012), pp. 102-103. For statistics on incarceration rates by country, consult the World Prison Brief, International Centre for Prison Studies website: http://www.kcl.ac.uk/depsta/law/research/icps/worldbrief.

[53]Peter Finn, "No-frills prisons and jails: a movement in flux." *Federal Probation* 60 (September 1996), p. 36.

[54]*Ibid.* See also W. Wesley Johnson, Katherine Bennett, and Timothy J. Flanagan, "Getting tough on prisoners: results from the National Corrections Executive Survey, 1995." *Crime and Delinquency* 43 (January 1997), pp. 24-41; Brandon K. Applegate, "Penal austerity: perceived utility, desert, and public attitudes toward amenities." *American Journal of Criminal Justice* 25 (No. 2, 2001), pp. 253-268; Nygel Lenz, "'Luxuries' in prison: the relationship between amenity funding and public support." *Crime and Delinquency* 48 (October 2002), pp. 499-525; Richard Tewksbury and Elizabeth Ehrhardt Mustaine, "Insiders' views on prison amenities: beliefs and perceptions of correctional staff members." *Criminal Justice Review* 30 (September 2005), pp. 174-188.

[55]Francis T. Cullen, Francis T., Cheryl Lero Jonson, and Daniel S. Nagin, "Prisons do not reduce recidivism: the high cost of ignoring science." *The Prison Journal* 91 (No. 3, 2011): 48S-65S; Shelley Johnson Listwan, Christopher J. Sullivan, Robert Agnew, Francis T. Cullen, and Mark Colvin, "The pains of imprisonment revisited: the impact of strain on inmate recidivism." *Justice Quarterly* (forthcoming); M. Keith Chen and Jesse M. Shapiro, "Do harsher prison conditions reduce recidivism? A discontinuity-based approach." *American Law and Economic Review* 9 (No. 1, 2007), pp. 1-29.

[56]See, for example, Elliott Currie, *Crime and Punishment in America.* (New York: Metropolitan Books, 1998), pp. 12-36; Natasha A. Frost and Todd R. Clear, "Understanding mass incarceration as a grant social experiment." *Studies in Law, Politics, and Society* 47 (2009), pp. 159-191.

[57]Alfred Blumstein and Joel Wallman (eds.), *The Crime Drop in America.* (New York: Cambridge University Press, 2000); Franklin Zimring, *The Great American Crime Decline.* (New York: Oxford University Press, 2007).

[58]Tonry, *Thinking About Crime*, p. 119; Tonry, *Crime, Punishment, and Politics in Comparative Perspective*; Zimring, *The Great American Crime Decline*, pp. 107-134.

[59]Richard Rosenfeld, "Changing crime rates." Pp. 559-588 in James Q. Wilson and Joan Petersilia (eds.), *Crime and Public Policy.* (New York: Oxford University Press, 2011), pp. 575-579. See also Blumstein and Wallman, *The Crime Drop in America*; Zimring, *The Great American Crime Decline*; Graham Farrell, Andromachi Tseloni, Jen Mailey, and Nick Tilley, "The crime drop and the security hypothesis." *Journal of Research in Crime and Delinquency* 48 (No. 2, 2011), pp. 147-175.

[60]For a summary of the research on incapacitation effects, see Cullen and Jonson, *Correctional Theory*, pp. 99-126.

[61]William Spelman, "What recent studies do (and don't) tell us about imprisonment and crime." Pp. 419-494 in Michael Tonry (ed.), *Crime and Justice: A Review of Research, Volume 27.* (Chicago: University of Chicago Press, 2000), p. 481.

[62]William Spelman, "The limited importance of prison expansion." Pp. 97-129 in Alfred Blumstein and Joel Wallman (eds.), *The Crime Drop in America.* (New York: Cambridge University Press, 2000), p. 123.

[63]Anne Morrison Piehl and Bert Useem, "Prisons." Pp. 532-558 in James Q. Wilson and Joan Petersilia (eds.), *Crime and Public Policy.* (New York: Oxford University Press), pp. 540-543. See also Steven Rapheal and Michael A. Stoll (eds.), *Do Prisons Make Us Safer? The Benefits and Costs of the Prison Boom.* (New York: Russell Sage Foundation, 2009).

[64]Spelman, "The limited importance of prison expansion," p. 97.

[65]Research suggests that the criminogenic effect of prison might be most pronounced for low-risk offenders. See Paula Smith, *The Effects of Incarceration on Recidivism: A Longitudinal Examination of Program Participation and Institutional Adjustment in Federally Sentenced Adult Male Offenders.* (Unpublished doctoral dissertation, University of New Brunswick, Canada, 2006).

[66]Cullen, Jonson, and Nagin, "Prisons do not reduce recidivism"; Daniel S. Nagin, Francis T. Cullen, and Cheryl Lero Jonson, "Imprisonment and reoffending." Pp. 115-200 in

Michael Tonry (ed.), *Crime and Justice: A Review of Research, Volume 38.* (Chicago: University of Chicago Press., 2009); Patrice Vellettaz, Martin Killias, and Isabel Zoder, *The Effects of Custodial vs. Noncustodial Sentences on Re-offending: A Systematic Review of the State of Knowledge.* (Philadelphia: Campbell Collaboration Crime and Justice Group, 2006).

[67]Pew Center on the States, *State of Recidivism: The Revolving Door of America's Prisons.* (Washington, D.C.: Pew Charitable Trusts, 2011).

[68]*Ibid.*, p. 2. Note that this 40 percent figure excludes California, because the state's "size skews the national picture."

[69]Mark R. Kleiman, *When Brute Force Fails: How to Have Less Crime and Less Punishment.* (Princeton, N.J.: Princeton University Press, 2009). See also Steven N. Durlauf and Daniel S. Nagin, "Imprisonment and crime: can both be reduced?" *Criminology and Public Policy* 10 (No. 1, 2011), pp. 13-54; Irvin Waller, *Less Law, More Order.* (Westport, Conn.: Praeger Publishers, 2006).

[70]Candace Kruttschnitt and Rosemary Gartner, *Marking Time in the Golden State: Women's Imprisonment in California.* (New York: Cambridge University Press, 2005), p. 15.

[71]Page, *The Toughest Beat,* p. 29.

[72]Kruttschnitt and Gartner, *Marking Time in the Golden State,* p. 14.

[73]Cited in Page, *The Toughest Beat,* p. 28.

[74]*Ibid.*, p. 29.

[75]Jonathan Simon, *Poor Discipline: Parole and the Social Control of the Underclass, 1980-1990.* (Chicago: University of Chicago Press, 1993), p. 13.

[76]Joan Petersilia, "California's correctional paradox of excess and deprivation." Pp. 207-278 in Michael Tonry (ed.), *Crime and Justice: A Review of Research, Volume 38.* (Chicago: University of Chicago Press, 2008), p. 209.

[77]*Ibid.*

[78]Blake McKelvey, *American Prisons: A History of Good Intentions.* (Montclair, N.J.: Patterson-Smith, 1977), p. 356.

[79]Petersilia, "California's correctional paradox of excess and deprivation," p. 209.

[80]McKelvey, *American Prisons,* p. 357.

[81]*Ibid.*, p. 340; Department of Corrections, *California Prisoners 1960: Summary Statistics of Prisoners and Parolees.* (Sacramento, Calif.: Research Division, Department of Corrections, 1960), p. 6.

[82]Francis A. Allen, *The Decline of the Rehabilitative Ideal: Penal Policy and Social Purpose.* (New Haven, Conn.: Yale University Press, 1982), p. 27.

[83]Department of Corrections, *California Prisoners 1960,* p. v.

[84]*Ibid.*, p. vi.

[85]Kruttschnitt and Gartner, *Marking Time in the Golden State.* The discussion to follow is based on Kruttschnitt and Gartner's work. Specific citations are included for quoted material.

[86]*Ibid.*, p. 72.

[87]*Ibid.*, p. 74.

[88]*Ibid.*, p. 73.

[89]*Ibid.*, p. 74.

[90]*Ibid.*, p. 65.

[91]*Ibid.*, p. 66

[92]*Ibid.*

[93]*Ibid.*

[94]*Ibid.*, p. 66.

[95]*Ibid., p. 18.*

[96]Zimring et al., *Punishment and Democracy*, pp. 201-211.

[97]*Ibid.*, p. 211.

[98]See, for example, John Pratt, *Penal Populism.* (London, U.K.: Routledge, 2007).

[99]Petersilia, "California's correctional paradox of excess and deprivation," p. 211.

[100]Kruttschnitt and Gartner, *Marking Time in the Golden State*, p. 13.

[101]Department of Corrections, *California Prisoners 1976: Summary Statistics of Felon Prisoners and Parolees.* (Sacramento, Calif.: Policy and Planning Division, Department of Corrections, 1976), p. 1.

[102]Page, *The Toughest Beat*, p. 4; Petersilia, "California's correctional paradox of excess and deprivation," p. 211. Between 1852 and 1965, California built 12 prisons. Between 1984 and 1997, the state erected 21 facilities, one of which was deactivated in 2003. A final prison was constructed in 2005. See the Home Page of the California Department of Corrections and Rehabilitation, California State Prisons Chronology. Retrieved July 3, 2012 from http://www.cdcr.ca.gov/Facilities_Locator/index.html.

[103]Petersilia, "California's correctional paradox of excess and deprivation," p. 209; Department of Corrections, *California Prisoners and Civil Narcotic Addicts, 1981 and 1982: Summary Statistics on Felon Prisoners and Parolees and Civil Narcotic Addict Inpatients and Outpatients.* (Sacramento, Calif.: Administrative Services Division, Department of Corrections, 1985), p. 1; William J. Sabol, Heather C. West, and Matthew Cooper, *Prisoners in 2008.* (Washington, D.C.: Bureau of Justice Statistics, U.S. Department of Justice, 2010), p. 18.

[104]Petersilia, "California's correctional paradox of excess and deprivation," p. 211.

[105]See *Brown v. Plata* 53 U.S. 2011. By the time the court decision was issued, the reductions that were required were 33,000 inmates due to falling prison populations in California. They affirmed a lower court decision requiring the state to release as many as 46,000 offenders.

[106]Page, *The Toughest Beat*, p. 4.

[107]Petersilia, "California's correctional paradox of excess and deprivation," p. 211.

[108]*Ibid.*, p. 211; see also p. 222. The $34,000 figure is in 2006 dollars. The 2011-2012 budget for the California Department of Corrections and Rehabilitation is estimated to be approximately $10 billion. See California Department of Corrections and Rehabilitation, *Corrections: Year at a Glance 2011.* (Sacramento, Calif.: Author, 2011).

[109]*Ibid.*, pp. 234-236.

[110]Simon, *Governing Through Crime*, pp.152-154; see also Simon's *Poor Discipline*, pp. 259-261.

[111]Simon, *Governing Through Crime*, pp. 152-153.

[112]Kruttschnitt and Gartner, *Marking Time in the Golden State*, p. 97. Note that the authors also examined the CIW in the 1990s. They found that this institution retained some of its rehabilitative orientation from the past, which made it differ from VSPW. Still, CIW was affected by the prevailing correctional emphasis at this time on custody and punishment.

[113]*Ibid.*

[114]*Ibid.*, p. 47.

[115]*Ibid.*, p. 97.

[116]*Ibid.*, p. 100.

[117]*Ibid.*, p. 98.

[118]*Ibid.*

[119]Petersilia, "California's correctional paradox of excess and deprivation," p. 253.

[120]*Ibid.*; see also Simon, *Poor Discipline*.

[121]Petersilia, "California's correctional paradox of excess and deprivation," p. 253.

[122]See California Department of Corrections and Rehabilitation, *Corrections: Year at a Glance 2011*, p. 3.

[123]Robert Weisberg and Joan Petersilia, "The dangers of Pyrrhic victories against mass incarceration." *Daedalus* 139 (No. 1, 2010), pp. 124-133; Joan Petersilia, "Looking back to see our future: prison downsizing in America." Keynote Address, National Institute of Justice Conference 2012, Alexandria, Virginia, June 19.

[124]See, for example, D. A. Andrews and James Bonta, *The Psychology of Criminal Conduct*, 5th edition. (New Providence, N.J.: Anderson/LexisNexis, 2010); Doris Layton MacKenzie, *What Works in Corrections: Reducing the Criminal Activities of Offenders and Delinquents.* (New York: Cambridge University Press, 2006); Francis T. Cullen and Cheryl Lero Jonson, "Rehabilitation and treatment programs." Pp. 293-344.in James Q. Wilson and Joan Petersilia (eds.), *Crime and Public Policy*. (New York: Oxford University Press, 2011). For those who played an instrumental role in advancing the rehabilitative ideal, see Francis T. Cullen, "The twelve people who saved rehabilitation: how the science of criminology made a difference—the American Society of Criminology 2004 Presidential Address." *Criminology* 43 (February 2005), pp. 1-42.

[125]Robert Martinson, "What works?—Questions and answers about prison reform." *The Public Interest* 35 (Spring 1974), p. 25. For the larger report on which Martinson's article was based, see Douglas Lipton, Robert Martinson, and Judith Wilks, *The Effectiveness of Correctional Treatment: A Survey of Treatment Evaluation Studies.* (New York: Praeger, 1975).

[126]Francis T. Cullen and Paul Gendreau, "From nothing works to what works: Changing professional ideology in the 21st century." *The Prison Journal* 81 (September 2001), pp. 313-338.

[127]Robert K. Merton, *The Sociology of Science: Theoretical and Empirical Investigations*, edited by Norman K. Storer. (Chicago: University of Chicago Press, 1972), pp. 277-278.

[128]Michael R. Gottfredson, "Treatment destruction techniques." *Journal of Research in Crime and Delinquency* 16 (January 1979), pp. 39-54.

[129] Mark W. Lipsey, Gabrielle L. Chapman, and Nana A. Landenberger, "Cognitive behavioral programs for offenders." *Annals of the American Academy of Political and Social Science* 578 (November 2001), pp. 144-157; MacKenzie, *What Works in Corrections*, pp. 112-134.

[130] Robert Martinson, "New findings, new views: a note of caution regarding sentencing reform." *Hofstra Law Review* 7 (Winter 1979), pp. 243-258.

[131] Over the last decade, calls for evidence-based corrections have become more plentiful. See, for example, Francis T. Cullen and Paul Gendreau, "Assessing correctional rehabilitation: policy, practice, and prospects." Pp. 109-175 in Julie Horney (ed.), *Criminal Justice 2000: Volume 3—Policies, Processes, and Decisions of the Criminal Justice System*. (Washington, D.C.: National Institute of Justice, U.S. Department of Justice, 2000), pp. 158-160; Doris Layton MacKenzie, "Evidence-based corrections: identifying what works." *Crime and Delinquency* 46 (October 2001), pp. 457-471.

[132] See, for example, Andrews and Bonta, *The Psychology of Criminal Conduct*; MacKenzie, *What Works in Corrections*; James McGuire (ed.), *What Works: Reducing Reoffending—Guidelines from Research and Practice*. (Chichester, U.K.: John Wiley and Sons, 1995).

[133] Ted Palmer, "Martinson revisited." *Journal of Research in Crime and Delinquency* 12 (July 1975), p. 142. See also Ted Palmer, *Correctional Intervention and Research*. (Lexington, Mass.: Lexington Books, 1978), and *The Re-Emergence of Correctional Intervention*. (Newbury Park, Calif.: Sage Publications, 1992).

[134] Palmer, "Martinson revisited," pp. 137-143. See also Cullen and Gendreau, "Assessing correctional rehabilitation," pp. 126-128.

[135] See, for example, the reviews of Paul Gendreau and Robert R. Ross, "Effective correctional treatment: bibliotherapy for cynics." *Crime and Delinquency* 25 (October 1979), pp. 463-489, and "Revivification of rehabilitation: evidence from the 1980s." *Justice Quarterly* 4 (September 1987), pp. 349-407.

[136] See, for example, Mark W. Lipsey, "Juvenile delinquent treatment: a meta-analytic treatment inquiry into the variability of effects." Pp. 83-127 in Thomas D. Cook, Harris Cooper, David S. Cordray, Heidi Hartmann, Larry V. Hedges, Richard J. Light, Thomas A. Lewis, and Frederick Mosteller (eds.), *Meta-Analysis for Explanation: A Casebook* (New York: Russell Sage Foundation, 1992); "What do we learn from 400 research studies on the effectiveness of treatment with juvenile delinquency?" Pp. 63-78 in James McGuire (ed.), *What Works: Reducing Reoffending—Guidelines from Research and Practice*. (Chichester, U.K.: John Wiley and Sons, 1995); "Can rehabilitative programs reduce the recidivism of juvenile offenders? An inquiry into the effectiveness of practical programs." *Virginia Journal of Social Policy and Law* 6 (Spring 1999), pp. 611-641; "The primary factors that characterize effective interventions with juvenile offenders: a meta-analytic overview." *Victims and Offenders* 4 (No. 2, 2009), pp. 124-147; Mark W. Lipsey and David B. Wilson, "Effective interventions for serious juvenile offenders: a synthesis of research." Pp. 313-345 in Rolf Loeber and David P. Farrington (eds.), *Serious and Violent Juvenile Offenders: Risk Factors and Successful Interventions*. (Thousand Oaks, Calif.: Sage Publications, 1998); Mark W. Lipsey and Francis T. Cullen, "The effectiveness of

correctional rehabilitation: a review of systematic reviews." *Annual Review of Law and Social Science* 3 (2007), pp. 297-320.

[137]Friedrich Lösel, "The efficacy of correctional treatment: a review and synthesis of meta-evaluations." Pp. 79-111 in James McGuire (ed.), *What Works: Reducing Reoffending— Guidelines from Research and Practice.* (Chichester, U.K.: John Wiley and Sons, 1995); James McGuire, "What works in correctional intervention? Evidence and practical implications." Pp. 25-43 in Gary A. Bernfeld, David P. Farrington, and Alan W. Leschied (eds.), *Offender Rehabilitation in Practice: Implementing and Evaluating Effective Programs.* (Chichester, U.K.: John Wiley and Sons, 2001).

[138]See, for example, D. A. Andrews, Ivan Zinger, Robert D. Hoge, James Bonta, Paul Gendreau, and Francis T. Cullen, "Does correctional treatment work? A clinically relevant and psychologically informed meta-analysis." *Criminology* 28 (August 1990), pp. 369-404. See also Andrews and Bonta, *The Psychology of Criminal Conduct.*

[139]Francis T. Cullen, John Paul Wright, and Brandon K. Applegate, "Control in the community: the limits of reform?" Pp. 69-116 in Alan T. Harland (ed.), *Choosing Correctional Interventions That Work: Defining the Demand and Evaluating the Supply.* (Thousand Oaks, Calif.: Sage Publications, 1996); Francis T. Cullen, Kristie R. Blevins, Jennifer S. Trager, and Paul Gendreau, "The rise and fall of boot camps: a case study in common-sense corrections." *Journal of Offender Rehabilitation* 40 (Nos. 3-4, 2005), pp. 53-70; Gail A. Caputo, *Intermediate Sanctions in Corrections.* (Denton, Tex.: University of North Texas Press, 2004); MacKenzie, *What Works in Corrections*; James M. Byrne and April Pattavina, "The effectiveness issue: assessing what works in the adult corrections system." Pp. 281-303 in James M. Byrne, Arthur J. Lurigio, and Joan Petersilia (eds.), *Smart Sentencing: The Emergence of Intermediate Sanctions.* (Newbury Park, Calif.: Sage Publications, 1992).

[140]Travis C. Pratt, Francis T. Cullen, Kristie R. Blevins, Leah E. Daigle, and Tamara D. Madensen, "The empirical status of deterrence theory: a meta-analysis." Pp. 367-395 in Francis T. Cullen, John Paul Wright, and Kristie R. Blevins (eds.), *Taking Stock: The Status of Criminological Theory—Advances in Criminological Theory, Volume 15.* (New Brunswick, N.J.: Transaction Publishers, 2006). See also Francis T. Cullen, Travis C. Pratt, Sharon Levrant Miceli, and Melissa M. Moon, "Dangerous liaison? Rational choice theory as the basis for correctional intervention." Pp. 279-296 in Alex R. Piquero and Stephen G. Tibbetts (eds.), *Rational Choice and Criminal Behavior: Recent Research and Future Challenges.* (New York: Routledge, 2002).

[141]See, more generally, Norval Morris and Michael Tonry, *Between Prison and Probation: Intermediate Punishments in a Rational Sentencing System.* (New York: Oxford University Press, 1990); James M. Byrne, Arthur J. Lurigio, and Joan Petersilia (eds.), *Smart Sentencing: The Emergence of Intermediate Sanctions.* (Newbury Park, Calif.: Sage Publications, 1992); Caputo, *Intermediate Sanctions in Corrections*; Cullen, Wright, and Applegate, "Control in the community," pp. 71-75.

[142]Joan Petersilia and Susan Turner, "Intensive probation and parole." Pp. 281-335 in Michael Tonry (ed.), *Crime and Justice: A Review of Research, Volume 17.* (Chicago: University of Chicago Press, 1993). pp. 310-311.

[143]*Ibid.*, p. 311.

[144]*Ibid.*, p. 315.

[145]Francis T. Cullen and Cheryl Lero Jonson, "Labeling theory and correctional rehabilitation: beyond unanticipated consequences." In David P. Farrington and Joseph Murray (eds.), *Empirical Tests of Labeling Theory: Advances in Criminological Theory, Volume 17.* (New Brunswick, N.J.: Transaction Publishers, forthcoming).

[146]Lawrence W. Sherman, "Defiance, deterrence, and irrelevance: a theory of the criminal sanction." *Journal of Research in Crime and Delinquency* 30 (November 1993), pp. 445-473.

[147]For early statements of the RNR model, see D. A. Andrews, James Bonta, and Robert D. Hoge, "Classification for effective rehabilitation: rediscovering psychology." *Criminal Justice and Behavior* 17 (March 1990), pp. 19-52; Andrews et al., "Does correctional treatment work?"

[148]See Ian Ayres, *Super Crunchers: Why Thinking-By-Numbers Is the New Way to Be Smart.* (New York: Bantam Books, 2007). More generally, see Daniel Kahneman, *Thinking, Fast and Slow.* (New York: Farrar, Straus and Giroux, 2011).

[149]For research on the predictive validity of the LSI, see Andrews and Bonta, *The Psychology of Criminal Conduct*, pp. 314-317; Paula Smith, Francis T. Cullen, and Edward J. Latessa, "Can 14,737 women be wrong? A meta-analysis of the LSI-R and recidivism for female offenders." *Criminology and Public Policy* 8 (March 2009), pp. 183-208; Brenda Vose, Francis T. Cullen, and Paula Smith, "The empirical status of the Level of Service Inventory." *Federal Probation* 72 (December 2008), pp. 22-29.

[150]See Paul Gendreau, Tracy Little, and Claire Goggin, "A meta-analysis of the predictors of adult offender recidivism: what works!" *Criminology* 34 (November 1996), pp. 575-607.

[151]Andrews and Bonta, *The Psychology of Criminal Conduct*, pp. 58-59.

[152]*Ibid.*, pp. 59-60.

[153]*Ibid.*, pp. 49-50.

[154]*Ibid.*, p. 405.

[155]*Ibid.*, p. 404.

[156]*Ibid.*, p. 405.

[157]*Ibid.*, pp. 405-406; Francis T. Cullen and Paula Smith, "Treatment and rehabilitation." Pp. 156-178 in Michael Tonry (ed.), *The Oxford Handbook of Crime and Criminal Justice.* (New York: Oxford University Press, 2011), pp. 172-173; Christopher T. Lowenkamp, Edward J. Latessa, and Paula Smith, "Does correctional program quality really matter? The importance of adhering to the principles of effective intervention." *Criminology and Public Policy* 5 (August 2006), pp. 201-220.

[158]For statements of the full set of principles in the RNR model, see D. A. Andrews, "The psychology of criminal conduct and effective treatment." Pp. 35-62 in James McGuire (ed.), *What Works: Reducing Reoffending—Guidelines from Research and Practice.* (Chichester, U.K.: John Wiley and Sons, 1995); Paul Gendreau, "The principles of effective intervention with offenders." Pp. 117-130 in Alan Harland (ed.), *Choosing Correctional Interventions That Work: Defining the Demand and Evaluating the Supply.* (Thousand Oaks, Calif.: Sage Publications, 1996); Andrews and Bonta, *The Psychology of Criminal Conduct*, pp. 46-47.

[159]See, for example, James R. P. Ogloff and Michael R. Davis, "Advances in offender assessment and rehabilitation: contributions of the risk-needs-responsivity approach." *Psychology, Crime and Law* 10 (No. 3, 2004), pp. 229-242; Devon L. L. Polaschek, "An appraisal of the risk-need-responsivity (RNR) model of offender rehabilitation and its application in correctional treatment." *Legal and Criminological Psychology* 17 (2012), pp. 1-17; Frank Porporino, "Bringing sense and sensitivity to corrections: from programmes to 'fix' offenders to services to support desistance." Pp. 61-85 in Jo Brayford, Francis Cowe, and John Deering (eds.), *What Else Works? Creative Work with Offenders*. (Cullompton, U. K.: Willan Publishing, 2010). See also Peter Raynor and Gwen Robinson, *Rehabilitation, Crime and Justice*, revised and updated edition. (Basingstoke, U.K.: Palgrave Macmillan, 2009).

[160]Francis T. Cullen, "Taking rehabilitation seriously: creativity, science, and the challenge of offender change." *Punishment and Society* 14 (January 2012), pp. 94-114.

[161]For the best compilation of evidence in support of the RNR model, see Andrews and Bonta, *The Psychology of Criminal Conduct*. See also Paul Gendreau, Paula Smith, and Sheila French, "The theory of effective correctional intervention: empirical status and future directions." Pp. 419-446 in Francis T. Cullen, John Paul Wright, and Kristie R. Blevins (eds.), *Taking Stock: The Status of Criminological Theory—Advances in Criminological Theory, Volume 15*. (New Brunswick, N.J.: Transaction Publishers, 2006); Paula Smith, Paul Gendreau, and Kristin Swartz, "Validating the principles of effective intervention: a systematic review of the contributions of meta-analysis in the field of corrections." *Victims and Offenders* 4 (No. 2, 2009), pp. 148-169; Paula Smith, "The psychology of criminal conduct." Pp. 69-88 in Francis T. Cullen and Pamela Wilcox, *The Oxford Handbook of Criminological Theory*. (New York: Oxford University Press, 2012).

[162]Polaschek, "An appraisal of the risk-need-responsivity (RNR) model of offender rehabilitation and its application in correctional treatment," p. 1.

[163]Andrews and Bonta, *The Psychology of Criminal Conduct*, p. 47.

[164]Francis T. Cullen, Andrew J. Myer, and Edward J. Latessa, "Eight lessons learned from *Moneyball*: the high cost of ignoring evidence-based corrections." *Victims and Offenders* 4 (No. 2, 2009), pp. 197-213. See also Michael Lewis, *Moneyball: The Art of Winning an Unfair Game*. (New York: New York: W. W. Norton, 2003); Scott Gray, *The Mind of Bill James: How a Complete Outsider Changed Baseball*. (New York: Doubleday, 2006); Alan Schwarz, *The Numbers Game: Baseball's Lifelong Fascination with Statistics*. (New York: Thomas Dunne Books, 2004).

[165]See, for example, Stefan Timmermans and Marc Berg, *The Gold Standard: The Challenge of Evidence-Based Medicine and Standardization in Health Care*. (Philadelphia: Temple University Press, 2003).

[166]Cullen et al., "Eight lessons learned from *Moneyball*."

[167]Cullen et al., "The rise and fall of boot camps"; Jeanne B. Stinchcomb, "From optimistic policies to pessimistic outcomes: why won't boot camps either succeed pragmatically or succumb politically?" *Journal of Offender Rehabilitation* 40 (Nos. 3-4, 2005), pp. 27-52.

[168]Edward J. Latessa, Francis T. Cullen, and Paul Gendreau, "Beyond correctional quackery: professionalism and the possibility of effective treatment." *Federal Probation* 66 (September 2002), pp. 43-49.

[169]*Ibid.*; Francis T. Cullen, "Making corrections work: it's time for a new penology." *Journal of Community Corrections"* 21 (Fall 2012), pp. 5-6, 15-18.

[170]Lawrence W. Sherman, "Why crime control is not reactionary." Pp. 171-189 in David Weisburd and Craig Uchida (eds.), *Police Innovation and Control of the Police.* (New York: Springer-Verlag, 1993); David Weisburd and Anthony A. Braga, "Introduction: understanding police innovation." Pp. 1-23 in David Weisburd and Anthony A. Braga (eds.), *Police Innovation: Contrasting Perspectives.* (New York: Cambridge University Press, 2006).

[171]Weisburd and Braga, "Introduction."

[172]Franklin E. Zimring, *The City That Became Safe: New York's Lessons for Urban Crime and Its Control.* (New York: Oxford University Press, 2012), pp. 100-150.

[173]Eli B. Silverman, "Compstat's innovation." Pp. 267-283 in David Weisburd and Anthony A. Braga (eds.), *Police Innovation: Contrasting Perspectives.* (New York: Cambridge University Press, 2006), pp. 268, 272.

[174]For a more extended discussion of these issues, see Francis T. Cullen, Cheryl Lero Jonson, and John E. Eck, "The accountable prison." *Journal of Contemporary Criminal Justice* 28 (February 2012), pp. 77-95.

[175]Friedrich Lösel, "It's never too early and never too late: towards an integrated science of developmental intervention in criminology." *The Criminologist* 32 (September/October 2007), p.6.

[176]For a discussion o change and desistance from crime among adult offenders, see Shadd Maruna, *Making Good: How Ex-Convicts Reform and Rebuild Their Lives.* (Washington, D. C.: American Psychological Association, 2001).

[177]For a review of theoretical perspectives in this area, see David P. Farrington (ed.), *Integrated Developmental and Life-Course Theories of Offending—Advances in Criminological Theory, Volume 14.* (New Brunswick, N.J.: Transaction Publishers, 2005); Francis T. Cullen, Michael L. Benson, and Matthew D. Makarios, "Developmental and life-course theories of offending." Pp. 23-45 in Brandon C. Welsh and David P. Farrington (eds.), *The Oxford Handbook of Crime Prevention.* (New York: Oxford University Press, 2012).

[178]For reviews of research on criminal development, see John Paul Wright, Stephen G. Tibbetts, and Leah E. Daigle, *Criminals in the Making: Criminality Across the Life Course.* (Thousand Oaks, Calif.: Sage Publications, 2008); Terence P. Thornberry and Marvin D. Krohn (eds.), *Taking Stock: An Overview of Findings from Contemporary Longitudinal Studies.* (New York: Kluwer Academic/Plenum Publishers, 2003).

[179]Magda Stouthamer-Loeber, Rolf Loeber, and Christopher Thomas, "Caretakers seeking help for boys with disruptive and delinquent behavior." *Comprehensive Mental Health Care* 2 (No. 3, 1992), pp. 159-178; Magda Stouthamer-Loeber, Rolf Loeber, Welmoet van Kammen, and Quanwu Zhang, "Uninterrupted delinquent careers: the timing of

parental help-seeking and juvenile court contact." *Studies on Crime and Crime Prevention* 4 (1995), pp. 236-251.

[180]For reviews of effective early intervention programs, see David P. Farrington and Brandon C. Welsh, *Saving Children from a Life in Crime: Early Risk Factors and Effective Interventions*. (New York: Oxford University Press, 2007); Peter W. Greenwood, *Changing Lives: Delinquency Prevention as Crime-Control Policy*. (Chicago: University of Chicago Press, 2006); Brandon C. Welsh and David P. Farrington (eds.), *The Oxford Handbook of Crime Prevention*. (New York: Oxford University Press, 2012).

[181]Cullen and Jonson, *Correctional Theory*, pp. 180-181.

[182]*Ibid.*, pp. 198-202; Francis T. Cullen, Brenda A. Vose, Cheryl Lero Jonson, and James D. Unnever, "Public support for early intervention: is child saving a 'habit of the heart'?" *Victims and Offenders* 2 (No. 2, 2007), pp. 109-124.

[183]For research confirming this finding, see James D. Unnever, John K. Cochran, Francis T. Cullen, and Brandon K. Applegate, "The pragmatic American: attributions of crime and the hydraulic relation hypothesis." *Justice Quarterly* 27 (June 2010), pp. 431-457.

[184]For summaries of this research, see Francis T. Cullen, Bonnie S. Fisher, and Brandon K. Applegate, "Public opinion about punishment and corrections." Pp. 1-79 in Michael Tonry (ed.), *Crime and Justice: A Review of Research, Volume 27*. (Chicago: University of Chicago Press); Cheryl Lero Jonson, Francis T. Cullen, and Jennifer L. Lux, "Creating ideological space: why public support for rehabilitation matters." In Leam Craig, Louise Dixon, and Theresa Gannon (eds.), *What Works in Offender Rehabilitation: An Evidence Based Approach to Assessment and Treatment*. (London: Wiley-Blackwell, forthcoming).

[185]Francis T. Cullen, "It's time to reaffirm rehabilitation." *Criminology and Public Policy* 5 (November 2006), pp. 665-667.

[186]Alexis de Tocqueville, *Democracy in America*, edited by J. P. Meyer and translated by George Lawrence. (New York: Harper and Row, 1969; originally published in 1835 and 1840), p. 287. See also Cullen et al., "Public support for early intervention," pp. 117-121.

[187]Francis T. Cullen, Jennifer A. Pealer, Bonnie S. Fisher, Brandon K. Applegate, and Shannon A. Santana, "Public support for correctional rehabilitation in America: change or consistency?" Pp. 128-147 in Julian V. Roberts and Michael Hough (eds.), *Changing Attitudes to Punishment: Public Opinion, Crime and Justice*. (Cullompton, U.K.: Willan Publishing, 2002), p. 137.

[188]Julian V. Roberts and Ross Hastings, "Public opinion and crime prevention: a review of international trends." Pp. 487-507 in Bandon C. Welsh and David P. Farrington (eds.), *The Oxford Handbook of Crime Prevention*. (New York: Oxford University Press, 2012), p. 492.

[189]Cullen et al., "Public support for correctional rehabilitation in America," p. 136.

[190]*Ibid.*, p. 137.

[191]Abramsky, *American Furies*.

Name Index

Subject Index